F. S. D Ames

Marion Howard

Trials and triumphs

F. S. D Ames

Marion Howard
Trials and triumphs

ISBN/EAN: 9783741143397

Manufactured in Europe, USA, Canada, Australia, Japa

Cover: Foto ©Thomas Meinert / pixelio.de

Manufactured and distributed by brebook publishing software
(www.brebook.com)

F. S. D Ames

Marion Howard

MARION HOWARD.

LONDON : BURNS AND OATES.

MARION HOWARD;

OR,

TRIALS AND TRIUMPHS.

BY THE AUTHOR OF

*"MAGGIE'S ROSARY AND OTHER STORIES," "LADY OF
NEVILLE COURT," "PETER'S JOURNEY," &c.*

New Edition.

LONDON: BURNS AND OATES.
1880.

This Little Work

IS DEDICATED

TO

SAINT ALBAN,

PROTO-MARTYR OF ENGLAND,

UNDER WHOSE PATRONAGE

IT IS HUMBLY PLACED.

PREFACE TO THE SECOND EDITION.

MARION HOWARD has been a long time out of sight; may we venture to hope that she is not yet altogether out of mind? The kind reception given to this work on its first appearance nine years ago, as well as the numerous applications made for copies during the time it has remained out of print, induce the author to hope that such is not the case. She gladly avails herself of the opportunity afforded her, by the issue of a new edition, to thank her friends for their kind encouragement in her endeavours to help on the great work of supplying wholesome light literature for Catholic homes.

EALING, 1880.

PREFACE.

THERE exists in the present day a dearth of Catholic light literature. Several writers have laboured, and are labouring still, to supply books suggestive enough to leave matter for thought behind them, and yet light enough to make their perusal a pastime. But as this kind of literature must be abundant, if it is to meet its object, a regret is still felt in every class of Catholic society that such books are so few.

The writer of "Marion Howard," therefore, hopes that there can be no presumption in trying to do what more able writers seem slow in doing. This is her principal reason for venturing to expect that Catholics generally, and influential Catholics especially, will give it their support and patronage.

The tale embodies an explanation of religion to those outside the Church, and the subjects are suited particularly to Evangelical Protestants, with whom the writer is best acquainted, and who may be disposed to read her unpretending exposition of Catholic truth.

As the work touches upon important doctrines of the faith, the author has not trusted to her own knowledge or judgment, but has submitted every word to ecclesiastics of position and learning.

NOTTING HILL, *May,* 1871.

MARION HOWARD;

OR,

TRIALS AND TRIUMPHS.

CHAPTER I.

IT was Sunday afternoon. Tea had been over some time, and
Mrs. Howard, leaning back in her chair, looked out into her trim
little garden, with a far-away expression in her dark-grey eyes.
Opposite, her weekly budget not yet exhausted, sat Miss Leicester,
news-purveyor in general to the good people of Ennington, too
happy in securing a listener to criticise the amount of attention
bestowed by her. This was certainly not very great; for, keen as
was Mrs. Howard's sense of the ridiculous, her wit was flown at
a higher quarry than the sayings and doings of the Ennington
shopkeepers. But even Miss Leicester's gossip was better than
nothing on Sunday afternoon, with its dull monotony; and so,
listlessly reclining, the lady of the house listened to her visitor as
long as she interested her, and amused herself with her own
thoughts when she did not.

But everything must have an end, and even Miss Leicester's
subjects were growing threadbare at last. She had discussed the
congregation, from Mrs. Stebbing and her blue bonnet to the
butcher's wife and her red shawl. She had shaken her head over
many things that were true, and many more that were not, and
made quite an Alpine chain out of a few straggling molehills.
Truly, as she contemplated the shortcomings of her neighbours,
Miss Leicester thanked the Lord that she was "not as other
men."

And all this time a little maiden had been sitting on a low seat
near her mother, her long curls drooping over her book, trying to
find something fresh in "Pilgrim's Progress." Miss Leicester had
not even bestowed a thought upon her, so engrossed had she appeared
in her book, and she was not a little startled by a very deep sigh
proceeding from the low seat in question. It was so evidently

A

the result of her last observation that the village gossip felt uneasy, for, in common with the rest of her class, she had a decided objection to "little pitchers," as she styled them. The look of vexation which she directed towards Mrs. Howard was, however, quite lost upon that lady, who only bent down to her child.

"What a sigh Marion dear! what was it for?"

"I was only wishing that people were good, mamma."

"Well, dear, we all wish that, of course; but you know the world is naturally wicked."

"Yes, I know," said the child mournfully; "but sometimes, when I think about it, it seems so dreadful that I feel quite tired," and, closing her large book, she rested her hands and cheek on its marbled edges, and looked up into her mother's eyes.

"You are a strange child, Marion," said Mrs. Howard, softly stroking the bright curls; "but was that all? was that the only reason of the sigh?"

"Yes, there was nothing else, mamma."

"Ah! my dear," exclaimed Miss Leicester, "you have many things to learn yet. All Christians mourn, of course, the corruption of the world at large. Well, it only remains for us, who have received greater advantages, to set the example. If all were what they ought to be, what a world this would be, to be sure!"

Perhaps it did not strike Miss Leicester that, should that halcyon period arrive, "Othello's occupation would be gone." Neither did it strike our little girl, she never having read Shakespeare; but she certainly had a strange thought or two of her own about her mother's friend, as she turned back to old Christian and his peregrinations.

"It is time for you to dress for church, my love," observed Mrs. Howard, taking out her watch.

"Will not you come too, mamma?"

"Not this evening. I feel rather tired; for I did not sleep well last night. Miss Leicester will stop and keep me company, I know."

Mrs. Howard's will was Miss Leicester's law, and that lady simply nodded her head.

"Try to remember the text, Marion," was her mother's parting injunction, as the child bent over to kiss her.

"Pray do," exclaimed Miss Leicester, "and the sermon too, if that dear Mr. Lisle preaches. I must say I hope he will not, for I shall feel disappointed if he does."

"I am sure you shall feel nothing of the kind on my account," rejoined Mrs. Howard. "I would not detain you for the world. Marion shall wait for you."

"My dear friend, you quite misunderstand me, indeed you do!" exclaimed Miss Leicester. "I have not the smallest wish to leave you. How can you talk so when you know how I appreciate your society? Why, Mr. Lisle himself would not teach me more than I know I shall learn from you to-night."

Mrs. Howard's lip curled perceptibly, but she only signed to Marion to go.

"Yes, indeed," continued Miss Leicester. "I count these evenings passed with you as golden moments. One gets so little intellectual society in this out-of-the-way place, while with you one finds the 'feast of reason and the flow of soul!' But do not you consider Mr. Lisle a sweet preacher? Oh, his sermon this morning—'Little children, love one another!' How beautiful, how exquisite, how touching it was! I could hardly restrain my feelings, I declare, but you know I am such a creature of impulse! Now, if I had only your firmness of character, your depth of intellect, my dear Mrs. Howard, I would—ah, what would I not do?"

Again the lip curled, and Mrs. Howard looked into the garden.

"You are such a dear undemonstrative creature : but tell me now, what do you think of Mr. Lisle? I should so like to know."

"Mr. Lisle?" replied the other, without turning her head, "he is all very well. He preaches good common-sense sermons, though he is far from brilliant. But whatever he may be, he is too good for Ennington, where I consider old Doctor Stebbing just in his place."

Toady as she was, poor Miss Leicester smarted under the innuendo, and the little old maid sat silent for nearly five minutes.

Marion started on her walk. It was the middle of June, and all things were bright and beautiful, as June alone can make them. As she passed down the street, she overtook many of the persons mentioned by Miss Leicester in her catalogue of woes. But she shrank from them all ; distrust had entered her heart, and nobody seemed good. When she reached the church, a tall, awkward country lad was leaning over the gate, who grinned sheepishly as she approached, and offered her a bunch of cottage flowers. Poor Bill Rogers! All that Miss Leicester had said and prophesied concerning him came into Marion's mind, and she shook her head.

"No, thank you ; I don't want them ;" and with the refusal she passed into the churchyard.

Bill looked after her. "Proud little puss !" he muttered, "but she warn't allers like that. She used to smile on a body pleasant-like, onst. It's all along o' that mother o' hern. Never mind, if she won't have 'em, here goes!" He flung the flowers into a ditch, and more than ever out of conceit of the "gentry" went his way.

It was an old-fashioned church, and one that had stood the wear and tear of centuries and fanaticism ; but its carved oakwork and rich stained glass contrasted strangely with the rough pews with which it was filled. Certainly, the alterations, reparations, and modifications it had undergone, would have puzzled an antiquary, and outraged an architect. But Marion knew nothing of all this, and only thought the church looked very nice as the sunshine flooded through the crimson glass. Nor did she wander back, as some might have done, to those days gone by, when a more glorious sunlight gilded its sanctuary and hallowed its walls. "I wish it was always like this," she thought, as, having reached her seat, she looked round ; "it is so different generally, so dull and dark."

Marion Howard was her mother's only child. Reared as she had been in the village of Ennington, it comprised her whole world. And a circumscribed one it was ; for Dr. Stebbing and his young wife, the curate, Miss Leicester, and Mr. Bernard the doctor, were the only friends that Mrs. Howard and her little daughter could number. Of these, the rector was too fussy, and his wife too prim, to please Mrs. Howard's fastidious taste ; but Mr. Lisle she liked better than she chose to acknowledge to Miss Leicester, though, as his stiffness somewhat awed her, she rather stood aloof from him, while the little old maid and her chatter were only tolerated when nothing better could be had. Mr. Bernard was an exception to every rule, for even Mrs. Howard unbent with him, while Marion found in the good-natured old bachelor the merriest of playfellows and the warmest of friends.

Distant, however, as she was to the world at large, Mrs. Howard was a kind and affectionate mother. She loved Marion dearly, and, being herself an accomplished woman, she carried on the work of her education unassisted. But she was not a Christian parent ; and had the child's qualities been less genuine, Marion would have been spoiled from her cradle. Excellent as was her training for the head, her culture for the heart was sadly defective, and Marion was principally indebted to the instructions of her old nurse, and to a disposition inherited from her father, for the gentleness and amiability that endeared her to all hearts.

Entrenched in the citadel of her pride, Mrs. Howard made all things subservient to it, and seldom glanced beyond. Endowed with only a modest competency herself, she shrank haughtily back from the advances of her more wealthy neighbours. Those in her own position she loved, shunned, tolerated, or ridiculed, according to circumstances ; her inferiors she simply ignored.

In Ennington, engrossed in her child, she was simply supine ; and there Marion neither learned from her the golden rule of love, nor the worldly one of censure. But in London, where the little girl occasionally passed a few weeks with her mother, and where the latter condescended to shine, things were different. Gathering brilliance from her imagination, there even Miss Leicester's humdrum stories were struck into sparkling anecdotes, and went off with a flash. Marion, young as she was, imbued with the simple piety of her kind old nurse, shrank from this, and loved her mother far better in the village home, than when she shone, the admired and courted visitor, in her aunt's stately drawing-room in Mayfair. Her impulse was to love all men, for the evil influence had not yet begun to work its way. She had not yet learned to grow suspicious of human virtue, nor to look for weeds rather than flowers in the great garden of human life.

At the time our narrative commences, Mrs. Howard had been

for some years a widow. Of all the bright points in her character, true devotion to her husband had been not the least conspicuous; and her grief at his loss was no sickly sentiment. Captain Howard had been twice married, and the fruit of his first union was a son, who had been brought up in India from his childhood, and who was now about three-and-twenty. To this half-brother Marion's heart turned with real affection. No ancient warrior, no hero of romance, no celebrity of modern days, shared the pinnacle to which she had elevated him. The soldier-brother stood "alone in his glory." Mrs. Howard was naturally far less ecstatic; her love for her truly noble husband made her read Edward's letters with interest; but the idea of a stepson of twenty-three had its drawbacks, and she discouraged Marion's deep affection for him with a jealousy, not unnatural, perhaps, in the mother of an only child. He was not her brother—she would never see him—he did not really think much about her,—were phrases that wrung Marion's heart and made her silent, but which made her love for brother Edward a deeper idolatry than ever.

Much as Mrs. Howard had loved her husband, her affection had never extended to his family; and for years, so many that Marion could only just remember when it was not so, there had been a wide breach between her and them. Two or three years after the death of Captain Howard, his mother had visited her daughter-in-law; but wearied out at length, notwithstanding great forbearance, by a haughtiness and assumption she could not understand, she had departed sick at heart. The kiss she bestowed on her little grandchild, with a gift to the old nurse, were her only leave-takings; and she had never seen or written to her daughter-in-law since.

On this bright summer evening, which probably tempted many of the villagers into the green lanes and smiling meadows of Ennington, the attendance at the service was but small; and when the sunshine faded once again out of the old edifice which it had brightened for a while, Marion grew gloomy too. It was with real pleasure that, the prayers being ended, she saw Mr. Lisle mount the pulpit-stairs. He was, as we have already said, the curate of the village, and truly and deservedly beloved. Intelligent as he was, the talents that would have shone in a wider field of action were not lost even in a narrower sphere. Unpretending in his piety, unostentatious in his charity, untiring in the weary labour of pastoral ministrations, he was the friend alike of rich and poor. Eagerly sought by all, he was nevertheless more frequently welcomed as a guest at the humble tea-board of the villager than at the stately dinner-tables of the county families round. The poor, the sick, and sorrowful, hailed in him an angel of mercy. But he had his faults; for he was bigoted, intolerant, and dogmatic. In religion he formed his own creed, preached it, and, of course, inveighed with the greatest vehemence against every one who differed from him.

This evening, however, his sermon was a plain, practical address, in which, continuing the subject of the morning, he urged upon his flock the duty of Christian forbearance. He was very earnest, and even a fashionable preacher might have felt satisfied with the attention of his rustic congregation. But at last all was over, the sermon preached, the blessing given ; every head was bent for a silent minute, and then all rose to go. Why should they linger, where all was redolent with decaying timber and mildewed baize, when God was quite as near in the bright green fields around ? Why remain bowed within four mere walls, while His Presence shone so much more vividly in the setting sun, the waving trees, and the farewell warble of the sleepy birds ?

Marion paused in the churchyard to watch the various groups chatting and laughing around ; lengthening, as it seemed, the little space now left between the Sunday leisure and the threshold of the morrow's toil. There a knot of old men were comparing the prospect of the crops with bygone harvests ; here a cluster of aged matrons discussed the sermon and the preacher ; while many of the younger ones, gliding away in cosy couples, were soon lost in the winding lanes. Who that knows country life cannot picture them, those stalwart old English yeomen and their red-cloaked dames ? The cherry-cheeked damsel, hiding her laughing eyes in a posy of "old man" and "sweet-william," while the awkward young fellow beside her places the flower he has been stealing from her in his button-hole. Who has not seen such a village as this, with its ivy-covered church, rising from amid the tombs of generations only to be numbered by the historian ? Who has not even sometimes almost envied the quiet existence that begins and ends in such a sweet monotony, with joys and sorrows, virtues and vices, all its own ? Marion stood and looked upon the scene, much interested, for the sermon had calmed her. She almost longed to join one of the merry groups, instead of going home to keep her own company in the garden, or Miss Leicester's in the parlour.

"Good evening, little dreamer," and a hand was laid lightly on her shoulder.

"O Mr. Lisle, how you startled me !"

"What were you thinking of ? for I suppose for some time to come one may ask you plain questions."

"Of so many things that I can really hardly tell you. I was looking more than thinking."

"What were you looking at, then ? " he asked, as, having by this time reached the gate, he half seated himself upon the low wall, whilst his little companion leaned against the railing of the gate.

"I was looking at the people talking together, and wondering whether any of the dead persons buried here could know what they were talking about."

"No ; how could they ? "

"I don't know ; though, if they could, there are many things I should like to tell papa."

" You have a Father in heaven, my dear child ; you must learn to talk to Him."

" How ? " asked Marion, looking suddenly up. " I wish I could," she added.

" In prayer."

" Yes, I say my prayers, of course ; but that is not like talking. It seems to me that nobody talks to God now," continued Marion, with a sigh.

" I do not understand you, Marion. It is our own fault if we do not do so. Has He not said, ' Pray without ceasing ' ? "

" Mr. Lisle, if I tell you something that I often think, will you be angry ? "

" Certainly not."

" Well, it seems to me that God is hardly fair and just. Please don't look like that. I really do not mean anything wicked. This is what I think. In the beginning He used actually to talk to Adam and Eve ; and even after their time He often came in the form of an angel, and talked to different people. It was God Himself who wrestled with Jacob, and who spoke in the burning bush to Moses. Then He might always be seen for so many years in the pillar of fire that went before the Israelites as they passed through the desert. After this, He was always over the mercy-seat, and though the Israelites themselves were not allowed to see Him, still they knew that He was there, looking at them through the thin veil, and the high-priest actually saw the bright cloud often."

" Only once a year," interrupted Mr. Lisle.

" Was it not oftener than that ? I had forgotten. Well, this cloud was God's own glory. It was the shadow of Himself. Then, Mr. Lisle, after all these things came Jesus in the form of a man, and every one could even touch Him. Was He at first like any ordinary baby ? "

" Exactly."

" His mother knew He was really God, did she not ? "

" Of course she did."

" She must have been very good."

" She was a very holy woman."

" But how strange it must have been to have washed and dressed Him. Should you think He ever cried ? "

" Hush, my dear child. Marion, we never think about such things. Like pictures of the crucifixion and crown of thorns, these things show us Christ too much in His humiliation, and we ought to turn all our thoughts to Him glorified. But what is all you have been telling me to lead to ? "

" I was going to say, that as long as Jesus was here, He talked to people and they talked to Him, just as you and I are talking now. He cured them, and helped them, and made them happy in many ways. But then He died, and since then, except once when He spoke to Paul, God has kept in heaven. And really, Mr. Lisle, this seems hardly fair to me. Why do you think it is that these people should talk to Him for thousands of years face to face almost, and that we should never see Him, or be able to speak to Him at all? If there were only a room always shut up, and I only knew He were inside, as the Jews did, I could talk to Him through the door. Do you understand me?"

"Quite, but I do not agree with you. The veil that lies between us and Christ in heaven is as thin as that which lay between the Israelites and the Shechinah. Marion, we live by faith; the old order of things has passed away, and with it the ordinance of things visible."

"But did not the people who followed our Lord live by faith too, else how did they know that He was God?"

"Of course they did. But do you think the Apostles loved Him less and prayed less to Him after He had gone from them?"

"No; because they had really seen Him and knew Him as He really was. But I always fancy they said very different prayers to us. Do not be vexed, Mr. Lisle; but I fancy if I could only see the land where Christ once walked and talked, He would seem more real to me. Of course I believe in Him; you know I do; but the sky seems so very high, and they say space goes on for ever, and so I cannot imagine where God and heaven are!"

"Everywhere, Marion."

"Yes, I know that too, because God is a Spirit. But this idea of God is too grand for me, and I love to think of Him rather as the Man Christ Jesus. This is what I mean. His body was not everywhere when He walked about Galilee, nor when He was crucified, and the last time the Apostles saw Him, before the cloud received Him out of their sight, He was still a man; and yet, now, He seems to be once again a great grand Spirit, that loves us and takes care of us, but who does not come near us any more."

"You are a strange child," exclaimed the curate, looking up at her from the ivy leaf he had been playing with during the conversation, "but do not be alarmed; your ideas are more fanciful than wrong. You must not, however, indulge in them. When you are older, these things will be more clear. We cannot be too careful in watching, lest, unknown to ourselves, we should try to penetrate the mysteries of God. He manifested Himself once for His own wise purposes, He hides Himself now for the same. It must have been very glorious to have talked face to face with Jesus; but prayer is still left us, and we must pray."

"But I would rather talk to Him," still persisted Marion.

"And was this what you were thinking about all the time you were standing in the porch?"

"No, I did not think of this at all then; I was wishing I was poor."

"Poor! Why?"

"Because then I should have some companions. All the cottage children seemed so happy together when they came out of church, that I quite dreaded going home to be by myself."

"Have you not dear mamma?"

"Yes; but Miss Leicester is spending the afternoon with us, and she talks all the time to mamma, and so I have nothing to do but to walk about the garden, and read Sunday books, unless I go and talk to Nursey, who likes to read herself, and does not want to be bothered. I can amuse myself many ways on other days with such things as my music, but all the hymns I know are the Sicilian Mariner's and the Evening Hymn, and I can't play anything but sacred music on Sunday."

"Of course not. And so Sunday is a dull day, is it?"

"Yes, very."

"I am sorry to hear it."

"I cannot help it : it is not my fault. What ought I to do?"

"Read, pray, and meditate."

"So I do, Mr. Lisle, as well as I can and as much as I can; but though I like religious books, some of them very much, I do get tired of reading them after a while, and then comes my dull time. Why, I get so sick of doing nothing, that I get quite tired for the evening service. If you had not preached such a nice sermon this evening, I should have gone to sleep."

The clergyman smiled. "I am glad you liked it."

There was silence for a few minutes, during which Marion seemed very thoughtful.

"I want to ask you a question, Mr. Lisle, about something that makes me feel very sorry," she said at length.

"What is it?"

"Are people generally, do you think, as wicked as they are in Ennington?"

"In Ennington! What do you mean?"

"Miss Leicester says there is hardly a good person anywhere about here. Did you not know it?"

"I do not understand you," replied the curate, with a face of blank astonishment.

"Would you like me to tell you all Miss Leicester said?"

"Yes," said Mr. Lisle, after a moment's hesitation, and rising from the wall on which he had been seated.

"Well, she says Greaves the butcher is a cheat, and so are Mr. Scott and Farmer Gribble; and that Bill Rogers is sure to be hanged, for he is going all the wrong way. It seems everybody is wicked, even that pretty little Mary Dawson that used to work for us."

"Is this all?" he asked.

"No, indeed, it is not. She said something about my dear kind Mr. Bernard that has made me feel quite wretched. She says he kills more people than he cures. Do you think he does it on purpose? He seems so very good."

"Mr. Bernard!" exclaimed the curate. "Good heavens, what will she say next! What a "—— he stopped with an effort. "No, my child, Miss Leicester is mistaken. Mr. Bernard is a clever doctor, and one of the best men I know."

"So I thought. I will tell mamma what you say."

"No, do not mention him ; I will call on mamma myself to-morrow, and then I can speak to her about him. Are these all the wicked people ? "

" No, not nearly all," and she repeated the slanderer's tale, in which so many a fair fame had been blackened that the clergy-man's heart was fairly wrung.

" Marion," he observed, as they left the churchyard, "it will be better for you to say no more to any one else about all this you have been telling me. I do not, of course, suppose that Miss Leicester has been telling your mamma wilful untruths in all this ; but she is quite mistaken : the people of Ennington are very good. Of course they have their faults, but who has not ? The greater part of them are poor, and want brings with it many temptations of which those more favourably situated rarely dream. It is our place to try and make them better, to teach them from our superior knowledge, and help them with our time, advice, and money, as far as we are able. Would you like to visit for me, and teach in our schools ? "

" Mamma would not let me, or else I should, very much. But what could I teach them ? "

" To love God and to be good."

" But I am not good myself."

There was so much ingenuousness in the reply that Mr. Lisle could hardly repress a smile.

" Suppose I ask mamma about it ; if she will let us have you, we shall know how to make you useful—that is, if you would like it yourself."

" Oh, I should, indeed I should !" and the blue eyes danced again.

" How old are you ? "

" Twelve. Mamma says I am a great baby for my age, and so I suppose I am. My cousins in London are quite women by the side of me, and they are very little older." And Marion looked down almost dejectedly.

" You are quite womanly enough to please me, Marion," replied the curate gently.

" Am I ? " said the child, chasing the shadow with a very bright smile.

" Have you heard from India lately ? "

" No, not for a long time. Mamma says that perhaps, as Edward is only my half-brother, as he grows older, and makes new friends, he will not write to us so often as he did once. This makes me feel very unhappy, for he used to write me such dear nice letters. But I think mamma must be mistaken, you know ; for the very last time he wrote he said he would save money as fast as he could, to come over to England to see his little Golden-hair. Isn't that a funny name for him to call me by ? but he always does. I am quite used to it now."

The curate glanced at the lovely curls that shaded the sweet face.

" Would you not like to see him ? "

"Of course I would; but I have a portrait that he sent me last summer, and I kiss that every night, and so feel a little as though I had him. He seems much more real than he did before the portrait came."

"I can well understand that," replied the curate.

"Then, that is very much what I feel about our Lord. Even a picture of Him makes Him seem more real, because I can fancy what He used to be. Mamma has one called the 'Man of Sorrows,' that I could look at for ever. This is not wrong, is it?"

"Very wrong; so wrong that you make me almost uneasy to hear you talk so. 'Worship God in spirit and in truth,' and do not trouble your head about any such nonsense. Take care, little one; the lamb must keep very close to the fold of the Good Shepherd. Good-night."

"Won't you come in?" asked the child, opening the garden gate.

"Not to-night. Tell mamma I will call to-morrow morning." He took her hand, and looked earnestly into her blue eyes. There was something in the little form before him that interested him very deeply. "Good-night, Golden-hair."

Had another spoken the word, she would have resented it almost as a sacrilege. But a smile mantled over her face as she watched his retreating figure down the little street. "I wonder if Edward is at all like him," she mused. "Mr. Lisle is only three years older; but one is a soldier and the other a clergyman. They must be very different."

CHAPTER II.

Mrs. Howard was not displeased with the curate's message. Even she could hardly fail to be gratified by the friendship of a man so universally beloved, notwithstanding her indifference to Ennington society in general. Whether, however, she lingered longer than usual over her morning toilette, we shall not inquire, or whether Marion would have been permitted to pluck quite so bright a bouquet, had it not been in honour of the anticipated visitor. Be all this as it may, it would have been hard to determine whether the lady herself, her child, or the flowers, looked the most blooming when the curate was ushered into the room, where, under the direction of her mother, Marion was copying a bust of Ulysses.

"I am afraid I am interrupting the lessons," he observed, drawing back.

"Not at all; we were just about to put by, for Marion has been very industrious."

"May I look?" he asked, taking up her drawing. "You have

caught the great hero's expression exactly," he continued; "I had no idea you were such a skilful little artist! One hardly knows which to admire most, the science of the teacher, or the aptness of the pupil; both must have had their share in producing such a sketch as this."

Marion blushed with pleasure, for she felt the kind criticism was sincere.

"How long has she learned?" he asked.

"Ever since she could hold a pencil," replied the mother; "but Marion has a decided talent for drawing. Run and fetch your portfolio, perhaps Mr. Lisle would like to look through it."

"Indeed, I should. The idea of a child of her age producing anything like that outline is most surprising," he observed, as Marion closed the door behind her. "It is boldness itself!"

Mrs. Howard smiled a warm, genuine, gratified smile, no relation at all to those she bestowed on poor little Miss Leicester.

Mr. Lisle was a long time examining the portfolio. "You seem fond of religious subjects," he remarked, as he turned over copies of Raphael's Madonna, and more than one Ecce Homo.

"Yes," replied Mrs. Howard, "and as I wish her to cultivate her own taste rather than an acquired one, I have taken some pains to procure the copies. Do not you like them?"

"I prefer other subjects."

"May I ask why? You surely do not see any harm in them?"

"There may be, or there may not," he replied gravely. "Marion has imagination, which is a bad element to bring into religion, when all should be simple matter-of-fact. You, as her mother, can best judge whether these pictured representations of mighty truths have an evil effect upon her."

Mrs. Howard was a woman of the world, and could talk well and wisely of its learning, science, and fashion; but things "not of the world" were out of her scope, and of everything, except the broadest doctrines of Christianity, she was profoundly ignorant. Whether imagination was, or was not, a legitimate element of religion, it had never entered into her mind to question, and she hastened to change the subject, lest she should get beyond her depth.

"Are you fond of flowers, Mr. Lisle?"

"Very," was the laconic reply, as he continued to turn over the drawings, admiring and criticising by turns.

"And so this is your idea of your brother Edward, is it?" he asked, holding up a pencil-drawing of a soldier, under which "Edward" was written in a very round hand.

"No, not at all now, for I have his proper portrait. Shall I show it to you?"

It was certainly the portrait of a brother of whom one might be proud, and Mr. Lisle thought so as he looked at it.

"He is a noble-looking fellow, this son of yours!" he exclaimed, glancing up at Mrs. Howard.

The flush of annoyance that passed over her countenance showed him at once that the relationship was not a pleasing one;

but remembering that "a rent is sometimes better than a darn," he continued, without appearing to observe her vexation—

"I suppose I shall some day have the pleasure of knowing him. I hope so, for I am sure I should like him, from his fine, open face. Although so different, I can trace a likeness between him and his sister."

Marion crept nearer to the speaker; to be considered like Edward was almost too delightful.

"I am so glad you think so!" she exclaimed; "but I should wish to be like him in other things, too. Mamma and I saw a gentleman last year in London, the one who brought us this photograph, and he says no one has any idea of the good he does among the soldiers."

"Indeed! Then, if he sets her such an example, little Golden-hair must certainly try to follow in his footsteps, and this is no bad introduction to the main object of my visit; for, do you know, mamma," he added with a smile, "that I have come to ask you to let Marion help us a little with our schools and poor. I know we have tested your liberality often, but we really need workers in our little vineyard, almost as much as means for carrying on its operations. I am sure you will try and let her do something for us. I know she would soon grow to like the work, and I promise not to overburden her. It would help to form her character in many ways."

Mrs. Howard was silent. She did not wish to give a flat refusal, but to mix with the lower classes in any way, was a formation of her daughter's character which she by no means desired. Calm, cold, and unapproachable, she was one who never unbent with her inferiors. Money she rarely withheld, but her sympathy she as rarely bestowed; and, though often munificent, was never charitable. No gentle word ever accompanied her gift, no smile her still rarer advice. The poor felt it was their interest to conciliate her, but they hated her for the indifference with which she treated them. With her servants she was the same. She expected from them no more than the duties for which she paid them, though she seldom excused their faults, but she never sought their confidence in their joys or sorrows, nor advised them in their difficulties. They waited on her unthanked, the villagers made way for her unnoticed; even the little children, who bobbed down before her on the path, were unrewarded by a single smile.

"I really cannot say," she replied at length; "Marion is so perfectly unaccustomed to anything of the kind, that I am afraid you would find her more plague than profit."

"Not at all," returned the curate, "I should only impose very light duties on her for some time to come yet, and we should soon train her with the co-operation of Mrs. Stebbing."

"Mrs. Stebbing! I did not know that she took any active part in the parish."

"But she most certainly does. I have heard her husband say repeatedly that she is as good to him as a second curate."

"I understand," sneered the lady ; "it is to please him she does it."

"Not altogether," replied Mr. Lisle, hurt at the tone ; "she does it first from a high sense of duty, and secondly to gratify him. Do these motives displease you ?"

Mrs. Howard smiled incredulously.

"Your flowers are very beautiful," observed the gentleman, rising and walking to the French window ; "might I ask a nearer view of them ? I have never been round your garden yet."

"Come, then, now, by all means," said the lady, stepping out upon the lawn. The clergyman followed, and for some minutes they rambled among the flower-beds in silence, until they reached a bench in a little corner, fragrant with honeysuckle and jasmine.

"I can see, Mrs. Howard, that you do not admire our friend, Mrs. Stebbing. May I ask why ?" asked the curate suddenly.

"It is no case of either admiration or dislike," answered the lady ; "but I was rather amused at your considering her desire to gratify her old husband a praiseworthy motive of action, as though it were her interest to do anything else."

"Pardon me, but I do not understand you."

"Well, Mrs. Stebbing is, I can see, a favourite of yours ; but you have asked me a question, and must not be offended at a frank answer. I have not a word to say against her ; she seems a quiet, good-natured, prim little woman, though one, I should imagine, without much soul. But do you suppose that any one with any discernment cannot see that she married the doctor for his money, and that therefore it is clearly her interest to please him ? I do not blame her for trying to do so ; indeed, she would, I suppose, be wonderfully wanting in common sense were she to act otherwise."

"But what has given you this idea, my dear madam ?"

"For what other possible reason would a nice-looking girl of two or three-and-twenty shut herself up with an old man of sixty, to find her sole recreation in beating the alphabet into the heads of stupid little children, binding up old men's cuts and bruises, and going from cottage to cottage listening to old women's twaddle ? Excuse me, Mr. Lisle, but I must tell you that my ideas of district-visiting are not very elevated."

"I can see they are not," replied the gentleman, "and I hardly know whether your idea of Mrs. Stebbing or her labour of charity is the more erroneous. But, if you will permit me, I will tell you the truth, as it stands. Dr. Stebbing is eight and forty, old-looking for his age, I grant, though such it is. His wife is twenty-seven. She is an heiress, but her property is entirely settled on herself by her husband. If he carries out all the plans of improvement he has projected, his own money will be spent during his lifetime, so that she will have but small expectations at his death. It seems she first learned his worth about seven years ago at the death-bed of her father, whom Dr. Stebbing attended as an old college friend. He saw the impression his kindness had made on the orphan girl, but wishing her to see more of the world before linking herself to him for life, he left her undisturbed for three years. Finding, however, that she refused the most eligible offers, he presented himself to her as a suitor, and a happier couple I have never seen."

"It seems, then, I have been misinformed, but I have been given clearly to understand, by a person who knows the rector and his wife, that my original surmise was true."

"Then may I advise you to set that person right at your earliest opportunity, and give me as your authority in doing so? How deeply grieved poor Mrs. Stebbing would be, could she know the unworthy motives that have been imputed to her! Never was scandal more unjust than in this case. But I should have thought that you, who have lived so much longer in the parish than I, would have known Mrs. Stebbing intimately."

"Our old rector had only been dead a year before you came, and the rectory was vacant some little time, so that I have only known Mrs. Stebbing a few months longer than you; and although we occasionally exchange visits, we are still comparatively strangers to each other—we have so little in common."

"True," was on the curate's lips, but he repressed the word, and pondered the difficult task before him instead. Now or never must he come to the object of his visit; now or never must the proud woman at his side be humbled. Should he give way and suffer yesterday's scandal to be repeated? He leaned his cheek upon his hand apparently absorbed in the contemplation of a bee struggling in the depths of a blue-bell. The morning was very still, calm with that sweet summer stillness peculiar to a June day, when the sky above, radiant in its blueness, is unflecked by a single cloud. The trees over their head stood motionless, while in the midday heat the very birds were silent. The only stirring sounds were the ripple of the little stream that bordered the garden with the hum of the mill it turned, the quiet clucking of the hens on the opposite bank, and the sweet clear trill of Marion's canary from the house. Yet all these distant sounds only made the silence round them the more palpable, and the more difficult for the Rev. Henry Lisle to break with his homily. It was not until his bee, having risen like an old toper from his cup, indulged them with an animated buzz that he commenced.

"Mrs. Howard, will you give me leave to tell you one of the main objects of my visit?"

The lady started: there was something so earnest and yet so timid in his manner, that she hardly knew what to think. Did he forget the years between them? It would not, even if he did, be the first time that she had known infatuation bridge such a discrepancy. In an instant, however, she was collected, and adjusting the cuff of her dress. He had just mortified her; was he going to give her her revenge?

"Last night," he commenced, turning a little pebble with his stick, "I had a long conversation with Marion. Did she tell you of it?"

"She simply said you had been talking to her. What was it about?"

"About many things; but, led to the subject by her own child-like thoughts, our principal conversation was of all the sad things she had heard Miss Leicester tell you concerning the village people; and allow me to say, my dear madam, for the greater part they were most untrue. You will perhaps think that I ought rather to have addressed myself to Miss Leicester; but she is, I fear, too far gone in this most miserable failing for anything I could say to take any effect. She will always make mischief. It seems to be the very air she breathes; nothing can win, or shame her from it. But will you allow me to remind you, my dear Mrs. Howard, that you at least have too much at stake, if only in your child, to encourage her in her most mischievous propensity. There is hardly one whose character she last night aspersed before you and little Marion whom I could not as easily justify as Mrs. Stebbing. I am only a young man, I know, and anything bordering on censure would be impertinence, but do let me warn you as a friend to discountenance Miss Leicester's stories before Marion, and, let me add, yourself. 'For every idle word that man shall speak, he shall give account thereof in the day of judgment.' Are not such words as these worse than idle? Marion began last night by asking me if the people were everywhere as wicked as in Ennington. Is this the spirit with which she should regard those among whom she has grown up from babyhood, this the light in which she should look on God's poor? Are there not bright and beautiful things around to give us subject for conversation, without descending to the shadows of human frailty, if not to the actual degradation of sin? I only repeat a fact patent throughout all the village when I say that Miss Leicester is a dangerous woman. Oh! for the sake of Him whose every breath was love, discourage her. I am very anxious to see Marion useful amongst the poor, but it was rather to say all this to you than for anything else that I troubled you this morning. You must not be angry with me."

"Not at all," replied the lady with constrained politeness. "And may we have Marion?"

"I am afraid not. She has much to do in her studies for many years; besides, surely Mrs. Stebbing is enough for this small parish."

"So far from that, we have work enough for five or six tract-distributors."

"Mr. Lisle, I detest tract-distributing,—now you have the truth! Shall I give you my experience of it? My sister was what most people call a thorough Christian, and a district visitor."

"Not much family likeness," was the uncharitable thought that slipped through the gentleman's mind.

"That was when she was about eighteen; she grew rather worldly afterwards, for at five-and-twenty she eloped from a ball with a half-pay captain."

The curate made no reply.

"But she was really very pious for all that," she continued, curling her pretty lip. "Now, shall I give you the programme of her proceedings? Her district was a crowded, dirty, narrow, ill-smelling court, rejoicing, as such localities often do rejoice, in the name of 'Beattie's Gardens,' I remember. Well, she used to knock at a door—if the poor things were dining, so much the worse ; if they were not, so much the better. In either case the last week's tract must be sought for amid the grumbling of the husband and wife and the squalling of the children, the former accusing each other of having lost it, the latter cuffed by their parents for not finding it. Then the mockery, at other times, of visiting a house where the cupboard was bare, and presenting them with a tract. Well, Mr. Lisle, I do not profess the cant of brotherhood with the working-man, nor do I see a sisterhood in starving seamstresses, but I could not do this. And what were these tracts after all? Sometimes a tirade against Romanism, in which Popery and Paganism were strangely jumbled ; anecdotes of precocious children, who always died singing about Canaan, as a reward for being good (an inducement to many children, I should think, to keep naughty), remarks on temperance, from the pens of reformed drunkards, publicly confessing their enormities with the greatest possible zest and effrontery,—the whole seasoned with just the sort of ideas on religion one expects to hear in the vestry prayer-meeting of a Baptist chapel. Now with such an experience as this of tracts and tract-distributing, could I conscientiously give you Marion?"

"Perhaps not," replied Mr. Lisle, who saw that his companion was thoroughly annoyed. "But let me say that, although what you have just said is in a measure true, you have stated the abuse, not the legitimate work and end, of tract-lending. As a reverse to your picture, I would say that to visit the sick and poor is to follow in the footsteps of Him, who came not to be ministered to but to minister ; and though in large towns the work is attended with all the difficulties you enumerate (especially if the visitors be inexperienced or wanting in discretion, as young ladies sometimes are), still in the country it is different. Here we seem to know, and take an interest in, each person visited."

"Granted, but the system remains the same. It seems to me to involve an unnecessary contact with uncultivated spirits and rough manners, from which the refined mind naturally shrinks. If a poor man wants aid, let him come and ask it, well and good ; but do not go to him. There is no necessity for it, for, depend upon it, the poor are never behindhand in making known their necessities."

"That the generality of the respectable poor are not intrusive with their wants, short as my ministry has been, I know from experience ; while, if there is anything, my dear Mrs. Howard, that can exalt the already-refined mind, it is the contact with God's own poor. By this one sees the utter worthlessness of human distinction and human wealth. What would not Dives

have learned, think you, had he communed with Lazarus? What
girl could give all her time to pleasure, all her heart to vanity,
and all her money to dress, if she felt that her fellow-creatures
were perishing from want? But if poverty has its own peculiar
troubles, it has its own peculiar pride. You look incredulous,
but it is true. As a rule, the respectable poor are behindhand
in proclaiming their wants. I do not, of course, allude to those
whom idleness has reduced to an indigence which they prefer to
labour, but to those who, having fallen through misfortune, struggle
on, as hundreds, thousands do, unassisted, until discovered by
some friendly passer-by. And in the ordinary course of a
labourer's life, there must be seasons when, even without misfortune, he needs assistance. Depend upon it, it is our duty to discover
this, and to lend, when it is in our power, the helping hand,
counselling him in his perplexities, guiding him in his difficulties,
and teaching him through all to look to God, and live for heaven.
Oh, Mrs. Howard, can you dislike such a work of love as this,
undertaken for Christ, continued in Christ, ending only with
Christ?"

She was silent, and once more the summer stillness prevailed.
Again the hens clucked, the canary sang, and another bee buzzed
in the bluebell. Their reflections were very different; he rejoicing truly that his task was over; she silently fuming, fretting,
and chafing. He had done his duty as a pastor; she had been
lectured like a cottager, scolded like a child, talked to like a
heathen. But the sun beginning to creep round among the roses
and honeysuckles, their retreat began, like their conversation,
to grow warm, and the curate rose to take his leave. They walked
down the path together. "May I have a rose?" he asked as they
passed a cluster of bright buds.

"Certainly;" but she neither stopped nor aided him to gather
one.

He plucked the flower himself, at the same time presenting one
to her.

"Thank you," was the cool acceptance; "will you stay luncheon?" she asked, as they entered the house.

"You must excuse me this morning, I have not yet been to the
schools. Good-bye, Marion: your bird sings very nicely; he is
the prime pet, I suppose?"

"No, there is my real favourite, Mr. Lisle, my spoiled child,"
and Marion pointed to her large grey cat sunning himself on the
lawn. "Come here, Tyrza."

Tyrza loved his little mistress, but he loved sunshine better, so
he blinked his green eyes and stayed where he was.

"There, Mr. Lisle, what could I do with children, when even
my cat is disobedient to me?"

"You are not going to try, Marion," replied her mother very
quickly. "I have told Mr. Lisle that you have enough to do, for
the present, in your studies."

Marion's countenance fell, but she stole a glance at a pair of quiet eyes, which said as plainly as eyes could speak, "Patience, little Golden-hair."

So Mr. Lisle departed to the village school, with its motley children and sleepy hum; Mrs. Howard went upstairs to get over her discomfiture as she best might; while Marion sat in the summer-house with her needlework and pussy, and thought of India and Edward far away.

CHAPTER III.

IT was on the morning of the day following that the postman handed Marion a letter over the railing of the little garden, where she was bustling about in her own fashion, tying, sticking, arranging and watering. Passing it to her mother through the open window, she continued her work, every now and then interrupted by Tyrza, who was amusing himself with springing out, tiger fashion, on his mistress's string, and then rolling over with it in the exuberance of his feline joy.

"You are a nuisance, Tyrza, really you are," was, however, the only rebuke he met with, as half-a-dozen yards of the ball lay unwound on the path.

"Marion, come here a minute," was the summons from the window; and Marion jumped up with so much alacrity that Tyrza pretended to be startled, and scuffled off under a box-tree.

Mrs. Howard, in the prettiest of little caps and the neatest of morning dresses, was seated at the breakfast table, not yet cleared, with the letter open in her hand, which she handed to her little daughter. It ran thus—

"MY DEAR FRIEND,—You know it has always been a promise, even when our home was smoky, dirty Manchester, that you should visit us. While located there, however, I could never find it in my heart to urge you to leave your dear little retreat, much as I often longed for your society. You know, this is not the language of compliment, for, linked as you are with my earliest recollections, I always look upon you, after my husband, children, and brother (all that are left me now), as my nearest and dearest friend on earth. You are surprised, I can well imagine, that we have not been over to see you, considering that we have been here since March; but there is so much to be done in settling and arranging such a large household as mine really is now, that I could not manage it, nor did I wish you to come here until I could entertain you, and give you up my time as I could wish. All is now straight, so when may we expect you, not for a day or two, but for a long, long visit, to make amends for our weary separation? Only tell us the day you will be ready, and my husband will fetch you and dear little Marion, whom I long to see;

and heartily, most heartily, dearest Margaret, shall we welcome you to the Cedars.   MARY DARRELL."

"Mamma, how delightful! when will you go?" cried Marion, whose eyes were sparkling with rapture.

"Really, my dear child, I can hardly say. There are so many things to attend to, that I cannot see how I can possibly accept this invitation just now. Indeed, it is not improbable that I may have to go up to London next week; for, in consequence of poor Captain Thompson's death, who was the last remaining executor of your papa's will, it is very likely I shall be wanted there; and business, you know, must stand before everything."

"Of course it must," replied Marion, trying not to look disappointed.

"How would you like to go without me?"

"Oh, not at all, mamma! let me stay with you."

"Spoiled child!" said her mother, drawing her to her and kissing her. "Well, we need not trouble ourselves about it now, as I shall not answer the letter till this evening; meantime I will think it over, and see what will be best for us to do. Now run back to your gardening."

Marion thought a great deal about the Cedars, but no more was said upon the subject during the day, which happened to be rather a busy one for Mrs. Howard, and it was with a palpitating heart that the little girl saw her mother seat herself at her desk in the evening.

"Marion, come here."

Marion obeyed, and marched up to the little table to hear sentence pronounced.

"Now, my dear child, I have considered the matter well, and we must be reasonable, you know. I see I must go to London, and it would make me very uneasy, all the time of my stay there, to know that you were here by yourself, with no one to keep you company but Turner."

"But cannot I go with you?—I always do," pleaded Marion.

"No, my dear; this time your aunts are out of town, and I shall have to be poor Mrs. Thompson's guest; and even if she had given you an invitation, which she has not, the house of mourning would be a dull scene for your midsummer holidays. I think, therefore, if Mrs. Darrell will kindly take charge of you, I should like you to go to her."

"Very well, mamma. I dare say I shall be very happy, but you know I have never been anywhere without you, and I am afraid I shall feel very strange. Tell me about Mrs. Darrell. What is she like? Have you known her long?"

"She and Mr. Darrell are, I think I may say, Marion, the two nicest people I ever knew, and when I saw their children, which was, however, many years ago, when they were quite little, they bade fair to be as good as their parents; at any rate they have, I know, been well brought up. The only peculiarity about the family is that they are Catholics. This is not surprising in Mrs. Darrell, who is an Irish woman, but I can never understand why her husband should be one. There seems to me something so un-English in a Catholic."

"Roman Catholic, you must say, mamma," laughed Marion; "Mr. Lisle says we are Catholics!"

"Ah! Mr. Lisle says a great many things," replied Mrs. Howard angrily.

Poor little Marion looked astounded.

"Well, it does not much matter, Catholics or Roman Catholics, they are very nice and very good people. When I first knew Mrs. Darrell she was a girl at school. You have heard me speak of Mary St. Leger and her wild tricks?"

"Yes, very often; but I did not know that she was the same as Mrs. Darrell, or that she was not a Protestant."

"With regard to her religion, school girls seldom trouble themselves much about that. She belonged to an old Irish family, who prided themselves as much on their Popery as their pedigree, though one was pretty nearly as inexplicable to me as the other."

"Did you ever try to make her a Protestant?"

"I? Marion, what a notion! No, such an idea never came into my head; and if it had I should have been puzzled where to begin, for, however thoughtless we Protestant girls may have been, Mary St. Leger certainly had her religion at her fingers' ends, and could have silenced any one of us in two minutes."

"Where were you at school with her, mamma?"

"In Paris; we were there together for two years."

"Used you ever to go to the Catholic church with her?"

"Not with her particularly, but on great days we English girls used to go with the school; but I could never make much of the services."

"Did you ever ask her what they meant?"

"Not that I remember. Although I was young at the time, I was old enough to see the folly of worshipping God with so much show and nonsense. I had been told to take care that they did not make a Catholic of me, but there was no occasion for the warning. As I never spoke to Mary of her religion except to ridicule it, she was not likely to make it a theme of conversation. In everything else we were very great friends, and in after years, on our return to England, circumstances cemented us more closely. Mr. St. Leger's family, as well as my own, lived in London, so that Mary and I frequently interchanged visits. It was at a ball given by Mr. St. Leger, when his daughter came of age, that I first met your papa. Mary was already engaged to Mr. Darrell, and our weddings took place within a month of each other. As I had been married five years before you were born, her children are all rather older than you. When you were a year old, they went to settle in Manchester, and except once, about four years ago, and then only for a few hours at your aunt's, I have never seen them since. I know you will like them both, and I am quite certain Mrs. Darrell will do all in her power to make you happy."

And so a letter was written, explaining how matters stood,
and by an answer, received the next day, it was arranged that
Marion should be fetched the following week, and remain Mrs.
Darrell's guest during her mother's absence.

It was again Sunday, and again came the usual Sunday routine.
Marion rose at eight, said her prayers, read her chapter, and then
walked round and round the garden till breakfast time. After
breakfast came another walk up and down the path with solemn
old Baxter in her hand, and after this the morning service in the
little grey church, with a very "ponderous sermon" from Dr. Stebbing, while the hour between church-time and dinner was spent in
dressing and redressing her mother's beautiful long hair. But
with the afternoon came the time that poor little Marion found so
weary, and yet it was better to-day than it had been the Sunday
before, for Miss Leicester did not come, and the little girl and her
mother had it all to themselves. Mrs. Howard was soon asleep,
not so Marion. She read Pilgrim's Progress and the Holy War
till she was tired, and littered her Sunday library about in all
directions, in the vain hope of finding something fresh. Naughty
child ! how longingly she glanced at her drawing-case and paint-
box, at the piano and the long row of "Chambers's Works," not
half read through. "Now, if it were not Sunday," she began,
but checked herself immediately. The recollection of Mr. Lisle's
grave look in answer to her complaint that "Sunday was a dull
day," flitted across her mind. This brought with it a thought that
had occupied her not a little during the last few days. "Why is
mamma so vexed with Mr. Lisle? I was afraid she would be
angry at the idea of my teaching in the Sunday-school, but I wish
very much she would have let me do something, for I am so dull
like this. This time next week I suppose I shall not be here."

A host of anticipations here somewhat distracted her awhile,
and walking out again into the garden she seated herself with
Tyrza on the little bench, the scene of Mrs. Howard's conversation
with her spiritual pastor. "Pussy," she exclaimed at length,
growing tired of her musings, "cats must be very happy, I should
think, to be allowed to do what they like on Sundays. God made
you as well as me, and I wonder why He lets you catch mice and
frisk about and purr, while I cannot do anything. I suppose it is
because you have no soul : is that the reason, should you think,
little pussy? I wonder what people do in heaven," she continued,
after a short pause ; "Dr. Stebbing says it will be an eternal
Sabbath. Dear me, how strange ! I am sure it must be something very different to this, or many people would not be happy
there at all."

At this moment she caught sight of old Turner, who in her
Sunday gown, white apron, and quaint old-fashioned cap, with
its bow of black ribbons on the top, was walking slowly down to
her.

"O nursey, I am so glad you have come. I thought you had
gone out, and I want some one to talk to."

The old woman smiled. "Well, deary, it's not much you'll get by talking to the likes of me."

"Nursey, do you like Sunday?"

"Bless you, Miss Marion, of course I do; isn't it the Lord's Day?"

"Yes, but, for all that, don't you sometimes get tired of it?"

"No, never, Miss Marion; it's all too short for me."

"What do you do to amuse yourself, then, all the afternoon and evening?"

"I read my Bible, my dear, and sometimes I think about my poor old husband, and how him and me used to sit together in the old times, and how we shall be together again some day, in the Lord's good time, in heaven."

"Nursey, what do you think heaven is like?"

"A beautiful bright place, child, where the angels are flying about singing, and where we shall always be together all dressed in white, with golden crowns on our heads, and playing hymns on golden harps for ever."

"Don't you think, nursey—at least, don't you think, perhaps—people will get tired of doing this always?"

"Of course not; it isn't right to talk like that, Miss Marion. But," added the old woman tenderly, seeing Marion's abashed look, "come here, deary, and I'll tell you what I think. We oughtn't to worrit ourselves any way about it; heaven, perhaps, is something very different to that, we can't tell, but we know it is as beautiful as God Almighty can make it, and, any rate, that ought to satisfy us."

"Yes," returned the child thoughtfully, "if He has made this world so beautiful, heaven must be something better. I see. But, nursey, I do not fancy it as you do."

"Never mind, child, what you fancy, as long as you try to get there, by putting your trust in your Saviour."

"Nursey, there is one thing that always puzzles me, and that is, how very good and clever people can have just the same happiness as those who are only pretty good or who know very little."

"Well, I'll tell you, Miss Marion, a thing as has sometimes come into my head. If you fill a half-pint pot up to the brim, it can't hold no more, nor a quart pot neither. If you was to try to pour a quart of water into the little measure, it couldn't hold it, because, don't you see, it wouldn't be in its nature, but half a pint of water would leave a very big gap in the quart pot. This is how I think it is in heaven. St. Paul is the quart pot, I, p'raps, am the half pint. The glory God will give to him will be more than I could bear, while my glory in heaven will be enough for the likes of me, but hardly more p'raps than St. Paul had here."

"O Turner, what a funny notion!" exclaimed Marion, laughing heartily, while the old woman joined her; "but, I am sure it is very true. Even Mr. Lisle never said anything better than that in his sermons!"

"Mr. Lisle! the Lord love his sweet face!"

"He is very good, isn't he, nursey ?"

"As good as gold!" cried the old woman enthusiastically. "He's been here only two years, but the people all about love him as much as if he had been born and bred among them."

"Do you know where he came from ?" asked Marion.

"From Scotland. This is the very first ministry he was ever in. He was ordained, so I'm told, only a month before he came here. His father and mother have been dead some time, and I heard some one say as he has no near relation but one sister married, and that's all I know about him."

"Is he rich, should you think ?"

"They say he has only what he gets for being here, but howsomever, he does more with the little he's got than some people do with thousands on thousands. There's more than one old man and woman in the place, as would be on the parish if it wasn't for him. The Lord love him, I say !"

At this moment the summons arrived to tea, and, with a kiss on the old nurse's withered cheek, Marion ran into the house.

Mrs. Howard did not go to church, but stayed at home to write letters instead. Again Marion started on her quiet walk up the sunny street, again the villagers lingered on the side paths and by their doors. Was it that nature's holiday-dress was gayer, or was it that the cloud of distrust had cleared away since her conversation with Mr. Lisle ? However it may have been, Marion felt very happy, and returned each friendly greeting with her own bright smile. Again Bill Rogers met her. "Do you think you could get me a few more primrose roots this week ?" she asked gently.

Bill looked up, the repulse of last Sunday evening was neither forgiven nor forgotten, but the bright eyes were too much for him.

"Lots on 'em, miss."

"I am so glad ; how is your mother ?"

"Much about the same," answered the boy. "She'll never be much better, they say," and, uncouth as he was, Marion saw something very like a wet eyelash.

"Will you give her this ?" asked Marion, taking sixpence from her little purse. "Good evening."

Again Bill stood and looked after her.

"Miss Howard !"

Marion stopped.

"Would you like a nest of young linnets ?"

"Oh no, no, indeed I would not !" replied Marion, most emphatically ; "please, please, Bill, don't rob the poor little things of their young ones for me. It is so very cruel !"

Bill grinned, not knowing what else to do.

"No, get me the flower-roots if you can, but not the birds. Are you going to church ?"

"No, I can't say as I be," replied the boy. "I was there this morning, and at school this afternoon, and I think that's enough for a lad as works hard all the week. Some folks don't seem to think so though, but I can't help that."

Marion glanced at the bronzed and freckled face and toilworn hands of the ploughboy. "He is right," was the judgment of the warm little heart.

Mr. Lisle was to take his ease, it seemed, to-day, for once again Dr. Stebbing mounted the pulpit, and the result, as usual, was a very dry sermon, extremely uninteresting to Marion, who thought more of the Cedars during its delivery than of justification by faith. On leaving the church she was joined by the rector's wife, and the reverend gentleman himself soon after overtaking them, they all three walked together towards the rectory.

Marion could not have said why, but she always felt a vast amount of awe in the presence of Dr. Stebbing. It was not his face, which was good-humour personified, nor his antique dress, nor his rather blunt manner, but there was something in the *tout ensemble* that always made her feel nervous.

"It is such a lovely evening, will you not come in and walk a little with us round the garden?" asked Mrs. Stebbing. "Mamma will hardly expect you yet."

"Do, my child," said the rector kindly.

Marion entered the door which he held open, and having spent some time in inspecting the cabinets and curiosities ranged round the old-fashioned library, the little party adjourned to the garden. It was very pleasant; the evening was so calm and still, with the sun setting amid a gorgeous pile of blood-red clouds, stretching from one side of the horizon to the other. The mill-stream, with which the rectory garden, like their own, was bounded, flowed lazily on, unruffled save by the flutter, now and then, of a minnow below, or the kiss of a dragon-fly above. Crowds of merry gnats danced around, bees hummed their homeward flight, and birds twittered in the trees above. The gossamer, too, spun her silken toil, the frog croaked in the meadow, the grasshopper chirped at their feet. Everything lay hushed in a silent, dreamy beauty, now broken by the voices of our friends, as they walked backwards and forwards by the side of the stream. Marion's share in the conversation was, however, extremely limited, for notwithstanding all the efforts of her host and hostess to make her feel at home with them, all they could get from her were monosyllables in reply. A step on the gravel made them turn their heads, and Mr. Lisle joined them.

"Here, Lisle!" exclaimed the rector, after a few minutes' conversation on parish matters, "see if you can make this young lady talk, she is wonderfully silent with us. Try what your magic words can do."

"What is the matter, Marion?" asked the curate, pulling one of the long curls, as the rector and his wife turned off down a side path.

"Nothing at all, Mr. Lisle, but really there has been nothing for me to say. I answered all the questions I was asked."

"But you manage to chatter very merrily sometimes, don't you ? "

"Yes, when I have anything to say ; but people should not talk for the sake of talking, should they ? "

"Well, Marion, it depends. Sometimes, to talk for talking's sake is a great kindness, but it is certainly more often a great folly, as in the case of half the small-talk we are doomed to listen to."

"Small talk ! What is that ? "

"It is the uttering of a great many words, without any aim but that of simply passing the time God has given us to improve. I have heard it spoken of as an acquisition to a person's style, that he or she had plenty of small-talk at command, but for myself, I have generally found such people more wearisome than anything else one meets with in society. I do think, however, that a man or woman with real conversational powers is a social treasure, to be highly prized for its rarity."

"I would rather be always silent than talk about nothing."

"Well decided !" laughed the clergyman. "Are not those clouds beautiful ? " he asked, pointing to the west. "Might not one almost imagine it was a little glimpse of heaven shining through to encourage us ? "

"I hope it will be fine to-morrow for my journey. Do you know I am going away ? "

"No: where are you going, and for how long ? "

"I do not know for how long, but we have received an invitation from Mrs. Darrell, a very old friend of mamma's. Mr. Darrell has just bought an estate at Harleyford, called the Cedars; do you know it ? "

"Yes, Harleyford is about nine miles from here, and a nice, clean, brisk little town it is. Let me see—the Cedars. Surely I have heard something about that house."

"It is rather an old one, I believe, and takes its name from two beautiful cedar-trees on the lawn at the back."

"The Cedars—Darrell," continued the curate thoughtfully ; "to be sure, I remember ; he bought the property last March ; but, Marion, somebody told me they were Romanists ! "

"So they are ; won't it be strange ? "

"Strange ! child, you do not mean to say you are going ! "

"Yes, I am really, to-morrow."

"What ! to stay in the house of a Romanist family, at your tender age and with your imagination ? "

"Why, Mr. Lisle, what harm will it do me ? Do tell me what Catholics are, for really I do not know."

"Roman Catholics ! " said the pastor crossly. "What are they ? —as people, they may be very well, but their religion ! "

"Is what ? " asked the child nervously.

"Is a gigantic lie. Were it only the thing of mummery and buffoonery it appears at first sight, it would not mislead bright spirits, as it has done, and is still doing. You are too young to understand all its mighty pretensions, claiming, as it does, infallibility and authority direct from God, or the intense presumption that says to every other religion and sect upon earth, I am right, and you are wrong. Marion, it is Antichrist, it is the Babylon denounced in Revelation, it is the masterpiece of Satan ! In the place of Christ, of that Saviour who died for them, they place the Virgin Mary, and where they pray once to God they pray many times to her. And no wonder ! Why should they look to Heaven for pardon, when the words of a priest, laughing in his sleeve at their folly, can forgive their sins ? or why look to the blood of a Saviour for redemption, when a few penances here, and a little purgatory hereafter, is a sufficient atonement for the blackest crimes? Ah ! little one, little one, your mother must indeed have confidence in her maternal influence ere she trusts you in such an atmosphere as this. Oh, Marion ! keep as close to her as possible, and away, as much as you can in common politeness, from even the children, should there be any. Should you get to love them, their priest, by an influence they dare not resist, will force them to wrest this very innocence of your heart to your eternal ruin. The more amiable Romanists appear, the more they are to be shunned ; for, depend upon it, Satan baits his hooks with the morsels sweetest to human nature. Believe me, I do not say all this in any uncharitable spirit, but the danger is imminent, and little Golden-hair is dear to us all. But keep near mamma, and I pray all may be well."

"Mr. Lisle, I am going alone," cried Marion, pale with excitement.

"Then may God have mercy on you !" exclaimed the curate.

There was a dead silence. The child trembled, Mr. Lisle groaned.

"Marion," he said at length, "you are going among all these dangers ; do you really think their blandishments will have no power to turn your young heart from God ?"

"No, I am sure they will not."

"Beware of presumption," he replied sternly. 'Watch and pray, lest ye enter into temptation.'"

"I mean that ; really, I do !"

"Well, then, my child, I commend you to God. Now, look here," he added, drawing a small book from his pocket; "this has been my companion for some years now, it once belonged to a friend that I shall never see again. One who—well, never mind, I shall be quite upset if I begin upon that. Now, promise me, whenever you see anything wrong, or, worse still, anything that appears to you inviting, to take this out and read a chapter ; or if you have not time for that, a few lines. Then you will be safe, for no girl ever read her Bible and became a Romanist. But come, it is getting chilly, and I must not let you stand here any longer or you will take cold."

They walked towards the house as he spoke, and found the doctor and Mrs. Stebbing waiting at the door.

"And has our little friend found her tongue?" asked the good-humoured rector, seizing her by the chin. "Why, what's the matter, Lisle?" he exclaimed, that gentleman's vexation being plainly visible.

"I have been grieved to hear that Miss Howard is going to visit a Roman Catholic family, and that Mrs. Howard will be unable to accompany her."

"Whew!" whistled the doctor. "Dangerous work that."

"How inconsiderate!" whispered Mrs. Stebbing, aside to the curate.

"Don't you be turning Papist!" cried the rector, "or you shall not come back into my parish, where there is not one but poor O'Leary, the cobbler. As for him, though, he is a perfect pattern of religious zeal. Why, that man walks over to Harleyford and back every Sunday to church! I wonder which of our parishioners would do that, Lisle, eh? Eighteen miles every Sunday! Sunshine, rain, snow, or hail, he never misses, unless he is ill."

"I have always heard it said that we might do well in copying the zeal of the Roman Catholics in their religion," observed his wife.

"How fast they are increasing!" exclaimed the rector. "I cannot understand it."

"And growing bolder every day," said Mr. Lisle; "but, no wonder, with the encouragement they get. Look at their churches and convents!"

"What! are there convents in England?" asked Marion, astonished.

"To be sure there are," replied the rector.

"With monks and nuns inside, like those we read of, hundreds of years ago?" continued Marion.

"Yes, just the same," said Mr. Lisle. "It is one of Popery's proudest vaunts that she never changes. What she is now, she was in the time of Mary and Catherine de Medicis. The lion's nature is the same, whether chained or ranging in his native woods."

"They were very dreadful then," said Marion. "They say Queen Mary burned even children and little babies. What a dreadful woman she must have been!"

"Stop, my child!" exclaimed the rector, "we must make allowance for the times, which were very barbarous. I believe Mary to have been a bigoted fanatical woman, but not the demon incarnate most historians paint her."

"But if the Catholic religion teaches people such dreadful things," said Marion, "for I remember now that somebody once told me that they even worship images, why does not God put a stop to it? Why does He let them increase?"

"Almost as puzzling a question," exclaimed Dr. Stebbing, laughing, "as when Friday asked Robinson Crusoe, 'Why God no kill de devil?' I do not know, my love; for purposes we cannot fathom. But we must not be uncharitable in talking even of what we know to be wrong; Roman Catholics do not worship images, they only reverence them with the same species of affection that we show to earthly things. In the same spirit exactly that you would kiss and fondle a portrait of your poor papa, the Romanist kisses his little crucifix; and as the peers of the realm bow even to the vacant throne of their sovereign, when she herself is absent, so do Catholics bow to the images of their saints, absent from earth."

"I do believe you are a little bit of a Papist yourself, John," whispered his wife, while Mr. Lisle looked decidedly blank.

"No, not at all," laughed the good-natured old doctor, "but 'fair play's a jewel;' and, I must say, the Catholics seldom get it from us. For instance, how often do we hear people say that they have expunged the second commandment altogether, finding it too hard upon their so-called idolatry?"

"Where is it, then, if they have not done so?" asked the curate.

"Where it ought to be; in their prayer-books and books of instruction."

"Pardon me, Dr. Stebbing!"

"Pardon me, Mr. Lisle, but I know what I am talking about. You must remember that the Bible did not stand originally as we have it now, divided into chapters and verses. Just look at the commandments as they stand in the twentieth chapter of Exodus. imagine them from beginning to end without division, and see if you would not have considered the matter of our first and second commandments as fitly suited to form the subject of one commandment. This arrangement the Catholic Church has adopted; and, though, of course, it matters little how you divide them, provided you get the whole sum and substance of the decalogue, I certainly think her division is the more perfect of the two. But you are quite under a delusion if you imagine that anything has been expunged from this version. With the exception of this difference, and a trifling deviation in the translation, the Protestant and Catholic tables of commandments are alike."

"But, believe me, Dr. Stebbing, that I have seen Roman Catholic catechisms in which the second commandment has been left out," triumphantly objected Mr. Lisle.

"And I have seen Protestant catechisms in which the commandments ran thus—

> " 'Thou shalt have none other Gods but Me,
> Unto no idol bow the knee,
> Take not the name of God in vain,
> Do not the Sabbath day profane.' &c.

Now, will you tell me, that that is the decalogue as delivered from Mount Sinai?"

"Of course not, but those catechisms were only for young children, and so only the substance of each commandment is given."

" And so were the Catholic catechisms that you saw for young children. And as only the commencement of each commandment is given, it naturally follows that in such catechisms a great portion of what we call the second commandment is left out. If, however, you should happen to come across the Douay catechism, and others authorised to be taught in Catholic schools, you will find the first commandment to the following effect :—

" ' I am the Lord thy God, who brought thee out of the land of Egypt, and out of the house of bondage. Thou shalt not have strange gods before Me. Thou shalt not make to thyself any graven thing, nor the likeness of anything that is in heaven above, or in the earth beneath, nor of those things which are in the waters under the earth. Thou shalt not adore them nor serve them. I am the Lord thy God, mighty, jealous, visiting the iniquity of fathers upon the children unto the third and fourth generation of them that hate Me, and showing mercy unto thousands of them that love Me and keep My commandments.' Depend upon it, there is quite enough to reprehend in their version of graver doctrines, without descending to hair-splitting and unworthy quibbles."

Much as Marion was interested in the conversation, she felt that her mother would be growing uneasy at her absence, and hastened to bid good-night to the doctor and his good little wife. Mr. Lisle accompanied her, not sorry to take leave of his rector, whose opinions, for the first time, he felt strongly inclined to censure.

"Good-night, Marion," he said, holding out his hand at the little gate. "Remember!" The child tripped into the house, and over supper retailed the conversation to her mother, nor did she omit Mr. Lisle's disapprobation of the proposed visit.

"I had better send my keys round to Mr. Lisle, and ask him to come and take the entire charge of my affairs," exclaimed the lady, reddening with anger. "You may safely go, my child, where your mother sends you." Marion crept into her arms, and nestled in her motherly embrace, and reassured that she was not going into the nest of dragons she had begun to dread, went to bed radiant with anticipation. "But I will keep my promise," she murmured, as she sank to sleep with the little black book under her pillow.

CHAPTER IV.

THE sun shone brightly from an unclouded sky as Marion sprang out of bed early next morning, awakened by the rural concert of cows, rooks, cocks, and bees, that came wafted through the open window, mingled with the perfume of summer flowers and new-mown hay. Had it not been for the one dull thought of leaving mamma, it would have been a morning of unmixed pleasure to our little girl, as she ran backwards and forwards, assisting her mother in arranging and packing her little fairy-like wardrobe of summer dresses. And when it was all finished, and the two little trunks were corded and carried downstairs, how very gladly Marion would have gone over all again.

"You will, of course, write to me often, Marion," said her mother.

"Yes, mamma, very often, and you will come yourself and fetch me, will you not?"

"If I can. Mrs. Darrell will, I know, see that you go to the Protestant church on Sundays. By the by, I expect you will find the Sunday rather a strange day to you. I do not know how Catholics spend it in England, but in Paris it seems to me very much like a week day. I quite forget how the St. Legers spent it in Manchester; it may be that I never passed one with them."

"May I just go to church with them once, if they ask me, to see what it is like?"

"Certainly, my dear, go to your own church in the morning, and then you may go with them wherever you like; I have never been into a Catholic chapel here, but I suppose it is much the same thing as in France. I have more confidence in you and them than Mr. Lisle seems to have in any of us, and it would be very dull for you to stay at home by yourself. Of course, however, my little girl will not forget to keep the Sabbath day holy, whatever she may see others do."

"Oh no, mamma! If I see anything you would not like, I will read or do something else. I will try and set them an example," and Marion looked very demure. "Now, I think I am ready," she exclaimed, as her mother put the finishing-touch to her little daughter's toilette, by twisting one of the bright long curls round her finger; "let us go downstairs and have a nice talk till Mr. Darrell comes."

"Hark!" said Mrs. Howard, and Marion's heart went pit-a-pat as the roll of a vehicle ceased at the gate.

"Mamma, it is Mr. Darrell!" she exclaimed, as from the window she caught sight of a tall figure walking up the path.

"Yes, it is Mr. Darrell," repeated the widow, almost mournfully, "and not much changed." A shadow passed over her face, for, notwithstanding her pleasure in meeting him, he brought back old times very vividly. A minute more, and they were all three in the parlour.

"Mary is dreadfully disappointed that you are not coming too," said Mr. Darrell, "and so are we all; but, I must say, I think you are doing right in going up to London at this particular juncture of your affairs; as for Edith and Emily, they are on the tiptoe of expectation, looking out for our little friend here. I thought at first of sending Joe for her with Tom to drive them, for I am literally obliged to make hay while the sun shines; but I thought

my legal experience might be of some use to you, so I drove over
in the dog-cart for her myself."

Here followed some business conversation between the two
elders, about as uninteresting to our readers as it was to Marion,
who ran out to order the luncheon. "I wonder what a dog-cart
is ?" she mused, and stopped to take a look at the vehicle; but the
varnished sides and plated harness flashing in the sun fully satisfied her scrutiny. "So that is a dog-cart; what a funny name for
such a handsome thing!"

Lunch was soon despatched, for Mr. Darrell, to use his own
expression, "never let the grass grow under his feet," and he felt
that just now his many haymakers required a master's eye. And
so little Golden-hair was mounted on the dog-cart, where she felt
very high, and rather frightened too, as Black Prince pranced till
his harness jingled all over. But she swallowed some salt tears
that would come, and tried to smile at her mother who stood kissing her hand at the gate, then off they rolled as fast as Black
Prince could carry them. For some few minutes Mr. Darrell left
her to herself, and talked to Tom over his shoulder about the
farms and estates through which the turnpike road led. But the
little head beside him was soon lifted up, like a daisy after a
shower of rain; and, quite at home with her new friend, Marion
forgot her tears in the full tide of chatter, and in less than an hour
and a half they stopped at the lodge of the "Cedars."

It was a charming residence, along the steep carriage-drive of
which Mr. Darrell and his little companion slowly passed. For
some distance, after leaving the lodge, the path lay between broad
flower-beds, planted with beautiful shrubs and flowering annuals ;
while, peeping between the trees of the shrubberies, green park-
like meadows stretched far away on all sides. After a time the
view widened, and the drive wound past a lawn interspersed with
parterres gay with flowers. The house, an old-fashioned building
of red brick, was shaded by its patriarchal cedars, while at the
back, rising to the very summit of the hill, towered a magnificent
wood.

A warm motherly embrace welcomed little Marion. "My
darling, I am so glad to see you," and the child looked up and
smiled confidently in the sweet strange eyes gazing upon her.
All that Mrs. Howard had loved in the Irish school-girl, clung
to her still. Time had tempered her faults, ripened her intellect,
changed her name, but in all else, with the same impulsive,
gushing temperament, the mistress of the Cedars was Mary St.
Leger still.

"Where are the girls ?" asked Mrs. Darrell, looking round.

An instant afterward the door flew open, and a glad little
spirit seized Marion by the hand. "How late you are! I have
been watching and watching for you; why didn't you come sooner ?
Naughty little thing," and she threw her arms round her new
friend's neck, who, all unused as she was to children, stood almost
aghast at this most lively salutation.

"Emily, my love, you must be more gentle; you are quite frightening Marion. Remember she has no brothers nor sisters, and will have to get used to such a wild little girl as you. You are really not half polite enough."

Emily drew a little back. "Are you afraid of me?" she asked, with her mother's roguish twinkle in her eye.

"No, not at all," replied Marion, smiling; "I was only a little startled."

"Come upstairs, then, and take off your things; don't you think you will be very happy here with us all? We are going to make hay this afternoon, and Joe says you are to have his pony every day, as long as you are here," she added all in a breath, as they passed along a broad oak passage at the top of the stairs. "What a dear little thing you are!" she added; "what pretty long curls you have! do you know what you put me in mind of when you smile?"

"No—of what?" asked Marion, laughing.

"Of sunshine! I don't know why, but somehow the word sunshine comes into my head when I look at you. Do you think you will like me?"

"I am sure I shall."

"Well, I think you will, just a little, but you will like Edith better."

"Who is Edith?"

"Don't you know? Why, my twin sister; everybody likes her; and so they ought, she is so good, and not at all wild, like me. I don't mean to be wild, you know, but somehow I cannot help it. Sometimes I feel as if I could laugh and dance and sing all day. This is to be your room: now come and see Edith's and mine; they lead one into the other, so that we are never lonely."

Fit emblem of the sweet twin sisters were the two little chambers to which her guide conducted Marion, chattering all the way. Draped with pure white muslin, with blue carpet and paper, and clustering roses peeping in at each window, Marion thought she had never seen anything half so pretty. But that which riveted her attention was a table covered with white, placed in a small recess in Edith's room, on which stood the image of a queen, surrounded with flowers and tapers. High above it was suspended a large image of Christ crucified, and the figure of an angel on either side. The cloth was richly trimmed with lace, and a small lamp burned before the statue.

"What is that?" inquired Marion.

"What?" asked her companion, glad of some new topic of conversation.

Marion pointed to the table in question.

"That is our altar, where Edie and I say our prayers."

"Do you?" said Marion.

"Yes, come and look at it. Did you never see one before? See, this is an image of our Lady, and there is our Blessed Lord upon the cross."

C

Both children looked very grave.

"And what are those?" asked Marion, pointing to a string of beads suspended from a nail.

"That is my rosary."

"What do you do with it?"

"I will explain that to you another time, because dinner will soon be ready now. I say some of my prayers with it."

"How strange!" and Marion laid her hand on the little black book in her pocket.

"Did you never know any Catholics before?"

"Never," said Marion.

"Oh then, I daresay you think we are funny people, and worship images and all that sort of thing?"

"No, I don't; Dr. Stebbing told me last night that you only reverenced them."

"Did he? Well, all Protestants don't think that. Father Stirling says some people think we really pray to our crucifixes."

"What a number you have!" said Marion, glancing round.

"Because we like to think of Almighty God and all He suffered, whichever way we look. Don't you?"

"I don't know; not always, not when I am merry, you know."

"But we ought to like it even then, to be sure that we don't get too merry, and do anything wrong."

They went back to the room where Marion had taken off her things. "See, here is a crucifix at the head of this bed, too. If you sleep here, will you mind its being there?"

"I would rather not have it," replied Marion. "Our clergyman, Mr. Lisle, says it is very wrong to represent Christ in His humiliation, so I don't much like looking at it."

"I don't understand that," said her little friend; "but if you don't like it, I will take it away;" and, getting a chair, she reached it down, and, kissing it reverently, laid it gently in a drawer.

That kiss was a simple action, but it touched her companion. It was something human and tender, and yet it was showing homage to God. A step along the corridor made them turn, and Edith Darrell joined them. Her greeting was quiet but affectionate, for in everything were the twin sisters opposite to each other. Emily was a blonde, bright and beautiful, pure as wax, with fair hair and laughing eyes, who reminded one in her perpetual change and merriment of the dashing mountain torrent, while Edith, the brunette, the principal charm of whose countenance was the pensive beauty of her large dark eyes, seemed like a tranquil lake, ever reflecting the silent heaven above. And truly, most truly, were the things of heaven reflected in that quiet spirit, shining forth perpetually in a hundred silent ways. Interesting at first sight, even by the side of the fascinating little Emily, Edith, when known, was the general favourite. Unpretending, generous, and self-denying, her very meekness was the charm that held all hearts captive with a magic chain, and gave her the pre-eminence over her equally generous, but high-spirited and sometimes petulant, little sister.

"Where have you been?" asked the latter, half reproachfully; "Marion has been here such a time."

"I would not have been out for the world, but I went to meet them. I am so sorry we missed you," she added, turning to Marion and taking her hand, while the smile that lit every feature was as genuine as the little heart within.

"Which way did you go?" asked her sister.

"Towards Harleyford."

"Past the church? Oh, I know now! O Marion! she is such a little saint; come, confess; you went into church and forgot all about Marion, papa, and everything else."

"Emily, what a teasing child you are!"

"It is all very fine, Miss Edie, but you know very well that I am right."

"Yes, I did go in, of course, just for a minute or two, but I cannot think how wheels could have passed without my hearing them, for everything was so still, and I was listening all the time."

"Your guardian angel made them pass silently, to save you from distractions, I suppose," said Emily.

Marion looked, but said nothing. The dinner-bell rang, and she was soon so busily engaged in discussing the good things provided that altars and guardian angels were forgotten.

"What shall we do now?" asked the mercurial little Emily, when the cloth had been removed, and grace said with a certain sign that made poor Marion feel very uncomfortable.

"Go into the hayfields, I think," said Mrs. Darrell. "Run and get your hats on as quickly as you can, for they are carting now, and an empty waggon is just going back to the field, so you can all ride in it."

Although Marion had lived in the country all her life, she had very little of the country girl about her; Mrs. Howard had kept her so exclusively to herself, that anything like companionship with young people was new to her, and especially those amusements in which gregarious youngsters find such exquisite delight, but from which the solitary child is naturally excluded. The ride to the hayfield therefore in the jolting, jogging waggon was as delightful to her as to her companions, whose experience of life in the cotton metropolis had given them a keen relish for the country and its pleasures. What a picture it was to see them all holding on by the side of the waggon, as old Dobbin broke into a clumsy run with his laughing, screaming freight behind him! How the carter enjoyed it too, as one by one they slipped down to the bottom of the cart, rolling about like so many little landsmen in a gale at sea! And then the romp they had when they

actually arrived in the hayfield; how they smothered brother Joe,
and old Jack the Newfoundland dog, who had come up in the
cart with them, and who always pushed his big, good-humoured
head out just when he was least expected, and then, wriggling
out of the hole, walked off with a mountain-load of hay upon his
broad curly back.   Never had Marion had such fun, never had
the lower croft meadow echoed to such peals of laughter.   Never
were haymakers so helped and bothered, for the execution the
little folks did with rakes and pitchforks was quite exemplary,
or would have been, had they not tumbled the cocks over again
in romping, as soon as they had built them.

But even haymaking grows warm work under a June sun, so
Joe made them a sofa of hay, " sub tegmine fagi," as he phrased
it, and then rode home on the top of the next waggon-load,
promising to see about something good in the shape of what he
denominated bever.

"Joe is very good-natured," said Marion, when at last they had
all arranged themselves, Eastern fashion, on their rustic divan,
and were ready for a chat.

"Oh, he's a dear old fellow !" exclaimed Emily, enthusiastically.

" Does he go to school ? "

" He has not been anywhere since we left Manchester ; but he
is going to college in September.   He has a holiday for the
haymaking, but he generally studies very hard with papa.
Mamma does not know yet what we girls are going to do, for
Miss Horton, our governess, who has taught us up till now, is
going to be married."

" I think we shall go to the convent Father Stirling was telling
mamma about, after the holidays," said Edith.

"To the convent !   What for ? " asked Marion.

"To learn."

" Why, do they teach in convents ? "

" Yes, in some," said Edith.   " What did you think they did ? "

" Do tell us, Marion, what you think nuns are like ! " exclaimed
Emily, sitting suddenly upright, and looking very mischievous.

"Really, I don't know," replied Marion, "I never saw one in
my life.   They are all dressed in black, are they not ? "

"Some are ; well, what do you think they do all day ? "

"I don't know exactly, but I have heard that they are always
praying, and that they never go out of doors."

"Would you not like them if they always did that ? " asked
Edith ; " it would not be wrong, would it ? "

" Yes, I think it would be idle to spend our life so."

" What ! to be always serving God ? " asked Emily quickly.

" Well, Marion, dear," said Edith gently, "nuns do many things
besides that.   There are many orders.   One kind visit the poor
and teach in the poor schools, and some attend the sick.   One
order take old men and women into their house, do everything
for them to make them comfortable and happy, and, to enable

them to do this, even beg for them. Some nuns, as you fancy, spend their time in prayer ; and others, like the sisters Emily and I are perhaps going to, have schools for young ladies. Then, their dresses are different ; sometimes the habit is black, sometimes white or brown, or even blue. Indeed, there are so many different kinds of nuns, that even if I knew them it would take hours to tell you all about them."

"Nor are they always shut up," observed Emily ; "some nuns are obliged to go out a great deal, and those who do not have generally beautiful large gardens to walk in."

"But they must be very unhappy," replied Marion. "If I were they, I would run off when I found myself all alone, some day, in the street ! "

Emily shouted with laughter, and Edith smiled.

"Why, Marion," said the latter quietly, "if they did not wish to stop, they need not run away."

"I thought they were shut in with great locks and keys."

"When your mamma has the street door locked at night, is it to prevent you from getting out ? "

"The very idea, Edith ! just as if I should want to get out into the dark cold night. Of course not ; it is to prevent robbers from getting in."

"Which is just the reason why nuns lock their doors," returned Edith.

"Yes, Marion," added the other sister, "what the cold dark night would be to you out of your warm snug house, such would the world be to the nun who has given up everything for God. To understand what a nun's life really is, one must be a Catholic ; but any Protestant, who loves our Lord, can see, I should think, that a woman who does every little thing to please Him must be happy."

"Yes, I can fancy that," replied Marion, after a few moments' silence ; "but she must long sometimes to be home with her father and mother, and those she loves, for all that."

"What ! love them better than God ! " cried Emily.

"O Emily, darling, Marion is right," said Edith ; "it must be very hard to give up one's home even for God."

"Edie !" exclaimed her sister reproachfully.

"Well, Emily, I really think so ; you know how much I love the nuns, and I know that convent girls are always happy, but I could not leave papa and mamma for ever."

"Could you, Emily ?" asked Marion.

"Who, I ?" exclaimed Emily, opening her eyes,

'I won't be a nun, I won't be a nun,
I'm so very fond of pleasure that I can't be a nun.'

But, I tell you what, Marion, we have some one coming here in a day or two who will tell you a great deal more about nuns and convents than we can, and that is Miss Horton, the young lady I told you of just now, who used to be our governess. I am sure you will like her; she was a Protestant once."

"How dreadful!" thought Marion, putting her hand in her pocket, but the little black book was quite safe.

"Well, girls, are you asleep?" cried Joe, making his appearance. "Come along, all of you; tea is being carried round to the dell, and we are going to boil the kettle, gipsy fashion, in the wood, and all sorts of fun. Come."

No second invitation was needed, and a very few minutes saw them all in the dell, awaiting the coming viands.

"Bravo!" cried Joe, seizing upon the first importation, which chanced to be the tea-kettle, "all right, Tom, there's a good fellow. You need not stop, we are going to manage for ourselves."

Tom disappeared, grinning from ear to ear, while Joe proceeded to build his fire and erect his tripod for the kettle.

"Jolly work this, isn't it, only rather warm?" he exclaimed, blowing vigorously at the flame he had kindled. "I think that will do now," he added, rising from his knees, and looking complacently at the result of his labours, as the sticks began to crackle and the kettle to sing. "I shall leave you girls to do the rest, for I must go wood-gathering."

"Here is the tea!" cried Emily, diving into the basket Tom had placed on the ground.

"And a pot of jam," said Edith, in her turn.

"What a little loaf! I am sure it will not be large enough: call Tom back."

"He has gone too far: never mind, we must make it do."

"There's the milk in a bottle, and the butter in a cabbage leaf."

Tip! Hiss! there lay Joe's kettle on its side, singing, like the dying swan, a parting lay.

"What shall we do?"

"Build it up again. Don't let us call Joe," cried Emily, "we can do it just as well ourselves."

And so Emily made another fire in a dry place, while Marion and Edith set off to fill the kettle. But even when that was once more singing, their misfortunes were not over, for Emily cut her finger as well as the bread-and-butter, and no sooner was that bandaged up in a pockethandkerchief than the tea was discovered to be missing. And a rare hunt they had for it, until it was found under a dock leaf, when, all being ready, Joe was summoned, somewhat astonished to find his fire transplanted during his absence, and never did greenwood echo to merrier voices.

The first cup was just poured out, and Joe had been persuaded to promise them a wonderful tale, when a low growl from Jack arrested their attention. Edith set down her tea-pot, while Joe started to his feet.

"What can it be?" asked Emily.

"Hush!" said her brother, "it is some one going across over there. I wonder who it is? No one has any right to come into this wood. Hush!"

They listened, and this time a voice was heard, while the bushes crackled as a path was forced through them.

"Mammy, mammy, do carry me!"

"Whist! whist! Mammy can't carry you and baby too; come, Johnny, walk like a man."

"Oh, I can't! I can't!" And the weary child sank on the ground, just as the poor mother came in sight of the little tea-party.

Joe stepped forward. "Do you know you are trespassing?" he asked, gently but firmly; "this is private property."

"I beg your pardon, sir, but I have lost my way; if you will let my little boy rest one minute, I will go any way you will show me to get to Harleyford."

"But this child is too tired to walk as far as that this evening: it is almost a mile from here," said Edith.

"He will have to do it some way, poor dear; though, if I could get him on my back, I think, perhaps, I could carry him. O children, children, may God in His mercy keep the dark day of trouble far away from your young hearts! Now, Johnny, my man, try and get on mammy's back."

But the child's eyes were fixed wolfishly on the food, and he did not stir.

"Come, dear." She strove to lift him, but she was too much exhausted; nature gave way, and she sank on her knees.

"I cannot go on yet," she exclaimed; "I am too tired and weak; let me stop only ten minutes."

"Ten minutes!" cried the boy; "do you think I would send you on as tired as you are? no, stop as long as you like."

"Joe," whispered Emily, "they are starving. Look at the child!"

"Are you hungry?" he asked bluntly.

"My children have had one piece of bread, I nothing all day," replied the woman, with a gloomy despairing smile.

An exclamation burst from all the children, followed by a whispered consultation between Edith and Emily. "Marion, what shall we do? would you mind our giving the tea to them?"

"I do so wish you would," replied Marion, delighted at the idea, "it is so dreadful to see them like that." In two minutes a wonderful transformation-scene had taken place. Edith was once again at the head of her rustic table, with the poor woman by her side. Emily had seized upon the baby, whom she was regaling with an unprecedented amount of sopped bread, while Marion and Johnny, already capital friends, were as busy as hunger and compassion could make them. As for poor Joe, his long legs, just before so fatigued, were now flying rapidly homeward for a fresh stock of provisions.

"You would never have reached Harleyford without food or rest," remarked Edith compassionately,

"Ah, my dear young lady, I only asked the way to Harleyford because it lay on my road, but my journey will not stop short this side of Ennington. I thought, however, that we might get a lift in a waggon or cart going there, if we once got to Harleyford."

"But you don't live at Ennington, do you?" asked Marion.

"I did live there once, but I have not seen the dear old place for many years; and now, whether my poor old mother is even living I do not know, and I dread getting to the town to ask, for an awful feeling comes over me sometimes that she is dead."

"What is her name?" asked Marion. "I live at Ennington, and know almost everybody there."

The woman paused; her very life seemed to hang on Marion's answer. "Mary Turner," she faltered.

"Mary Turner! why, that is the name of our old servant, who has lived with us so many years."

The woman looked as though in a half dream. "My mother lived with a Mrs. Howard," she said at length.

"This is Miss Howard," cried Emily, clapping her hands. "Now, are you not happy? you see your mother is living."

"Thank God! thank God!" ejaculated the poor woman, covering her face with her hands.

"And quite well and happy," added Marion; "poor dear nursey! how delighted she will be!"

"Does she ever speak of me?" asked the woman, glancing up.

"Very seldom; but she told me once that she thought of you and prayed for you always."

"But why have you not written to her?" asked Emily; "you might have done that."

"First from pride and then from shame. Ah, child, child, but mine is a sad story. I was just fourteen years old when I left my poor dear mother, not long after my father died, to go to service in London. I had very good places, for I was quick with my needle, and I got on from one thing to another, till at the end of six or seven years I went as lady's maid. I travelled about with my mistress in foreign parts, and saw a good deal of the world, for two or three years; and I grew fond of pleasure and fine clothes. Up to this time I wrote regularly to my mother, and used to send her presents, and I had begun to save up some money to go back and live with her. I meant to take the little cottage again that I was born in, to get my living by dressmaking, and to have her to live with me, and to make her happy in her old age. But then the love of foolish nonsense came over me, and I grew quite changed, and just about this time my lord took a new valet, and though my mistress warned me against him again and again, for she never liked him, I would talk and laugh with him, and more than once I went to the theatre with him. He was a Frenchman, and not, as my lady said, in any way suited to a young girl religiously brought up, for he was an atheist and feared neither God nor the devil. But I did not care, although I knew what a bad companion he was for me; but I did not know all then that I learned afterwards. At last my mistress told me she had written for my mother to come up, for that she was certain if I was left to myself I should go all wrong. I told Adolphe, and he went into a dreadful passion, and persuaded me to go away with him. We were married, and I went to Liverpool with him, where I have lived ever since, but from that time to this I have never heard one word of my poor mother."

"And where is your husband?" asked Edith.

"Dead, miss. I need not tell you now all I have gone through, for my married life was as wretched as it deserved to be, but whatever my poor dead husband's sins may have been, I believe he died repentant. He had to be buried by the parish, and my baby was born in the workhouse about a month after his death. As soon as I was strong enough I came out again, and tried to get a little home for my children, but it was of no use. At last, one way and another, I got ten shillings together, and set off to come here. It has been hard work, I can tell you, ladies. We came partly by railroad, and sometimes we managed to get a lift for a few miles in a cart, but great part of the way we have come on foot, sleeping in barns, or on fine nights under hedges. I spent my last penny this morning, and—you know the rest."

"Well, you will be able to get to Ennington now; we will see about a cart or something to take you."

"Thank you kindly, most kindly, young ladies; but only think, after all, when I get there, what a disgrace I shall be to my poor mother."

Marion was silent, for she knew very well that this would be just such a disgrace as Mrs. Howard would not relish.

"I wish something could be done to make you more comfortable before going home to your mother," said Edith. "We must see."

At this moment Joe arrived with fresh provisions. A plate of cold beef and a glass of strong ale brought real life once more into the poor woman, and half an hour afterwards she rose to depart.

"Why, you don't suppose you're going off to Ennington or even to Harleyford to-night, do you? Come, youngster, get on my back," cried the undignified Joe, in whose bright black eye something very unwonted was twinkling. "You are not going farther than the Cedars this evening, I can tell you. They are making up a bed already in one of the men's rooms, which just happens to be empty. Bring the baby, Em, and set Jack to watch these things till we send for them. Now then, hurrah! off we go." And with the dusty but pretty child clinging to his back, Joe Darrell started across the fields, followed by the girls and the poor woman, the former all wanting the baby at once, and carrying it by turns.

"Good-night, Marion dear," said Edith, as she kissed her at her bedroom door; "does it not make you happy to think that the poor woman is comfortable for at least one night? Betsy says she is so grateful and looks so happy. I do not know how she has managed, but she has found them all clean clothes. Good-night."

"Poor dear old nursey," cried Marion, the tears glistening in her eyes, "how thankful she will be! Edith, darling, your mamma is very good."

CHAPTER V.

"And what are you going to do next with your protegée?" asked Mr. Darrell of his little Emily, 'as for the twentieth time she recounted the adventures of the preceding evening.

"We want you to help us to decide that," said his wife. "I certainly cannot see what good she will do by going to Ennington. It is very certain Mrs. Howard will have no place for them, and what can an old woman like poor Turner do towards the mainten-ance of a woman and two children?"

"Eliza must work for herself," said Mr. Darrell.

"Which she tells me she is only too ready to do, in any way, and at anything," observed his wife.

"Papa," said Edith, "I have a little idea in my head, but you must not be vexed if you do not like it. It is only a sudden thought, you know."

"Go on, dear child, what is it?"

"Well, papa, you know Jarvis at the lodge is going. Could you not put Eliza in instead? I think, from her being up between four and five to alter the old clothes Betsy gave her, and from the nice natty way in which she has dressed the children, that she is naturally quick and neat. Even yesterday they were rather dusty than dirty."

"And to-day they look lovely, like two little angels," broke in the impetuous Emily.

"Not at all a bad idea, Edith, for providing a shelter, but what could she live on? We could not let her take in washing at the lodge, and if she went out charring she could not open the gate."

"But, papa, dear, she could take in needlework, which is her real business. Mamma herself could give her a great deal to do, and if she is clever she would be a real boon to the neighbourhood, where mamma says, though there are plenty of dress-spoilers, there is not one dress-maker."

"What think you, Mary?" he asked, turning to his wife.

"That Edith has an old head on young shoulders. If Eliza is clean, neat, and handy, she would be certainly the right woman in the right place."

Nothing could exceed the gratitude of the poor creature when the plan was proposed. Jarvis was willing to retire at once, Mrs. Darrell found a few articles of plain furniture besides those already in the lodge, and within twenty-four hours from her arrival in the dell, Eliza found herself and her little ones sheltered in a sweet little home, embowered in roses and summer flowers, under the kind and gentle guidance of the mistress of the Cedars.

Merrily rolled the week along, with the cricket match, boating, strawberry feasts, and haymaking in the higher croft, and last, not least, the runs backward and forward to Eliza, and the romps with her children, the baby especially being a most untiring plaything. Besides this, there were visits to be paid and received, for Harley-ford was a sociable old-fashioned town, and already Emily and Edith had made many nice friends. Many amongst these were, of course, Protestants, but this difference of creed made none in the spirit of kindliness that pervaded the little parties that met from time to time in the hayfields, cricket-ground, and each other's houses. Marion liked them all, although, as Emily had prognos-ticated, she did learn to love Edie with a deeper love than the rest; and when sometimes Mr. Lisle's words rose before her mind warning her even against the children, it was with a feeling almost akin to indignation that she thought of them.

"Who could look at Edie and doubt her?" she whispered one evening, almost passionately, as, having read a chapter in her little book, she was about to get into bed. "I wish I slept with her, for I feel lonely to-night; but I did not like the idea at first, because of what Mr. Lisle said. It is very strange that he should hate this religion so. I hardly remember what he said distinctly, but he looked awful when he spoke. I know he said that they loved the Virgin Mary more than Christ, but they have more images of Him than of her. Well, I do love a crucifix, notwithstanding what I said to Emily. I wonder which drawer she put it in; I should love to have a look at it all by myself. It cannot be wrong to look into the drawers, because Mrs. Darrell said I might use as many of them as I liked." Obeying a strong impulse, Marion took out the crucifix, and gazed at it long and steadfastly. And the dark scene of that crucifixion passed before her mind, with the scourge, the thorns, the nails, the bitter gall, and still more bitter insult. The words so gently spoken from the depths of that Sacred Heart fell in imagination on her ear, "Father, forgive them, for they know not what they do;" and while more than one tear fell on the image in her hand, the little Protestant trembled with emotion. "I do love a crucifix, in spite of all Mr. Lisle says," she exclaimed suddenly. "I could love it as I do Edward's pic-ture, only more, much more. Edward is very dear, but what is even he to Jesus Crucified?" And in her turn kissing the little crucifix, she laid it once more in the drawer. "I will ask the girls to let me sleep with one of them to-morrow. I know they will. I am half inclined to run in to-night," she added, glancing at the large bed with its heavy cornices and crimson hangings, "it is so very lonely here, and the rain makes such a noise." A sudden gust of wind against the casement decided her movements, and, opening her door, she ran quickly along the oak passage that sepa-rated them from her; but her light becoming extinguished by a sudden draught, so increased her nervousness, that she ran into their room as white as a sheet.

The twins were kneeling side by side before their little altar, now bright with lights. Marion, fearful of disturbing them, was about to withdraw, notwithstanding her fright, but Emily, who had turned at her sudden entrance, rose at once from her knees and prevented her.

"Get into Edith's bed, dear," she whispered; "we shall soon have finished. You are timid, and have come to sleep with us, have you not?"

"Yes," said Marion, "if I may."

Emily returned to her place, and Marion tried to catch the words, but in vain. "Ora pro nobis" she did not understand, and remembering something about "an unknown tongue," she put her head under the clothes, regretting that her little black book had been left behind in her flight. It was not until all was finished by something, though she could not hear what, in honest Queen's English, that our little girl felt relieved, and inclined for the merry chat that followed.

Marion was so tired that the sun was shining brightly on the still dripping leaves when she awoke. To her surprise, her companion was no longer by her side, and on rising and peeping into Emily's room, she found the other little couch vacant also.

"Oh dear, how late I shall be for breakfast! Why did they not call me?" and she began dressing in good earnest, expecting the bell to ring every moment. But no bell rang, and when she was partly dressed a peep at the staircase clock told her it was only half-past seven. "They must have gone out for a walk," was the conclusion she arrived at. "What a strange thing they did not call me! I suppose they thought I was tired."

Her toilette being ended, Marion said her prayers, and, having fetched her little book, sat down to read. But her ideas were wayward, and it was in vain she tried to fix them, so, half closing her book, she sat and thought. She looked at the little altar, with its sweet flowers, burnished candlesticks, and stately image, round which a curtain of white lace fell in graceful folds from a wreath of blue flowers above. "It is very pretty; I wonder what Mr. Lisle would say to it. I think it is very nice to have a little corner in one's room given to God; and if He does not like things to be beautiful, why did He have the old Tabernacle and Solomon's Temple so grand? I know, of course, religion was altered after Christ came, but God Himself remained the same. He never changes, and if He liked things as splendid as everything belonging to the old Temple was, it seems strange that He should not like this splendour now. If I could make a religion of my own, and if I were rich, I would still be a Protestant, but have things as beautiful as I could. God likes flowers surely, because He Himself makes them, so I would put them in my church, and lights too, in imitation of the candlestick in the Jewish sanctuary. I would have pictures of the life of Christ hung up in different places, and a crucifix where every one could see it ; then people must think of Him. I suppose Mr. Lisle would say that all this is wrong, but I can't help it. I must keep these thoughts a great secret from everybody, I suppose, though I am sure, if I ask Him, God will take them away if they are not right. It says nowhere in the New Testament that churches must not be beautiful, but in many places in the Old that they must. I have thought of this before, but never very much. Why, I do think," she added, springing suddenly from her seat, "from what Mr. Lisle said a little time ago, that I must be a Puseyite !" The blood flew to her face and neck with the excitement of the thought, and she started as she caught sight of herself in the glass. "When I am older I will see what Puseyites really believe, and if I find them what I fancy they are, I will be one, for I am not satisfied with my religion. God seems too grand to be thought as little of as everybody but Mr. Lisle and old nursey seem to think of Him !"

Her ruminations were here interrupted by Emily, who danced into the room, whirling her hat by the string.

"What! up and dressed already !" she exclaimed.

"O Emily, I should so have loved to have gone out with you: why did you not call me ?"

Emily laughed. "We have been to church."

"To church ! What ! so early, and on Saturday !" .

"To be sure ! We go every morning. Mamma, Edith, Joe, and I, and sometimes papa."

"Always before breakfast ?"

"Yes, in the summer, because we have mass at seven ; in the winter it is at nine."

"What is mass ?"

Simple question, asked by the little Protestant in childish curiosity. Could Michael, as he bows his radiant head before the eternal throne, give the reply ? Could Mary herself, crowned in the highest heaven, Queen of created intelligences, Daughter, Mother, Spouse of the Triune God, tell in fitting words what is the mystery of the altar ? For a moment the question overpowered the child of thirteen. What could she say ? How make her companion understand ?

"The principal service of our religion," was the answer at last.

"How strange to go to church every day ! We only go on Sundays."

Edith now entering, the conversation took a turn, and at the sound of the bell they all ran downstairs to breakfast.

It was with a very mixed feeling that Marion lay awake the next morning, partly watching the flies chase each other round and round, settling every now and then on the knots of the curtain fringe, and partly questioning much what this day, certainly not a little dreaded, was to bring forth. "I wonder what they will do ? Perhaps they will be like mamma says the Catholics are in Paris, and go on with everything just the same as

usual. It would seem very dreadful to see Mr. Darrell busy with
his farm bailiff as he was yesterday, or to see Mrs. Darrell and the
girls sit down to needlework. If they do not keep Sunday
properly, but work on it like any other day, I shall know they are
wrong, because any child can see it is wicked to break God's
commandments. Really, really, I do not know what to think!
What Mr. Lisle says makes me so uneasy all the time, and yet
they all seem so very good. Perhaps I shall see to-day, better
than I have done yet, what their religion really is. I like Miss
Horton very much. Whatever could make her turn Catholic? I
suppose she has gone to church, too."

Yes, Miss Horton was at church, with her head bowed low after
her communion, praying fervently at this very moment, among
other intentions, for the little Protestant, whose winning manners
and sunny curls had wonderfully attracted her the night before.

Marion met the little party at the lodge, where Eliza, looking
quite smart in a new print dress, was just setting Johnny down
to his bread-and-milk. She looked the very picture of grateful
happiness, and her room, as Emily phrased it, "like a little
palace." Mrs. Darrell stepped in to kiss the children, while her
husband slily slipped a shilling into Johnny's little chubby
hand.

The breakfast-table at the Cedars was a very happy one. There
was something so joyous, yet subdued, in the cheerfulness of the
three elders, and they naturally gave the tone to the rest of the
family. For the first time since Marion's arrival, the conversation
was thoroughly Catholic. Miss Horton having resigned her
engagement in the family upon their leaving Manchester, this was
her first visit to Harleyford, and she asked many questions as to
the position of Catholics in this part of the country. Marion was
astonished to find, from Mr. Darrell's replies, that the Catholic
Church was a regularly-organised establishment; she had always
imagined that it consisted of a few people with very strange ideas
scattered here and there, without order or arrangement; and she
was astonished to hear Mr. Darrell speak of its archbishops and
bishops, its dioceses and parishes, its colleges and schools. But
wider still the blue eyes opened as he talked of distant missions,
and of the number of converts each week swelling the ranks of
the Catholic Church even in England. The wisest heads in
Ennington knew but little of the great world beyond, save,
perhaps, the broadest politics of the day, and it is not to be
wondered at that little Marion listened in astonishment to Mr.
Darrell's description of the machinery of a Church, upon whose
very existence, until the week before, she had hardly ever bestowed
a thought.

"Betsy will take you to church this morning, my love," said
Mrs. Darrell.

"Thank you. Would you mind my going this afternoon with
Edith and Emily?"

"I am afraid your mamma would not like it, dear child."

"Yes, she said I might go if you would let me ; that is if I went to the Protestant church in the morning."

"Then I am sure you shall go ; the girls will, I know, be very pleased to have you with them, and so will Miss Horton, and you must tell Father Stirling that we are expecting him to spend the evening with us."

It was with a beating heart that Marion entered the little Catholic chapel of Harleyford. It was a small building, and to an eye accustomed to nobler edifices decidedly simple, but it was clean, well kept, and well arranged. An altar of white stone occupied the centre, with smaller ones on either side, dedicated to the Virgin Mother and St. Joseph. As it was a feast day the church was more than usually decorated, and bright flowers adorned every altar and image, while the solemn light of the red lamp was reflected in a ruddy glow from the gilded door of the tabernacle. Altogether the scene was very striking to our little girl, who gazed around her from her seat beside Miss Horton in silent wonder. The service commenced by the Rosary, which, to Marion's ear, accustomed only to Dr. Stebbing's sonorous mouthing of the Church prayers, or to Mr. Lisle's emphatic enunciation of the same, was quite unintelligible. Then followed a sermon from Father Stirling, on the commandments, and lastly came Benediction. If the chapel was pretty before in little Marion's eyes, it certainly was something far more brilliant now, as row after row of tapers glimmered on the altar. When Father Stirling appeared in his rich vestment, and the white-robed acolytes, swinging the fuming censer and bearing the lighted torches, passed on before, Marion wandered back, in imagination, to the days of Solomon, and fancied herself actually in the temple of the Jewish monarch. What had been her thoughts, child as she was, could she have read the Mystery of Mysteries, could she have pierced, like the hearts around her, the humble veils, and recognised by the eye of faith the Dweller on the altar ? No, little Golden-hair, your eye may be charmed by Catholic ceremonies, your ear entranced as the music of the grand old master peals forth in the " O Salutaris," your imagination may be led captive by flowers, lights, and incense, but God will not yet reveal to you the Secret of the Tabernacle.

More to the children's surprise than to Miss Horton's, who already began to understand her, Marion asked no questions concerning Benediction. It had been such a complete realisation of her religious dreams, that, almost unknown to herself, she laid it by among the secrets of her heart, to be "read, marked, learned, and inwardly digested" for years to come. Not so the rosary ; here was all curiosity.

"What did the priest and all of you keep on saying when we first went in ?"

"Our Fathers, Hail Maries, and Glorias, couldn't you hear ?" asked Emily, laughing.

"No, I should think not, you rattled on so fast. What are Hail Maries and Glorias ?"

"The Gloria, you know well enough, my dear, because you say it in your own church at the end of every psalm," replied Miss Horton ; "the Hail Mary is a prayer to our Blessed Lady," and she repeated it.

"May I see your rosary ?"

"Certainly ; here it is."

"What a strange-looking thing ! it is very handsome, though ; is this silver ?"

"Yes, but I prize it most of all because the priest who received me into the Church gave it to me."

"Then you say first the Lord's Prayer, and then, let me see, ten Hail Maries, and then Glory be to the Father, and then begin the same over again till you come to where you started from ?"

"Exactly so," said Miss Horton, stepping behind with Edith, while Emily and Marion passed on before.

"What do you think of her, Miss Horton ?" asked her companion ; "is she not a dear little thing ?"

"One of the sweetest girls I ever met, and one, I should imagine, who thinks deeply and silently.   We must pray as hard as we can for her."

"Miss Horton !" cried Emily, turning suddenly round, "Marion says she thinks our Lord meant just such things as the rosary when He says, 'Use not vain repetitions.'"

"You must not be offended, really, Miss Horton !" exclaimed Marion, blushing : "I do not want to say rude things about the Catholic religion, but I want to understand it."

"Do not for one moment imagine, my dear child," replied Miss Horton, "that anything you can possibly say will be deemed rude by any of us ; we all understand you too well for that."

Marion smiled.

"Moreover," continued the elder lady, "your objection is very natural, and generally, I suppose, the first thought excited in the mind of a Protestant by the rosary, the principal part of which is, however, the contemplation of the mysteries. Did you explain these, Emily ?"

"No, I left that for you."

"Then, Marion, you are only half enlightened ; and, you know, proverbially, 'a little knowledge is a dangerous thing.' The rosary consists of fifteen mysteries ; of these five are joyful, five sorrowful, five glorious. First among the joyful mysteries is the Annunciation, when the angel came to the Blessed Mary in her little silent room and told her that she was to be the Mother of God. Now, we think of this while we say the first Our Father, the ten Hail Maries, and the Gloria, which altogether we call a decade, and then pass on to the next, which is that of the Visitation. Here we see Mary, notwithstanding her dignity, visiting the mother of Christ's forerunner as the simple Jewish maiden. Then, in the next decade, we meditate on the birth of our Lord in the stable, when man refused Him a shelter, and He found it among the beasts of the field. Next comes the Presentation in the temple, where Simeon, the old prophet, and that pattern of anchorites, the aged Anna, who made her home in the temple day and night, passing eighty years in prayer and fasting, took the Divine Infant in their arms. The last decade is the finding of Jesus in the temple by His Mother and St. Joseph, after He had been lost for three days. Now, do you imagine you would find it hard or strange to meditate on these beautiful things of God?"

"Oh, no, Miss Horton! I should like to do that by itself very much, but I cannot see how people can say other prayers at the same time."

"I can well fancy it seems strange to you at first sight, my dear child, but I think I can illustrate it to you. Do you never perform actions whilst your mind is imbued with the spirit of something to which these actions tend, but of which they form no immediate part? For instance, in a visit of condolence to a bereaved friend, the departed one is perhaps barely mentioned, and yet the loss sustained is never absent for an instant from the mind of either the mourner or the comforter, and every word uttered, though perhaps only commonplace, is tempered more or less with the spirit of grief. Again, on Christmas Day, with its scenes of joyous merriment and family union, how, amid all, does the spirit of the first Christmas insensibly pervade each thought, word, and action of a Christian. Good-bye, slips lightly off the tongue that looks for re-union to-morrow, but how is it spoken on the eve of a life-long separation? Then, Marion, dearest, can you not understand a little of the spirit of the rosary? Holy Mary, Mother of God, pray for us! says the sinner, as he meditates on Jesus prostrate in the garden. Pray for us! he cries again, as the Blood shed for the guilt of the whole world, and for him in particular, falls upon the ground of Gethsemane. Pray for us! again and again he exclaims, as the alternate view of God's humiliation, and man's wretchedness, bursts upon him, till lost in the wonders of redeeming love, he cries, Glory be to the Father, and to the Son, and to the Holy Ghost! Again, he contemplates, amid the glorious mysteries, the Coronation of our Lady. Jesus has entered the Holy of Holies, and there, in faith, he sees the Virgin Mother too. Holy Mary, Mother of God, pray for us! he exclaims, lost in the contemplation of her dignity. Crowned Queen of Heaven! Then pray for us! and again and again through all the decade, he invokes her blessed name, and thinks of the infinite love of God, and the power and gentleness of her to whom God refuses nothing."

"I understand," said Marion thoughtfully; "I quite see what you mean."

"The Rosary is more like a string of meditations than a prayer, is it not, Miss Horton?" asked Emily.

"It is both, my dear, hence its great beauty and efficacy."

"You have only told me the joyful mysteries yet," said Marion, "what are the others?"

"The sorrowful are, the Agony in the Garden, the Scourging of Jesus, the Crowning with Thorns, the Carrying of the Cross, and the Crucifixion."

"Those are beautiful," replied Marion, "any one could meditate on those, even a Protestant."

"So they could on all, except, perhaps, the two last glorious ones, which are certainly essentially Catholic."

"Tell me those."

"The Resurection, the Ascension, the Descent of the Holy Ghost, the Assumption, and the Coronation, are the glorious mysteries. The two last refer to our Blessed Lady. You know, we believe that after her death she was carried, body and soul, up to heaven, where Jesus crowned her Queen of archangels, angels, and men."

"I do not understand that," said Marion: "but the rosary is enough for me to think of for to-night. I do like that very much. You nice little beads," she added, seizing Miss Horton's chaplet, "who would think there was so much in you? But I should never remember the mysteries; will you write them down for me?"

"I will, as soon as we get in," said Emily; "but, Miss Horton, mamma said Edie and I might run round and fetch Dora and Jessie Seymour home to tea. Do you mind walking gently on with Marion? I daresay we shall catch you before you get far."

"Certainly not, my dear; I am quite sure we shall get on very well together. If we get tired, we shall sit down, and make ourselves comfortable. I hope this little lady will not convert me, though!"

"I shall not try," said Marion, laughing, "for it would be only labour lost. I know you are as firm as a rock."

"I hope so," said Miss Horton, laughing in her turn; "I have not much disposition, certainly, to travel back again."

"I cannot fancy that you were ever a Protestant," said Marion, "it seems such a strange thing."

"Well, so it does, Marion, I can scarcely fancy it myself sometimes," replied Miss Horton.

"Ah, yes! but I do not mean it as you do," cried Marion; "I cannot fancy how people feel, who take such a tremendous step as to change their religion. It seems natural for Emily and Edith to be Catholics, because they were born so, but it is different with you. Will you tell me why you changed?"

"I think we had better do as I said we would, and sit down here first. Yes," continued Miss Horton, as soon as they had arranged themselves, "I will give you one reason which, I think, you can understand, why I learned to like the Catholic religion, though this is by no means one of the chief ones."

"What was it?" asked the child, anxiously.

"When I was a little girl, Marion," returned her companion, "like most other little girls, I was giddy, thoughtless, and fond of play ; I very seldom thought about anything seriously, and though I could not conscientiously have neglected my religion, I fear it was little more to me than a thing of daily routine. As I grew older, however, my father, who was a very scientific man, wishing to give me a habit of reflection, gave me some books ; and, among others, elementary works on the sciences. From this time I changed, a great fancy for this kind of study seized me, and, indeed, to this day, there are few things in which I take so deep an interest. My father's intention in giving me these volumes had been that I should study nature, but I studied God ! I saw the world as He had made it, bright, glorious, and beautiful, and I saw more ! I saw creation as a great harmonious whole, and the world in which we live and move, had now a fresh charm for me. The grand secrets of the past, revealed in the 'Stone Book of Geology,' the mighty speculations of astronomy, the magnificent discoveries of the telescope, the marvels of the microscope, each, and all, threw new ideas into my hitherto circumscribed notion of the Creator Father, and a deep conviction gradually stole over my soul, that for a world so beautiful there must be one grand religion. As I looked at Protestantism, with its numerous sects, I felt how little it was in unison with the harmony of this creation ! Marion, my child, believe me, I am now thirty years of age, I have had friends in many sects and of many opinions, but never among them all have I found two Protestants who thought alike. Now, in worldly matters this diversity of ideas is of little or no consequence, but it is not so with the things of God. He has revealed Himself, and by that revelation man must stand or fall ! Depend upon it, He who made the material world so fair, has not left the spiritual one in mist. You look surprised, and perhaps, my dear, I have said too much, not a difficult thing to do upon a subject on which one feels very deeply. But now we shall have to leave our little nook, for I hear our young friends coming, and so we must reserve the rest of our conversation for another time."

CHAPTER VI.

OTHER friends had arrived at the Cedars during the absence of Miss Horton and the children, and in the course of the afternoon the party was still further increased by the arrival of Father Stirling, the parish priest. He was a man of not more than forty summers, but care had cast her shadow upon him, for the stately figure was already slightly bowed, and the dark hair interwoven with many a silvery thread. But his look, his voice, his manner, were still young, and there was such an expression of fatherly kindness and benevolence in his whole mien that he was a uni-

versal favourite, not only with his own flock, but even with some
of the Protestants of the bigoted little town of Harleyford.

They were certainly a merry party ; so much so, that [when,
after tea, they gathered into little sociable knots in different parts
of the drawing-room, Marion, escaping from the rest, seated herself upon a retired ottoman, close to a French window, looking
out upon the lawn. She felt so uncomfortable that, had she
known how to beat a retreat unobserved, she would certainly
have done so ; for though, as yet, conversation had been the order
of the evening, it was something so unusual to our little girl that
she felt positively frightened. What then was her horror, when
Joe suddenly appeared with card-box and counters, while Edith
placed chess, draughts, and other games before them ! It was not
long before the young people had obeyed Joe's summons, and
were rapidly seating themselves round the centre table. Father
Stirling and Miss Horton engaged in a game of chess, the others
made up a whist party, while Jessie Seymour, seating herself at
the piano, accompanied herself in an Italian song. Marion withdrew still deeper into her nook, and snatching her little black
book from her pocket, pressed it almost convulsively to her
heart.

"O Mr. Lisle, what would I not give to be talking to you in
Ennington churchyard, as I was this day fortnight ! He is quite
right ! the Catholic religion is a wicked thing ! I did like what
Miss Horton told me, but I don't care, I hate it all now."

"Marion," said Edith, "they want you to play at cards, but
you would not like to do so, would you ?"

"No, indeed, I should not," replied Marion, very decidedly.

"Shall I come and sit with you, or would you rather read your
book ?"

"I would rather read, please : do not distress yourself about
me, I am getting on very well."

"Protestants do not do anything on Sundays but read, do
they ?" asked Edie.

"No, nothing," replied Marion, over whose bright little brow a
very dark shadow was perceptibly gathering ; "but do go back to
your friends. I would really rather read than do anything else."

"It seems so strange to leave you here to yourself."

"No, not at all."

And so Marion was once more left unmolested, save by the
peals of laughter from the round table, which now and then
sadly disturbed her equanimity. But she only tried to read the
harder.

"What did she say ?" asked Dora Seymour, taking up her cards,
as Edith once more resumed her place.

"She seems quite vexed," said Edith.

"Are not Protestants ridiculous ?" continued Dora. "Just as
if there could possibly be any harm in anything Father Stirling
sits by and allows."

A smile was Edie's answer.

"I suppose they never do anything but read, pray, and talk scandal all day."

"O Dora!"

"Well, really, I mean it. I have a religious horror of a Protestant Sunday. What is she reading?"

"The Testament, I think."

Dora laughed. "Hard work to be recollected just now, I should imagine. I find it difficult enough to make a meditation in church. I should get awful distractions if I tried to make one here."

"So should I," said Emily; "but she is only reading."

"Well, but spiritual reading is almost like a meditation," said Dora. "Do you like that song Jessie sung just now, 'Il Segreto'?"

"Very much; she sings it beautifully. You have both great taste for music."

And so the evening flew by, everyone happy except little Golden-hair in her corner; gentleness and good-humour prevailing on all sides. After a time the whist party broke up and a varied conversation ensued, in which the members of the round game took their part, as well as the two chess-players. Many persons spoke to our little heroine, but she seemed so disinclined for conversation that all, even Mrs. Darrell, gave up the attempt and left her to herself. The fact was that Marion's heart was divided. Young and lighthearted, she felt severely not being able to take part in the pleasures around her, while all that Mr. Lisle had told her, and the promise she had made him, so mingled with her feeling of disappointment, that she not only felt sorry for what she considered their impiety, but felt positively miserable herself. It is true she pored over the pages of her little book, but though St. Paul's words glided before her eyes, the meaning did not enter her mind, and, at last, sinking her head on the heap of cushions beside her, she closed her book. "O mamma, I wish I was with you!" she whispered again and again, almost crying.

"Well, little lonely bird, what have you been doing all the evening?" said a gentle voice behind her.

Marion started. Father Stirling had walked round to the other side of her ottoman, and was seated close to her elbow.

"Nothing," she replied, looking up and trying to seem bright; "I was only thinking about mamma."

"Is she very far away?"

"No, only nine miles," said Marion, feeling rather ashamed of appearing so babyish.

"That is not quite a seven days' journey, is it?" asked Father Stirling, smiling, "and what do you think of Harleyford?"

"It is a very pretty, clean, little town."

"And the Cedars?"

"The Cedars! I do not think I ever saw such a lovely place. I like it better and better every day. I could stop here for ever, I am sure, and still find something fresh. Edith and Emily ought to be very happy."

"And so I think they are, do not you?"

"Yes, very, and they are both so good. If you only knew how kind they were, the day I came, to a poor woman we found in the wood ; and Joe, too, is as good as his sisters." And she related, with sparkling eyes, their adventure with poor Eliza.

"And so you are very happy here?"

"Yes, generally, that is———, except this evening," and she paused.

"And this evening our little friend thinks us all very wicked, and feels very unhappy," returned Father Stirling, smiling.

Marion hung her head. It was so exactly what she did think that she had no reply to make.

"What have you been reading?" asked the priest, laying his finger on Mr. Lisle's book.

" St. Paul's Epistle to the Ephesians."

"And very beautiful it is!" said Father Stirling, gently taking the book ; "do you think you understand it?"

"Yes, very well," answered Marion, with a little shadow of assumption in her tone ; "the Bible is so simple, any child may understand it. God meant His word for ignorant people as well as wise ones, and so He made it very plain."

"Did you ever notice," asked the priest, "that the whole of the third chapter is in parenthesis?"

"In what?" asked Marion, opening her eyes.

"In parenthesis, all except the first verse, which reads on to the first verse of the fourth chapter, when it repeats the words, ' the prisoner of the Lord;' so that, leaving out the twenty parenthetical verses, the exhortation begins thus : 'For this cause I Paul, the prisoner of Jesus Christ for you Gentiles, beseech you that ye walk worthy of the high vocation wherewith ye are called.'"

"I see," said Marion, much interested, "but I never noticed it before."

"Then how, my dear child, could you possibly understand the epistle? Do not misunderstand me," he continued, as Marion reddened with sudden surprise and vexation, "I do not for an instant think you intended in any way to deceive me just now, but I wished you to see that you were deceiving yourself, for, notwithstanding what you say about God's word being so easy to understand, there are few things of which the meaning lies less on the surface than St. Paul's Epistles. They are far more difficult than you imagine, and I question much whether there is a child or unlettered person in England, let him be ever so great a Bible reader, who could give anything like a clear explanation of any twelve consecutive verses in the whole of this great apostle's epistles. Will you try?"

"No, indeed," said Marion, drawing back from the book he held towards her; "for one thing, I have not been reading at all to-night, though I held the book in my hand."

"I can well imagine that ; you rather wanted something to amuse you. Devotion in the wrong time and place burdens the spirit, and even becomes distasteful. You do not like to confess it, even to yourself, but St. Paul was too dry for to-night."

Marion smiled in spite of herself.

"There are some pretty books of Emily's there; you should have taken one of those."

"On Sunday! You do not know what they are."

"What! are they bad books?" exclaimed the priest, in well-feigned astonishment.

"No, but they are not religious books."

"Do they speak lightly of God and holy things?"

"No," said Marion, who could not help laughing amid her vexation, "but I am sure you know what I mean."

"Well, I suppose I do," said Father Stirling; "the fact is, my little friend, you have been taught that Sunday not only has its peculiar duties, but its own amusements also, and you are consequently shocked at the admixture of anything not positively religious in the observance of it."

"Yes."

Father Stirling was here called upon by Joe to decide a knotty point with regard to a "natural vingt-et-un," which, having arranged to the satisfaction of the card-table, he returned to Marion.

"Will you have a little walk round the garden with me?" he asked.

"Yes," replied Marion, who already began to like her companion.

More than one significant smile was exchanged as they passed through the open window, and at least one fervent prayer ascended from the card-table, that the little stranger might this night hear the first whisper of her call heavenward.

"How calm everything is!" said Father Stirling, as they stood watching the setting sun, just as Marion had done the week before in Dr. Stebbing's garden. "It seems such a soft and peaceful ending of God's own day. I think the Beneficent Father has shown His love for His creatures, perhaps, more in the institution of the day of rest than in any one other earthly blessing He has bestowed upon us. 'The bow of Apollo is not always bent,' said the ancients, and sweetly indeed is the bow of the week's toil relaxed by the sweet repose of the Sunday."

"It is very nice here," said Marion, as they wandered up and down a pretty alley, carpeted with turf as soft as velvet, and bordered on either side by a high yew hedge. "It is much nicer here than in the house."

The clergyman smiled. "Both have their charms, I think, but change is always pleasant; do you not think so?"

"Yes, I do; but for the first time since I have been here, I longed to be by myself to-night."

"Do you want me to go away?"

"No, I like you now."

"But you did not like me at first."

"I did not like you when you were playing chess, or when you were watching the others playing cards."

"Why not?"

"Because, Father Stirling, I think such things are wicked. You puzzle me; for one minute you talk so nicely about Sunday, when just before you have been"——

"Breaking it! Out with it, you will not offend me."

"Well, that is really what it seems to me, and I promised before I came, whatever I might see, to keep Sunday properly myself. The first part of the day was very nice—stricter, I think, even than we are ourselves; but since tea it has all seemed so dreadful, that when you first spoke to me I was actually crying."

"I know you were, and I liked you all the better for it."

"Did you?" asked Marion. "Why?"

"Because I saw you were conscientious. You would dearly have loved to have joined in the gaiety around you, but you were afraid of offending God and disobeying your mother, and so you begrudged us even a glance. I was watching you with one eye and my chess with the other, and though I of course believe that, in common with other Protestants, you are mistaken in your Sabbatarian ideas, I nevertheless believe you will not lose your reward for this night's firmness. I should have been as grieved to have had you for a partner this evening as I was pleased to have Miss Horton."

"And yet Miss Horton was once a Protestant."

"And so was I. Yes, my child, you may look surprised, but I used to keep Sunday far more strictly than you, or perhaps any one you ever knew. My family were Presbyterians, for I am a Scotchman, and it is not permitted by that sect to touch the piano on Sunday, even to play sacred music, with many other notions peculiar to themselves."

"Father Stirling! I could never have thought you had been a Protestant. But why is it Catholics keep Sunday in such a strange wrong way?"

Father Stirling laughed good-humouredly. "First of all, tell me what you have seen wrong. You say the early part of the day was quite as you could have wished."

"Yes, indeed, perfectly so."

"And setting aside the fact of its being Sunday, have you seen anything to displease you? Have you seen any sin committed, or heard anything in any way improper?"

"No, every one is too good for that. I do think the whole family would be perfect if"—and she paused.

"They were not Catholics," exclaimed Father Stirling. "Well, I am very glad you acquit us of everything but Sabbath-breaking, for I think that I can show you that, thinking as we do, we have by no means committed that sin."

Marion shook her head incredulously.

"First of all, my child, we must remember that 'the Sabbath was made for man, and not man for the Sabbath.' These were the words of our Blessed Lord, as He rambled through the corn-fields one Sabbath-day, talking to His disciples, who were plucking the ears of corn, and rubbing them in their hands, as they passed along. The Jews grumbled even at the works of love that He performed on that day, so we see there is no pitch of absurdity too great for man to arrive at, when he begins in any way to alter, strain, or add to the commandments of God. But even Protestants admit that works of piety, charity, and necessity are lawful, so that, however strict they may be, they pray, preach, attend the sick, relieve the unfortunate, eat, drink, and even make no scruple of poking their fires and snuffing their candles on Sunday. According to their creed they are more or less particular. But we go further: God says, ' Keep the Sabbath day holy.' Any Catholic missing Mass, commits, by the law of his Church, a deadly sin. God says, ' Thou shalt do no manner of work,' and take the only Catholic family you have ever visited, and which, let us hope, may stand as a fair type of the rest, and what do you tell me? They are, if anything, stricter than your own house-hold." He paused, but Marion made no reply.

" With regard to keeping it holy, the Sabbath cannot be too much hallowed. Good Catholics generally sanctify it, at its very commencement, by a union with God, sweeter, holier, deeper than I could make you understand, namely, by Holy Communion. This I know, dear child, is beyond your present experience of things divine ; may the Almighty Father enlighten you ! but I tell you, because it is an action with us so sacred that any sin committed during the day would seem, if possible, after this, doubly terrible. Many of our congregation, indeed I may safely say all, whose duties will permit them, regularly attend two Masses, as the family here have done to-day, and prayers and benediction in the afternoon, while, should we ever be able to maintain another priest, we should have an evening service, which I have not the slightest doubt would be well attended. Nor is this lip service alone ; I am quite certain any stranger visiting our church this afternoon must have felt, looking on the bowed heads around, that every heart was praying."

" Oh, yes ! I did think so. Everything was so beautiful, I could have stayed in the church for ever."

" Very well, then, you admit so far that we hallow the Sabbath day, and that we abstain, as far as possible, from all servile work."

" Yes, I do, but yet "——

" ' Is a jailor to bring forth some monstrous malefactor ?' " added the priest, laughing. " Well, let him come."

" It is not at all difficult to tell you what I mean. Why do you play cards and chess, sing songs, and read novels on Sunday ? "

" Because God never forbade us to do so."

" What do you mean, Father Stirling ? "

" Simply what I say, dear child, that God, in commanding us to hallow the Sabbath day, never forbade us innocent recreation. He does not even allude to the subject. God instituted the

Sabbath for two ends, for His own honour and glory, and for the repose and renewal of the mental and physical powers of man. We fulfil the one end by our devotions, the other, as I have already said, by harmless amusements. Now, this is our rule: whatever amusement has in it a shadow of evil, is wrong on Sunday, and consequently forbidden; but mark, it is also wrong on Monday, Tuesday, and all the days of the week, and forbidden, too. A simple game of vingt-et-un bears with it no sin, it is perfectly harmless; but were a man to gamble on Sunday night he would commit a sin, though his sin would be equally bad every other day. Jessie Seymour has well attended to all her religious duties during the day, let us hope; to-night she relaxes our spirits and her own by the charm of her beautiful voice. Nor would we have had her melody sacred, for one likes not to hear holy things without attention, and therefore in the light-hearted mood of the company secular music was both more appropriate and more agreeable."

"But mamma says that in Paris the shops are many of them open, and the cafés, theatres, and all kinds of places of amusement. Do you approve of that?"

"Miss Howard, I know few things more distressing, and yet, at the same time, sweeter, than Sunday in Paris. You may well look surprised, for this is, certainly, what we call a paradox. For one who has been all his life accustomed to the solemn stillness of an English Sunday, I know few things more painful than to walk the streets of Paris on a Sunday morning, where open shops, itinerant vendors, bustling purchasers, loaded carts and carriages meet the eye at every turn. To a Catholic, finding himself, for the first time, in a country professing his own faith, it is more than painful, it is overwhelming. But let him ask one fervent Catholic that he meets, what he thinks of it, and the reply will be that of my own friend, M. l'Abbé B——, 'C'est un vrai scandale.' France is essentially Catholic; look at her mighty body of faithful priests, her monks, her nuns, her incomparable, ever-devoted Sœurs de Charité, and last, not least, her beautiful crowded churches, and he will find religion doing her mighty, but silent work. But, my child, there is another element in France besides Catholicity, and that is Infidelity. Fatal offspring of the wretched Voltaire, nourished by the blood of the Revolution, and fostered by the impious publications with which France is still inundated, its fruit appears in evil of every possible shape. How can a man who writes on the gates of the graveyard, 'Death is an eternal sleep,' be expected to close a wicked romance, to turn from an evil play, or still less to shrink from the desecration of the Sabbath? No, it is very mournful to walk through crowds intent on breaking God's commandments; but, remember, amid all its sadness, it is Infidel, my child, it is not Catholic."

"But what do you like in their Sunday then, Father Stirling?"

"I like to walk on Sunday afternoon, or evening, in the more rural parts of their metropolis, and to see the merriment, gaiety, and heartfelt glee that prevail on all sides. I like to see groups of people wandering here and there, and young men, boys, and children engaging in what are really innocent amusements. For instance, I love a ramble in the Bois de Boulogne, as the evening is closing in, and all are on the qui vive for a display of fireworks. I love to see the crowds in the Louvre, the Palais d'Industrie, the gardens of the Tuileries, and Luxembourg, and the more fashionable Champs Elysées. I like to see the carriages wheeling past, when you know the hour for devotion is over, and that the exercise to the spirited horses is not labour. I love the afternoon excursion to Versailles, or St. Cloud, to see the waters play, and I like to see the merry parties seated outside and inside the gay cafés and restaurants on the Boulevards, because all this may be innocent, and is recreative."

"And would you go to theatres and balls then too ?"

"No! a decided, unmitigated, no! and for the simple reason, that I would not go to theatres and balls on other days. There is the possibility that these places may be sinless, but I question much, whether any young person ever left a theatre or public ball-room, as good and pious as she entered it. Should you know more of Catholic society, as you grow up, you will find that really serious people rarely frequent either one or the other, and you will moreover see that in the private evening party, the strict Catholic will be much more guarded than many a good Protestant. For instance, I should be surprised to see Emily or Edith, when they grow up, dance anything more than a quiet quadrille, unless it were a circular dance with each other, or some other young girl."

"Is it wrong, then, to dance polkas and waltzes ?" asked Marion, opening her eyes very wide.

"I do not say that, but I hope no one in whom I am interested will ever dance them. And, as you see. I do not like polkas any day," he added, smiling, "you are not likely to find them in my list of Sunday amusements. Do you think you understand us better now ?"

"Yes" returned Marion, frankly, "but I should be very sorry to join in amusements myself."

"Nor does any one desire you to do so, my dear child; act up to your own conscience; all I ask of you, is not to be scandalised when other people act up to theirs. Prejudice goes a great way with us all; we live in a Protestant country, and its stiffness finds its way even into Catholic families. We are all bound to keep Sunday holy, under pain of sin, but certainly beyond making ourselves dull and mopy, we should do nothing worse, if after church we took up our Bibles and prayer-books, and never lifted our eyes from them till we went to bed. We should lose much happiness, but we should commit no sin; while were you, on the contrary, in your present belief, to engage in amusements which you thought to be displeasing to God, however innocent they might be in themselves, you would do decidedly wrong. It was for this reason, I was pleased with you this evening, and much as I should like to hear you sing," he added, smiling, "I should be very sorry for you even to favour me with the 'Last Rose of Summer.'"

Marion was silent. Father Stirling's words were, she felt, reasonable, and her agitation of spirit had quite subsided. Beneath the soft influence of his words, she felt the vitality of the atmosphere around her, and saw that, however she might disapprove of Catholic Sundays, they were not, in their gayest moments, freed from the restraints of Catholic piety.

"And now shall we go back to the others, or do you still shrink from the drawing-room?" asked the priest.

"No, not at all; you have done really as you said, and I do feel that the Sunday amusements of Catholics are no sin to them."

"On the contrary, my child, you see one may almost call them a part of their religion, since, by them, they recreate their souls for God's better service."

Marion looked up. "Amusement is a strange part of religion though," she answered, musingly.

"It is astonishing," replied Father Stirling, "into what trifling actions of our lives religion does enter. Did it ever strike you, that in eating your dinner, you perform not only a necessary, but a religious action?"

"No," said Marion, laughing.

"And yet, the Bible says,.'Whether you eat, or drink, or whatever you do, do all to the glory of God.' We eat to sustain life, and surely the great end of the life He has given us, is God. No, my child, not the smallest action of a Catholic is unsanctified by his religion. I say Catholic, because Protestants do not, with few exceptions, think of these things in a religious light, and consequently lose many little graces, lurking even in the ordinary routine of every-day life."

At this moment some other members of the party made their appearance.

"Where is papa?" asked Father Stirling of Emily, who had been saying "Hail Maries" innumerable for Marion, but who, seeing the tête-a-tête ended, came bounding towards them.

"There he is, talking to Jessie; but, really, Father, you must not go to him yet, please; I have just been to fetch the battle-dore, for you are such a nice player! Do stop five minutes!" she added, pleadingly, holding it out to him.

"Certainly, till supper-time, if you like; there!" he added, sending the shuttle-cock spinning into the air, "catch that, if you can!"

But Emily did catch it, while Father Stirling, on his side, let it fall, amid a peal of laughter from Marion and his little antagonist. But notwithstanding this mishap, he really was a good player, and they kept the little shuttle-cock in a constant whirl, Emily springing from side to side like a fawn, till poor Father Stirling, who was not quite so agile, began to grow very warm and red.

"Well done! Well done!" cried Mr. Darrell, for by this time quite a group had assembled on the green sward. "Talk of gladiators and chariot races, I wonder whether ever the Forum witnessed such a trial of skill as this!"

"That you may safely say it did not!" exclaimed Father Stirling, aiming a blow at the shuttle-cock, "nor anything half so sensible."

"I wonder how you would get on, if I were Nero, ready to kill and fry the first who let the shuttle-cock down."

"Rather nervously, I expect ; but what a barbarian you must be, to make a man talk during such hard work as this," cried Father Stirling, almost out of breath.

"Oh, go on ; seeing that I am weaving a laurel crown for the victor," said Mr. Darrell, cutting a branch.

"Each of them has let it fall once," said Edith, "so they are quite even. Jessie is counting, they will soon reach three hundred."

"Let us go on to a thousand, Father !" cried Emily.

"Thank you, you would have to play with my ghost ! There," he added, throwing down the battle-dore, and seating himself on the grass, "I am quite done for, and ready to be crowned."

"Rather a cool request for the vanquished, I must say !" exclaimed Mr. Darrell. "No, I adjudge the wreath to Emily, the victor, and death to the vanquished by starvation. See, I hold down my thumb, he shall go without his supper."

"Misericordia !" cried Father Stirling, from the grass, while Emily was adorned by her father with a very spiky crown of laurel.

Marion was wonderfully amused by the merriment around her. "But is it possible," she thought, "that that joyous face belongs to the same man who stood preaching so gravely this afternoon, and who afterwards performed that very solemn service ?" She could no more have fancied Mr. Lisle playing at battle-dore and shuttle-cock, than he could have imagined him in Father Stirling's vestments.

After supper, of which, notwithstanding Mr. Darrell's judgment, Father Stirling did partake, there was a general move among the guests.

"Edie, dear," whispered Emily, "don't you wish Father Stirling would come and say the rosary and night prayers with us in the little chapel?"

"Yes," replied Edith, delighted with the idea ; "see, there he is, walking up and down the terrace ; let us go and ask him ;" and the twins were soon by the side of their pastor.

"Certainly, my children, there is nothing I should like better. We must go at once though, for it is getting late. Call Joe."

The chapel in question was a pretty little building, deeply hidden in a copse of trees, which Father Stirling himself had blessed a few days previously.

A large image of the Mother of God surmounted the altar, which the care of the twins kept always bright with flowers. Edith soon lighted the tapers, and Father Stirling was on the point of commencing, when Marion's voice was heard calling her companions, in evident perplexity at their absence.

"Shall I go to her, Father?" asked Edie.

"Yes, tell her what we are going to do ; and if she likes, let her join us."

Edith accordingly ran off, and in a few seconds returned with Marion.

"So you have come to say your prayers, while we say ours," said the priest, "but we are going to say our beads first, and I am afraid they will scandalise you."

"Do you mean the rosary?"

"Yes, see," and he held it up.

"Oh, no! Miss Horton told me all about it, and if the prayers were only to God, instead of the Virgin Mary, I should very much like to think of all the different things she told me."

"By the bye, that reminds me that Miss Horton would, I am sure, like to join us. Run, Joe, and see!"

For a few minutes the little party were silent.

"Father Stirling," said Marion, at length, "if you will tell me the things you are going to meditate upon, I will try and think about them, too ; that is, of course, without saying the prayers."

"Very well, come and kneel then by me, and I will tell you what each mystery is before we begin the decade. But will you promise me just one little thing?"

"If I can," said Marion.

"I assure you it is nothing difficult."

"Then, I do," answered the child.

"Ask our Blessed Lord before you begin, that He will teach you to love and reverence His holy Mother, as far as is pleasing to Himself."

"Yes, I will," and the head was immediately bowed.

The devotions commenced, and Marion followed Father Stirling through the first three glorious mysteries. The Assumption and Coronation were of events unknown to the little Protestant, but she wandered back in spirit to those she could understand, happy in the very presence, as it were, of a risen, glorified Redeemer.

"Father Stirling," whispered the child, as they crossed the lawn, now bright in the gleam of the summer moonlight, "your religion is very beautiful, I sometimes think I should like to be a Catholic myself."

"Deo gratias," ejaculated the priest, but his only answer to Golden-hair was a smile.

CHAPTER VII.

IT was evident to her young companions that Marion Howard was attracted towards their religion, but, following the advice of Father Stirling, they refrained from saying anything to her on the subject, although she went with them every morning to mass. "Leave her to herself," said the priest, "and let her overcome those little prejudices, so small in themselves, but such insuperable barriers to a reception of the faith. A farthing is not very large, yet, if held before the eye, it may hide a colossus."

One morning, about ten days after Marion's conversation with Father Stirling, detailed in the last chapter, Mrs. Darrell was surprised, in the midst of her morning duties, by a visit from that gentleman.

"I have called in to ask you," said he, "if you think we might make up a little party to-morrow to Burnett's Wood. The weather is beautiful, and as we have holidays just now at the schools, I am a little less busy than usual. What do you think?"

"O mamma! O Father Stirling! How delightful!" cried Emily, springing up and clapping her hands.

"Stop, stop, mad-cap, you do not know whether you are going yet. Things require a little consideration," said the priest.

"Oh, I am sure mamma is quite ready!"

"But how about papa?" objected the sober Edith.

"The carting will not be finished before to-morrow night, I know," said Joe, who had been chatting to the girls from the garden, through the open window, "but I think papa will be quite free on Thursday."

"Joe is right," said Mrs. Darrell. "I am very sorry, but I am afraid Mr. Darrell would not be able to leave his men to-morrow."

"What a pity!" cried all the children in a chorus.

"Couldn't you manage to make it Thursday, Father?" asked Emily, coaxingly, and sidling up to him.

"Well, really," he replied, stroking his chin, "I don't know, but I suppose it will not be quite impossible even to do that."

"Mr. Darrell could go with us then, I know," said their mother.

"Very well, then," said Father Stirling, "I must contrive it, too. As for getting Seymour to join us, that is, I suppose, quite out of the question. Country doctors get few holidays, but I am sure Mrs. Seymour and the children would enjoy the day very much, if we could contrive to pack them."

"Oh, yes, I think we can manage it if we take the phaeton and dog-cart," replied Mrs. Darrell.

"Suppose I were to borrow old Jackson's gig, and relieve you of myself and one of these little people?" suggested the priest.

"Oh, please take me, Father!" cried all the children together.

"Let us draw lots," said Joe, and, amid a great deal of fun and laughing, it was agreed that Emily should ride to the wood in the gig, and that Marion should be Father Stirling's companion back.

Mr. Darrell's hay had been all safely housed the night before, and the June morning rose without a cloud. Miss Horton and the children went to Mass, and brought back Father Stirling in

triumph to breakfast. All were in rampant spirits ; Emily alone
was sufficient to have sustained a whole regiment in merriment.
How she sang, and danced, and frisked, running up and down
the drive every five minutes to see whether Rufus was coming !
and when at last he did arrive, with the unfashionable equipage
lumbering behind him, Boadicea never sat more proudly in her
chariot, than did Emily Darrell in old Jackson's gig beside Father
Stirling.

What a sensation they created as the three carriages rolled on,
one after the other, through little villages, where staring peasants
and gaping children greeted them from every house, old women
smiling, the girls grinning, and the ragged urchins waving their
caps, hallooing and hurrahing after them till they were hoarse !
On, through turnpike roads, past hayfields dotted with haymakers, and smiling cornfields ripening fast. On, amid singing
birds and gurgling brooks, past loaded wains, and roadside inns
with dingy signs creaking in the wind. On, past dusty travellers
who turned and gazed with wonder at the merry cavalcade, past
hedges gay with dog-roses and honeysuckles, past cottages covered
with woodbine and jessamine, and village churches buried deep
in ivy. On, through the sweet green lanes of dear old England,
where spreading trees met high above their heads, through country
scenes with cows and sheep scattered in the meadows, and boys
swinging on the gates, or riding heavy cart-horses to water. On,
through summer heat and summer stillness, broken only by the
rattle of their own wheels, and the joyous laughter of their own
light hearts. And, then the wood ! Oh the delight of running
wild beneath those grand old trees—of leaping through masses
of fern that waved high above their heads — of tying up the
horses—of jumping in and out of the empty carriages, in search
of viands stowed away in all conceivable places—and of seeking
a clear smooth place to spread the cloth, and decking the branches
of a tree with hats and bonnets ! Oh, the charm of all those
thousand-and-one delights to be found only in a picnic !

"See," cried Joe from a distance, "here are the remains of a
fire."

"Some one has been here before," sapiently remarked Emily.

"Gipsies, perhaps," suggested Marion.

"What fun if they would come now," cried Emily ; "I should
so love to see some real live gipsies. What a splendid life theirs
must be ! "

"Do you think so ? " asked her father. "I question it very
much. A picnic is all very well, but for my part I would rather
be a Christian and live in a house."

"O papa ! now listen, if I could have my way I would be a
gipsy girl living in the woods, like a bird. I should like you to
be the great king of the band, and me the little queen. Fancy
how beautiful it would be, always living in a wood like this, or
travelling about from one place to another on a white donkey
crowned with flowers ? "

" You or the donkey ? "

" Me, of course ! And for all the other gipsies to gather round ready to defend us. O papa ! I am sure the gipsies must be the most delicious people in the world. They seem so good and innocent, so unlike other people. As for their stealing children, everybody knows that is nonsense."

" Very likely, at anyrate we will give them the benefit of the doubt ; but I wish their consciences were equally clear in the matter of fowl-roosts and clothes-lines. Delicious people ! So much for the romance of young brains ! Yes, very like a king I should look certainly, tinkering away at old pots and pans, while your majesty went round cheating servant girls out of their sixpences. I wonder if you would be brave enough to sleep on the grass in summer, with frogs, spiders, and beetles walking over you, and how you would like hiding yourself in the winter in the worst holes and corners of the town ? Emmy, Emmy, what a set of scamps you have chosen for your favourites ! "

This picnic was, of course, no exception to the general rule, for a whole hamper of glasses, small plates, and the corkscrew were found to have been forgotten. But what did that matter, while three laughing mouths could drink out of one glass, while tarts could be eaten in the fingers, and bottle-necks broken off ? They had come to enjoy themselves, and enjoy themselves they did, laughing so immoderately that Tom and Betsy were obliged to run away to preserve a decent gravity, while the very horses turned from their feast of leaves to shake their ears in astonishment. But, delightful as they are, picnic dinners will not last for ever ; all was over at length, and again a wild troop rushed through the ferns. But the day had grown very warm, the first excitement was over, and tired out, even with fun, the children at last sank down to rest beneath the spreading branches of a right royal oak, not far from the elder party, who were quietly conversing on subjects very uninteresting to our little friends, whatever they may have been to themselves.

" Now, Joe, tell us a story," cried Emily, as she and Marion settled themselves very comfortably against the tree stump.

" What a notion ! " cried Joe ; " go and ask Father Stirling to preach you a sermon."

" Thank you, we would rather have the story."

" But ' story, I have none to tell,' " cried Joe, unconsciously quoting Shakespeare.

" Make one up then," said Jessie.

" By George, you might as well set me to make a pudding."

" Nonsense, Joe, you know you can think of plenty, if you choose ; you read enough."

" Tell us the one you were reading all last evening," said Edie.

" It is too long."

" You can make it short ! " cried Emily. " I know the one Edie means ; it is called ' Rosalind.' I caught Joe crying over it last night."

"O Em, what a shame! I declare I was only blowing my nose; but you girls had better get your handkerchiefs ready, for it is very sentimental, I can tell you. Well, here goes," he continued, and clearing his throat after the most approved fashion, and blushing up, as only a boy of fifteen can blush, he commenced the story of

ROSALIND.

Once upon a time there was a princess, great, rich, and beautiful, and her name was Rosalind. She was the daughter of a mighty king, and the fame of her beauty was so great that her father's court was always crowded with knights and noblemen, princes and minstrels, and each and all were the suitors of the lovely Rosalind. But amid all this homage she was sweet and innocent as a mountain daisy. She would run away from the state of the royal palace, to roam the woods with her maidens, and would turn away from a grand speech, it had cost some unfortunate lover a week to concoct, to play with her pure white fawn. This fawn had been her mother's once, and now that that mother lay in the cold grave, Rosalind clung to it fondly, and loved it better than anything in the world, except her father. As the months rolled by, they found Rosalind every day more beautiful, and her lovers more despairing, for she grew more indifferent to them than ever, and so some of the poor fellows went off in desperation and found other brides, or went to the Crusades, or sat at home and turned misers and woman-haters, and all for the sake of Rosalind.

One night there was a great storm, and amid flashing lightning and pealing thunder, a great knocking was heard at the castle gate. The warder looked forth, and he beheld a tall knight on a coal-black charger, who asked for shelter. The warder bade him welcome in the name of his royal master, and the tall knight rode into the courtyard, and raised his visor. And the Lady Rosalind looked forth from her casement, and she gazed with wonder at this knight, more handsome than the heroes of her wildest dreams, and for the first time the white fawn licked her hand unnoticed. A splendid banquet was spread in the hall below, for it was a day of high festival, and when the Lady Rosalind sat down beneath the gilded canopy, by her father's side, the stranger knight came and bowed himself almost to the ground before her. And Rosalind trembled. But as for the knights, when they saw their wit unnoticed, and the minstrels' songs unheard, they grew positively green with jealousy, and kicked the white fawn on the sly, and scowled on the handsome stranger.

"My name is Rodolph, and I am bound for Palestine," he said; and the king glanced at the red cross, and the golden spurs, and was silent.

Days and weeks flew by, and still the stranger lingered; and

Rosalind grew pale, the white fawn desolate, and the lovers almost raving mad with jealousy.

One night, the king found Rosalind weeping, and Rodolph on his knees, and certainly the old gentleman was rather astonished.

The knight rose, towering to his full height, " Sire, I love the Lady Rosalind."

" And you, my child ? "

" Father, I will be obedient."

And the old king was so charmed with the answer that he joined their hands then and there.

The next day there was a grand feast in honour of the betrothal of Rodolph and Rosalind, and as the despised lovers were obliged to drink the health of the happy pair, most of them ate a good dinner, to comfort them in their disappointment. And then Rodolph went to fulfil his vow at the Crusades, and Rosalind shut herself up with her maidens and white fawn, inconsolable for many days. But when they talked to her of the time when Rodolph should come back and make her his bride, she smiled again and fondled her fawn, and again her laugh was heard in the green-wood, as she rambled with her maidens.

But sorrow cast her heavy shadow over the royal castle. One night the watch-dog howled, the bat flapped his black wings, the screech-owl hooted in the ivy, and when the morning dawned the Lady Rosalind was an orphan and a queen. Her maidens spoke in vain of comfort now, as she lay on the ground, beside her father's bier, and sobbed.

But as time went by, even this grief grew paler, and Rosalind was the crowned queen of a great nation, with crowds watching for her at her palace gates, and hailing her with shouts and smiles. But though she smiled in return, her heart was very heavy, for the past was buried in her father's grave, and the present, dreary without Rodolph, made the future a blank. She heard no tidings of her absent lover, and Rosalind drooped, but grew each day more lovely in her sadness, like the lily of the valley.

One day she rambled on the seashore, alone with her fawn, for even her maidens seemed wearisome in her grief, and she watched wave after wave roll in, gilded by the setting sun, and she thought of Rodolph till she wept aloud, kneeling on the bleak and lonely shore.

" Daughter of an ancient race," said a deep, strange voice, and turning, she beheld an old man standing by her side. His robe was long and flowing, his beard and hair white as snow, and his whole frame bowed with the weight of years. But the Princess shrunk beneath the glance of two piercing eyes that entered her very soul.

" What will you ? " she asked proudly.

" To comfort you, Princess."

Rosalind, smiled scornfully. " Do you hold the reins of fate in your hands, old man ? " she asked.

"I do! Come and see!"

Spell-bound by a power she did not try to resist, Rosalind followed the stranger. Their way lay along the coast, and as she went on, the scene grew wilder at every step; large rocks and heaps of sand, covered with coarse herbage and sea-shells, stretched away far as the eye could reach on one side, and the wide roaring ocean on the other. Her guide at length stopped before the entrance of a cavern in the range of gloomy rocks, and turned and gazed upon her.

"Enter," he said.

"To what end ?" asked the maiden. "I have followed you thus far because you spoke of comfort, and for this my weary soul yearns with a longing indescribable. But can there be aught to comfort in such a spot as this ? Let me go back; I see my folly."

But the wrinkled hand still pointed inflexibly to the cave. "Enter," he said again.

"No, it would be of no avail. Who are you ?"

"One in whose grasp lies the past, the present, and the future, and at whose nod the very fates bow low. My name is Azor, royal maiden. Trust me and enter; heaven, earth, destiny, veil no secrets from my glance."

Rosalind hesitated for an instant, and then, with a faltering step, followed her guide through the dark portal of his dwelling; the white fawn trembled, but left not her mistress' side. They passed along a tortuous passage cut in the solid rock, and Rosalind shrunk as she walked through the dreary darkness, for the cold earth-damp struck to her very soul. But the pride of her warlike race sustained her, as she followed the glimmer of her guide's lamp; the passage gradually widened, and at length she found herself in a spacious chamber.

It was a strange-looking room, hung with skins, and lighted by dull red lamps, that shed a murky glare around. A furnace burnt in one corner, over which a dwarf, hideous in its light, bent to replenish it. A curtain fell from the roof at one end of the apartment, and Rosalind trembled as she thought what might its heavy folds conceal.

The wizard gazed on his lovely guest, a smile, almost of satisfaction, hovering on his lips, though his arms folded on his breast gave him an aspect of deep humility; but, beneath the lurid glow of those fearful eyes, again the maiden trembled.

"Princess, give the sign, and that mirror, unveiled, shall reveal the absent Rodolph."

Rosalind started, and gazed fearfully round her, then, clasping her hands firmly, bowed her head.

As the curtain slowly rose, a large surface of crystal appeared before her. Rosalind at first could see nothing more, but while she gazed, a majestic forest rose to the surface, glorious with waving palms, and the luxuriant vegetation of the East. A figure appeared in sight, and with a bounding heart Rosalind recognised her lover.

Breathlessly she watched him as he made his way through the tangled brushwood. "He lives! He lives!" she cried. "Father! you have kept your word, take what you will as your reward," and she glanced at the jewels that adorned her neck and arms. But the wizard stirred not, his glance was riveted on the glass. Again she looked, Rodolph was there still, but, horror of horrors! a monstrous lion, crouching beneath a tree, was about to make his fatal spring on the unconscious warrior, intent only on breaking his way through the jungle.

A shriek rang through the cavern, and echoed from gallery to gallery.

"Save him! Save him!" she cried, falling on her knees before the wizard.

But Azor stood motionless, and the lion quivered with expectation, as his prey approached nearer and nearer.

"Azor, he is so young to die!"

"You alone can save him."

"How?"

"Renounce your crown for ever."

"I do!" An arrow pierced the lion's heart, and the curtain fell.

Again Rosalind and her fawn stood upon the shore. "When next you need me, you must summon me," said the magician; "I shall seek you no more. Three blows upon my door, will bring me to you."

That night the troops of a mighty king surprised her castle, and Queen Rosalind fled away with her jewels, her maidens, and her fawn, and she reigned in the land no more.

Three months passed by, three months of adversity, anguish, and incertitude, and though the Lady Rosalind recoiled in horror from the wizard and his cave, love prevailed, and once again she found herself before the magic mirror.

It was the camp of the crusaders that she beheld, glorious in the setting sun, with its fair white tents, its waving banners, and stalwart warriors in gleaming corslets, hurrying to and fro. And there, in the shadow of his tent, upon a couch of leopards' skins, lay Rodolph, locked in the deep slumber of a weary man. Long did Rosalind gaze upon the face so calm in sleep, every lineament of which was so deeply traced in her innermost soul. Of what is he dreaming? A smile flits across his features, and he murmurs "Rosalind." Entranced, she turns to look at Azor, that this time, at least, he may participate in her joy, but the rock of his own cavern is not more immovable, and she turns from him to gaze again on Rodolph. The scene has changed, a turbaned form hangs over the sleeper, a gleaming dagger quivers in the air, as the bead-like eyes of the assassin gloat over their victim. There is no time for words, she grasps Azor's arm in anguish unspeakable.

"Your beauty," he hisses.

That night the Lady Rosalind lay upon her couch, raving in

the delirium of a malignant fever.   Her maidens fled, and the
white fawn licked her mistress' hands alone.   An aged hermit
found her, sick to death, but beneath his skilful hands she lived
again for misery and Rodolph.

The evening sun is setting once again upon the billows, rolling
ever onward in the restlessness of their power, and a woman,
weird-looking in her ugliness, knocks at the wizard's door.   It is
Rosalind, but the brightness of her eye is dimmed, unsightly
blotches mar the once fair cheek, the stately form is bowed as
though with age, and a thick black veil floats behind in the place
of the fairy tresses.   Again she stands before the mirror, but
when Azor would withdraw the curtain, she grasps his arm in fear.

"It is too late," he mutters, and Rodolph, bound hand and
foot, lies before her in a dreary dungeon.   No friend, no food,
no gleam of heaven's light, but darkness, manacles, starvation !

"What will release him, Azor?"

"All you possess."

"My jewels?"

"Not enough."

"The miserable shelter I still call mine?"

"More than that.   This is not enough to ransom Rodolph from
his deadliest enemy."

"It is all I have."

"It is not enough."

"Alas ! I have nothing but my life besides ! "

The wizard laughed scornfully.   "Not yet, not yet," he muttered.

"And must he perish?"

Azor pointed to the fawn.

"I cannot ! I cannot ! Oh, my mother !"

"Then Rodolph dies ; for four days he has not tasted food.
He faints already, see !" and the mirror showed her Rodolph in
a swoon.

"Last of my friends, adieu !" cried Rosalind, and the white
fawn leaping into the air, as though struck by a sudden dart,
licked her hand and died.

Alone in the wide, dreary world, a beggar-woman wends her
way from door to door, and lives on the charity of strangers.
But she is ever welcomed ; mothers pour their troubles into a sympathising ear, while little children run in flocks to meet her.

"She is good as she is ugly," says an old woman, gazing after
her as she limps away from her door.

"Aye, cummer ! and as wise as she is poor," is the hearty
response.   "Poor Rosalind is an angel in disguise !"

"What will you?" asks the wizard, sternly, as three trembling
knocks bring him to his threshold.   "Who are you?"

"All that remains of her that was once a queen."

"Aha ! my pretty Rosalind ! welcome !" and his cruel eyes
shoot fire.

"Where is Rodolph?"

"Come and see."

Even before the curtain was withdrawn, the roar of waves, the howling of the storm-wind, the pealing of thunder, and the hoarse cry of sailors in distress, broke upon her ear, and the murky glare of the red furnace revealed, in the depths of the mirror black as night, a ship foundering in a tempest.

"There he is! I see him plainly, struggling in the waves, O Azor! Azor!"

"And just nearing home," cried the wizard; "two hours more would land him on our shores. Will you save him?"

"Do you mock me?" cried Rosalind; "what have I that I have not given, for my life you spurn! O Azor! be merciful, miserable as it is, take it for his!"

"Not yet! not yet!"

"Then, Rodolph, adieu for ever!"

"You have yet the chief ornament of your race. That which your ancestors vaunted more proudly than riches, rank, or power —your honour. Learn to be spurned as vile and outcast, and Rosalind shall ransom Rodolph."

"Keep my integrity, and lose my name?"

"Keep what you will," cried Azor, "though when you shall hear yourself branded and stigmatised, what shall conscious innocence avail?"

"Enough, I submit. One day more, and then with Rodolph, all shall be forgotten!"

A mocking laugh ran through the cavern, and the curtain fell.

A gallant ship rides proudly into harbour, bearing marks of a recent storm. A precious freight is hers; jewels, spices, and stuffs from the far East, while many a knightly form, bending over her bulwarks, hails with a tearful eye the land of his birth. Burgesses crowd round to deal with traders from afar, fair ladies gaze with rapture on their lords returned, and churchmen flock to welcome the warriors of the cross.

Decrepit, weary, clothed in rags, jostled by all—for poverty finds few friends—a woman passes through the crowd, and gazes, with a life history in her glance, upon the deck of the stalwart ship.

"Thief! liar! witch!" bursts from the idlers round, but she heeds them not; Rodolph alone fills ear, and eye, and heart, and the contumely of a few short moments matters nothing.

"Prithee, peace, good friends!" says a stout burgess, "this woman harmeth none. Faith!" he whispers, beneath his breath, "but, by our Lady, she is wondrous ill-favoured!"

"She is looking for her lord!" cry the crowd, in mockery.

A form springs to land. Many are stately there, but not one steps forth like him; many are fair to look on, but the glory of his martial beauty surpasses all. In an instant Rosalind has threaded the crowd, her hand is on his arm—"Rodolph!"

He had seen her from the vessel's deck, and he knew her well, but he recoiled from her touch, and shuddered.

A jeer rose from the crowd, "The lady has found her lord!"

Alas! poor souls, they knew not how the random arrow of their
jest flew home.

"Rosalind, you are wondrous changed," he muttered, "but we
will meet anon," and as he passed on his way, a troop of gallant
knights and fair ladies followed in his train.

"'Tis the great Baron Rodolph," cried the crowd, falling back on
all sides.

"Witch! liar! thief!" again assailed Rosalind, as she passed
through the crowd, but again she heard it not, nor quailed beneath
the shower of missiles that fell around her. She turned away,
and passed along the dreary shore, and though the dark night fell,
and the winter wind swept across the sea, and howled around her
like the voices of a hundred demons, still she passed onward, and
Azor found a form rigid as marble lying across his threshold. He
bore her through the vaulted gallery, and Rosalind woke once
more to life.

He was gazing at her with folded arms, when she raised her
head.

"Where am I?" she asked, "where is Rodolph?" but the glare
of the fiery eyes recalled her to herself, and she sprang shuddering
to her feet.

"Why do I find you at my door?" he asked; "for what have
you come?"

"To show you your work," she cried, bitterly.

"A masterpiece, truly!" was the reply.

"Is this the comfort, this the solace, you promised me when
first we met?"

"What more will you?—is not Rodolph safe?"

"He spurns me like the rest. He, for whom I have borne all,
abandoned all! My crown, my beauty, my reputation. All that
woman holds dearest. O Rodolph! Rodolph!"

"Will you have revenge?"

"Not for a thousand worlds! faithless as he is! But why
should he spurn me? Man, show me myself!" The mirror
reflected a form, from which Rosalind shrank dismayed.

There was a long silence, broken only by the roaring of the
furnace, the bubbling of the crucible, and the sullen moan of the
sea without.

"Maiden," said the wizard, at length, "since you refuse my
vengeance, will you call back his love? Shall I give you once
again your crown, your beauty, your name, more lustrous than
before? Shall even the white fawn come back from the land of
shadows, to welcome the Rosalind of old, and shall Rodolph,
loving and repentant, kneel once more at her feet?"

"Azor!" cried Rosalind, "have you such power as this? Who
are you?"

"Lucifer the supreme! Lucifer the light-bearer to the benighted!
Lucifer the refuge of the soul-weary and crushed! Listen, sweet
Rosalind, soon to be queen once more! Swear fealty to me, and
all that I have promised shall be yours." And terrific in his

fallen grandeur, the prince of darkness stood unveiled before her.

"Monster, depart!" cried Rosalind, with a shriek; "think you, for Rodolph, I would lose my soul? Avaunt, in the name of God!"

A mighty convulsion shook the rock to its foundation, and the mirror flew into a thousand fragments. A shriek, echoing far and wide, broke from the baffled demon; he himself, his chamber, the dwarf, and the furnace, disappeared in a whirlwind, and Rosalind lay panting and breathless, on the bleak sea-shore alone . . . . .

Far in the depths of an ancient forest, whose giant oaks had reared their proud forms for centuries untold, unmolested by the woodman's axe, there stood a modest hut. Built of clay, and thatched with boughs, it gave but little shelter from the summer's heat, or winter's cold, and yet, within it dwelt a woman, high-born and young. The fruit of the forest was her summer's food, while in the winter she wandered forth for charity, and husbanded her little store till spring. Rumour spoke of her wondrous wisdom, and deep sanctity, and how, with tears and groans, she washed away the sins of early days. And rumour spoke truth, for on her knees, until the very stones were worn, Rosalind wept over her rebellion to the decrees of Heaven. If there were times when earth would mingle with higher aspirations, and when forms once loved would glide from the spirit-land of the past, Rosalind only bowed the lower in the fervour of her devotion, until even Rodolph's memory paled into a picture in the volume of the past; a name to be forgotten except in prayer.

One day the gentle hermit was weeping even more bitterly than her wont, and though the evening shadows lengthened in the grotto, the frugal meal lay still untouched. Six long years had passed since she had stood before the ship from Palestine, but she watched not the flight of time. Devotion counts not years and seasons, and life was now only a short cold passage to a glorious home, through which she trod in haste. The ravages of sorrow and disease had passed, and, fair with the beauty of holiness, the Recluse of the Forest shone with a more hallowed beauty than Rosalind the princess. Nearer, nearer through the forest, came the tramp of a horse's hoof, but she heard it not, as she sat in the rude doorway of her tent, pondering the past in bitter self-humiliation, and a knight was kneeling at her feet before she could drop her veil.

"Rosalind, Rosalind!" he cried, "is it thus I find thee! sought through long years!"

"Hush!" said the Recluse, "Rosalind is dead!"

That same hour a tall horseman, with a drooping plume, rode away beneath the green-wood trees. Rosalind had given all things up for Rodolph,—the Recluse gave Rodolph up for God.

"O Joe!" cried Dora, "what a shame! Only fancy, just as we thought poor Rosalind was going to be happy, after all her troubles, to leave her in the wood in such a miserable manner. Why, I could make a story with a better ending than that myself."

"What would you have done with her ?"

"I would have made her forgive her repentant lover, who should have carried her away with him, on his coal-black horse, into the world again. Then he should have killed the king who had taken her crown, and they should both have lived happily all their lives."

"And died at a good old age, I suppose," said Joe, "a very orthodox ending."

"Well, but, Joe," said Edie, "such a life as you have left Rosalind living, is, I must say, a very gloomy termination to the story. Still," she added, "I think it ought to be something of the kind. Dora's ending would have been more interesting, but the one in the tale is more just."

"Why ?" asked Dora.

"Because Rosalind had committed a very great sin in consulting the magician, and she did not deserve to be happy."

"But she repented, Edie," cried Jessie.

"Yes, I know she did, and so she ought. But mamma says stories have not a good moral in them when wicked actions go unpunished."

"Well, it seems to me," chimed in Emily, "that both Dora and Edie have their own way. Rosalind was wretched when she did wrong, and happy when she repented. I like the story myself as it is."

"O Emmy," cried Dora.

"I do ; not though, perhaps, in the same way that Edith does, for I think the story really has a happy ending. To me there is no life more delightful than a hermit's."

"Except a gipsy's," said Joe, mischievously.

"Oh, that was only my fun, Joe ; a passing thought that ran through my mind on first finding myself in the wood. But the other is what I should really love." And Emily's cheek flushed.

"She has been reading the Fathers of the Desert lately, I guess," cried Joe, with a comical look at Dora.

At this moment the heads of Father Stirling and Mr. Darrell peeped round on either side of the tree.

"Have you been listening ?" cried Emily, springing to her feet. "O Joe !"

"To be sure we have, for a long time, and have been much entertained by Joe's powers as a story-teller."

"And even more so by your various moralisations," said their father.

"And what is your opinion of the tale, papa ?" asked Emily.

"Why, that its moral quite bears out the old proverb, that the 'Devil's wheat is all chaff.' But it is rather hard upon our sex. What say you, Father ?"

"That it is a fair picture of the women of every age. Depend upon it, my dear sir, they set us an example in constancy and fortitude. There are not many men who would have endured one tithe of Rosalind's privation for a woman, or who would have shrunk like her into patient fortitude under her crushing disappointment."

"I felt a drop of rain, I am sure," cried Joe, suddenly springing up.

He was right. The sky, which had been for some time growing gloomy, was now quite overcast. A general panic ensued.

"It will be a thunder-storm, sir," said Tom, "and a pretty tidy one. Look at the sky over there; the wind is blowing them clouds up fast, sir."

"We must get out of the wood, then, at anyrate," said his master. "You had better, my dear," he continued, turning to his wife, "all of you set off, as fast as you can, to the inn at the village of Ilcombe. It is half a mile at least, so you have no time to lose. These trees would be dangerous in a storm. Father Stirling, Tom, and myself will follow with the carriages as soon as we can get the horses in. Are all the hampers packed?"

"Yes, sir," said Tom.

"Then Betsy can go too. Now, Joe, you must go with your mother, and do the best you can."

"I wish Father Stirling would go, and let me drive his gig up. He would be of more use to them than I shall. Besides, if he catches cold, he is sure to be ill, and I can stand a wetting."

"Thank you, my boy, but I should be very sorry to trust you with old Rufus in a storm. He and I are old friends, and he knows he must obey. He knew me in more fiery days," he added, half to himself.

Notwithstanding the hurry they were in, it was a merry party that ran through the lanes leading from Burnett's Wood to Ilcombe, which, with its sharp-pointed spire, lay in a valley at their feet. It was a long half-mile, but they arrived at last at the little inn, just as a peal of thunder growled in the distance.

It was a quiet old-fashioned little house, with a garden, gay with flowers, and surrounded with clean white railings, on one side, and a little farmyard, with thatched stables and cowhouses on the other. A large tree shaded a horse-trough in front, by the side of which rose the sign-post, a wonderful work of art, executed by some village Raphael, and setting forth in all the glory of royalty his most gracious Majesty, King William.

"Can we have a private room?" asked Joe, stepping into the little sanded red-curtained bar, and addressing a buxom landlady, glorious in red ribbons, and still redder cheeks.

"Well, sir, there be a gentleman who has been dining here, as has got the best parlour. He be a minister, sir, but I don't suppose he'll mind you. Anyways, I'll go and see, and I'll be bound for it, if you don't mind him, he'll make no objections. He seems very civil and gentlemanlike."

"Oh, stop, my dear," cried Mrs. Darrell, from the doorway; "I should be very sorry to disturb the gentleman. You have nowhere else you could put us, I suppose?"

"No, that I haven't, ma'am."

"Is there no other inn ?"

"No, ma'am, never a house will you find atween this and Higher Ilcombe. No, no, I'll just step in and ask him ; it's very likely he'll be glad o' company hisself." And the old lady bustled off.

It was not long before she returned, followed by the gentleman in question.

"I beg, madam," he exclaimed, bowing to Mrs. Darrell, "that you will not scruple to make use of the parlour I have been occupying for my dinner. It is, believe me, quite at your service. A very small corner of it will serve for my accommodation," he added, smiling. "Our good landlady here is quite right in her surmises : I shall be very glad of company."

"Mr. Lisle ! Mr. Lisle !" and Marion darted up the steps to the clergyman.

"Why, Marion, my child, this is a surprise." And a shadow fell at once over the face so bright just before in the energy of kind politeness.

"There is no need of an introduction now," said Mrs. Darrell, smiling ; "this is indeed a pleasant rencontre for Marion."

The whole party followed the curate into the parlour of the little inn, and, for some time, a general conversation was carried on between Mr. Lisle and the elder ladies. But it soon began to flag, as fears for the absent gentlemen began to arise.

"It is very dark," said Mr. Lisle, rising and walking to a window at the further side of the room, overlooking the little farmyard, "but I think it will hold up for a few minutes yet."

"When it does begin, there will be no mistake about it," said Joe, who, with his mother and Miss Horton, was stationed at the front window, in hopes of catching sight of the delayed vehicles.

"There are no [signs of them yet," said Mrs. Darrell ; "they cannot, I am sure, escape the storm."

"We must hope for the best," replied Mrs. Seymour, moving towards the window, round which they all now stood, grouped in anxious expectation.

Marion walked across the large room to Mr. Lisle, who still stood looking out into the farmyard, where ducks, geese, pigs, and hens were indulging in a concert in disapprobation of the weather.

"Well, Golden-hair, and how have you been getting on ?" he asked, stroking the glossy curls.

"Very well indeed," said Marion ; "I am enjoying myself very much. Have you seen mamma ?"

"No ; but I met Turner this morning, and she told me that Mrs. Howard left for London yesterday, and that she expects to remain there some little time. And so you are very happy. Who are those little girls ?"

"Edie and Emily Darrell, and the other two are the Miss Seymours. Do you not think Emily, the one by the side of Mrs. Darrell, very pretty ?"

"Remarkably so. I never remember to have seen a more perfect face. How old is she?"

"Thirteen. I am sure you would like her, she is so amiable and so full of fun. But Edie is my favourite."

"Why?"

"Because she is so good and generous; she never seems to think of herself in anything. She is very thoughtful, and talks very little, but when she does, it is always about something sensible."

"I hope she does not talk of religion," said the curate, with a glance that pierced to her innermost soul.

Marion recollected her secret about Puseyism, and began to feel uncomfortable. Suppose Mr. Lisle should find it out!

"They all talk of religion very often," she replied; "it seems to be the principal thought of their lives: but they never try to convert me."

"That is, they never, on any pretext, mention the subject to you?"

Marion paused. "Yes, they do sometimes, but only when I ask questions. That is, when I ask why they do such and such things."

"And do you mean to tell me," he asked, in a low tone, "that you, Marion Howard, ask questions about Romanism? Then take my advice, and leave off saying the Lord's Prayer; for it is only mocking the Almighty to say, 'Lead us not into temptation,' and then to go and thrust yourself in its way. You may just as well put your hand in the fire, and pray not to be burned. 'Come out from among them, and touch not the unclean thing.' To think you should ever have come here! I wish I could take you back with me."

"Really I could not go, Mr. Lisle; Mrs. Darrell would be offended. You cannot think how kind she is to me."

"Of course, I know you cannot go," he replied, crossly; "I only spoke of what I should like to do. O Marion, my child! you are endangering your soul."

The tone was so inexpressibly unhappy that Marion was really touched, though at the same time not a little vexed.

"Any one would think they were all trying to convert me," she exclaimed, half pettishly.

"And so they are, there is no doubt about that," replied Mr. Lisle; "and your only safety lies in your obedience. Promise me not to say one word more about religion, and I shall be satisfied. Refuse to do this, and I will write to your mother the instant I get back to Ennington."

"But I like to talk about it just a little, especially to Miss Horton, that young lady dressed in black; she was a Protestant herself once."

Mr. Lisle was far too angry to speak.

"Mamma said I might go to church sometimes, just to see, so I am not disobedient when I go, and I have only been very few times as yet. And then, this is generally (indeed always, except once) to the early Mass before breakfast on weekdays, when there is no incense nor music, nor anything grand, and I sit and read my Bible all the time. Surely there is no harm in that. How can I promise not to talk of religion, and sit fancying something very terrible, which after all is only very simple, as I did with the sign of the cross?"

"You are an obstinate girl."

He spoke so angrily that Marion was really pained, and felt very much inclined to cry.

"I am not obstinate, Mr. Lisle, and how can I be doing wrong, when I am only doing what mamma said I might? Besides, I know there is not one here who cares whether I am a Catholic or not."

Innocent falsehood! Could she have heard the prayers that rose for her night and morning, she could not have said that.

"Father Stirling will be here directly; he is a very good man. He is the priest of Harleyford. I am sure you would like him, Mr. Lisle, though he is a priest."

"Stirling!" said the curate with a gasp.

"Yes, Father Stirling. He is a Scotchman."

"A Scotchman!"

At this moment a shout was heard from Joe, announcing the arrival of the carriages. Hardly had the gentlemen entered the room, before the rain commenced pouring down, while the artillery of heaven flashed and rolled in all the awful grandeur of a terrific thunderstorm.

CHAPTER VIII.

No sooner had the new-comers entered the room, than Marion, the storm, the strangers surrounding him, were all forgotten by Mr. Lisle, who seemed absorbed in contemplating Father Stirling. His whole frame heaved convulsively, and his cheek, but lately flushed by his conversation with the child, became ashy in its whiteness.

"Just in time," said Mr. Darrell, "what a flash!"

All stood silent with awe, as a peal of thunder seemed to break over the house, shaking it to its foundations. Edie, pale and trembling, clung to her mother, and Dora hid her face in Miss Horton's dress, sobbing with fear. It was certainly a fearful storm, and older people than Dora and Edie grew alarmed, as the flashes of forked lightning succeeded each other with awful rapidity.

"Courage, my dear children," said Father Stirling, "remember that the danger surrounding us is not sent by the malevolence of man, or the wrath of evil spirits. It is God, our own Father, who directs every flash. Shall we not trust Him?"

It was, at least, half an hour before the storm began to abate, during which time hardly a word was spoken.

"It is beginning to grow lighter now, I think," said the priest at length, closing the breviary he had been reading. "I wonder how it is at the back," and, advancing as he spoke towards the other window, he perceived, for the first time, that they were not alone.

No, they were not alone. In the sanded parlour of the village inn, for the first time for ten long years, Father Stirling met the son of his benefactor—met the man he had loved and cherished as a younger brother, and from whom he had been separated by estrangement worse than death. Ten years had worked their will on both, had changed the stripling to a man, and matured the elder, even sprinkling his hair with grey, and yet at the first glance each recognised the other. For a moment not a word was spoken, till Father Stirling, recovering himself, advanced towards his early friend with outstretched hand.

"Henry !"

The arms remained folded, and save by the quivering of the mouth the salutation was received unmoved.

"Henry," repeated the priest, "have you forgotten me ?"

It was too much ; the stiff arms unbent, and the hand of Father Stirling was wrung convulsively.

At this juncture Mr. Darrell chanced to turn. "Bless me !" he exclaimed to his wife, "I had not the slightest idea that any one besides ourselves was in the room."

"Yes, Mr. Lisle, the curate of Ennington ; he was exceedingly polite when we first came in, but the storm so confused me that I quite forgot to introduce you ;" and she related the circumstances of their arrival at the King's Head.

"Father Stirling knows Mr. Lisle, it seems," said Marion, "how funny !"

"I was not aware of it either," said Mrs. Darrell.

"I see nothing extraordinary, though, my dear," observed her husband, "that two clergymen, residing within nine miles of each other should be acquainted."

Mr. Darrell was less wise than he imagined. The priest and the curate had been ignorant till this moment of each other's vicinity.

A light rain and a distant rumbling were all that now remained of the storm. Mr. Darrell endeavoured to raise the spirits of his little ladies, and so well succeeded that Dora forgot her fears, Marion her scolding from Mr. Lisle, and all were soon laughing heartily over his droll tales. But amid the laughter of the picnic party, a different kind of conversation was going on at the further end of the room.

"And so we meet again," said Father Stirling, after the short pause that had followed their first salutation, "and so we meet again. Oh, my friend, amid the changes and chances of ten long years, how have I prayed for this !"

A sigh was the only answer.

"I have sometimes thought of writing to you," he continued, "but the sight of a letter long ago returned, and growing yellow in my desk, told me it would be of no avail. The memory, too, of a door closed behind me, as I turned from the house that had sheltered me from childhood, banished every idea of revisiting Scotland. But, though absent, I have still known all. Believe me, Henry, during my ten years' estrangement I have both mourned and rejoiced with you. With a sorrow that could only be exceeded by your own, did I mourn over your father's death, my generous, noble-minded guardian. Boy of sixteen as you then were, you called me ungrateful, and that for following the dictates of my conscience. You were young and angry, Henry, and time had not tried the purity of my motives, but will you not give me credit now, for having acted then in conformity with what I felt to be the will of God ?"

"Misguided man ! "

"Misguided ! then, by God Himself !_ But perhaps we had better talk no more of this. Mine has been a hard fate, but God's holy will be done. It is sad to see the grave close over prejudices unremoved."

"You said just now that you had rejoiced as well as sorrowed with us since your departure : when was this ? " asked the curate.

"When Agnes married."

"Indeed ! Who told you of her marriage ? "

"Herself. Two days before, she wrote and told me all. Told me how the old affection had grown into a quiet sisterly remembrance, and how Frank Gordon had gradually taken the place of the companion of her childhood : and none wrote her, I know, a warmer, heartier letter of congratulation than George Stirling."

"She never told me this. Strange ! "

"Search your own heart, and it will tell you why. Much as you had loved me as a boy, have you ever striven in any way to close the breach between your family and me ? "

"Never. And while you bear the hated name of Romanist, I never will. O George ! George ! to think that I should live to see you in that odious garb ! Stirling ! the companion of my childish romps, the confidant of my later years, my elder brother, a Roman Catholic priest ! His fine mind degraded to the superstition of the Middle Ages, and his ingenuous character practising wiles from which the frankness of his boyish nature would have shrunk. What would his friendship avail me now ? How can two hearts, whose aims are devious, know anything of unity ? Can travellers north and south bear each other company, or vessels sail to opposite ports side by side ? "

"Our roads are devious, I know: ought not our goal to be the same ? "

"Yes ; but it is not so. Mine is God, and you are travelling from Him. The monstrous Juggernaut of dogmatism and superstition, that man has created, hides the Essential Truth from you.

You are like the Egyptians, wandering in the darkness caused by your own errors, while those of a purer faith bask in a more than summer light. George, do you remember my mother's death? Do you remember how, with her dying breath, she prayed for you with her children?"

"I do. I was thinking that you must have forgotten it. Perhaps at this very moment, in the land where the weary are at rest, she reads our hearts in the clearness of the beatific vision. Could souls in heaven weep, I believe she would be weeping now over such disunion."

"Say, rather, over the errors of him she had loved and cherished as her own," replied the curate. "But do you mean to say that you believe that those who are out of the pale of the Romish Church can be saved?"

"Yes; if their ignorance is invincible; and who but God can read their hearts?"

There was a long silence. Both looked steadfastly out of the window, and strangely into the past.

"Well, Henry," said the priest at length, brightening up, "I am glad indeed that we have met at last, although you are still so hard upon me, but tell me how you come to be in such an out-of-the-way place as this?"

"I have had a curacy at Ennington from the time of my ordination, three years ago, and I came here to-day on parish matters," answered Mr. Lisle, coldly.

"During the whole of which time I have been living at Harley-ford," answered the priest. "Well, we know each other's whereabouts now, thank God, and can often meet."

"Pardon me," returned the curate, "we have been strangers for the last ten years, and as far as I am concerned, I prefer that we should remain such."

"Henry, is this resentment worthy of a Christian?"

"It is not resentment. Here is my hand to prove it to you; and believe me, George Stirling, that above all men, yes, above every soul on earth, you have my pity, and shall have my prayers."

"And must we part like this? In the name of Him whose ministry we both profess, and who is the God of charity, why cannot the old friendship bind us still?"

"Because I mistrust you, thoroughly mistrust you, Stirling; I know that Romanists will countenance any means to work their ends. I have learned much in a few years, something even this afternoon, and that from a little one whose innocence and artlessness might have rendered her sacred in your eyes. But hear me, and I at least am candid, be it the business of *my* life henceforward, to circumvent the end and aim of *yours*, and such as you, for while I have life and strength, never will I cease from the combat! Adieu, and for ever, unless you see the error of your ways, for then indeed shall David and Jonathan mingle, as of old. Good-bye." He held out his hand.

"Dominus tecum," said the priest, pressing it almost abstracted-

F

ly. With a bow to the rest of the company, without so much as
thinking again of Marion, Henry Lisle passed from the room,
and was seen a few minutes later riding off through the restored
sunshine towards Ennington.

Marion looked after him much surprised.

"Did you tell him about Eliza, my dear?" asked Mrs. Darrell.

"No; I meant to do so, but we were talking of other things at
first, and I was too frightened to think of anything during the
storm. Then I could not go to him, of course, while he and
Father Stirling were talking together, but I thought he would
have come and spoken to me before he went away. It is very
strange he should go without even saying good-bye to me. He
seems very much vexed about something; I wonder what it is?"

"I did not observe it."

"Because you do not know him well enough, Mrs. Darrell, or
else you would have seen that he was quite pale."

"Perhaps Father Stirling has been trying to convert him,"
exclaimed that lady, laughing, as the priest came slowly towards
them.

"You are right," he replied, sadly, "though not perhaps in the
sense you imagine."

"Mr. Lisle seems a very gentlemanly man," said Mrs. Darrell;
"have you known him long?" Unwittingly she had touched the
vibrating chord too suddenly. A deep groan burst from the priest,
and sinking into a chair he covered his face with his hand.

"I shall be better presently," he whispered, "but I do not feel
well."

Miss Horton motioned the children from the room, Mrs. Seymour and her daughters followed under pretence of looking round
the farm, and Father Stirling was left alone with his friends.

"You are astonished at seeing me so strangely moved, I know,"
said he at length, "but I will tell you all. It was Henry Lisle's
father who, when I was left an orphan, took me home and adopted
me as his own. His was a bereaved household; child after child
had passed away in their infancy, and when I entered it, one little
girl alone remained of a large family. After I had been with
them two or three years Henry was born, and this boy and girl
were all that Mr. and Mrs. Lisle ever reared. It would be impossible for me to describe to you the kindness of my self-con-
stituted guardian, or the maternal affection lavished on me by his
wife. Mr. Lisle was not rich, neither was I, but he husbanded
my little store, and partly from his own resources, partly from
mine, he gave me a liberal education, and when I was old enough
received me as partner in the firm, of which he himself was the
head. Things went on quietly enough until I reached the age of
six-and-twenty, when, by events I need not now particularise, the
whole current of my life became changed. A desire to dedicate
myself to what I then considered the ministry, took possession of
me, and all in which I had hitherto taken an interest grew distasteful to me. But there were ties, one in particular, that bound

me to my post, and I remained at it, the prey of many a mental conflict, for two long weary years, until, in a moment of impulse, I revealed my wish to Mr. Lisle. To my surprise, for he was a staunch Presbyterian, he thoroughly approved of the idea, and so smoothed the pecuniary difficulties that lay between me and the wish of my heart, that within two months from that time I was at Oxford. I remained there two years : you know the result. I returned to Scotland and told my adopted father all, and I shall never forget the scene. Early associations, old affections, all were forgotten ; he tried arguments, persuasions, even threats, but, thank God, in vain. He told me I was disgracing him, thatI had no right to bring distress upon a family with whom I was united by ties as strong as brotherhood. Henry, at that time a youth of sixteen, heard my determination apparently unmoved, only I who knew his disposition understood his grief, as he stood motionless as a statue beside his father. 'Go,' said Mr. Lisle, as he held the door open, 'go, and may God forgive you, for I never can.' This is ten years ago. Mr. Lisle is dead, Henry is curate of Ennington, I priest of Harleyford. All are changed, or gone, or dead, except the bitterness and estrangement, and these remain still, for Henry Lisle refuses my friendship till I give up my God."

"I had no idea that you were talking seriously," said Mr. Darrell as the priest concluded, "the children were making so much noise."

"How very sad ! " said Mrs. Darrell, with tears in her kind eyes.

"Yes, I feel it just now, but it will soon pass away amid the pressure of daily cares and duties. Hard work leaves us little time for brooding over our troubles, and a good thing too. Come, the weather is beautiful now ; suppose we go and order the carriages."

"Suppose we have tea, first," said Mr. Darrell, ringing the bell, "I expect their fright has given our young people an appetite."

Mr. Darrell must have been right in his surmises, if the matter could be judged by the celerity with which the landlady's bread-and-butter disappeared. Then came a walk round the farm and garden, out of which the good-natured hostess picked them a round red nosegay of country flowers—flowers that people loved in those old-fashioned days, when some would have been puzzled to spell rhododendrons and fuchsias. Such a substantial bunch it was, that Emily's fingers could not compass it, with its damask roses, London pride, rockets, stocks, and ladies' needlework, blending in rich if not harmonious colouring.

"Marion is to ride home in the gig," said Emily.

"Will you tell me a story, Father Stirling ? " asked Marion.

"Tell her the one you told me, abut the hermit, and the robber who turned a saint," suggested Emily.

"Does Marion like stories about the saints ? " asked Miss Horton.

"Of course she does," replied Father Stirling ; "I hope we shall live to see her a saint herself one of these days."

"It must be a Protestant one, then," said Marion, who began to think of her conversation with her pastor.

Father Stirling and his little companion maintained a profound silence for some time after they had started, he pursuing the gradual unfoldings of the last ten years, she thinking of Mr. Lisle, and whether he would fulfil his threat.

"Father Stirling," she said, timidly, having at length determined to tell him her troubles.

"Yes, my child."

"Mr. Lisle, the gentleman you were talking to, comes from the same place that I do."

"So I believe. I suppose you know him very well."

"Yes, I have known him for three years; he has always taken a great deal of notice of me, and he speaks to me as he likes. But I think he was very unkind in something he said this afternoon. What do you think it was?"

"How can I possibly guess?"

"He said that unless I promised him faithfully not to speak to anyone about the Catholic religion during the rest of my visit, he would write to mamma to-night."

"Did you promise?"

"No, I did not. Mamma has confidence in me, and I think that is enough, for as I told him, it might even happen that I might make very silly mistakes for want of asking a little question. But I should not like him to write to mamma. Do you think he will?"

"I am sure he will if he said so."

"It seems to me so strange that people should be afraid of being converted," said Marion, musingly; "no one would be so silly as to join a religion they did not believe was made by God; and surely if God made it, everything in it will bear looking into."

"Exactly so. Everything that comes from the hand of God will bear scrutiny; therein lies the difference between His works and those of man. The more powerful the microscope, the more exquisite does the insect's wing, otherwise insignificant, appear; the mite becomes a monster of magnificent proportions, and a piece of mouldy cheese a forest of majestic plants. Take, on the other hand, the works of man. Beneath the lens the finest needle is a rough-hewn pike, and a piece of dainty lawn becomes coarse as the coarsest canvas. So it is with the Church of God. The more you gaze into her innermost depths, the more you will be astonished at the glory, the holiness, the perfect beauty of the whole, while in its imitations made by man, disorder, confusion, disunion, meet the wearied eye on all sides. Fair perhaps may they be to the naked eye, but failing, signally failing, beneath the all-revealing glass of Truth."

He had spoken more to himself than Marion, and relapsed once again into his own thoughts. After a few minutes his reflections were again interrupted.

" Mr. Lisle is very good, but he is rather bigoted. Do you not think so, Father Stirling ? "

" Yes, very good, very bigoted."

" Mamma is not so at all."

" I am glad to hear it."

" I do not think I shall ever be a Catholic," pursued Marion, " but somehow I fancy when I grow up I shall not be what I am now. I do not think our religion is right in some things."

" You have as good a right to judge it as any one else," said the priest, half to himself, but looking much amused.

" People must be what they think to be right," continued the child. " If mamma told me always to wear a blue dress, or a red one, I could do that easily to please her, however much I disliked it ; but if she told me to believe a red one blue, or a blue one red, it would be impossible ! With regard to believing or disbelieving anything because she wished it, I could no more do that than I could see at this moment two horses before me instead of one. For religion cannot be what we wish or like ; it must be what it really is to us."

" Yes ; but you know there is such a thing as believing, and yet being ashamed to own our belief. Many people would be content that you should believe what you liked, if you would only keep it to yourself. But then this is really denying God. Do you not think so ? "

" Yes, of course, and then He will deny us. If I were to change my religion though, mamma would not be my greatest dread."

" Who then ? Mr. Lisle ? "

" No, though I should dread him more than mamma. I mean my brother Edward."

" Your brother ! I thought you were an only child."

" I am mamma's only child, but I have a half-brother who has always lived in India. I really think, from all I have heard, that he is as good as any one can be. He is coming to England some day, and I cannot think what he would say if he found Golden-hair a Puseyite, or anything else but the firm Protestant he thinks her."

" A Puseyite ! " cried Father Stirling, " why, whatever put that into your head ? "

" Oh, myself," replied the child, gravely ; " there seems too much in the Catholic Church, and not enough in ours, and so I have been thinking I should like to be a Puseyite."

" So much for private judgment," cried the priest, laughing heartily. " Oh dear, oh dear ! "

" What are you laughing at, Father Stirling ? "—Question never answered, but there came instead the crash of a falling vehicle, the shriek of a child, the plunging of a frightened horse. When Mr. Darrell reached the spot Father Stirling was lying powerless with a broken arm on a heap of stones, and unconscious near him, the warm blood trickling through her golden curls, lay Marion white as a marble image.

.   .   .   .

It was a melancholy party that wound up the drive of The
Cedars, very different from that which had issued in the morning
from its gates. In compliance with his desire (for the Darrells
would fain have tended him at their own home), Father Stirling
was left at the Presbytery, under the care of Mrs. Seymour, until
her husband, the only medical man of the neighbourhood, could
arrive.

"And then let him come to us," cried Mrs. Darrell, as she
pressed Marion, now conscious of bitter suffering, to her heart.

"Don't cry, Emily, I shall be better soon ; it does not bleed
so fast now. I am afraid your dress will be spoiled, Mrs.
Darrell."

"What matter that, my darling?" and again they were silent.

Hardly a moan escaped her as they carried her upstairs, and
laid her in Edith's little bed. Without waiting for Mr. Seymour,
Mrs. Darrell bathed the wound, which was a deep incision, and
swathed the throbbing head with linen bands.

"It will not be much, I trust," said Mr. Seymour, "she will
soon be all right. I wish I could say as much for the Father, but
his is, I fear, a compound fracture. He must be in great pain,
but all he seems to think of is, how he is to get a priest for Sunday."

"I expect my brother on Saturday," replied the lady; "I will
write to him and ask him to come directly."

"Poor Father Stirling!" said a voice from the little bed; "do
you think it was my falling on him that broke his arm?"

"No, I do not think you would have brushed a fly off him."

Marion tried to smile, but the attempt was very sickly.

She was worse than they thought. The blow had been very
severe, the weather trying, and the last few days full of excitement; before morning the poor child was quite delirious. Once
more, too, the storm broke forth, and roused from their sleep by
the thunder, the twins rose and joined their mother in her sad
vigil beside the little sufferer's bed.

"Go to bed again, my dear children, you can do no good;"
but they pleaded hard, and remained trembling at Marion's
strange words. Her mother, the thunder, Rosalind, and the
Puseyites, were strangely jumbled, and then 'she talked of Father
Stirling and Mr. Lisle, every now and then raising her hand to
her aching head.

"I will send for her mother in the morning," said Mrs. Darrell,
who began to grow seriously alarmed; "I hope she has not
started for London."

"What a sad ending to our happy day!" exclaimed Emily; "if
we could only have foreseen it."

"Ah, my child, in nothing has our Father in Heaven more
shown His love for us than in the thick veil He has cast over
the future. Could we pierce this we should never have one happy
day."

"What a vivid flash!"   .

The thunder, like a peal of cannonade, rolled forth at the same moment, and Marion grew even more excited.

"What shall I do with her?" cried Mrs. Darrell.

"Come, Emily, let us pray for her," whispered Edith.

Side by side, unmoved amid the storm and the low moans of their little friend, the twins knelt before their altar, their rosaries in their hands. Before three decades had been offered to the Mater Dolorosa, the little sufferer lay asleep in Mrs. Darrell's arms.

CHAPTER IX.

"CAN you give me Mrs. Howard's address in London?" asked Mr. Lisle, as old Turner opened the street door in answer to his summons. "I called to ask it last night, but you were out."

"Yes, sir, I was; Mrs. Jones said she would mind the house a bit for me, while I ran out for two or three little odd things, and very sorry was I when I came back, to find as how you had had your walk up for nothing. Will you step in, sir?" added the old woman, curtsying.

"No, thank you, I only want the address."

"Dear me, now I come to think, my missus forgot to give it to me. But if you'll step in a moment, sir, I'll just run over and see if Miss Leicester has got it."

"Thank you, Turner," said the clergyman, walking in. "Who do you think I saw last night?"

The old servant glanced up inquiringly.

"Your little pet, Miss Marion."

"Did you, now! The Lord love her! And how is she? if it's not making too bold."

"She looks very well, and says she is very happy. I had business at Ilcombe, and dined at the little inn there. While I was waiting for the storm to give over, a picnic party ran in for shelter, and among them was Miss Howard."

"God bless her," cried Turner, "for she deserves it, indeed she do."

"Yes, she is a sweet child," said the curate, thoughtfully; "you must miss her very much."

"Miss her! Bless you, sir! but the house ain't the same thing without her. Of course a lady like missus has got something better to do than to talk to the likes of an old woman like me; and though Sally has a downright feeling heart, and is ready to do a hand's turn for anybody, she has what I call a glumpy sort of way with her, and says very little to any one. Miss Marion seems to do one good just to look at her, and to hear her talking to her cat, and singing about the house, for she does sing beautifully.

It's not much as I know about such things, but it seems to me, as that child is very clever. You should hear her talk French with her mamma; why she rattles on just as fast as the missus herself, and she draws wonderful pretty pictures. Look at that pretty creature now, a-hanging up by the side of the fireplace," she added, pointing to a crayon head, "that's all Miss Marion's doing. Oh, deary me! she's just what her poor dear father was. He was a real gentleman!"

"I did not know you had lived with the family during Captain Howard's lifetime. Sit down, Turner; see, I am making myself very comfortable," and he threw himself back in the arm-chair as he spoke.

"I have lived with Mrs. Howard, sir, fourteen years come Martinmas. My poor dear husband had been a private in Captain Howard's regiment, in his young days, before ever the captain thought of going to India. They came from the same part of the country, don't you see? and so Captain Howard took a good bit of notice of him like, and took him for his servant. Oh! he was wonderful fond of him! My poor man and me were a-keeping company when the master went away, and soon after we got married and had a snug little place of our own near Portsmouth. But somehow or other things didn't go so well with us at last, and when, just fifteen years after he had gone away, we heard the master had come back again and was going to settle down in England, nothing would serve Turner but that he must go back and live with his old master. Well, sir, the long and short of it was, that we gave up our cottage and came over here to Ennington, where Captain Howard had just bought this house. I was cook at first, until Miss Marion came, heaven bless her, and then I was nurse. And now missus keeps me like an old horse, to do what I can, which I'm afeard, sir, is very little. She gets more out of Sally's big arm in one day, than my old withered stumps can do in six!"

"Ah! but you find head, Turner; do you see that?"

"Well, sir, thank you, sir, but I suppose I have had some little experience in my day. It's true that you can't put new feet on old legs, as you do with stockings, but at the same time you can't put old heads on young shoulders."

"When did you lose your husband, Susan?"

"When missus lost hers, sir; master went out to India to see about his property out there, and to fetch Master Edward to England."

"That was his son by a former marriage, I believe?"

"Yes, sir."

"Go on."

"Well, sir, as I was saying, he went out to India, and to please missus, who was nervous like about him, for he was subject to fits; my poor man went too. It's a sad story, sir, and of course you know it. I went up with missus to see them off, and it was a sight of a ship they went in. But a storm came on after a bit, and the 'Ocean Queen,' as they called her, struck upon a rock, and she went to the bottom of the sea. Only two men escaped, who got into a little boat, and sailed about till they were picked up by a vessel coming home."

"Mrs. Howard and you may well be attached to each other ; whatever your position as mistress and servant, you are own sisters in grief."

"She is very good to me," said Turner, quietly.

"Had you never any children ?"

"Yes, sir, a daughter."

There was something so altered in the voice that the clergyman started. Her tone in relating her story had been naturally mournful, but there was almost a hollowness in this short response, that made him at once regret the question. He remained silent.

"Yes, sir, I had a daughter once, but whether I have one still, God only knows. When we came to live here, I was obliged to let her go to service in London. Well, sir, she went on very well, for I saw her when I went up to town with missus, and when my poor man died, she came to stay with me a bit while Mrs. Howard was stopping with her sister. But then she went back to her place, and I have never seen her since. She used to write and tell me how she was saving up money to take the old cottage again at Portsmouth, where she was to be a dressmaker, and I was to get a little by the garden. For you see, sir," she added, lowering her voice, "although I have been so long with missus, I do find it hard to get along with her sometimes, and in those days it was rather worse than it is now, for I was a little proudish like, and the missus was young and handsome, and Captain Howard—well, it's not for me to say—but, anyway, she liked her own way, and he had let her have it. And then young missuses and old servants don't always agree, so I had a bit of a notion of leaving. But then the letters came fewer and fewer, and at last, one morning, I got a note from Lady Jane, her mistress, telling me to come at once if I would save my child. I went, but I was too late. Eliza had already got married, and gone off with the valet, and from that moment to this I have never set eyes upon her. My poor, poor girl !"

"She will come back some day to you, you will see," replied the curate in a sympathising tone.

"If it was only for this world, sir, I feel as though I could bear it, almost cheerful like, but with such a sin as hers unrepented of, how can I hope to meet her in heaven ?"

"How do you know she is not repentant ?"

"Would she not write to her old mother if she was ?"

Mr. Lisle was silenced.

At this moment a knock was heard at the outer door ; Turner rose to open it.

"Is Mrs. Howard at home ?"

"No, sir, she went to London yesterday."

"What shall I do!" exclaimed Mr. Darrell, for it was he; "what is her address there?"

"She has forgot to leave it, sir, but if you will leave a message for her, I expect her back in a few days."

"A few days! It may be all over then."

"All over!" exclaimed the old woman with a shriek, for the first time recognising the speaker; "Mr. Darrell, sir, is Miss Marion ill?"

"She is, indeed; in great danger, I fear."

"Come in, sir, come in, please do. O Marion! my darling, my little one, that I was the first in all this world to nurse, to think of you dying away from your mother and old nursey."

"But I trust in God that she may not die," exclaimed Mr. Darrell, as he entered the parlour, where Mr. Lisle, who had overheard the conversation, had risen from his seat in great alarm.

"Excuse me, sir, but do I hear that Marion Howard is ill? She seemed so well last evening."

"In the midst of life we are in death," replied Mr. Darrell, and he described the accident and its consequences.

"Is Mr. Stirling in danger also, do you think?" asked the curate so anxiously that he seemed for the moment to have forgotten Marion.

"I trust not, but one can hardly tell. Do you think," he added, turning to the old woman, who was sobbing violently, "that you could leave the house in charge of any one, and go back with me? it would be a great comfort to Mrs. Darrell to have you."

"To be sure I can. My fellow-servant is away for a holiday, but I will get a woman from the village, and be ready directly."

"And if you will permit me," said Mr. Lisle, "I also will intrude myself upon you this afternoon. I shall not be able to rest till I know that this poor child is out of danger."

"Come, by all means," was the hearty response. "Perhaps in the meantime you may be able to ascertain Mrs. Howard's address from some of her friends."

"I will go to Miss Leicester's immediately," said the curate, taking up his hat.

It was a melancholy ride for Mr. Darrell, as he wended his way back, with the old servant by his side. A lovely morning had followed the storm, but both were too much absorbed in their own sad reflections to notice the beauties of nature. As Black Prince stopped before the lodge, a little boy, brown as a berry, but neat as a new pin, ran out to open the gate.

"What do you think of him?" asked Mr. Darrell, looking at the old woman, for amid all his anxiety he had not forgotten that at that very moment a mother was passing the threshold of a long-lost child, and that the little chubby face was not an alien to the good old soul beside him. "Is he not fit to be a prince's child?"

"Pretty cretur!" said the old woman, looking fondly after him, as he tripped into the lodge, when Eliza, who had caught sight of the coming vehicle, sat with her face buried in her hands.

"At last! at last!" she muttered; "oh, my God, this is too much!"

She had not expected her mother; the idea of her coming had never entered her mind, but she had recognised her instantly.

"O mother!" she cried, with bitter tears, "I have sinned before Heaven and against thee, and am no more worthy to be called thy child."

Marion was still hardly sensible, though more tranquil. Mr. Lisle came and saw her, but left, unrecognised by word or glance. Towards evening, consciousness returned, but found the little patient so exhausted that Mr. Seymour shook his head in reply to the anxious glances of Mrs. Darrell and old Turner.

"Would you not tell her of her danger, Mr. Seymour?" asked Mrs. Darrell.

"I tremble to say yes, but I dare not say no," replied the doctor; "this constitutes, my dear madam, the real pain of our profession. It is a hard thing to disturb the mind when the body is racked with suffering, but it is harder still to let the soul glide away in a moral lethargy into the presence of its God. Speak to her as gently as you can."

He left to visit his other patient, who needed his services little less than Marion.

"You yourself would tell her, would you not?" asked Mrs. Darrell, appealing to the old nurse, whose good sense and gentle manners had already won her heart.

"Indeed, I would, ma'am, it would be hard to lose her; but if she is to die, let her say at least, 'Lord Jesus, have mercy upon my soul.' I will go into the other room; you will feel freer like without me. Oh, deary, deary me! to think it should have come to this!" and the poor old soul sobbed as though her heart would break.

"Marion," said Mrs. Darrell, bending over her, "you are very ill, is there anything you would like?"

"My Bible."

"But, dear child, you cannot see to read."

"But nursey can read for me."

"Very well. Is there nothing else?"

"I should like to see Mr. Lisle, but he is too far off."

"He has been to see you, but he has gone again, love. Would you like to see Mr. Gardiner, the clergyman of the church near here?"

"Yes, please. Was I asleep when Mr. Lisle came? I wish you had awakened me."

"Very well, so we will another time, he is coming again soon."

There was a grand dinner-party that night in Harleyford, and the Rev. Mr. and Mrs. Gardiner were among the guests invited. The latter stood in her sylph-like dress before her cheval-glass, directing her maid, who was putting certain finishing-touches, while her husband fidgeted up and down the library, straightening the fingers of his gloves. The brougham was already at the door, the grey horse prancing till his harness jingled, as impatient as his master.

"A groom from Mr. Darrell's, at The Cedars, is waiting to speak to you, sir, if you please."

"Darrell! The Cedars! What on earth can he want with me?"

"If you please, sir," said Tom from the doorway, "if you please, sir, a young lady, who is stopping at The Cedars, is dangerously ill, and my mistress says she would be glad if you could come and see her at once. She would have written to you, but she could not leave Miss Howard when I came away, and the young ladies are too much shaken to hold a pen."

"But how is this?—is she not a Catholic?"

"No, sir, a Protestant."

"What is the matter?" asked Mrs. Gardiner, entering the room in full trim.

"A sick person that I am afraid I must go and visit: how shall we manage, my dear?"

"Who is it who is ill?"

Mr. Gardiner explained.

"What is the matter with her?" asked the lady, withdrawing herself from Tom's vicinity. "Is it a fever?"

"No, ma'am; she was thrown out of a gig last night, coming from a picnic; both she and the gentleman who was driving her had a narrow escape with their lives."

"Dear me!" said Mrs. Gardiner, who was a sharp little lady and generally spoke in jerks, "how dreadful! Well, you will go the first thing to-morrow morning, I suppose, Adolphus."

Mr. Gardiner hesitated. "Is there any immediate danger, do you know?"

"My mistress said, sir, I was to ask you to come at once."

"Impossible!" said the lady, under her breath, and puckering her forehead at her husband. "Why, we are awfully late now."

"What can I do, my dear?" asked the clergyman, looking at his better half. "The Cedars is not far?"

"The Cedars! Why it is not in your parish," said his wife, quickly.

"Yes, it is," answered Mr. Gardiner, shaking his head dolefully. "I think I had better go. Tell your mistress I will be with her in a quarter of an hour. It is very unfortunate," he added, as the door closed behind the servant, "but we must explain matters to Lady Harley; she cannot possibly be offended."

"I don't know that; we shall see."

"Why, Helen, what would you have me to do?" he asked, almost deprecatingly.

"How can I tell you?" she replied, shrugging her pretty shoulders still further out of her dress. "All I know is, that it is about one of the most aggravating things I ever heard of. If it had been one of your own parishioners even, but for these Catholic people, how intensely annoying!"

"What will you do, my dear? we are only wasting time now?"

"I don't know—pull off my things and stop at home, I suppose," and she began plucking angrily at her glove. "Oh, don't! leave me alone!" she exclaimed, giving herself a sharp twist, as her husband approached with the idea of coaxing the spoiled beauty. "Any one but you would have managed some way."

"You are very cross, Helen; I am sure I am as sorry as you are, but what do you suppose people would say if I refused to go? It would be the town talk, especially among the Romanists and Dissenters."

"Bother the Romanists and Dissenters!"

"The only way that I can see," continued the reverend gentleman, without noticing the rejoinder, "will be for John to drive me at once to The Cedars, and then come back and fetch you. You can take me up afterwards at the end of the lane. I will not stay an instant longer than I can help, and I am sure I shall be able to make it all right with her ladyship."

"Well, pray be as quick as you can, it looks so abominably stupid to be late at a dinner-party!"

Marion turned languidly on her pillow, as her spiritual comforter entered the room, preceded by Mrs. Darrell; but she asked no questions, she was too ill to feel curious.

Mr. Gardiner approached the bed, by the side of which Mr. Darrell and the two girls were standing, while old Turner, at some little distance, with her hands in her lap, looked the picture of silent despair. The clergyman just glanced at the mournful group and at the pale little figure extended on the bed, and then opening his book, commenced at once.

"'Remember not, Lord'"——

"Stop a moment, sir, if you please!" exclaimed Mr. Darrell. "If you will allow them to pass, my children will leave before you begin. Nor is there any reason, my dear, why you or I should remain," he added, turning to his wife. "Turner, you will stay with Miss Marion."

"Yes, sir," said the old woman, approaching the bed.

"You will excuse us," continued Mr. Darrell, in answer to Mr. Gardiner's look of astonishment, "but you are aware, I have no doubt, that we are enjoined by our creed to abstain as much as possible from assisting at the religious worship of others."

Mr. Gardiner simply bowed, but he looked unutterable things, which he was in too great a hurry to express.

"'Remember not, Lord,'" he once more commenced as the door closed.—"Have you anything you would like to say to me?" he asked, having arrived at that portion of his ritual, where he was enjoined to question the invalid with regard to his conscience, debts, and the arrangement of his worldly goods, &c.

"What did you say?" asked Marion, with the vacancy peculiar to extreme weakness.

"I asked you whether you would like to speak to me."

"What about?"

"Oh, the affairs of your soul, or anything of that kind."

"No, thank you," said Marion.

"You are very ill."

"Yes, I think I shall die."

The clergyman started. "Do you not feel afraid? are you prepared? would you not like to live?"

"Just to see mamma," replied the child, "that is all. I long to be in heaven with God and dear papa. Will you reach me that crucifix down, please."

"What for?"

"I like to have it in my hand. When I think of all Christ suffered in dying on the cross for us, the pain of my head seems so much better."

"You can have that when I am gone," said the clergyman. "You had better attend to me now, I have been sent for to pray for you."

"Have you?" said Marion. "I didn't know. Have you been here long?"

The clergyman thought of his wife, and fidgeted.

"No, not very long. Then if you have nothing to say to me I will go on."

"Please begin again, and I will listen and pray with you. I did not hear you reading at all.—Nursey!"

"Yes, darling."

Mr. Gardiner was in despair.

"Come and kneel here, and pray with us, too."

The old woman hid her head in the bed-clothes to smother her sobs.

"Now I am ready," said the child, folding her hands. "Please go on," and for the third time Mr. Gardiner recommenced the office of the visitation of the sick.

"Thank you," said Marion, when he had finished, "I like that very much, but I should like you to pray for me your own self better. Will you?"

The Rev. Adolphus Gardiner stood aghast, he could about as easily have preached an extemporaneous sermon. Besides, time was flying, and what would his wife say, and Lady Harley think? And yet, how refuse?

"Do you not think we have had talking enough for the present?" he asked: "you must not be excited too much, you know."

Marion only made large eyes at him.

"If I were to stay with you, though," he continued, "I should only read you some more prayers out of this book, for they are far more beautiful than any I could compose."

"Are they?" asked Marion.

"Yes, if you like I will read one for a sick child.—There," said he, at the conclusion, with a sigh of relief at having done his duty, "I think that will do for to-night. Go to sleep now, there's a good child, and I will call and see you to-morrow. Will you pass me my hat, if you please."

Turner obeyed, and the physician of souls hurried off to join his wife.

They were late, but all was excused on the plea of pastoral duties. Indeed the story of the little girl and her accident, the request for the crucifix, and the "wretched bigotry" of her popish friends, made quite an interesting little episode in the conversation of the dinner-table.

Another night passed in anxious watching, and Marion was better. When Mr. Seymour announced that all danger was over, old Turner smiled again, and the twins danced in their glee, and said rosaries by the dozen in thanksgiving. When Mr. Lisle came again, the bandage had been replaced by a plaster, the curls smoothly arranged, and Marion almost looked herself again. She knew him now, and a look of deep gratitude smiled from the blue eyes as he approached.

"Do you know that Father Stirling's arm was broken at the same time that I was hurt?"

A look of pain passed over the curate's face.

"Yes, poor fellow!"

"Will you go and see him?"

"No, not to-day. To-morrow, you know, will be Sunday, and I must go home to prepare. Dr. Stebbing is away, so I shall have to preach both morning and evening, and I have been so uneasy about you, that I have hardly thought about my sermon yet. If I do not go back soon, the people will go sermonless to-morrow, and you know that would never do."

Marion smiled. "I shall go sermonless, I am afraid, for many Sundays."

"I hope not; no, the fever has left you now, and I trust you will soon get well. I met Mr. Seymour as I came, and he says you are going on very nicely."

"Did he say anything about Father Stirling?"

"He says he is very ill, but," added he, his generosity triumphing over his reluctance to praise him, especially to Marion, "as patient as an angel."

"Just what I should have thought," said Marion.

"Well, good-bye, my child, for I must run away. Now, listen to me. Do not, for God's sake, let them talk to you of religion. Marion, I would not deceive you! However bright their religion may appear, believe me it is false. Your own pure simple faith is truth, but you are so young, so impulsive, so easily impressed! Oh, would to God that you had never come here, where everything around you combines to make the great lie alluring! Look at that little altar; pretty, I grant you, very pretty, but," he added, lifting up the cloth as he spoke, "what is it, after all? A wooden table! Would that I could expose to you the worthlessness of their larger mummeries, as easily as I thus lay bare the legs of Mrs. Darrell's altar." He dropped the curtain as he spoke, and returned to Marion. "Good-bye, my child, till Monday."

He had not long left the house when a letter arrived from Mrs. Howard, telling Marion of her intention of fetching her the following week. She had little anticipated the tale of disaster she was to receive in reply, sad enough to a mother's heart, even when softened by the exquisite tact and delicacy of Mary Darrell's pen.

"Mrs. Darrell, I have been lying and thinking about one thing almost all the time you were at church," said Marion, to her kind hostess as she sat beside her next day, while Turner went down stairs to her dinner.

"What is it, love ? Tell me."

"Why, about Eliza. I do so want her to see her mother. I talked to nursey just a little about it this morning, to see what she thought."

"And what did she say ? "

"She thinks she is dead, or else ashamed to write. O Mrs. Darrell! will it not be a delightful thing to tell her ? Sometimes I can hardly lie still for thinking of it ! "

"Now, Marion, if you excite yourself you will be ill again."

"I will not, really; but just listen, dear Mrs. Darrell : don't you think they might see each other this afternoon ? It would do more towards making me well again, than all the medicine Mr. Seymour could give me in a month."

"I shall tell Mr. Seymour how lightly you value his skill."

"O Mrs. Darrell! I don't mean that. I am very grateful to Mr. Seymour, for I think if he had not taken great care of me, I should have died. But I do so long to see Turner and Eliza together."

"Very well, then, so it shall be. I will send Eliza in to see you with her little boy; that will be a good excuse. Now, remember, you promise to be calm."

"Yes," said Marion, but she looked very much the reverse.

When Turner returned, Mrs. Darrell went down to her brother, who had arrived from Dublin only the day before, and to whom she was desirous of devoting as much of her time as possible. He had already said the two masses, and preached, and now had only a short time for a chat before the afternoon services.

"This is not much of a holiday for you, William," observed his sister.

"What ! do you call this work ? for shame of yourself, then ! " exclaimed the good-natured Irishman.

Turner was more than usually cheerful this afternoon. Marion was out of danger, and her mistress knew, or soon would know, of the state of her little girl. "Shall I read to you, deary ?" she asked, as she smoothed down her clean apron and put on her spectacles.

"Presently, but I want to talk to you first, nursey : I have been building castles in the air."

"What does that mean, child ? "

"Why, fancying things, you know. I have been fancying Eliza coming back, and living in a pretty little cottage, with a nice garden and two little children."

"Laws, Miss Marion, what's the use of troubling that poor little head of yours with things what's never likely to be? I shall never see her any more, deary."

At this moment Emily entered on tiptoe.

"Marion," she asked in a subdued voice, "would you like to see the lodge-keeper, she has asked after you so often?"

"Very much; please let her come."

In a few minutes Eliza entered the room, leading little Johnnie, her eldest boy, by the hand. To meet her mother face to face was more than the poor thing could do, and she slipped round the bed in such a way as to place herself by her side. Turner, who was busy arranging the pillows, hardly noticed her, much to Marion's disappointment, and the poor woman stood trembling after her first low salutation to the invalid, with her back half turned to her mother, trying to summon courage to throw herself into her arms.

"Come here, Johnnie," said Marion. "Come here, and kiss this dear, kind old grannie."

It was a term Marion often used in fun to the old woman, who, without noticing it, seated herself and took the chubby little rogue on her knee.

"Well, you are a pretty fellow!" she exclaimed, looking at him in unfeigned admiration. "Do you know, Miss Marion, but his eyes is wonderful like my poor man's!"

She did not observe, as Marion did, how convulsively a pair of thin hands were pressed together beside her.

Many were the questions put by the old woman to the little prattler, for the sake of hearing him talk. And all the time his mother kept her position, her eyes half averted, looking through the window into the tree-tops, and silent heavy tears falling one after the other upon the folded hands.

"He's a dear little fellow, and does credit to his mother, that he do," exclaimed the old woman at length. "He's been well brought up. So much the better. 'Train up a child in the way he should go, and when he is old he shall not depart from it.' People should never spoil children. It's far easier, I know, to let them have their own way at the time, but depend upon it, it's better to be a little hard upon young people, than to have them live to be hard upon you, as I know to my cost. Won't you sit down, ma'am! Go and fetch a chair for mammy, there's a dear."

A convulsive sob echoed through the room, and in another moment, Eliza was at her mother's feet.

"Mother! mother!"

Reader, shall we describe it, or shall we draw a veil over the scene so like that jubilee of the angels rejoicing over the sinner doing penance?

"My child! my child! now I can die happy!"

G

"Now, nursey, didn't I tell you Eliza would come back again?" cried Marion, emerging at last from under the bed-clothes with very red eyes. "Am I not a little prophet?"

"Yes, that you are," cried the old woman, kissing her fondly; "but I tell you what it is, deary, we shall have you ill again, and that will never, never do."

The twins kept watch that evening beside the little invalid, and there was a very long talk at the lodge. That talk might have made one think of April weather, but there were more smiles than tears, more sunshine than showers after all, gentle reader.

Marion made rapid progress from this afternoon. Mrs. Howard arrived in great alarm on the Tuesday morning, but found her child much better than her fears had allowed her to anticipate; and after spending a week or two at The Cedars, she found her sufficiently recovered to return with her to Ennington.

It was with sincere pleasure that Mr. Lisle welcomed Marion home, for he had trembled for her firmness. His kindness to her child completely obliterated from Mrs. Howard's mind every trace of her own angry feeling towards him, and in a very short time what in the beginning had been simply social intercourse between the curate and his parishioner, ripened into a deep and lasting friendship. In the expressive language of the Germans, Mr. Lisle became a "house-friend," and now that little Marion was once more actually beneath his eye, he no longer feared for her orthodoxy. He felt that she had been slightly touched by the dreaded evil, as he phrased it to himself, but finding that she resumed the even tenor of her old life apparently unaltered, he never spoke to her or her mother on the subject. Notwithstanding Mrs. Howard's "religious horror," Marion soon after became a district visitor and Sunday-school teacher, and all traces of anything like a leaning towards Catholicism so entirely disappeared, that when the next summer the twins spent a day or two with Marion at Ennington, they returned quite disappointed to their mother with the intelligence, that Marion was quite, quite Protestant.

"God's ways are not man's ways," said Father Stirling. "Marion will be a Catholic yet."

"If it had not been for the accident you and she met with, she might have been one now!" sighed Emily.

"Cannot the same God who willed the accident, will also her conversion in His own good time?" asked the priest.

Could they have read the heart of Marion, they would have seen the relics of more than one conversation, lying secretly germinating in the depths of that little spirit, and calm strange thoughts, growing with her growth, and strengthening with her strength, seeming to whisper even among the things she loved best in her religion, "This is not thy rest."

CHAPTER X.

FIVE years had passed by since the visit to The Cedars, and it was the twilight of a December afternoon. Marion, still the bright-haired Marion of her childhood, was sitting musing over the fire in the snug little parlour at Ennington all alone, for Mrs. Howard had not yet returned from a call on her old friend and adviser, Dr. Bernard. Snow had been falling lightly, and was lying fairy-white on the garden paths and beds, but the well-protected fuchsias and geraniums stood up black and gaunt in their grim prison clothes, and everything looked cheerless in the winter mist. Marion had been watching at the window for her mother, enjoy-ing the licensed idleness of the twilight, but she had grown so cold and sad withal, in thinking of fireless homes, and homeless little ones, that she was glad to shut out the dreary landscape. So she had drawn the crimson curtains, stirred the fire into a blaze, and pulling her mother's stool before it, sat down thereon to dream.

Many and varied thoughts passed through the busy little brain, as she wandered back in spirit through the gradual unfoldings of the last five years. One could not have imagined they would have furnished much food for thought, and yet in her inner life—that life that lies so deep down in the nature of us all—was hidden many a little treasure-house, known to herself alone. First came her visit to The Cedars, with its shadowy remembrance of soul-stirring thoughts, warm hearts, bodily pain, and Father Stirling. Next, a summer spent at home when the twins had visited her, and of which the distinguishing feature was the novelty of parish work, and the visits of Mr. Lisle. Then the two summers at the London school, and the holidays at her aunt's, amid London sights and sounds and gaieties. These things passed through Marion's mind, smiled at or sighed over as the case might be, but it was over the last bright summer-tide that she really lingered ; lingered in thought, until the fire burned almost down, and startled her with a rush of falling ashes ; and when it was replenished, and once more sparkled merrily, still she thought on, while Tyrza in her lap purred forth his very soul in a low com-placent hum. She is a sweet little picture, in her dark merino dress, relieved by the daintiest of little collars, as the soft firelight flickers upon her rounded cheek and glossy ringlet. What thought is it that shines at this moment in the bright blue eye ? Has Golden-hair a secret ? Crosses and candlesticks have been sinking lower and lower for a long time now, until the idea of them has almost faded, and she has lived to laugh merrily with even Mr. Lisle about her Puseyite notions. She is " thoroughly low church now," she says, and the old secret is one no longer. Has she another ? She could not tell you if she would, but there is a something, sunny and shadowy by turns, rooted in her very nature, bound .with her being, for life or death, and yet un-whispered in the deepest recesses of her heart. She has changed, but she does not see it ; she acts with other aims, but she does not know it ; she lives with another life, but she does not feel it ; for in all her thoughts, and words, and actions, Marion thinks, and speaks, and moves, only in Henry Lisle. And yet she deems she values him as her mother's friend, and would crimson to the temples, even in that lonely parlour, could she suspect the existence of an affection for which she would, at this very moment, lay down her life. No, Golden-hair is like the little flower of which the poet sings, she "must be wooed, and not unsought be won."

A knock at the door startled her from her reverie. "There is mamma at last," she exclaimed, giving the fire an energetic stir, that a blaze might welcome her. "I wish tea was on the table." But it was a very firm footfall that passed along the passage—so firm, that the young girl stopped in her progress towards the door. It opened, and two minutes later, Marion Howard and the curate of Ennington were seated tête-à-tête before the fire.

"And what has Golden-hair been doing all this dull afternoon ? "

"Thinking and thinking here by myself, till I feel half stupid ! "

"I hope not," returned the gentleman, laughing ; "we could ill spare one of the wisest heads in Ennington."

"I never thought before, you knew how to pay a compliment. I wish you would take mamma's large chair and make yourself comfortable. Sally will bring in the lights directly."

"An event for which I am in no way anxious," said Mr. Lisle, accepting her invitation to change his chair, and warming his hands ; "you know my penchant for firelight."

"Yes. I like it very much too. It is so dreamy."

"It is, when one is alone, and can give oneself up to its influence. On that account it is a dangerous luxury for young people, as is everything that helps to make them romantic and sentimental."

"Are romance and sentiment dangerous, Mr. Lisle ? "

"I think so."

"I am sorry for that," returned Marion, "because it really appears that our every-day business is the prose of life, and that the little flashes of sentiment, that come to enliven even the dullest lives from time to time, constitute its poetry. Our existence would be hard and dry without them, though in these days, nothing that is not hard, dry, and common-sense, as it is called, is understood. Yet, as mamma says, when people speak of romance, sentiment, or ideality, they only mean that power of extracting the beautiful from the commonplace, which God has given to every man if he will only use it. I know I seem to be talking nonsense, yet," she continued earnestly, "what I mean I feel, and very deeply. Of course, Mr. Lisle, I know that mine is a very ordinary mind, but I should be sorry to pass through life without some appreciation of the exquisite harmony of all things in the world around us, that man calls beauty. How would our little home look, do you think, if the flowers were cleared out of the garden, and cabbages and potatoes planted in their stead? Yet that is just my idea of souls without sentiment."

"And such it will remain, you obstinate little lady; like most quiet people, it takes a world of power to make you alter your notions. Perhaps my opinions are not altogether as matter of fact as you imagine, still I have a horror of anything exaggerated, —anything, for instance, like mysticism, which is almost as fatal to the character as enthusiasm is to religion. Simplicity is the touchstone of truth."

"Ah! now you are beyond me, I know no more about mysticism than Tyrza, though I cannot see why enthusiasm should be wrong in religion."

"It is not in conformity with the meek and gentle spirit of the gospel," replied Mr. Lisle, "which falls like light, silently irradiating all."

"But the Spirit of God is also fire," said Marion, looking at him, "and once fell on man like the noise of a mighty rushing wind. Was not this something like enthusiasm? You will laugh at me again, I know, but I cannot help thinking that when God took away Eden, He left some of its beautiful flowers behind, which they find in Eastern lands even now, and I also think that when He punished our race, He left one great impulse of unfallen man, and that was enthusiasm. O Mr. Lisle! really, really, this is the grandest thing in man's whole nature, and it cannot be wrong to bring it into religion. Who can contemplate God in His perfections, and not feel enthusiastic?" and Marion's eyes kindled, and her lips trembled with excitement.

"You are a singular compound of simplicity and earnestness, Golden-hair! It is strange that you and I get on as well as we do together, for really we seldom agree."

"Mr. Lisle!"

"Miss Howard! but indeed we seldom do. You have such a quiet way of differing from people, that it passes almost unnoticed; but you do very often differ from them, none the less for that. You will be surprised at my saying so, I daresay, but I really hardly consider you a plain common-sense Christian even now. You mingle that dangerous element, the imagination, too freely in religion to be perfectly orthodox."

"Do I?" asked Marion; "how?"

"It is difficult to express to you exactly what I mean," he replied, "but it is an opinion I have formed from little things you have said to me at various times, some of them even as a child. I remarked it, I remember, for the first time, in a chat we had together about five years ago in the churchyard, one Sunday evening. Do you remember it?"

"Yes, very well, but I am surprised that you do. You have a good memory."

"For some things, yes; at any rate I remember our conversation of that evening very well, and the wish you then conveyed to me in your childish words, that religion had something in it more tangible."

"I sometimes wish so still. I get lost in a species of rapture when I contemplate the Humanity of Christ. His Infant Life, His Childhood, His thirty years before His Ministry, have a wonderful fascination for me—the more so, I sometimes think, from the veil drawn over them by Scripture. I wish we knew something of that silent life at Nazareth."

"Marion," said the curate, "need I say more in answer to your question, asking in what way you mingle religion and imagination? Are you not desiring to lay bare those things that Infinite Wisdom has involved in shadow? Be reasonable, my dear young friend, and be content with those fords and shallows through which the 'Sun of Righteousness' plays on the ground beneath, or you will wander beyond your depth, and be carried away by the current. And that would break my heart!"

The last words were spoken in an almost whisper, but they reached Marion, who lifted Tyrza again into her lap, and looked gravely into the fire.

"Christmas is coming fast," said the clergyman cheerfully, not sorry to change the subject.

"Very."

"How are you going to spend it? Here as usual?"

"Mamma is going to London, and she wants me to go with her. But somehow I would rather not."

"Why?"

"Because, if we go, it will be to visit my aunt, Mrs. Burrowes. She is very rich, and her daughters are merry, dashing, fashionable girls, about my own age, rather what some people describe as 'fast.' Altogether, my life with them in London would be just the reverse of what I like. Even as a child, the excitement of my holidays was not altogether pleasure to me, and I expect that what then was only distasteful in London life, would be positive misery now. Of course I am 'out,' and should be whirled off to operas, theatres, balls, parties, concerts, and conversaziones, till the country-girl's brain would be in a perfect whirl. Besides, is it consistent to be engaged as I am, in district visiting and Sunday-school teaching at one time, and at another to be mingling in such constant dissipation, as I must be if I visit London with mamma? It would only be for a few weeks I know, but that would be quite enough to unsettle me for a year."

"By all means remain at home then," said the curate anxiously. "One season in London has been the narrow strait through which many a young and earnest soul has been hurried on to the great sea of worldliness, never again to find the bright haven of its childhood. O Vanity Fair! Vanity Fair! what fearful victories it has won!"

"And yet there is only one way in which I can escape it," said Marion, "and I think you will approve of it even less than my going to London."

" What is that ?"

" I have another invitation, a previous one, that I could accept."

" Why not do so then ?" asked the curate.

Marion's only answer was a very mischievous smile.

"Why should you not accept that invitation, Marion ?" continued Mr. Lisle, looking puzzled.

" So I can, only—Mr. Lisle, I cannot help laughing, please don't look so serious. Where do you think it is to ?"

" How can I tell ?"

" To The Cedars ! "

Scylla and Charybdis ! The frying-pan and the fire ! Never was man on the horns of such a dilemma.

" Which invitation shall I accept ?" asked Marion, whose eyes were brimful of mischief, for she knew in what horror he held London society, while, on the other hand, the Darrells—oh, what were they not !

" I see no necessity for accepting either," he returned crossly ; "stay at home."

" What ! all by myself ? I did not think you were so cruel !"

" Are you sure Mrs. Howard is going ?"

"Quite."

"And could you not really make yourself happy for a few weeks here, with your schools, and district, and books, and—and "——

" My cat, I suppose, for that is all I have besides."

" No, no, but seriously."

"Seriously, I should be very miserable on Christmas Day with my roast-beef and plum-pudding all to myself. No, Mr. Lisle, it must be one or the other, and the question resolves itself into whether I shall go to my aunt's, or to The Cedars. Which shall I do ?"

" In plain words, do I advise you to run the risk of becoming a worldling, or a Romanist ?"

"Neither one nor the other, I hope, but I think a visit to Aunt Burrowes might really be a source of temptation to me, for I am naturally excitable ; but with regard to Romanism, having been once just a little bitten, I will take good care to keep myself out of harm's way. 'Un chat échaudé craint l'eau chaude.'"

" Well, I am sorry to say it is a matter on which I cannot advise you. I suppose when you have made up your mind which invitation you will accept you will tell me. You are really very wilful !"

" I do not see it," she replied, this time very seriously, for she saw that he was pained. "I have so much confidence in you," she continued, "that I would follow your advice if it only entailed a dull Christmas for myself, but we must not offend my aunt, which I certainly should do were I to refuse her invitation without a sufficient reason. I cannot tell you how much I shrink from the bustle and gaiety of her house, while at Mrs. Darrell's I shall be almost as quiet as at home. I am older now, I should hope, wiser, and protected by my little black book, what can I fear ?"

"That little black book! Marion, you little know to whom that once belonged!"

She looked at him with a strange little creeping at her heart.

"Shall I tell you an o'er true tale?" he asked. "Long, long ago I had a friend, whom I loved as dearly as my own life"—he paused, more affected than Marion had ever seen him.

"Never mind, Mr. Lisle; it pains you to tell me, I can see."

"It does, still I would rather tell you, for somehow there is a kind of consolation in thinking of days that were very happy, even when they are gone for ever. When I think of our childhood passed in the same home, of our deep affection, and still more when I remember the tie that was to have united us, I feel—but let us not talk of that," and he paused again.

"Did she die?" asked Marion.

"She! who?"

"The lady you are speaking of," said Marion, who felt very strange.

"I was not speaking of any lady, Golden-hair," exclaimed the curate, an exulting twinge running through every fibre, notwithstanding his emotion, "but of an orphan boy many years older than myself, who was to have married my sister Agnes."

It was very strange that the tables should have been turned so soon, but it is a fact that the tears came into Golden-hair's eyes, just as the curate began to smile like a sunbeam.

"And did *he* die?" she asked, her confusion permitting no further attempt at originality than changing the gender of her nominative.

"Would to God he had, while clothed in his 'Robe of Righteousness.' No, he went to Oxford, and then, just as he was about to return, rich in honours, to those waiting so impatiently at home, he went to hear a Romanist preacher. From that moment, intellect, love, gratitude, honour, all lay prostrate at the feet of the Moloch of Superstition. He became a Papist. He gave up my father's protection, my sister, my own long-tried brotherhood. And for what? To follow a cold heartless system he does not believe. At last, separated from all he had loved, he put the finishing-stroke to his isolation, for cutting himself off irrevocably from human love and human ties, he became a priest."

"And have you ever seen him since?"

"Once, in your presence, I met George Stirling after ten years' separation, in the little inn at Ilcombe."

"Mr. Lisle! Was Father Stirling your old companion?"

"He was."

"And you never saw him until the day you met at Ilcombe, when he and I were afterwards so nearly killed in driving home?"

"Never, nor have I seen him since."

"And my little Bible really belonged to him: who could have imagined it?"

"Yes, it was my sister's gift to him in happier days. I found it among some books and papers he had left behind, and knowing that he had no further use for the Word of God, retained it. Did you never notice the initials, 'From A. L. to G. S.' on the fly-leaf?"

"Often, and wondered what they meant."

Both were silent. Marion dared not speak her thoughts, but her remembrance of Father Stirling was still so vivid, that she felt persuaded, that however he might have been misguided, he was at least sincere, and sympathised with him, notwithstanding Mr. Lisle's description of his heartlessness, far more than that gentleman would in any way have approved.

" Do you not think it was a sacrifice to him to give up all those he loved?" she asked.

"I suppose so, unless he had grown quite unnatural."

Mr. Lisle knew nothing of the supernatural. One eye alone had witnessed the early conflicts of the Oxonian, as he turned from home, respect, and error, to solitude, contempt, and God.

"Father Stirling!" ejaculated Marion again and again, "you and Father Stirling early friends! Who could have thought it!"

At this moment Sally entered with the lights, and Mr. Lisle rose to take his leave.

"Will you not stay to tea?" asked Marion : "I expect mamma in directly."

"Not this evening, thank you, I am engaged to meet Dr. Stebbing on business, for an hour or two."

"You understand my position now, do you not?" asked Marion, as Sally closed the door. "You will not be vexed with me in your own mind, for you see I cannot do as you would have me."

A slight pressure of the hand he held was the only response to the question.

"I wish I could follow you everywhere, Golden-hair, to shield you from every breath of error."

"As a guardian angel?" she asked, looking up into his face.

"Little riddle," thought he, as he once more took his way through the darkening street. "But how could she read what I have been so anxious to conceal? Sweet little Golden-hair!" and the curate walked on briskly through the snow.

"Mamma," said Marion, later in the evening, "I think if you do not mind it, I should rather go to The Cedars than my aunt's."

"Of course, my dear, I should like to have you with me, but do just as you please."

"Well, for one thing, you see, mamma, it would be a saving of expense if I went to Harleyford, for I must have so many things if I go to London. And then I am only eighteen, and I hardly feel old enough for a gay life yet."

"Well, Marion, just as you like ; please yourself, and you will please me."

"Then I will go to The Cedars, for the Darrells have asked me so often, and they are such good, kind people. How tenderly Mrs. Darrell nursed me after my accident."

"Very well; then, suppose you write at once and accept the invitation. You will, at any rate, keep Christmas in right old English style."

"What will Mr. Lisle do without us?" asked Marion: "he has dined with us for the last two or three Christmas days."

"Go to the Doctor's, perhaps, at least I hope so. If I thought he would be alone and dull, I should be very sorry, for he seems to me almost like my own son now."

That night Mr. Lisle sat in his bachelor parlour all alone, in a very discontented mood. Never had he felt so disinclined to get his own slippers, make his own tea, and keep his own company. His meal was a very dull one, and soon despatched. Then he looked at his writing-desk, but it was too much trouble to fetch it; he took up a book, but dubbed it detestably dry; certainly the reverend gentleman was very difficult to please. He looked round his little room. He did not know why, but never had it looked so half swept, half dusted, half arranged. Perhaps he was mentally comparing it with another, in the comfort of which he had not long since basked. At last, tired of doing nothing, he seated himself on a chair before the fire, put his legs one over the other, and lighted a cigar. The discomforted brow grew smooth once more, under the influence of the "fragrant weed," and a pleased expression stole over his wearied face, as he conjured up many a pretty vision in the graceful wreaths of smoke that curled lightly above his head. By the time his cigar had burned out, his fire had burned down, and the chilly air began to creep in through the shaking old window-frames. But a very sunny smile was on the curate's face, for a very bright hope was in his heart.

"Yes, I think she may be trusted even at The Cedars now," he muttered, "and when she returns, things will be more settled with me, and I will speak to her." After which cabalistic speech, he took up his candle, and dreamed that night of a living half promised him in the south. And a very strange dream it was, too, for he thought the mistress of the new parsonage was sweet little Golden-hair.

CHAPTER XI.

"'O Christmas is a merry time,
    When old and young together join;
    Then let our hearts with rapture glow,
    Nor mind the nipping frost and snow!'"

So sang Joe Darrell, as he sprang down the stairs, three at a time, to go and fetch Marion from Ennington the morning before Christmas Eve.

"Good-bye, girls!" he exclaimed, peeping in at the dining-room door, where his sisters, with Dora and Jessie Seymour, were busy with their decorations. "Any final commands ? I'm off to Ennington."

"What a cold drive you will have, Joe !" said Edith.

"Marion will, I am afraid ; as for me, I am cast-iron, nothing hurts me. A pretty fellow I should be for a gale at sea, if I couldn't stand a nip from Jack Frost !"

"You will take care of Marion, won't you ?" asked Emily. "Wrap her up well."

"Trust me for that. I have had the buffalo robe, and I don t know what besides, put into the trap on purpose for her."

"You are a dear old fellow, Joe ; be as quick back as you can, I am so anxious to see her. I wonder if she is as pretty as she bade fair to be," and Emily, the same merry little spirit as of old, tripped back to her decorations.

"When does Joe's ship start ?" asked Dora.

"In about a month," said Emily, with a sigh.

"And how long will he be before he comes back again ?"

"The same time as before, three years."

"He must have seen a great alteration in you and Edith."

"In Edith, because she is so tall, but not much in me."

"You are certainly not very big even now," returned Dora, smiling at the diminutive, fairy-like figure beside her.

"Little and good," said Emily ; "you know the old saying, that precious things are always in small parcels."

"How old are you, Emily ? I always forget."

"We are sweet seventeen, a year younger than you and Marion, and two years younger than the majestic Jessie."

"What a shame, Emmy !" cried Miss Seymour. "Whatever put it into your head to give me such a title as that ?"

"Because you look so dark and queen-like, with that red camelia that Joe fastened in your hair."

"Silly boy !" exclaimed Jessie, taking it out and throwing it on the table, "I had forgotten all about it."

The words were carelessly, almost haughtily spoken, but a few minutes after the red camelia had again disappeared from the table. That night one very like it stood in a glass on Jessie Seymour's toilette, and received a vast amount of attention too.

"Jessie is very handsome," said Edith, as Emily and Miss Seymour passed into the hall.

"I can well imagine that some persons find her so : for my own part, I consider Emily very much prettier."

"One can hardly compare them," replied Edith, "they are as different as red and white roses."

"They are both very good, I think," said Dora ; "as for Emily, she is almost my idea of a little saint."

"Is she, Dora? Most persons think her so merry and full of fun. Jessie told me the other day, that she had hardly ever seen her serious in her life."

"Jessie went too far there, as she often does ; papa used to call her Miss Hyperbole, when she was a child. I should like to know who could say her face was anything but serious in church. Did you ever watch her?"

"Very often."

"What do you think I sometimes fancy, Edith?"

"What?"

"That Emily will be a nun. I have thought so for a long time, ever since she was about fourteen years old."

"Suppose I tell you that I have felt *certain* of it ever since she was a little child!"

"Have you really, Edith?"

"Yes ; and I expect every day to hear her say, Let me go into a convent. Mind, I betray no confidence in saying this, for we have never in our lives mentioned the subject. I sometimes fancy that mamma thinks so too."

"And how would you like it?"

"O Dora! if it were not that God who calls her, will send us strength to bear the parting, I think I should die ! I cannot realise such a thing, try as I will."

"Do you think she would enter our convent,—I mean the one where we were at school?"

"No, I believe from many things she would choose a strict order—a cloistered one, probably."

"Impossible, Edith, with her disposition!"

"Well, we shall see. If Father Stirling could speak, he could surprise us, I have little doubt."

"Apropos of Father Stirling, Edie, how pleased he will be to see Marion again, though, poor man, his recollections of her visit cannot be altogether pleasant."

"You mean on account of his accident."

"Yes. How patiently he bore it, though he was a whole year without saying Mass. Papa says he must have suffered dreadfully, the bone was so splintered."

"I believe he would rejoice in any suffering," replied Edith, "thinking it brought him nearer to our Blessed Lord. But the girls are calling us, they are going to begin papa's study. Come."

It was a very cold drive from Ennington to The Cedars, but the wrappers were so warm, and Joe such a merry companion, that Marion really scarcely felt it. Besides, cold though the weather was, it was certainly very pleasant. Black Prince seemed in a thoroughly Christmas humour, and the dog-cart bowled smoothly over the frozen road, by the side of which boys were sliding in the gutters, and old men toiling homewards under shining loads of holly. Christmas shone in every face, echoed in every voice, and beamed in the cottage lights, that now began to twinkle like stars around them. The very stage-coach that passed was piled mountains high with hampers of Christmas presents, and the merry faces of expected visitors, or home-returning wanderers, smiled through the windows, or glanced down jollily from the roof.

"Now this is what I thoroughly enjoy," cried Joe, as with a

light touch of his whip he sent Black Prince careering on at a full gallop. "I sadly miss all this at sea."

"But you like sea life, do you not?" asked Marion.

"I should think I do!" replied her companion enthusiastically. "Why, England itself is a prison-house after the broad Atlantic! Depend upon it, a sailor's life is the only true liberty in the world."

"Now do you know, Joe, it seems to me just the reverse. You cannot walk on the water, and I should feel dreadfully cramped up in the narrow limits of a ship's wooden walls, which, after all, broad as is the Atlantic you sail over, is all you have to roam about in. London is a large place, but if a man were shut up in Newgate he would not be much the better for its size, even though he were permitted to peep as often as he liked through the windows. I never can bear to think about the sea. I suppose because poor dear papa was drowned in a voyage out to India, and poor Turner's husband too. By-the-bye, how is dear old nursey?"

"As right as ninepence! if you know what degree of perfection that implies. They are getting on very well; Eliza goes out making vanities for ladies, Mrs. Turner minds the lodge, and the elder lad is errand-boy to a chemist in the town."

"I am so glad; I missed Turner dreadfully at first, but I am very pleased she went to you: it is much better for her to be with her daughter."

"There is one thing about them will hardly please you, I am afraid; but perhaps I had better tell you, though I don't know—I think I will leave it for the girls."

"No, tell me now, Joe, please."

"Well, Eliza has become a Catholic, and is bringing up both her children as such."

"Is it possible?" cried Marion. "What does old Turner say?"

"She was very much put out of the way at first, it seems, but Father Stirling talked her into a good temper, and though she still sticks to the Methodists and the Reverend Howler Growler, or whatever you call him (for Mr. Gardiner's ideas were so elevated, that they took away the old soul's breath), she says Eliza certainly has a right to please herself."

"Well, I suppose she has, but I am really very sorry."

"Are you?" said Joe; "I don't think you look so, very. Now, Marion, don't say bigoted things, for I have always quoted you as the most respectable little heretic I ever knew. You used to be a jolly little thing when you were a child! I hope you haven't changed. As far as face goes, I see no alteration at all; you have grown into a woman with the same bright face and sunny curls you used to have five years ago," and the young midshipman gazed at his companion in unfeigned admiration.

At this moment they reached the lodge gates, and the next Marion's hand was seized and smothered in old Turner's kisses.

"Miss Marion ! Miss Marion ! my own blessed child ! how old nursey has longed to see you !"

"That will do, that will do, Turner !" cried Joe, laughing. "Black Prince won't stand, he wants his supper. Come to the house, and you shall eat Miss Marion up if you like. See, here's a shilling each for the youngsters to keep Christmas with—now, old fellow, go a-head !"

"What a pretty couple they do make, to be sure !" said the old woman, looking after them, "but there's one in store for her better nor even him. Poor fellow ! I hope he won't get to like her, for it's clear to me (and her mother too, I think) as another has her heart, leastways he had six months ago. And they do say too, as how Miss Jessie Seymour is wonderful set on Mr. Joe. But one can hardly say, young folks changes so in a little time. Bless me ! if that isn't four o'clock striking ! I shall have Eliza here directly, and I haven't got a cup of tea ready for her yet, and it's very certain she'll want it to warm her, poor dear, for it do be bitter cold !"

"Does not this look like old times?" asked Mr. Darrell, as he gazed round the cheerful tea-table. "We only want Father Stirling and Miss Horton."

"Both of whom will, I trust, be with us on Christmas day," replied Mrs. Darrell.

"You think a great deal of Christmas, do you not, Mrs. Darrell ?" asked Marion.

".Yes, my dear, I do indeed ; if it were possible, I would have the grate taken out in the dining-room, and have the fire on the hearth in the true old English style. The fireplace was evidently intended originally for that, but it was altered when the house was modernised."

"O mamma ! how delightful that would be !" cried Emily. "I should like to keep Christmas quite in the old way, like Squire Bracebridge in the Sketch Book."

"Well, I do not know that I quite agree with you," replied her father. "I cannot but think that a modern Christmas with its refined and quiet amusements is preferable to the boisterous mirth and noisy games with which our forefathers celebrated it in 'the good old times.'"

"But, papa," said Edith, "they were good old times in one sense—when they were Catholic."

"Yes, Edie,—but it is too bad to introduce the subject of religion now. Look at our little Protestant, how straight she is looking down her nose."

"Who, I, Mr. Darrell ? No, I was only thinking I should like to ask you a question," said Marion.

"Do, my dear ; I hope it will not be too deep for me, but you look so profound that I feel rather nervous."

"It is simply this. If you believe your religion to be the true one, how can you account for England, one of the most, if not *the* most Protestant nation, being at the same time the queen of all others?—for you do admit that she is this, I suppose."

"Undoubtedly I do, prosperous with an unrivalled prosperity! Why, Marion, I am a thorough-going John Bull! as English as I am Catholic! I believe there neither is, nor ever was, a nation in any way approaching her."

"And is not this a strange reward of error?"

"Ah, my child, here we differ; suppose I tell you that I believe England's prosperity to be the reward of her Catholicity?"

"Mr. Darrell! Why England is thoroughly Protestant! No one can deny that. Protestantism is not only established by law, but it is the universal sentiment of her people."

"Hardly that, my dear, in a country numbering as many Catholics as this. But we will not quarrel about trifles : England is undoubtedly a Protestant nation; I will say Protestant to the backbone, for the sake of argument, if you like."

"Then what did you mean just now?"

"Simply this. Whatever England may be now, in these her days of heresy, there was a time when, above all other lands, she bore the sweet titles of the 'Isle of Saints,' and the 'Dowry of Mary.' The Church cannot err, but individually her pastors may grow faithless, and her people stray from their allegiance. Satan was once an angel—Judas an apostle—Luther a monk. England, like the Israel of old, fell from her high estate, and God punished her through her most vulnerable part—her Church. Protestantism fell on her like a blight, and hid the ancient faith. For how long this punishment was adjudged to her we know not—there are those who believe that the term of God's anger is drawing to a close—we cannot say. But with this our dreadful punishment, the wrath of God seems to have been appeased, perhaps propitiated, by the prayers of her who pleaded for her 'Dowry.' He laid not His hand on the worldly prosperity of the land that had once done such great and glorious things in His Name, and sent Him so many great and glorious saints to heaven. No, Marion, my child, while the Catholic sees the names of a St. Alban, St. Cuthbert, St. Neot, St. Dunstan, St. Wulstan, St. John of Beverley, of the royal Edward and the patriotic St. Thomas inscribed on the pages of England's history (picked out from a hundred others), he at least will never marvel at the existence, nor question the source of her prosperity."

Marion smiled. "I dare say yours is a very satisfactory solution of my question to one who believed in the intercession of saints," she remarked. "But tell me, Mr. Darrell, do you seriously believe that England will ever be Catholic again?"

"I do."

"And yet you see what a strong hold Protestantism has on the hearts of English people."

"Pardon me, it is just because I believe that it neither has, nor ever had, any real hold on them, that I think so."

Marion looked down with a look even more compassionate than incredulous.

"If you could only know, Mr. Darrell!"

"Know what?"

"The great work Protestantism is doing. We had a French minister preaching at Ennington, a little time since, who spoke most beautifully in his broken English of the Church of England and its work. He also spoke of Protestantism in France. It is making such rapid strides there, he said, that Catholics themselves must see that their religion is losing its hold upon the French nation every day. Do you think so? I ask, because I really want to know what you think."

"Certainly not. No one who knows France as she is, with her faithful family of priests, her monks, her nuns (especially her devoted band of Sisters of Charity), can for one moment imagine it. No one who sees, as I have seen, marble tablets of gratitude covering almost the entire walls of many of her churches, the crowded congregations, the numerous communions at every Mass, could for an instant say such a thing. I grant you, at first sight the irreligion of France shocks an Englishman, be he Catholic or Protestant, with her vile literature, her desecrated Sundays, her many sins and scandals; but at the core, France, with all her faults, is truly Catholic still. And even if this were not so, do you think the ardent temperament that had rejected our religion, would embrace yours? A mighty convulsion once shook France to her foundations, bringing madness and infidelity in its train, but all the artillery of hell combined could never make her Protestant.

Marion smiled. "It seems to me that your ideas, Mr. Darrell, about Protestantism in France, and those of the French preacher about Catholicism in England, are very much the same."

"And yet, my dear, it is impossible to compare the two. Remember, I know both England and France well; mark the difference. In England the Catholic churches are rich, even elegant, well supported, wonderfully multiplied within the last few years, and wonderfully multiplying still; English in their priests, their congregations, and their style generally. They are objects of curiosity to those outside the Church, are crowded at every service by large congregations, and are visited by strangers of every denomination. In social conversation, in the pulpit, on the platform, in the press, the progress of the Catholic religion in England is the one unfailing topic that is canvassed with every shade of opinion. Now for French Protestantism. In France one occasionally meets with a French Protestant Church, and what is it like? Ill-conducted, ill-sustained, ill-attended, exciting a little contempt from both Catholic and sceptic, and still less curiosity. A few well-built churches have been erected by the English for themselves, with English chaplains and services, but these have nothing to do with any form of French Protestantism, as they are supported by the Anglican Establishment. I can prove to you that Catholicity is spreading in England by pointing to zealous converts, day by day swelling its ranks, to its hierarchy, to its growing power, to its literature, to the Catholic spirit that is beginning to pervade even Protestant society. Now can you show me any similar signs of the spread of Protestantism in France?"

"Not at this moment, Mr. Darrell, although that clergyman said at a public meeting that it is spreading. He really was a very nice man. He pleased the Ennington people so much that he made a very good collection after the sermon."

"What for?" asked Joe.

"To buy Bibles with."

"I see; do you intend that as a proof of the increase of Protestantism in France?" asked Mr. Darrell, mischievously.

"Now, papa, that is too bad," cried Emily; "remember Marion is unsupported."

"And yet, I think if we were to retrace our conversation, you would find that it was Marion who first threw down the gauntlet."

"I daresay I did, Mr. Darrell, for I like to know what reasons Catholics give for things, even while I cannot agree with them."

The fact was, Marion disliked controversy far less than either she or Henry Lisle imagined, or she would not have found herself located at The Cedars, with so little opposition on the part of her spiritual pastor.

"While the girls are at mass, I will run down and see old Turner," said Marion to her kind hostess the next morning after breakfast.

"Do so, my dear, the old soul will be quite fidgety till she sees you. You must not stay too long, though, for Joe wants to take you all to see some skating on the other side of Harleyford."

"I will get ready at once," cried Marion, jumping up. "Is not mass later than when I was here before?"

"Yes, dear, it is always at nine in the winter. It is inconvenient for us, but Father Stirling finds that it suits the generality of his congregation better than an earlier mass, so he does not mind fasting a little longer to accommodate them."

"Fasting! What do they want him to fast for, poor man?" Mrs. Darrell laughed one of her own musical Irish laughs. "Oh, they have nothing to do with that, Marion, but a priest cannot eat or drink anything before he says his mass."

"Why not?"

"Do you not know what the mass is, or, rather, I should say, do you not know what we believe the mass to be?"

"Yes, a solemn service, the most solemn service of your Church."

"Your answer is right as far as it goes," replied Mrs. Darrell. "But I must not stop to chat with you now, for Betsey never fancies the Christmas dinner complete unless I literally have a 'finger in the pie;' but if you will remind me at some time, I will tell you what we really believe. I like you to understand, even while you criticise, our religion."

Marion kissed the sweet motherly face, and tripped off to the lodge.

"O Miss Marion ! I did think you never were a-coming ! I felt quite disappointed like, when I saw the young ladies go out without you, till I began to think, perhaps, you were coming to see me instead."

"Why, of course I was coming to see you," said Marion, kissing her reproachfully.   "Well, nursey, so you are really happy now ! Where is Eliza ?"

"Gone to her work, and Ben has gone to see the skating, so I am here all alone, with nothing to do but to sit still and look at you.   How well you are looking, to be sure !   And how's missis, and Mr. Lisle, and the doctor ?"

Marion's answers appeared highly satisfactory to the old lady, and an animated conversation ensued concerning all the sayings and doings in Ennington for the last six months.

"And so Eliza is a Catholic ?" said Marion.

The old woman nodded her head, and peeped into a saucepan simmering on the fire.

"Yes, deary, she be," she replied at last, slowly resuming her seat ; "yes, she be, and though I felt dreadful about it at first, for it seemed like losing her twice, yet, somehow or other, I have got used to it, and I should be almost sorry to see her turn back again now."

"O nursey, how wrong of you !   Why ?"

"Because, do you see, Miss Marion, whatever her religion is, it comforts her, and to a poor thing like her, that has been knocked about from pillar to post, till her heart was almost broke, of course that is the chief thing. 'Liza,' says I, at first, 'why can't you worship God as you have been always taught ; what do you want more nor your Bible, and your Saviour to take you to heaven ?' Well, Miss Marion, I know I spoke cross, for my temper was up, and I was riled at the idea of her being a Papisher. But she answered me so quiet-like, that I felt quite ashamed. She was a long time trying to explain her religion to me, but that, you see, wasn't no manner of use.   I will let her be what she likes, and let her make her boys what she likes, and I'll be very civil to the priest when he calls—for really, Miss Marion, he do be one of the nicest gentlemen I ever saw ; but I won't change my religion for anybody !   I have lived by my Bible, and gone through all my troubles with it, and with God's help I'll die by it.   I know I'm a sinner, but I trust to God's mercy through Christ, and that's all I know, and all I care to know."

"It must make you very grieved, though, to see Eliza praying to the Virgin Mary, and all that sort of thing."

"Well, it used to do, deary, but I've got over it.   I am sure she's got real religion in her heart, so I don't seem so much to care, though I do think there's a good bit of nonsense mixed up with it, I must say.   I did feel queer when I first see little Bennie fumbling them beads. Oh, deary me, Miss Marion, what use can they be?"

"Well, I think the rosary one of the few beautiful things in their religion. I was much struck with it, I know, the last time I was here; I forget what they are now, but I remember at the time I thought the meditations beautiful."

"Did you, though! Well, of course you know best; it's all Greek to me together. To please Liza I went to church with her once, but I couldn't get on nohow. But it doesn't much matter, deary; when we get to heaven we shan't quarrel as to which road we came by, though people does make a mortal deal of fuss about it here below!"

"You go to the Methodist chapel, I hear, now?"

"Yes, I do, for as for that Mr. Gardiner, God forgive me! but I can't abear him. Only to think of him alongside of our own dear Mr. Lisle, or the doctor."

"Well, nursey, you know he came to see me once or twice when I was ill, and though I tried hard to like him, I thought him a most disagreeable man, especially for a clergyman."

"They say he only became a minister for the sake of this living, which they didn't want to go out of the family. It was in his father's gift, I think they call it; they say, too, it was his wife's money as made him marry her. But he has paid dearly for it, for, if what people says is true, he daresn't call his soul his own, poor man. Mr. Gardiner met me the other day," continued Turner, "and at first he was going to pass me by, though I made my best curtsy, but all on a sudden he recollected who I was, and didn't he just give it to me! First about Liza, and then about going with the Methodists. He told me I ought to be ashamed of myself."

"And what did you say?"

"I spoke to him civil, like, at first, and said as how Liza must do as she liked, and said I found the Methodist ways better for me somehow; but he still spoke so rude to me that I fired up and told him a piece of my mind. It isn't because a body is poor they are to be treated like that, you know, deary."

"Of course not," said Marion.

"If you had only seen Mr. Joe, when I told him what I had said to Mr. Gardiner. He laughed till it seemed as though his sides would crack. Oh, he do be a right merry young gentleman, do Mr. Joe! Bless him! But here comes the young ladies, deary," and as she spoke, two bright faces, fresh as rosebuds in the frosty air, peeped in at the lodge door.

"Father Stirling told us to remember him to you most kindly," said Emily, as Marion walked up the drive between the twins, "but he says he is afraid he shall not have the pleasure of seeing you before to-morrow at dinner; he is so busy just now with the poor."

"Poor Father Stirling!" said Marion gently, as, conjured up by his name, a flood of recollections passed through her mind.

Childish recollections, though mingled with them was the shadow
of a sad tale recently told. Strange fatality! had Henry Lisle
striven to enlist her sympathy on behalf of the priest, he could
not have done so more effectually than by the history of their
bygone and shattered friendship.

CHAPTER XII.

IF the home of the Darrells, when gay with summer flowers and
surrounded by lawns and leafy trees, was beautiful, it was hardly
less so in its pure white mantle of winter snow. When the giant
oaks, whose verdant honours had budded and fallen so many
times, stood erect in their brumal stiffness, and the magnificent
cedars, that gave the estate its name, bowed even lower beneath
their crystal load. Yes, it was a charming winter picture when
the sunshine, cold and bright, fell on the unsullied surface of the
snow, but even more beautiful when the full moon cast her light
and shadow on the scene.

"Emily, it is fairyland!" said Marion, who on crossing the
hall, about ten o'clock on Christmas Eve, had found Joe and his
sister looking out upon the night from the garden door. "it is
fairyland!" she repeated; I never saw anything so lovely."

"How would you like a walk?" asked Joe.

"Above all things; are you and Emily going for one?"

"We were talking of it," said the latter, looking at her brother.

"Oh, I see," said the sensitive little Golden-hair, shrinking back,
"I should be de trop."

"No, darling, you would not indeed, but"——

"Out with it, Em!" cried her brother. "Come, Marion, I will
tell you all about it. We always go to the midnight mass on
Christmas Eve, and we were just discussing what was to be done
with a certain little Protestant, who it is to be feared would not go
with us, and yet whom we could not make up our minds to leave
at home alone."

"But, Joe, I can stay with your mamma and Mr. Darrell."

"Unfortunately the Pater and Mater go too."

"Then I can amuse myself with a book, and if I get sleepy, go
to bed."

"What an entertaining Christmas Eve!"

"Nay, Christmas Eve will have passed by midnight," returned
Marion, "anyway, Joe," she continued, laughing. "I shall be
better off than you, for I can have my supper while you have
to fast. You will be very hungry by the time you get home."

"I think not: I had a good dinner at six, and that will do till
to-morrow morning."

"But, Joe, listen, it will be Christmas day when you get home,
so you can have what you like."

"Can I ? Thank you," replied Joe, looking aside at his sister.

"May he not have some supper even then ?" asked Marion.

"Yes, if he likes," said Emily.

"Joe," called his mother from the drawing-room door.

"Joe seems very strict," said Marion, "I should think he is a very good Catholic."

"Very conscientious," replied Emily, "but we always laugh at him, because, though he acts up to the iota in everything, he never goes beyond it. He is as religious as most boys of his age, but you must not look upon him as a model of piety. He would not eat a crumb over the collation allowed on fast days for the world, but at the same time he would decidedly grumble at anything short of it. He would not miss Mass on Sundays for an empire, but I hardly ever in my life knew him in the church ten minutes before eleven, or a quarter of an hour after the service was over. He would not eat meat on Fridays, I verily believe, to save himself from starvation, but he likes a very good fish dinner. There, now you have Joe,—he would, I am persuaded, die any death for his religion, but he takes things very easily."

"Then why will he not have any supper to-night after twelve o'clock, for I could see by his face .that he meant not to do so ?"

"That," said Emily, quietly, "is because he is to receive Holy Communion to-morrow. For that," she continued, "he will be in the church by half-past six to-morrow morning, to make his preparation before the seven o'clock Mass. Merry as he is, and self-indulgent in common with all boys, he can do, of course, something for Almighty God. I did not include these duties just now when I was laughing at him. God bless him !"

"Yea, and he shall be blessed, though I don't know who you are talking about," cried Joe's voice behind them : "I hope it was not the Rev. 'Dolphus, though."

"Who is he ?'

"He means Mr. Gardiner. Do not be so uncharitable, Joe ! I am sure I would bless him willingly if I could, especially at Christmas time ; and so would you."

"Would I !" said Joe. "Now, Marion, what are you going to do with yourself, without the light of our countenances ?"

"Anything; pray do not trouble yourself about me, I shall manage very well."

"I can propose a capital plan.

"What ? Something very outrageous, I know," said Marion.

"Come with us ; we shall have a jolly walk over the snow, first-rate music, best carpet and vestments, and I don't know what all. Last, not least, no sermon, so you will run no risk of being converted."

Amid all his fun, a prayer, nevertheless, was flickering up from the sailor's heart, that she might,

"Do !" cried Emily, clapping her hands, as in the days of old.

"What would *he* say ?" thought Marion, but she glanced at the moonlight and thought of the music, and the inducement was too strong.

"Very well, I will."

"Hurrah !" cried Joe ; "and now come in and sing that duet with Edith, which we all like so much."

And so Marion found herself once again in the Catholic church of Harleyfold. They arrived there some little time before the Mass commenced, and seated in the same seat, beside the same friends, before the well-remembered altar with its gilded tabernacle and massive candlesticks. Marion strove to recall and analyse the feelings with which she had regarded these things five years before. The church had been enlarged and adorned since her last visit, and the Christmas decorations were far more beautiful than she had anticipated ; but Marion was changed. She felt that lights, incense, flowers, and music, however sweet, would have little or no influence over her imagination now. "And of what else does this religion consist," she asked herself, "but in exterior show ?" and she glanced from gilding to alabaster, and from picture to image. "Beautiful, very, but religion is something more than a spirit of beauty."

The Mass commenced, but although she revelled in the music, Marion continued to criticise. Not a vestment, not a genuflexion, not a movement of the priest, passed unnoted or unjudged in that busy little brain. "Further off than ever !" she thought, as the creed concluded. But when the "Adeste Fideles" rose high through the vaulted roof, ringing out clearly from childish voices, our little heroine was moved, and a tear stole down her cheek. "Venite adoremus !" sang the choir, and Marion bowed her head over Emily's little book. Protestant as she was in every idea, and thought, and feeling, she felt the presence of the Child-God, and could not hold her head erect in pride, while every heart around her bowed before the cradle-shrine of Bethlehem.

"Are you pleased you came, Marion ?" asked Joe, offering her his arm, as she found herself again with her friends in the frosty air and winter moonlight.

"Yes, very, I should have been dull at home by myself."

"How did you like it ?"

"The music was beautiful."

"Yes ; we had some professionals, besides our usual amateurs."

"I am not at all converted," said Marion, mischievously.

"Very likely not ; did you expect you would be ?"

"No. It is a strange thing, Joe, but the last time I was here, I liked your religion a great deal better than I do now. I had then, I remember, almost an idea of being a Catholic, or at least a Puseyite. Now—you must not be offended—but I really hardly see an atom of sense in it at all. I should like to know the use of that perpetual kneeling down and getting up again, which Father Stirling went through towards the latter part of the service."

"You would have knelt, had you been in his place," said Joe, quietly ; " but, Marion, I am not at all surprised at what you tell me about your old and new ideas."

" Why not ? "

" Because I believe you too sensible now to be captivated by the forms and ceremonies of any religion ; and you must excuse me, but really that is all you know of ours yet."

" Nonsense, Joe! I know a great deal more of your religion than you think."

Joe smiled. " And yet you asked me why Father Stirling knelt."

" Yes, that is nothing; I mean that I understand the funda- mental doctrines of your Church, such as your worship of the Virgin and the Saints, Purgatory, &c."

" I see," said Joe, still smiling, " but, Marion, we have greater doctrines even than those ; shall I give you the words of one of your own divines, touching this very subject of genuflexion ? ' If,' he says, ' I believed what Catholics believe, I should lie prostrate on the sanctuary floor, day and night.' Come, that would be more extraordinary even than a genuflexion ! "

- " Then what do you believe ? "

Joe paused. " I wish," he said at length, " you would oblige me by asking my mother that question, instead of me."

" Joe ! " cried Marion, bursting into a fit of laughter, " I believe you do not know yourself."

" Not know ! " he exclaimed ; and the young man turned on her a look so intense that Marion was awed. " Not know ! But it is not from the mouth of a wild young fellow like me, that you must learn such a truth as this. Ask my mother, or Emily."

Marion changed the subject.

" Father Stirling looks very little older," she observed.

" Very little ; he wears very well."

" I am pleased to see him again. I used to be very fond of him as a child."

" So is everybody in Harleyford, I think, except the Rev. 'Dolphus."

" What ! Mr. Gardiner ? "

" Yes ; he has done a great deal to annoy Father Stirling, but as yet all his weapons have been turned on himself."

" I really am not surprised you do not like him," said Marion, " he is one of those clergymen, who, entering the Church as a profession, get through their ministrations without either heart or earnestness, with neither the zeal of the high-churchman, nor the piety of the low."

" Are these the distinguishing characteristics of the two parties ? " asked Joe.

" I think so ; little sympathy as I have with the Tractarians, I do consider them generally as a very zealous body of men."

" Well, now, Marion, you may think it strange, but though I am a Catholic, I infinitely prefer your even ultra low-churchman. The Tractarian clings mainly to the forms which, much as we think of them, are valueless detached from the mighty truths they symbolise. I remember once almost laughing when I was beguiled, by a friend and my own curiosity, into an Anglican place of worship. Shall I tell you what it reminded me of?"

"Yes, do; but please to remember I have no fancy for Puseyism now."

"I know that; but now for my story. Once upon a time, during the Chinese war, it came into the sapient heads of some of the long-tailed Chinamen, that as we gained such signal advantages over them by our steam-ships, if they only had them also, they could do great things. But the difficulty was to make them. Now you know the Chinese are first-rate copyists; so at last from a distance (for you may be sure we did not let them get very near), they made an exact imitation of one of our finest screws. There was the funnel, and all the et-ceteras, and they gazed with no little pride on this chef-d'œuvre, which was going to make the English tremble, and set free the Celestial Empire. Unfortunately, however, one thing was wanting to make the steamer complete."

"What was that?"

"The machinery, of which John Chinaman knew nothing, and when, having lighted some faggots under the funnel, they saw the smoke come out of the top in tremendous wreaths, they were wonderfully astonished to see their steamer stand stock still! Need I draw the parallel? The Tractarian may make crosses, and burn candles, chant his service, and set up his credence table, but it is only a poor imitation of things he does not understand after all."

"You are very wise about the Church of England."

"Well, I have not passed through my life of twenty-two years with my eyes shut, and I have talked a great deal to Father Stirling about these things, and that makes me wiser than I should otherwise be."

By this time they had emerged into the broad road, and falling back with the rest of the party the conversation became general. But a quiet spirit seemed to have fallen over the whole family; and Marion supped alone before the cosy fire in her own bed-room.

"The compliments of the season, a merry Christmas, and a happy new year," said a hearty voice behind her, as she next day sat alone in the drawing-room poring over an illuminated folio by the firelight. Marion turning, beheld Father Stirling, and it was with a feeling of sincere pleasure that she returned the kind greeting.

"Well, I suppose it is rather late to condole with each other now," said Father Stirling, gaily, after a few minutes chat, during which they were joined by the girls, "we are neither of us now, I suppose, whatever we were then, much the worse for our tumble; you were dreadfully hurt though, I believe, poor child."

"Oh, nothing to you, Father Stirling! I was well in a few weeks, and you were ill for a year afterwards."

"Yes, I was, but you see time heals all things; I am afraid though," he added, thoughtfully, "he is not so good a mediciner for the mind as the body. What say you?"

"I hardly know, I have had so few wounds of either kind for him to cure as yet."

"Happy child!"

At this moment the bell rang, and in a few minutes the whole party, including the entire Seymour family, were gathered round the dinner-table.

Christmas! Christmas! Where is the heart that does not revel in thy name—that does not thrill with a thousand recollections, while the circle still unbroken gathers around the festive board, and every thought, and word, and glance, is unity and harmony? When even the low sad whispers from old times that breathe around the elder ones are hushed in the joyous melody of the young home-birds, and when half-faded memories of Christmas past are illumined by the ruddy light of Christmas present. All is joy, for old hearts will not think, and young ones cannot forecast, cannot read those characters of change, with which the recesses of the future must be stored. O Christmas! dark would be the day, if thou couldst fall as a shadow rather than a sunbeam! But this can never be. There is indeed a danger, that amid the glare of the glowing fireside, the star of Bethelem may shine above unseen, that amid the sound of revelry and feasting, the angels' harps may swell unheard; but when the best beloved have passed away, and the snapt heart-chain drags listlessly in the dust, then perhaps the spirit, freed from the world, feels its true vocation. Gloria in excelsis Deo—the lonely hearth and vacant chair are forgotten beside the Crib, Pax hominibus bonæ voluntatis—while Jesus, Mary, Joseph, smile from heaven, who shall mourn and weep on earth?

But The Cedars, at least, are as yet unshadowed; and worthy of Emily's "good old times" is the mirth that circles among the younger members of the party at Mr. Darrell's stories. Nor is Father Stirling far behind, and his tales of adventures in foreign lands and college freaks, alternately melt his auditors into tears, or send them off into peals of laughter.

"Do tell us some more stories, please, Father Stirling," cried Emily, "we like them so much."

"Why you children are like the daughters of the horse-leech! If I go on much longer, I shall be making one up, and then you would never trust me again."

"Tell us another tale about the French."

"The French! I am sure I have talked Paris to you, till you must know it almost as well as I do myself. You will be like Mr. Bridges, who went everywhere but to Complet."

"But where?"

"Complet. Did I never tell you about that?"

"Never: do tell us, please."

"Well, once upon a time, there was a gentleman named Bridges,

who, having determined on treating himself to a fortnight's holiday, thought he could not possibly spend it better than in a trip
across the Channel. So one balmy day in June, he packed his
portmanteau, and off he started. His purse was better stocked
with money than his brains with French, but with the verbs
manger, *boire*, and *dormir*, a pocket dictionary, and sundry
pantomimic gestures, he stumbled through the first few days, and
did his best to think himself profoundly happy. He had come, as
he phrased it, ' to do Paris ; ' and he did it, and no mistake about
it. He wandered about, a solitary figure, at the Louvre, the
Luxembourg, the Tuileries, the Jardin des Plantes, the Gobelins,
the—— but it would take so long to tell you where he did go, that
it would be no use attempting it—the fact is, he went everywhere
but to Complet."

"Why didn't he go there?" asked Joe.

"Because they wouldn't let him. He started from the Palais-
Royal in all conceivable directions. He went to Passy, to Batig-
nolles, to Vaugirard, but as soon as ever an omnibus came in sight,
bearing the name of Complet above the door, he never could catch
it. And yet it was evident to Bridges, that it was a place of some
note, or why so many omnibuses constantly travelling thitherward?
for there was not a quarter that he traversed, but an omnibus
rumbled past, bound to that most mysterious locality.

"At last Bridges grew desperate ; he had only two days more,
and Complet he must visit, or how could he face those quizzical
friends of his, who knew Paris so well, if he had never been to
Complet? Yes, go he would, why shouldn't he? Just as he came
to this desperate decision, an omnibus crossed the Square of the
Palais Royal, bearing in unmistakable characters the name
Complet.

"'Now for it,' thought Bridges, setting his teeth with determination ; but the vehicle, as was usual, passed on before he had time
to reach it.

"'Never mind,' said the chivalrous Bridges, thinking of Jones,
Brown, and Robinson, 'I'll go this time. Complet!' he shouted
at the top of his voice, running after the omnibus.

"'Complet, Monsieur,' said the conductor, pointing to the board
over his head.

"'Oui! Oui! Complet!' cried Bridges, still running on.

"'Complet!' roared the conductor.

"'Complet!' shrieked Bridges, waving his umbrella.

"By this time all the people in and on the omnibus were on
the broad grin, which at any other time would have made Bridges,
who was rather bashful, feel nervous, but too much was at stake
now. His anger did not decrease when the conductor having let
down his bar, seated himself upon it shrugging his shoulders at
poor Bridges.

"'Complet!' now shrieked a voice or two from the pavement,
and thinking that the French accent might propitiate the conductor, where the English had so miserably failed, Bridges sped

on. In vain ! The omnibus quickened its pace, and at that very minute Bridges tripping over a stone, measured his length in the Rue de Rivoli.

"'*C'est un vrai Anglais*,' said a Parisian belle, which remark happening to fall within the limits of poor Bridges' French, in no way consoled him. But how retaliate, when the speaker was a lady, and had only spoken the truth, for Bridges was a Cockney born and bred, but with all his devotion to the fair sex, he could have eaten her without salt. But even if he had, he would not have felt much better for it, so he wiped off the dust, picked up his umbrella and limped off to his hotel. Two days after he left Paris sad at heart, for he loved the cafés, the restaurants, the Boulevards, and Champs Elysées, and last, not least, he had not been to Complet. On board the steamer, he met with another home-bound Englishman, and having grown communicative, they retailed their respective adventures.

"'There is one quarter of Paris,' said Bridges, 'that must be very populous, for I never saw an omnibus going to or coming from it that was not crowded.'

"'Which is that ?' asked his new friend.

"'Complet,' said Bridges. 'Those dunder-headed Frenchmen could never understand me, though I screamed Complet at them till I was hoarse,' and Bridges narrated his adventure of the previous day in the Rue de Rivoli.

"'Oh dear! oh dear !' said his companion, shaking with laughter.

"'Did you ever hear such a thing ?' asked Bridges.

"'No, that I never did ; why, man alive, Complet means *full !*'"

"Now, Father Stirling, you made that story up, you know you did !"

"And is that all the thanks I am to get for my trouble in telling it ?"

"Emily is very ungrateful," said Marion ; "I am sure we will believe it, every word."

"Will you ? well, perhaps you had better not, altogether, for though Brown, Jones, and Robinson contrived to worm it out of poor Bridges on his return, perhaps they may rather have embellished it."

The ladies now adjourned to the drawing-room, where they formed a cosy, chatting little party, and when shortly afterwards they were joined by the gentlemen, Marion found herself beside her old friend the priest.

"I had quite forgotten," she exclaimed, after a few minutes' conversation, "but do you know, Father Stirling, I meant to have been very stiff, for I am very angry with you ! "

"With me ! What have I done ?"

"Why, converted my old nurse's daughter."

"No. I have not."

"Who did then ?"

"Almighty God. It is paying me a vain compliment to give me the credit of anything half so glorious. Have you seen her?"

"Not yet, but I saw her mother yesterday."

"Well, and you found her more than half reconciled to it, did you not?"

"Yes; but you will never make a convert of her."

"Very likely not; poor old soul, I believe her to be a thoroughly honest, straightforward woman."

"Her creed is a simple one," observed Marion.

"Very," replied the clergyman, "faith, hope, and charity."

"And do you believe this is enough to save her?" asked Marion.

"I do; for I believe she is in invincible ignorance.'

CHAPTER XIII.

It was New Year's night, and there was an evening party at The Cedars. Nothing so delighted the kind-hearted master and mistress of this hospitable home, as to see their young people merry around them, and to-night it certainly appeared that in the furtherance of this object, the usually quiet house had (to use Joe's own phrase) been turned out of windows. The whole was a scene of lights, flowers, and flitting drapery. The conservatory was hung with Chinese lamps, the large dining-room converted into a ball-room, while quiet coteries of elderly people clustered round the card-table, or sat talking politics and news, in the drawing-room. Radiant amid them all passed Mr. Darrell, a perfect spirit of sunshine, now animating the dancers, now lingering behind a whist-player's chair, now turning over the pages at the piano, explaining prints and pictures, or chatting with some aged dowager in her quiet corner by the fire. Can he be forgiven, if amid all he gazed with unwonted pride on his lovely Emily, certainly pronounced by all the belle of the country, far and wide? Many a manly form hovered around her, many a whispered compliment fell on her ear, many an eye beamed in the light of hers, but though she smiled, and chatted, and danced with all, not one could claim the preference; and Mr. Darrell sighed.

"Unusual in a pretty girl of seventeen," he whispered to his wife, "that quiet Edie is twice as much of a coquette as she. See how pleased she is with the soft nothings of that moustached hero. Little puss! They have put the quadrille out twice already by their inattention. There is little Emily, on the other hand, treats all attention with the greatest possible nonchalance. She is a darling child, but I wish she was more like other girls. Look at her now, half hidden behind the curtain, talking to old Seymour."

"Marion Howard is a sweet-looking girl, with her beautiful floating ringlets," observed Mrs. Darrell.

"Very; but she is not as pretty as our Emily."

And now a polka struck up, on which the Darrells and Seymours, the only Catholic girls present, slipped off into the drawing-room, where they stood laughing and chatting with the old people, rather, perhaps, to the discomfiture of sundry scientific whist-players, who growled behind their cards.

"Emily," said Joe, putting his head in at the door, "come and have just a turn or two with me. You are such a jolly little dancer; there's not one of the girls there fit for anything after you. Come."

"Are you tired?" asked Joe, as, after two turns round the room, Emily stopped and put her arm in his.

"Rather. Come and have a walk with me upstairs in the long gallery. It looked so pretty in the moonlight, as I came through just now, and every place down here is so warm."

They passed up the broad oak stair-case, and, still arm-in-arm, were soon gazing through the large window at the end of the gallery upon the placid snow scene.

"It is very nice here?" said Emily, laying her head upon her brother's shoulder, while he stole his arm gently round her; "do you not think so?"

"Very; the music below sounds so subdued and sweet."

There was a silence of some minutes, broken at length by the sister.

"Joe!"

"Yes, darling."

"What are you thinking of?"

"Of many things—of the sea, partly, and how long it will be before I am captain, and partly of the people downstairs."

"Joe," said his sister, looking up at him archly, "I have made a discovery to-night."

"What is it?"

"That you are a desperate flirt."

"O Em! What an accusation! They say that, I know, of sailors generally, but I thought I was an exception to this rule."

". Then, 'lay not that flattering unction to your soul' any longer. You have been doing dreadful execution among the young ladies to-night, I fear!"

"It was not premeditated homicide, then, but one must be civil in one's own house."

"How do you like the Seymours?"

"Very well; they have wonderfully improved."

"What do you think of Jessie?"

"She is a good-looking girl, but I think she knows it."

"She cannot look in the glass without doing so. She is certainly the belle to-night."

"Jessie Seymour! Is she?" asked Joe, drily.

"Why, I thought you liked her very much."

"I do pretty well, but she is not one of my prime favourites."

"Joe, I am going to tell you something. I hardly know whether I am right or wrong in doing so, but remember, it is only what I think, not what I know "——

"Well, what is it ?' asked Joe, with all a man's curiosity.

"I think Jessie is fond of you."

"The dickens she is ! Nonsense, Em !" he added, very seriously, "you don't mean it !"

"I mean that, from many little things, I think she is, and up to this moment I half fancied you rather liked her."

"Oh, my dear little sissy ! for goodness sake tell her I don't ! At least, that is, give her a hint about it in some fashion. Girls have such nice ways with them, they can say a world of things in one word. O Em ! I wouldn't have anybody like me that I couldn't like again for twenty worlds. Why, what on earth have I ever said to her ?" And poor Joe's face looked the picture of consternation.

"Nothing, that I know of," said Emily, who could not help laughing, in spite of his distress ; "but you really have shown her a good deal of attention at different times. Look even at to-night, you have been flirting dreadfully with her."

"Nonsense, Emily ; I was the same to all the girls in the room !"

"No, Joe, you were not ; there is one that you have very much neglected. One reason why I brought you up here, was to scold you for it, but I had forgotten it again. I do not think you have once asked Marion to dance with you all the evening."

The grasp round Emily's waist tightened.

"Yes, I did once, but she was engaged."

"And why did you not ask her again ?"

"I don't know."

Emily glanced up, the young man's cheeks were crimson.

"Joe," she whispered softly, kneeling upon the broad window-sill, and throwing her arms round his neck, "tell me what is the matter ?"

"Nothing, child !"

"Yes, there is ! O Joe, darling ! I have read your secret—but a Protestant !"

"I know that, but it does not prevent her being an angel."

"And would you peril your faith, your soul, for her ?"

"No, Emily, she is as dead to me as though we had never met."

"Thank God !" cried the impetuous little creature, bursting into a passionate flood of tears.

"Come, Emmy, Emmy ! you will make such a fright of yourself, and that will never do."

"I cannot help crying, for I know that in spite of all your gaiety, you must be unhappy. Poor dear fellow !"

"No, I am not ; I have one hope left."

"What is that ?" asked his sister anxiously.

"That she may yet become a Catholic ; I have prayed for this ever since I first knew her."

"So have I, but I will pray harder than ever, now that you and she are bound, as it were, in one intention. Of all things I could desire, it would be to see Marion a Catholic, and you her husband. I should like to see Edie well married, too," she added musingly, after a pause.

"And for Emily to be the old maid of the family, eh ?"

"Just so, with a dog, and a cat, and a parrot."

"No, no, Emmy, that would never do ; we must have a baronet, at least, for you."

"A baronet ! Nothing short of a marquis will satisfy me, I can tell you."

"I wonder what will be the fate of us three ?" said Joe, thoughtfully. "If that young Gauntlet were only a Catholic, there is no one I should like better for you than he. He is really a good sort of a fellow."

Again they looked out upon the snow, and again there was silence.

"Joe," said Emily at length, "I have guessed your secret, shall I tell you mine ? A secret cherished in my heart of hearts for years, though never whispered except to one ; but, somehow, to-night, I feel that I must tell you, for, dear as Edith is, I cannot say things as easily to her as I can to you."

"Who is the one who knows it ?" asked Joe, with a sickly sensation at his heart.

"Father Stirling."

"I thought so ; then I can read it. O Emily ! Emily! would you break all our hearts ? If you were ugly, stupid, or cross, it would be different, but you, our pet, our sunshine, the most beautiful girl of half the country."

Emily smiled. "Are you trying to make me vain ? But this is not a right feeling," she continued ; "if I were all your affection loves to fancy me, would it be too much to give to God ?"

"No, but He does not ask it."

"He does."

"How do you know ?"

"By what I feel here," she replied, laying her hand upon her heart. "From childhood, He has never given me another thought."

"What does Father Stirling say ?"

"He told me yesterday, for the first time, that he believes I have a vocation ; and that is why I have been so happy all day. Joe, darling, you should rejoice with those who do rejoice, and weep with those who weep."

"I shall have a great deal more weeping than rejoicing to do, then," replied her brother ; "for though you are so jolly about it, I expect you will break our father's and mother's hearts ! "

"God will strengthen them," replied Emily.

"And when are you going ?"

"Not yet ; Father Stirling says I must wait at least two years. I shall be nearly twenty then."

"What order do you wish to enter ? the convent where you went to school, I suppose. Bother those old nuns ! I was always afraid of them. They could coax a very broomstick into taking their habit, I believe ! "

"They must first learn whether it had a vocation, which might be rather difficult to determine. Now, you know, Joe, you do not believe one word you are saying ; you only talk so because you are cross. You are quite wrong ; I do not wish to go to the sisters."

"Where, then ? "

Emily hesitated. "I would rather not talk to you about it this evening, you are not the dear boy you generally are."

"Well, I won't be cross any more, only tell me."

"I do not know yet, but I should like the Carmelites, or perhaps the Poor Clares."

"O Emily ! this is too much, I could not bear that ! "

"Yes, you could," said his sister, kissing him, "or anything else, for the love of God. I am not going yet, so don't look so dull, but come downstairs again. Now I know your secret, and you know mine, we shall get on better."

"I don't know that ; it would be a comical fashion of helping an overburthened horse to put a fresh load on him."

"Ah, but, Joe ! we must bear one another's burdens."

"That may be all very well, when one is empty-handed, but when each has a good tidy load of his own, the other's help is little assistance. At any rate, I cannot say I feel much the better for your communication. Fancy me at sea, thinking of you in a convent without shoes, and Marion married to somebody else. Comforting that for a fellow, certainly ! "

"I wish I had not told you now," said Emily, drawing her shawl round her.

"And so do I ; " but seeing the shadow on his sweet little sister's face, Joe stopped. "Forgive me, my own darling ! " he exclaimed ; "be what you like, and may God bless you. You are shivering with the cold. Come down directly."

Once again they mingled with their friends, and were soon again buoyant with the buoyancy of youth. At the end of half an hour, Joe and Marion were whirling round in a polka.

"I engage you for the first quadrille at the county ball," said Joe.

"If I go," answered his companion, "but if I can possibly get myself excused, I shall. I have never been to a public ball in my life."

"Neither have the girls, but papa wishes to take them, and so they will not refuse."

"As much as to say, I must not do so either. Will Mrs. Darrell go ? "

"No. It would be too much for her. It is seven miles off."

"Perhaps I may stay and keep her company."

"I do not think you will be let off very easily. Mind, I shall vote against you."

"Thank you. Though I do not know why you should throw your sword and belt into the scale; you will have enough to do in looking after Miss Seymour."

"Her father is going," said Joe, "so I shall have no need to do that."

"Mr. Seymour has been here all this evening, but you have evidently seen great necessity for attending to her, notwithstanding."

"What a teaze you are, Marion! the girls have been giving you these notions, I know."

"My own eyes have," replied Marion.

"Then do not trust them for the future, for, believe me, they are false guides;" and the young sailor cast an earnest reproachful glance upon his companion. He could not help it, and her woman's instinct read the interpretation.

That night, in the solemn solitude of its darkness, three hearts pondered a secret newly read.

"Poor dear boy! How anxious and unhappy he must be! I must pray very hard for her conversion, for both their sakes;" and, with her rosary in her hand, Emily sank to sleep.

"Emily, my pet! my darling! I cannot bear it!" and the sailor sobbed in his great grief, and wetted the pillow with his tears.

"Does he really like me? I never thought of it till to-night. I wish he had been at sea! He is such a good kind fellow, I would bear anything rather than make him unhappy; but, really, it is not my fault. Perhaps it is only fancy, after all, though." And Golden-hair fell asleep, and dreamed of Henry Lisle.

Marion did not go to the county ball, notwithstanding all Joe's persuasions and opposition, for, as she had a cold, Mr. Seymour and Mrs. Darrell took her part, and so the carriage drove off with Mr. Darrell and his children, leaving Marion and the mistress of The Cedars in quiet possession of its snuggest chimney-corner.

"Now, Marion," said the latter, stirring the fire, and drawing the large screen closer, "we will make ourselves cosy; where is your knitting? I quite agree with you in preferring this to a seven miles drive through the cold in a gauze dress, and I think a warm bed infinitely more comfortable than dancing till four or five o'clock in the morning. I shall be the only one at Mass to-morrow, I presume."

"No, that you shall not, for I will go with you."

"Will you? then you and I will breakfast first by ourselves."

"You seldom miss Mass, do you?" asked Marion.

I

"Not very often, my dear, thank God."

"I cannot think why Catholics should think so much more of their churches than we do. Do you not believe, dear Mrs. Darrell, that God hears prayer offered to Him, before the duties of the day, in one's own room?"

"Certainly, dear, I do."

"Then do tell me, why you should go every morning through the cold, and sometimes even in the rain, to church, when you can pray just as well at home?"

"Marion, I shall answer your question by asking you another,— do you ever hear from Edward?"

"Yes; very often."

"Why, then, do you long so anxiously to see him?"

"Dear Mrs. Darrell," replied the young girl, "what are his written words, in comparison to his own dear self?"

"Such is the feeling of the Catholic, my child," returned her friend: "his communion with his Father in heaven may be fervent anywhere, but his most ardent devotion is in the actual presence of his Lord."

"But God is no more present in the church than anywhere else; in this room, for instance."

"Did I not once tell you, Marion dear, that you knew but very little of our religion? Suppose I told you that we believe that Jesus, God and Man, is really present on our altars; what would you say?"

"That it was not possible you could hold such a belief."

"Nevertheless we do, and strange as it seems to you, it is the one grand point of the Catholic religion. Like the heart in the human frame, it is the centre of its vitality; take it away, and every doctrine, every sacrament, has passed with it."

"I always thought your religion strange," exclaimed Marion, "very strange, but I never dreamed for an instant of such an idea as this in it. Do you mean to say, that when you go into a Catholic church, you believe God is actually there?"

"Yes; as truly as He was in Bethlehem, in Nazareth, on the Mount of Olives, by the Lake of Tiberias, or on the cross; as He was in His resurrection and ascension, as He is at this moment in heaven. All this is expressed in the word, Transubstantiation. Did you never hear of this doctrine of our Church?"

"Yes, sometimes, but I never stopped to consider what it meant. I thought it had something to do with your celebration of the Communion."

"And you were right," said Mrs. Darrell; "the Blessed Sacrament on our altars, is what we receive in Holy Communion."

"What! God Himself!" said Marion, starting. "You surely cannot believe such a thing as this!"

"Not when Christ says, 'This is My Body, this is My Blood?'"

"Yes, but He meant it figuratively, of course," said Marion, decidedly.

"Who told you so?" asked Mrs. Darrell.

Marion paused, her eyes brimful of astonishment.

"Who told you so ?" repeated her friend. "These are the words that God actually pronounced, and I believe them—you accept the same words, and you do not believe them ; what is your authority for this ?"

"But I do not disbelieve them, Mrs. Darrell !"

"Not when God asserts one thing and you another ? Protestants talk a great deal about the wresting of the Scriptures, but this is more, it is an absolute denial of the grandest institution of Christianity, and this revealed perfectly, purely, openly, in their own Bibles."

Marion looked thoughtfully in the fire, and for a time both ladies maintained a profound silence.

"If I believed such a thing, I am certain I should die."

"No you would not," replied her companion. "Our Lord abides with us, not to destroy, but to save. On the contrary, I have heard many converts say, that from the moment they believed in the Blessed Sacrament, the whole world was changed to them. But such a feeling as yours is very natural. I have no doubt that the sentiment of a soul upon whom this truth first dawns, must be one of unmitigated awe. If you had been in a dark room for some time, and a person suddenly entered with a light, you would be dazzled, though after a time you would grow accustomed to it, and even use it as a means of sight. Yet this would not be because the lamp grew duller, but simply because you grew more habituated to its beams. And so it is with the Blessed Sacrament, for those who are first most overwhelmed by Its glory, are those who afterwards bask most freely in the beams of Its light and heat."

"But it all seems so confused to me," exclaimed Marion : "how do you believe that the Blessed Sacrament comes upon the altar ? "

"I will explain this doctrine to you, my dear, as well as I can, but the subject is so tremendous that one almost trembles to approach it. You know we all believe that Christ died upon the cross for man's salvation, for this at least is an article of Faith common to both Catholic and Protestant ; but we believe, moreover, that the one great Sacrifice, though perfectly consummated on the cross, is still continued in the Sacrifice of the Mass. The Blood of Christ is the universal medicine, the Mass the living fountain that keeps it perpetually flowing, bright with the ever-fresh and unchangeable love of the Heart of Jesus. Holy Communion is the stream of life, that, issuing from this living fountain, carries its whole efficacious power to heal down into each of our weak and suffering souls, and the power of all the other sacraments likewise takes its rise in this one same glorious spring, this living presence of our Redeemer."

"What do you mean by the Sacrifice of the Mass, dear Mrs. Darrell ? Surely you believe that the Sacrifice of our Lord, once. offered on Calvary, was sufficient to save the whole world ? "

" Undoubtedly it was, Marion, but our faith teaches us that the Sacrifice of the Cross and the Sacrifice of the Mass are one and the same thing. Thus, you see, the death of our dear Lord is not for us, as for you, an historical event that took place some eighteen hundred years ago, but an ever-present reality; for He who had power to lay down His life, and to take it up again, chose to perpetuate the moment of His death until the end of time. And as we believe that these two sacrifices are identical, so we believe that Jesus Christ is offered, and sin atoned for, as perfectly in one as in the other. In the great sacrifice of our Lord, therefore, the two ancient priesthoods are combined and fulfilled. That of Aaron, with its constant stream of blood, flowing ever as sin abounded and increased, and that more glorious and mysterious priesthood of Melchisedech, who offered bread and wine, and whose superiority, Abraham, the very foundation-stone of the Aaronic dispensation, acknowledged by giving him tithes of the spoils he had taken from the enemies of God. Like that priest of the Most High God, the priest of later days takes bread and wine; all he does is to pronounce the words of consecration that Jesus Christ Himself pronounced eighteen hundred years ago, ' This is My Body, this is My Blood;' and those words bring down the King of kings from heaven, to remain under those humble veils of bread and wine, until He glides into the hearts of His children in Holy Communion."

" Is the Blessed Sacrament always on the altar ? "

" Yes, dear, in the tabernacle; that is why that red light burns · before it."

" And that is why you always kneel when you enter the church! Now I understand what Joe meant, when he said on Christmas Eve that I should have knelt, had I been in Father Stirling's place."

Once again there was silence, during which Marion pushed back her chair, and sat down upon the hearthrug at Mrs. Darrell's feet, where she remained, apparently absorbed in the red coals.

" It is a strange thing," she exclaimed at length, " but this, or something like this, has been my dream almost from my babyhood. Of course, dear Mrs. Darrell," she added, suddenly looking up through her curls into that lady's face, " of course I cannot think it true, but I can well imagine that those who do, live in a different world. Why, you believe that you almost talk to God, face to face ! "

" Of course we do, dear, and carry all our troubles to Him, as we should have done in the days of His visible sojourn on earth."

" And I always fancied I understood the Catholic religion so well, while it seems I had never so much as heard of its principal doctrine, or at least never heard of it to give it a moment's thought. But it cannot possibly be true ! "

" Then it is a magnificent deception," said her friend.

" You know, Mrs. Darrell, we consider the Lord's Supper as a figure of His death upon the cross," observed Marion.

"Are you not sufficiently acquainted with Bible history, my child, to know that the figure invariably precedes the thing signified? Where can you find a more beautiful one of our Lord's death and atonement than the Passover? A lamb without blemish was slain, and its blood sprinkled over their houses saved them from destruction. Not a bone was broken, but it was divided among all the family, and entirely consumed with bitter herbs. Here certainly was a figure of the one great Sacrifice, perfect in all its parts. Our Lord came on earth and fulfilled it, and what then? Protestants say that having done so, and abolished this exquisite figure of the paschal lamb, before He left the world He instituted in its stead another figure. Even supposing it to represent our great Redemption as past, and to be taken in memory of it, what is it? Why the representation of His Body by a square of wheaten bread, and the representation of His Blood by a drop of wine sipped out of a chalice. Catholics are at least reasonable in believing that our Lord worked a stupendous wonder, and veiled His Divinity and Humanity under the humble appearances of bread and wine, while Protestants in denying the mystery assert what outrages reason."

"I understand what you mean. You adore a mystery, where we only see a figure."

"Exactly so ; and you must remember that our Lord once said in speaking to His chosen twelve, 'to others I speak in parables, but to you it is given to know the mysteries of the kingdom of God.' Now would it not have been much more like a parable, than the explanation of a mystery, to speak of the simple representation of a thing as the actual thing itself? And this, moreover, on the very eve of His death, when even men couch their last will and testament in unmistakable terms, lest when they are no longer living to explain, their intention should be taken in a different sense from what they had intended. But there was another occasion besides the institution of the Holy Eucharist, upon which our Lord alluded to it. Of course you remember the long discourse in the sixth chapter of St. John, in which He talks so much of the 'Bread of Life' to His disciples, and says, 'Unless you eat the Flesh of the Son of Man, and drink His Blood, you have no life in Me.'"

"Ah! but of course that is a figure of speech."

"No, dear child, it is not. Do you think that for the sake of explaining this figure, if it had been such, our Lord would have suffered the Jews to have left Him as they did, for we hear that from that day many went back from Him, and walked with Him no more? Did He value His disciples so little as to let them depart, rather than say, 'My Body shall be represented by a piece of bread, and My Blood by a drop of wine?' Would it have been like the loving Jesus to let them go, when a word would have detained them? No, Marion, if the doctrine of Transubstantiation be not true, it is our Blessed Lord Himself who has misled the millions of rejoicing souls, who for nearly two thousand years have lived and died by the strength of this Bread of Life. For remember, my child, your Church is but a parasite newly sprung from the stem of an ancient tree; until the reign of Henry the Eighth, no other belief than that of the Catholic Church was known. Millions have feasted, as the twelve did on the night of that Holy Thursday, and have journeyed on to eternity, terrible to the devils, and independent of the evil world, because they have been in the family, and have eaten the Lamb that was slain to deliver them. Then again, my dear, what do you suppose St. Paul meant when he said, ' Whoso eateth and drinketh unworthily, not discerning the Lord's Body, eateth and drinketh judgment (or as your Bibles have it, damnation) to himself?' Marion, God does not deal judgment and damnation lightly round Him, and really I cannot see why Protestants are threatened with it here. How can they discern what does not exist? If the Body of Christ is not in that bread, nor in that cup, why this heavy denunciation for not discerning it? To Catholics this verse is plain enough, for surely judgment and damnation are due to him who would dare to receive that humble host or chalice, which veil the living presence of Almighty God, as common bread and wine."

"But, Mrs. Darrell, where is the man, let him be ever so holy, who would be worthy to touch God?"

"Nowhere, Marion. But men like our priests, who devote their lives to His service, are more worthy to touch Him than the men who crucified Him. Do you not think so?"

"That was different: Christ consented to the humiliation of His Passion for our sakes."

"And He consents to be handled by sinners now for our sakes. Can you not see that if He comes down upon our altars of His own free will, it is for the very purpose of being handled by our priests, and received by men less pure even than themselves? I can understand a priest prostrate on the ground beneath the sense of his unworthiness, and yet saying Mass ten minutes afterwards with the greatest confidence. Do you imagine the Virgin Mother of God considered herself worthy for one moment to perform the duties of that sacred maternity? Certainly not, but we can fancy her still less shrinking from those duties on the score of unworthiness. Had we scaled the heights of heaven to find the Blessed Sacrament and bring It to our altars, then, indeed, one might talk of God outraged by man; but while He Himself, of His own free will, visits His creatures in their nothingness, we may not shrink from Him. And who would wish to do so? O my child! you may love God; I believe sincerely that, in common with many Protestants, you do; but the warmest Protestant piety must be cold beside even ordinary Catholic devotion. You must not mistake me in saying this. God forbid that I should arrogate to ourselves, individually, warmer hearts in the cause of religion than you! It is not that. It is that there is a reality, a warmth, a home-feeling, if we may so style it, in the Catholic Church, that one looks for in vain elsewhere."

"Of course, dear Mrs. Darrell, with such a belief as yours, religion must be one golden, glorious dream. But it cannot be true."

"It is true," said Mrs. Darrell, kissing her, " true as God, for it is God Himself. To-night, of course, I have only given you a few points of this important subject; there are many more, and to-morrow I will lend you some books, and you shall read them for yourself. That is if you would like to do so."

"Of course I should like," said Marion, energetically; "let me take them to church and read them during the Mass. Somehow this idea seems the most beautiful one I ever heard of. Catholics ought to be good; I should think they would never dare to go inside a church, if they had done wrong."

Mrs. Darrell smiled. "That would be rather hard, Marion. God does not bear with sinners the less patiently because He hates sin with an inexorable hatred. Hence the Sacrament of Penance."

"Penance! O Mrs. Darrell! that is dreadful! I never hear the word without thinking of the pilgrims of Loretto with peas in their shoes. I never can understand how any one can believe in getting to heaven by doing penance."

"Ah, Marion, that shows that you know just as much of the Sacrament of Penance, as you did just now of the Holy Eucharist. But we will not talk of this to-night. You have quite enough to think of for the present."

"I have indeed."

At this moment the supper was brought in, and soon after they retired. But it was late before Marion's light was extinguished, for she sat a whole half-hour in a reverie before she commenced her preparations for the night, and then the sixth chapter of St. John was read and re-read many times. During all this time, Golden-hair never thought once of Henry Lisle.

CHAPTER XIV.

"I AM very sorry, my dear," said Mrs. Darrell, the next morning, to her little guest, "I have mislaid the key of the closet, in which I had placed several books, but I will look for it, and give you the volumes I promised you as soon as I find it. Do you think you had better go to Mass with me this morning, it is so very cold?"

"Surely, if you can bear it, it will do me no harm," said Marion.

"I do not know that; we Catholics get used to inclement weather and untimely hours; you hardly ever went out so early on such a cold morning in your life, I should think."

"If I were at home, I should very likely be just starting for the schools, to help the teacher cut out, and fix the work for the children. I generally go twice a week; it is so much for her to do by herself, poor thing."

"Well done, little Marion! I had no idea you were so handy or so industrious!" exclaimed Mrs. Darrell.

"What time did they come home from the ball?" asked Marion.

"Between four and five o'clock this morning. Betsy sat up for them, and had plenty of hot coffee ready. I do not expect we shall see any of them very soon."

At this moment the door opened, and Emily entered, beaming and bright as usual.

"Why did you get up so soon, my child?"

"Because I did not care to stay in bed; I never like to make the morning pay for the night's dissipation."

"Why, Emily, you are quite a little miracle; it is more than I could do, and I am stronger than you."

"I do not like missing Mass; things never seem to go right all the day afterwards, if I do."

Marion glanced at Mrs. Darrell, but she said nothing.

"Well, and did you and Edith make many conquests last night?" asked her mother.

"What do you suppose, mamma? Why, if these had been the days of chivalry, I expect you would have had half-a-dozen heralds at the door by this time, all making proposals for the hands of your daughters at once. But as they do things more quietly nowadays, I suppose they will not come."

"No; but seriously, Emily, how did the ball go off, and how did you enjoy yourself?"

"The ball went off very well: just as I expected, there was a great deal of dancing in a very small space; a great deal of dress, and very little taste; and a great deal of laughing, flirting, and talking, but very little said, and—shall I go on, mamma?"

"Yes, do; what?"

"Do not say anything about it to papa, or he might think me ungrateful, but it seemed to me that a great deal of time and money had been expended for very little enjoyment."

"I am sorry you did not enjoy yourself."

"I did not say that, mamma, dear; I really got on very well, but you know I do not care for these things. I love a quiet dance at home, or a cosy little party round a winter's fire, or a friendly picnic, or anything of that kind; but I am a thorough homebird, and should never care to put my nose outside The Cedars, except for church. I do love home!" and the sweet face brightened like a sunbeam.

"May you never tire of it, my darling."

"Tire of it! O mamma! that would be to tire of all of you; for if you were not here, The Cedars would be as indifferent to me as any other place."

"And how did Edith get on?"

"Very well indeed; she, at least, thoroughly enjoyed herself, and when she had danced a little time, and grew excited, she really looked very nice. Those red geraniums suited her dark hair and complexion so well. As for Joe, he spent the greater part of his time with Dora."

"With Dora! I thought Jessie was his favourite?"

"It seems not, for he took very little notice of her; nor do I think his attentions to Dora would have been so exclusive, but he knew so few of the girls there."

"Poor fellow! These long voyages make him quite a stranger at home," said his mother.

Emily glanced anxiously at Marion. "Whatever her feelings with regard to Joe, she is not jealous of him," she thought. She was certainly not, for she did not even notice that he had been mentioned. She was at that moment deeply engrossed in recalling the conversation of the previous evening. The fact was, that Marion could think of nothing else, and it was not till Mrs. Darrell had addressed her twice that she started from her reverie.

"It would be an insult to offer a penny for such thoughts as those," said Emily: "from the earnest expression of the face, I should say gold would not have bought them."

Marion laughed. "I hardly know what I was thinking of myself, but it led me to the conclusion that this is a very strange world."

"A conclusion more true than original," replied Emily. "It is a very strange world, and in some things a very silly world, and, I am afraid," she added, almost in a whisper, "in many things a very dangerous one."

"It is getting on for nine," said Mrs. Darrell, looking at her watch; "it is almost time to start. As I cannot get those books I want for you, here is a little one I should like you to look through. You read French, do you not? It is entitled 'Elevations sur la Sainte Eucharistie;' it is in no way a controversial work, but a book of devotion. The subject is the Blessed Sacrament. I have often thought that if such volumes as these found their way more frequently into the hands of Protestants, they would do much more in teaching them what our religion really is, than any amount of controversy and discussion. Of course the truth cannot be known unless it is explained, but I am sure, if Protestants were to read such works, they would be astonished at the depth of fervour they display—but come, it is time to go."

It was in vain that Marion tried to fix her thoughts upon her book, although it bore so completely on the subject engrossing her mind. She closed it soon after the commencement of Mass, and remained during the rest of the time with her eyes rivetted on the altar, weighing and re-weighing Mrs. Darrell's words of the night before.

"I can well understand," she thought, "that converts to the Catholic religion must see everything in the world very differently to what they did before.—God on the Altar! Jesus among His

people, as He was before His death ;" and then she added, for
about the twentieth time that morning, "it cannot be true, and
I will not think any more about it." But she did think for all
that, again and again, and it was not till Mrs. Darrell touched
her arm to tell her she was going, that she woke from her dream.
Yet amid all her pros and cons Golden-hair forgot to pray, forgot to ask the Dweller on the Altar to reveal His presence to her
in His own way, and so she questioned and wondered on.

As they were leaving the church porch, the little boy who had
served Mass ran after them, and turning round they saw the
priest standing at the door of the Presbytery.

"I wanted to see you," he said, as he ushered them into his
little parlour, where his breakfast was prepared, "to ask you to
go and visit an old woman for me, who, finding herself really ill,
is showing, they tell me, some signs of repentance, after staying
away from the sacraments for thirty years. I was just going up
to see her, when it struck me that a visit from you might do some
good by way of preparation, more particularly as I fear the poor
creature has been neglected during her illness. You have been
instrumental in helping to save so many lost sheep, that I really
should like you to see her. She lives in Spencer's Gardens ; you
will easily find her out, I think."

"Oh, I have a poor family there, too," said Emily, "so I will
go with mamma."

"But what will Marion do ?" asked Mrs. Darrell. "We had
better walk home with her first."

"Spencer's Gardens is a very short distance," said Father
Stirling ; "I should propose that Miss Howard stay here till you
return. I daresay she will excuse me if I go on with my breakfast, for I assure you I begin to need it. Shall it be so ?"

Marion answered with a smile. Father Stirling placed a chair
for her by the fire, and the two ladies took their departure.

"Don't you convert her, Father Stirling," cried Emily, running
back from the house door, where her mother was condoling with
the old housekeeper on her rheumatism.

"I am too busy," said the priest, pouring out his coffee.

"You have been very gay, I hear, up at The Cedars lately,"
said Father Stirling, after a short conversation, the topic of which
had been the warm hearts that had just quitted them.

"Rather."

"We shall have you going back to Ennington quite a dissipated
young lady. Did you enjoy yourself at the ball last night ?"

"I did not go," returned Marion, "on account of my cold."

"I was thinking that you were out rather early after such a
night of hard work."

"Emily went, though, and they did not get home till past four
this morning, yet she would not miss Mass."

Father Stirling smiled. "Quite right."

"A little longer sleep must have been a great temptation to
her, though ; I should never have resisted it."

" Perhaps not ; every one is not Emily Darrell. I suppose you were disappointed in not going to the ball ? "

"No, indeed, I was not. I do not like the idea of a public ball."

" I think, as a rule, they are best avoided ; but you see, in this instance, Mr. Darrell's party, with the friends they expected to meet there, would form quite a little coterie ; so that it was almost the same thing to Edith and Emily as a party at their own house."

"But I am glad I did not go," observed Marion. "I spent a nice quiet evening with Mrs. Darrell instead, and I made a discovery."

"A discovery! Of what kind? Did you get among Mr. Darrell's telescopes ? "

"No, we wandered among subjects higher even than the stars, and I learnt something I never knew before."

"What was that ? " asked Father Stirling, laying down his knife and fork.

" I learnt, for the first time, what you believe in your doctrine of transubstantiation, and why you believe it."

" And was that all ? "

" All ! that has given me something to think about for the next month."

" I could wish, dear child, that you had gone further still," said the priest, "and that beneath His Sacrament you had found the Author of that transubstantiation Himself."

"That could not be, Father Stirling," replied the young girl, "because He is not there. I have thought well over all that Mrs. Darrell said last night, but though I think the idea most beautiful, it is impossible."

" Remember you speak of God," said the clergyman.

" I know that," replied Marion, " but the day of miracles is past, and God now adheres to the laws of nature in everything. For one substance to be changed instantaneously into another would be contrary to those laws ; and though we know that God could set them aside (for He can do anything), still we know He never does."

." I understand," said Father Stirling ; "you meant to say our belief was improbable, not impossible."

" Well, yes, I think I did," said Marion, after a few seconds' consideration ; "the word impossible cannot, of course, apply to God."

" Very well, and you consider this doctrine improbable, because you say it is opposed to the laws of nature. But remember, to be opposed to the laws of nature is one thing, to be above them is another. For instance, the doctrine of the Blessed Trinity, which Catholics and Protestants hold in common, is not opposed to the laws of nature, it is above them. Human ideas of even the world around us are so limited, that things which at first sight have appeared utter impossibilities, have frequently become every-day facts in the end. What think you would our sires have said only a hundred years ago to the idea of their children travelling by steam, talking by the flash of an electric spark, painting by the sunbeam, and passing with rapidity through the air by the aid of an invisible fluid? And yet all these things now enter into the every-day occurrences of life.

"Do not, however, for one moment think that I bring down this glorious doctrine of the Church to such a standard as this. I merely wish to show you that if things as purely natural as these, have been treated as hallucinations, because they have been counted impossible, people may easily consider things super-natural—things that never can be brought within the scope of human reason—as contrary to nature too. It is very strange that, though in the material world men see things every day which they cannot explain, yet in the higher sphere of the spiritual world they reject everything that cannot be demonstrated with the nicety of a mathematical problem. A man who cannot read the thoughts of his own child, disbelieves and scoffs because he cannot penetrate the secrets of the Most High. Physicians tell us that in the course of a few years every particle of the human body has been renewed, but that the process has been so gradual, that not a scar or spot has been removed, and very often not a feature altered. Yet for all this, does a man lose his identity? Am not I—who, according to this theory, must have been renewed many times—the actual George Stirling of my youth? You may well smile, for this is a strange thing, and a thing hard to demonstrate, that a man should be at once the same, and yet a different being. A tiny infant comes into the world, and in a few years' time a man six feet high stands in that infant's place. Whence then has come this vast increase of bulk? Has not food, solid and liquid, been changed into flesh and blood, bone and muscle? This, my child, is no less strange than true. Suppose a being from another sphere, who knows nothing of our world, were told that the oak tree once lay in the acorn shell. Would he credit you? Would he not say 'impossible'? A man, Miss Howard, who lives in such a world as ours—a world that sprung into existence from nothing at one word of its Creator, must beware how he talks of things that are simply above his com-prehension as contrary to Nature. Even the spectacle of the world around us, may lead us to the appreciation of the far more wonderful things to be found in a higher sphere, though as earth is lower than heaven, so are God's operations in the natural, lower than His revelations in the supernatural. In the words of the poet, though in perhaps a different sense, man may look 'through Nature up to Nature's God,' for he may tread with a firm foot the path of scientific investigation, if he will but remember that he is on holy ground. Then every step as it leads him onward shall lead him also upward, and as he has found wonders in the Kingdom of Nature, so shall he be prepared for miracles in the Kingdom of Grace, and mysteries in the Kingdom of Glory.

"But then you tell me that the age of miracles has passed ; are you sure of this? If the Bible spoke of none after our Lord's Ascension, I could better understand your assertion, but the Acts of the Apostles contain several. Or had this miraculous power extended only to the chosen twelve, I could have understood you better, but the last chapter of the same book contains two miracles of St. Paul, and he never even knew our Lord during the time of His mortal life on our earth. When, therefore, did it cease? Never, my child. The same God who turned water into wine at the marriage feast of Cana, who changed the Egyptian river into blood, who transformed the rod of Moses into a serpent, and that serpent again into a rod, and who will one day call many a bright glorified body from death and corruption, works His miracles ever. Sometimes by human agency, as in the actions of the apostles and subsequent saints ; sometimes by visible interference, as in the conversion of St. Paul ; sometimes by a secret act of His Almighty Will, as in the mysteries of the Altar."

He ceased, but Marion remained silent.

"Doubtless," he added, "in all that I have said, I have only repeated Mrs. Darrell's words, for I have simply given you some plain and palpable reasons for not rejecting this doctrine, which must occur to every one."

"No," replied Marion, "Mrs. Darrell spoke in quite a different way to me ; she tried rather to make me understand what this doctrine is, and why Christ should institute such a sacrament, than to reconcile it, as you have been doing, with the dispensations of Providence generally. Father Stirling, I cannot tell you how I feel. Sometimes the idea of such a truth as this would be, seems heaven itself, and I feel as if I would give up everything to believe it ; but then the thought comes over me, that to do so I must be a Catholic altogether, and there are many things in your religion that seem so very strange, almost dreadful to me, that I could never, never believe them."

"Do not trouble yourself about them, my child ; bend all your thoughts and prayers to this one subject, to this doctrine which, in spite of all your conflicting doubts, you half believe already."

Marion shook her head. "It is impossible that it should be true, and yet that so many people should be ignorant of it."

"Do you know how stand the comparative numbers of the Catholic and Protestant world? In the last table I saw, the Catholics were computed at one hundred and ninety-five millions, and the Protestants at about ninety-seven millions ; so, you see, that although we make a comparatively small show in England, Scotland, and one or two other European countries, you must consider how we stand in Europe generally, in South America, and a very large portion of North America. Why, even the Greek schismatics almost equal the Protestants! But it is not by statistics that we can decide the truth or falsehood of a doctrine. Does not our

Blessed Lord Himself say, 'This is My Body, this is My Blood,' and dare we contradict Him?"

"I have just thought of something," said Marion, after a pause. "Christ says, 'I am the vine, ye are the branches,' does He not speak figuratively here?"

"Of course He does, in the same way as when He calls Himself the door of the sheepfold. He chose to be born the Son of an Eastern nation, and He loved to use Eastern metaphor."

"Then why may He not have used a metaphor in instituting the Eucharist?"

" In one sense He did, for bread, that is the support of human life, is a beautiful metaphor of Him who is the food and sustenance of our souls. But then our Lord had prevented His words from being understood only in a metaphorical sense, by having already approved and praised His apostles for accepting His promise, that He would give them His flesh to eat, in a literal sense. 'Then said Jesus to His disciples, Will you also go away?' Besides, bread and wine in themselves do not convey to us the idea of something else, as a statue or picture does, and you must remember, moreover, that when our Lord pronounced the words of consecration, He had not said anything from which the apostles could gather that He was going to institute bread as a sign of something else. So that when we read that He took a piece of bread in His hand, and emphatically declared, 'This is My Body,' the apostles could only understand Him as declaring *what* that was which He held in His Hand. And when He says that It is His Body, shall not I also believe Him and accept with my whole heart and soul the affirmation of Infinite Wisdom? I remember an answer once given by an old man to a scoffer, which afforded him a great deal of amusement, but which made a very opposite and indelible impression upon me, boy as I was at the time. He was a very old man with silvery hair, and I can see him now sitting at his cottage table, poring over his Bible.

"'You don't mean to say you believe all that, do you?' asked the person I alluded to (one of the would-be wits of the rising generation, young men who disbelieve because it is fashionable so to do, often without knowing why), 'you don't mean to say you believe all that!'

"'Every word, master,' said old William.

"'You are surely not fool enough to believe that the whale swallowed Jonah alive, and then spit him out again upon dry land?'

"'Master, I should believe that Jonah swallowed the whale, if the Bible said so,' returned old William, 'because it is the word of God.'

"And old William's answer is quite in the spirit of the Church. Our Blessed Lord holds a piece of bread in His hand, saying, 'This is My Body,' and I believe Him. Without pointing to any object, while showing His disciples how they must depend on Him in all their spiritual life, He represents Himself as a vine or door. Had He pointed to any object, however small, however strange, however apparently insignificant, I should have believed Him, had He only said, 'Behold Me!' But this He never did, nor was there ever any religion in existence that believed in the actual presence of our Lord under any form, save and except the Catholic Church, in the Sacrament of the altar."

A silence of many minutes ensued, as Father Stirling began to stir his cold coffee in an abstracted manner. When at length he raised his eyes to glance at his little visitor, he pitied her amid the shadow of perplexity that had fallen on the young face.

"I never thought," she said at length, "that the Word of God could be so difficult to interpret."

"Then do not try to interpret it, dear child, by your private judgment, or every moment you will advance still deeper in the mire of perplexity. Take, rather, the inspired interpretation of St. Paul, 'the Chalice of Benediction that we bless, is it not the communion of the Blood of Christ, and the Bread that we break, is it not the partaking of the Body of the Lord?' Or going higher still, bow in simple faith at the words of Jesus Christ, 'and the Bread that I will give is My Flesh, for the life of the world.'"

As the priest uttered these words in a tone intense in its devotion, Marion trembled. Once more there was silence, soon broken however by the sound of footsteps on the garden path.

"Mrs. Seymour and her daughters," said Father Stirling, glancing at the window.

"I could not speak to them just now, really," cried Marion, rising from her chair, " are they coming in here?"

"Yes, for a short time, but you need not see them; come with me;" and crossing the passage he opened a small door. "Go into the church, my child; you will find One there who will tell you more in a heart-whisper, than I could do in the years of the longest life-time."

Mrs. Seymour's visit lasted longer than Father Stirling had anticipated, and before it was concluded, Mrs. Darrell and Emily returned from their visit to Spencer's Gardens.

As soon as the former had taken her departure, and the latter had given an account, spiritual and temporal, of the old woman, Father Stirling entered upon the subject of Marion Howard. "She is even now," said he, in conclusion, "upon her knees, before the Blessed Sacrament. If, however, you will take my advice, you will not mention the subject of religion to her. Answer all her questions, pray for her very hard, offer your communions for her, and leave the issue to God."

CHAPTER XV.

ALTHOUGH from this time Marion's mind was in a great measure occupied by one subject, no casual observer would have said that anything more than usual interested her. She laughed, chatted,

danced, rode, and even, under the patronage of Dora and Jessie, began
to skate. She wrote regular accounts to her mother of her gay life
at Harleyford, visited the poor with Mrs. Darrell, helped with the
Christmas trees at the schools, seeming in all things to live only in
the excitement of the present moment. Only He who witnessed
those long night prayers, in which the little weary soul struggled
with its convictions at His feet, knew that amid all her merriment
one thought was ever uppermost.

"I cannot bear it any longer," she exclaimed, one Saturday
night, about a fortnight after her conversation with the priest, "I
cannot bear it! I must see Father Stirling again, and tell him all
I think and feel," and she gazed through her tears at "Keenan"
and the little black Bible, both of which lay open before her.
"This little book," she continued, taking up the former, "has been
like a fairy wand, revealing hidden treasure. The Catholic religion
must be true ; the chain of reasoning that proves it is so perfect !
But somehow, though I understand, I cannot feel it ; I seem half
stupefied by the rush of thoughts that the subject brings with it,
and hardly seem to pray at all. If I look into the future now, I
can realise nothing, and I feel frightened. It is all very well to
think about the Catholic religion here, at The Cedars, in the bosom
of a Catholic family, but what would it be to return to Eunington?
What would mamma say? what would she do? What would
every one in the village think and say—my class at the school—the
people that I visit—Edward—Mr. Lisle?" But on these two last
names Marion dared not, and did not, dwell. Notwithstanding
the pliability of her disposition, she could be firm ; and from the
moment she commenced to study the subject, it was with a strong
determination, come what might, to follow the truth. Her fire
burned very low, before she rose from her knees, and when at last
she lay down, it was not to sleep, for she tossed about restlessly
till the morning.

That day, Marion attended the service at the Protestant Church.
It is rather to be feared, however, that the pastoral address of the
Rev. Mr. Gardiner received but small attention from our little
heroine, whose thoughts would fly where she least wished. Then
more than one letter was written in imagination to Edward, and
more than one scene pictured with another, dearer still.

"How wicked this is !" was her self-accusation, as she shook
back her curls in vexation ; "I shall very likely remain a Protestant
after all."

Marion stayed a short time after the dismissal of the congregation, to look at some mural tablets. As she was about to pass out
of the church door, she perceived Mr. and Mrs. Gardiner on the
step before her. With a slight bow she would have passed on, but
her former spiritual physician, who had recognised her, held out
his hand.

"Miss Howard, I believe?"

Marion smiled.

"I am glad to see you looking somewhat brighter than when

I saw you, four or five years ago. And somewhat grown, too, eh ? How young people spring up, to be sure !—Miss Howard, my love."

The lady bowed very frigidly.

"Staying at The Cedars, I presume ?" resumed Mr. Gardiner.

Marion replied in the affirmative.

" I wonder you are not afraid to trust yourself there ! "

" Why should I be so ? "

" For fear of getting converted, or, rather, perverted."

" I love Mrs. Darrell's family too well to fear them."

" Humph ! Depend upon it they will try. Trust a Romanist for leaving no stone unturned to make a proselyte ! "

" Is that a discredit to them ? " inquired Marion ; " what good would it do them individually, if all the world were Catholic ? "

" This good, that they imagine their own salvation ensured, if they can only, by hook or by crook, make one convert."

" Excuse me, if I say I think you are mistaken in attributing such a belief to them," replied Marion, beginning to feel annoyed at Mr. Gardiner's manner, " but even if it were so, one could hardly blame them for zeal in saving their own souls, as well as another person's at the same time. Besides, however they may strive to further, or bring about conversions, we must remember that people can only become Catholics by their own free will and deed."

" Ah, young lady, you do not understand them quite as well as I do ! " returned Mr. Gardiner. " They have a hundred ways of making black white, and wrong right. The less one has to do with them the better, I say. I warn you especially, mind, against that priest—Father Stirling I believe they call him, a thorough Jesuit. He had better take care, or I shall be down upon him some day."

Marion's cheeks told that she was in a state of quiet suffocation.

" If he would keep away from my congregation," continued the clergyman, " and confine himself to his own Irishmen, I should not care. What business has he to interfere with Protestants, I should like to know, ' creeping into houses, leading captive silly women ! ' "

" What is the matter now ? " asked Mrs. Gardiner sharply.

" That he has induced one or two more poor silly fools to give up their religion, and go to his ginger-bread chapel. Only look at Mr. Darrell's lodgekeeper, he never rested till he had induced her to go over."

Marion could restrain herself no longer. " Father Stirling never spoke to her in his life, Mr. Gardiner," she exclaimed, " until she called on him of her own accord, to speak to him about religion. May I ask if you know Father Stirling personally ? "

" Not I, I never spoke to him in my life."

" It is a great pity, for I am sure you would like him if you knew him as he is. A more perfect gentleman I never met, and he is as amiable as he is intelligent."

K

"Humph," said Mr. Gardiner, "all the more dangerous; did you ever hear of 'whited sepulchres'?"

"Often, but what have they to do with Father Stirling?"

A sarcastic smile was the clergyman's only reply.

"Do you intend honouring our school-treat next Wednesday?" he asked, suddenly changing the subject.

"Next Wednesday? I am sorry to say I am already engaged for the Catholic one. Mrs. Darrell has given a Christmas Tree, and I have promised to help to distribute the presents."

"If I give you a little piece of advice, Miss Howard, will you be offended?"

"To tell you the truth, Mr. Gardiner, I think I very likely shall. You might say what you pleased of myself, and I would take it in good part, but when you speak of the religion and friends of Mr. and Mrs. Darrell, as you did just now, I do feel very angry. You will think me rude in saying this, perhaps, but although I have been among Catholics ever since I left home, I can assure you that your words this morning have been the only unkind ones I have heard all the time I have been at Harleyford. Good morning," and Marion passing quickly on, left the pastor at the gate of his own church, looking very angry and uncomfortable.

"How stupid you are, to be sure, about the Catholics!" exclaimed his wife. "I know you will never cease till you get into hot water with every one in the parish; you are already on bad terms with the Churchwardens, and at daggers-drawn with the Guardians. I wonder how much the Dissenters care whether you approve of their love-feasts or not, while, as for the Romanists, of course they make fun of you. Can they help laughing, when they see their very name act on you like the red cloak on a Spanish bull? How you bothered that poor girl, just because she happens to be staying with Catholics! Half the good families are growing disgusted, and you will soon have your congregation getting as sick and tired of such nonsense as I am."

"I must do my duty, nevertheless," replied her husband.

"Your duty!" she repeated impatiently, "it seems a strange kind of duty that consists in setting your own parishioners by the ears with each other! You must begin to practise what you preach, depend upon it, if you want to do your duty."

Poor Mr. Gardiner groaned under the yoke of his Xantippe, and writhed beneath the rattle of his golden fetters.

That afternoon, much to the delight of Joe and his sisters, Marion went with them to the church. Father Stirling preached, and his subject was the manifestation of Christ to the Gentiles. First he told the story of the Star of Bethlehem shedding its mild light over the pagan world, and of the three kings that followed it, leaving their thrones and diadems to seek an Infant lying in a manger. Then he spoke of the Star of Truth, whose soft ray gleams often suddenly on the hitherto darkened vision, and lights up a path that must be followed, even though it should lead from riches to poverty, and from honour to contempt. He counted the cost of such a passage, faithfully, but described the glorious recompense to be found for its sacrifices in the treasure-house of the Church, in the love of God, and the prayers of Mary. Then while his eyes gleamed with fervour, and his voice trembled with emotion, he spoke of the Sacred Heart, spoke of it with its human yearning and divine love, its earthly sympathies and its almighty power. He talked of the dying life to be lived for God, of the living death for the world, and of that interior life which is the soul that animates all the Christian virtues. And then, turning suddenly to the altar, he stretched forth his hand, and appealed to God Himself, as a witness to the truth of every word that he had uttered. The action was a momentary impulse, but it touched one little Protestant to the heart, and from that moment Marion Howard felt that Jesus, God and Man, was before her in the tabernacle. Her head had been convinced, her heart was now penetrated, and when the little bell tinkled amid the hushed breath of the congregation, when the benediction, not of earth, fell on the kneeling worshippers, Marion, like a second Thomas, cried, prostrate before the same Lord and Master: "My Lord and my God!"

The two sisters and Joe lingered in the church so long after benediction, that the afternoon twilight faded into darkness, but still Marion remained with Father Stirling, whom she had sought at the close of the service. It would be hard to say which of the three prayed the most devoutly in the dark church, whose only light was the fitful gleam of the tabernacle lamp. It was a solemn hour to each, especially to the young sailor, whose warm heart had clung to the little heretic, even from their childhood, and he bowed his head before the image of Mary, and prayed long and fervently.

When, at last, Marion joined them, it was in company with Father Stirling, and they all returned together to The Cedars. While the girls were upstairs, the priest mentioned Marion's visit to his friends. "She has commissioned me to tell you this," he observed, in conclusion, "and I can say that never in my life have I seen any one so resolved in so short a period of time. She has made good use of her visit to you, for she already understands all the leading doctrines of the Church quite well. I was many times astonished at the pertinence of her remarks, and the depth of her questions and answers. She seems very intelligent."

Joe's eyes danced with pleasure.

"Well, Father, you have indeed brought us good news," said Mr. Darrell.

"There are one or two points she is rather uninstructed in, even now," said Father Stirling. "But she must come to me as often as she likes."

"I wonder whether she will meet with much opposition," said Mr. Darrell, musingly. "I should not much like to have to play at cross purposes with that mother of hers. She has wonderfully softened down of late, I believe, but she used to have a tremendous spirit."

"As a school-girl, she certainly had," observed his wife.

"Oh, later than that, my dear. I never saw much of her before her marriage, but I know that poor Howard never got on so well with her, as when he let her have her own way. I have often heard him say, that she could bear anything better than contradiction, and this is unfortunately just what she will have now, and I feel half afraid."

"But she is very fond of Marion," returned his wife, "and as this is, I am sure, the first time that the child has ever acted contrary to her wishes in her life, I have no doubt the storm will soon blow over. At any rate, it will not do to meet troubles half-way. I think it is only natural, though, that Protestant parents should feel these things severely; fancy what we should endure if it were one of our children."

"If I turned Mormon, for instance, or went over to Mr. Gardiner," said Joe.

"The cases are not parallel," replied Father Stirling; "where is the Catholic parent who would not rather see his son dead, than that he should come to this? But, if Protestants felt as deeply, would they allow their children to read the books of other sects, and go to other places of worship, as they do?"

"I think Marion will make a good little Catholic," observed Mrs. Darrell.

"As far as I can judge," replied Father Stirling, "it seems to have been the doctrine of the Real Presence that first attracted her. She herself traces everything to her conversation with you, the evening before you both called upon me."

Mrs. Darrell smiled. "Does it not seem," she observed, "that there are some minds into which a belief in the Blessed Sacrament flashes instantaneously, like light into a room the moment the shutters are opened?"

"Exactly so; and you have been very happy to have been the first to unbar those shutters."

"Not so, Father," replied the lady, "they were too hard and high for me, though I tried my best; it was your strong hand, after all, that let in the light."

"'Non nobis Domine, sed nomini tuo da glorium,'" sang the priest, as the girls re-entered the room.

They spent a very happy evening; Joe was full of fun, and told sea stories and college scrapes by the dozen. Father Stirling and Mr. Darrell played at chess in the corner, while Edith and Emily played and sang. Every one was surprised when ten o'clock struck, none more so than Marion, who had been chatting with Mrs. Darrell during the greater part of the evening.

"You have not felt quite so uncomfortable about the Catholic Sunday to-night, as you did some few years since, have you?" asked the latter of her young companion.

"No; but even then Father Stirling made me so thoroughly see the spirit of Catholic Sunday recreations, that I could never misunderstand them again."

"The Church, dear child," said Mrs. Darrell, "is too jealous a guardian of her children's souls to countenance anything injurious to their spiritual welfare, and that she not only permits but encourages such recreations is shown by Father Stirling's presence amongst us to-night. Do as the Church tells you, and all responsibility is immediately shifted from you to her; she bears the burden while you go free. O Marion! if there be a liberty on earth, it is in the obedience rendered by the Catholic to his Church. Can you understand this? Perhaps not yet."

"Yes, I think I can. A Catholic is like a child, who acts simply in obedience to its mother."

"With this difference," replied Mrs. Darrell, "an earthly parent, with all her solicitude, may misdirect her child, whereas, the Church cannot err. I know, of course, that you already understand this well, but just let me hear you explain, in your own words, this 'terrific dogma,' the Infallibility of the Church. Fancy that I am mamma, and that you are trying to convince her that you have done right in becoming a Catholic."

A shadow fell across poor Marion's face, and she sighed heavily; but she shook back her curls, as was her wont in making a fresh determination.

"Really, Mrs. Darrell," she exclaimed cheerfully, "I have thought comparatively little about either the authority or the infallibility of the Church. My one idea has been the Blessed Sacrament. I know that our Lord is upon the altars with us, and I cannot think He would leave His Church in error, and yet be with it unceasingly."

"I perfectly understand you, my dear child," replied her friend, "but though this feeling of calm repose is, as far as I can judge, the best disposition for you individually, still it will not do for mamma, and still less for Mr. Lisle, for I suppose you will have to give a reason to him also for 'the hope that is in you,' will you not?"

The warm blood shot across Golden-hair's cheeks and brow, and then back again to her heart, leaving her paler than before. Not Curtius himself, not the Decii, ever gave life more heroically than Marion Howard now laid the happiness of her life upon the altar of conscience, nor was the sacrifice less precious that it was made in silence. Quick as she was, Mrs. Darrell did not read the troubled look aright, but supposed that it simply arose from dread of the controversy she had imagined.

"I dare not think yet of what any one in Ennington may say to me," replied she, "I can only put my trust in God. When the moment to answer their questions arrives, I must look to Him to tell me what to say, but it is a moment I truly dread." And absorbed by painful thoughts, Marion sat for some few minutes looking silently into the fire.

"May I ask what it is, that is so to be dreaded?" asked Father Stirling, who, having finished his game, now seated himself at the centre table.

Mrs. Darrell repeated the conversation.

"God Himself, my dear Miss Howard," said the priest, "has flashed the whole truth upon your mind at once, rather than suffered you to learn it word by word, and line by line. As to myself, it was much longer before I saw my way into the Church, though, looking back, I cannot imagine how I could ever have been so blind as not to see the marks that evidently distinguish her as the spouse of Jesus Christ."

"I wish, Father Stirling, you would tell me just a little about the infallibility of the Church."

"I am afraid it is rather late to commence such a subject this evening," said the priest, looking at his watch, "but I dare say I shall have time to say a few words upon it before supper; at any rate, I can give you the salient points, which you can afterwards study for yourself. To commence then, Miss Howard, I would remark that Protestants as well as Catholics admit the fact, that before our Blessed Lord left the world He established a Church. The former are, however, as usual, divided on the subject; for some by the term Church mean a distinct body, such as 'the Church of England,' while others, Dissenters for instance, take it simply to imply those who are faithful to God, let them belong to whatever denomination they may. The latter doctrine cannot, however, relate to the visible body of Christ's Spouse on earth, and it is to this that He has promised infallibility in His pastors, and which He has commanded us, as His flock, to obey; for a body of believers whose membership should consist only in internal acts, could be recognised only by the eye of God Himself, and could not be said to constitute a visible Church.

"According to the Catechism, the Church of Christ must have four marks—she must be One, Holy, Catholic and Apostolic. One, for there must be 'One Lord, one Faith, one Baptism'—holy, for God Himself is holy, and the Church that leads us to Him must be holy too—Catholic, for it must 'teach all nations'—Apostolic, because to the Apostles alone—'go ye and teach'—was delegated the care of souls. Let us consider first the question of unity. I can assure you," and he turned to Mrs. Darrell, "that, although I lived for twenty-six years among Protestants, I rarely found any two who thought alike on every doctrine of religion. Leaving individuals, however, out of the question, we will speak only of general disunion, and that only with regard to important doctrines. Take, for instance, the subject of Baptismal Regeneration. Can any article of faith be more important, more momentous than this? Now, I remember once when I was a young man, asking a clergyman of the Anglican Church, one of the 'evangelical party,' why infants were baptized. As a matter of course he could not tell me, because, poor fellow, he dared not say on tradition (which is the actual fact), and yet by no manner of means, could he wrest any text of the Scriptures into a warrant for infant baptism. So he said a great deal about 'Suffer little children to come unto Me,' which has nothing to do with the question, and talked of St. Paul baptizing the household of Stephanas, amongst which he said most likely there were some little children,* but that was all, and when I asked him what baptismal regeneration meant, he said it was a popish superstition, for though baptism conferred a certain grace on the soul, it could not in any way remit sin. What he made of our Lord's words, 'Ye must be born again of water and the Spirit,' I have not the slightest idea. Now not very long after this, I heard the following words from a Church of England pulpit : 'If your infant be sick, my brethren, bring him to the font, do not delay ; have him baptized at once, or you will never meet your child in heaven.' Which, then, is the teaching of the Anglican Church ? Does she believe baptism to be regenerative or not ? Christ promised to lead His Church into all truth, when the Spirit of Truth should come. Can Truth be coincident with two such extremes as heaven and no heaven for the unbaptized child ? The sweet and bitter water from the same fountain were nothing to this !

"Again, there are churches belonging to the Anglican Establishment, in which the communion is celebrated very frequently (in some, I have been told now, every morning). In this communion part of the communicants believe that what they receive is the Body and Blood of Christ ; while others, and indeed the greater number, believe that it is mere bread and wine. Now, what does this latter extreme say to the tenets of the first extreme of this same Church on this point ? Does it find any epithet too harsh with which to brand such papistical innovations, although both extremes are members of the same Church, both professing union with the one Lord, one faith, one baptism ? What does the Low-Churchman say to that answer in his own catechism touching the communion, 'that the inward part or thing signified is the Body and Blood of Christ, which are *verily* and *indeed* taken and received by the faithful in the Lord's Supper' ? What does he say to the confession heard in the Tractarian church ? or to the translation, almost verbatim, into English, of the absolution we give, and which, poor man, he is obliged to read in his visitation of the sick ? What does he say to the fasts still marked in his own prayer-book, and still practised so religiously by certain members of his own Church ? What of that proudly vaunted apostolic succession, so gloried in by some of his own brethren ? Why, he laughs at it all, and styles those brethren fools ! For the Low-Churchman looks upon his Puseyite brother as a sort of connecting link between truth and error, very much in the theological world what the ape is in the natural one, forgetting that as members of the same Church, they must stand or fall together. And what says the High-Churchman in his turn ? Why, he despises his Low-Church brother from his very heart, talks of him as bringing scandal upon the Church, classes him with the Dissenters, laughs at him, derides him, yet cannot ignore him, uncomfortable eyesore

* An answer actually returned.

though he be! 'Behold, He shall lead you into all truth,' is an
awkward text for a Church, one-half of whose children anathema-
tises the most cherished doctrines of the other.

"With regard to the second mark that is to distinguish the
spouse of Christ, her holiness, do we find it in the Anglican
Church? Can the respectability of her modern pastors and pro-
fessors merit this glorious attribute for a religion whose doctrines
were disseminated by secular authority, represented in the persons
of royal tyrants and sacrilegious nobles? A simple negative may
seem to be a summary disposal of the subject, but do we need
more, while the infamous characters of the first reformers, so-called,
are patent to every one who has courage to learn the truth, and
while the history of their so-called Reformation is familiar to us,
in all its hideous details, as the nursery rhymes of our babyhood?
Let Protestants answer the question that fell from the lips of our
Divine Lord: 'Shall men gather figs from thorns, and grapes from
thistles?' and then, if they can, let them look for holiness in the
religion of Luther, Zwinglius, or Calvin!

"The third point of the Church, her Catholicity, need hardly
be touched upon with reference to the English Church, and that,
for the simple reason, that she is only the Church of a portion of
one nation, having neither position, power, nor jurisdiction, in
any country but England and a few of its colonies. She is
essentially a National Institution, and nothing more.

"The fourth point, namely, the claim of Anglicanism to the
apostolic succession, we will consider presently. Let us now look
into the Catholic Church, and let us see on what she founds her
title to be the one, holy, catholic, apostolic Church of Christ.
Just now I told you I had never found two Protestants whose creed
was precisely the same; now, with my hand upon my heart, I tell
you, that I have rarely found two Catholics to differ. Go back with
me to those days when Jesus, seated among His chosen twelve,
first spoke these words: 'Thou art Peter, and upon this rock I
will build My Church, and the gates of hell shall not prevail
against it.' The ark floating on the dark waters of the flood, is a
splendid metaphor of that Church, within the precincts of which,
safety alone is to be found."

"But people may be saved who are out of the Church, you said
this afternoon," remarked Marion.

"Out of the visible Church, my child, but the Church of Christ
considers all as her children, who have been baptized. God is not
a hard taskmaster, looking to reap where He has not sown. And
we have, moreover, the hope, that he who has kept faithful in the
uncertain gloom, while others have sometimes, unhappily, stumbled
in the full light, receives his reward accordingly. But, to return
to the unity of the Catholic Church. Do not even her enemies
admit her unchangeableness? What she was in her earliest days,
when her bishops were ex-fishermen, and her temples the cata-
combs of Rome, such she is now. Does any proud spirit attempt
an innovation; the thunders of her excommunication fall upon

him, and he is cut off from her—plucked out—cast away, till he repent, or until he is summoned to answer for his despised birth-right, at the bar of the great assize.

"If you, Miss Howard, knowing as much as you do now of our religion, were to ask me what proof I should give of the holiness of the Church, I should tell you that the best and truest answer is the one that lies most deeply buried in the recesses of a Catholic heart. I speak of that sweet familiarity with the Sacraments and Sacrifice of the Church, that I trust will, in God's own time, flood with its intensity the whole of your being. But if a Protestant asked me this, your mamma, for instance, returning again to the little Catechism, I should tell her that 'the Church is holy because she teaches a holy doctrine, offers to all the means of holiness, and is distinguished by the eminent holiness of so many thousands of her children.' Of course she would say this was simply assertion, and would ask for proof. Then I should compare the Church to one of those grand old temples, raised by our fathers to the glory of God, and should show her that as in them, every line of their architecture points to and culminates in the sanctuary, so in the Church, every dogma, every doctrine, every symbol, every ceremony points to and culminates in the Hill of Calvary. Then I should speak of the seven Sacraments. Of Baptism that sets it seal for ever on the brow from which it has chased the shadow of original sin. Of Confirmation that seals the soul to all eternity, as the shrine of the Holy Ghost. Of Ordination that seals for life and death, the heart, the hand, the whole of the priest to God. I should tell her of Penance that removes the sinner from his sin, as far as the east is from the west; of Matrimony that blesses the joys and sorrows of life; of Extreme Unction that soothes the departing soul, and then I would tell her of the Holy Eucharist, the sun and life of man below. She could not tell me that these seven mystical pillars of the Church were not means of holiness, and I should go on to tell her of the eminent holiness of the children of that Church. Of the Martyrs, Confessors, Virgins, Widows, and Hermits; of her Clergy, regular and secular; of her Religious Orders, active, contemplative, and ascetic, that have graced every age of Christianity; and of the pious souls, not the less saintly because perhaps unseen, who are gracing it now. In answer to this, she would tell me of the purity of the Protestant religion. I should point inflexibly to its originators and promoters. She would tell me how Protestantism teaches the love of God, and belief in Jesus Christ as the Saviour. I should speak of the flower plucked off from the plant, fair to a certain extent with the beauty of the parent tree, preserved for a short time by artificial means, but doomed to die, nay dying, because it has no root. She would point finally to Protestant piety, and I to something deeper still, inasmuch as the fire-tried constancy of solid virtue is deeper than the regularity of a life free from gross sin. Protestantism takes a man as he *appears*, the Church as he *is* before God, tried and tested. If you only knew anything of the process of canonisation, and how strict and searching it is, you would understand better what I mean. Protestantism can appreciate good men, but that is all. She cannot go with the Church into highways and byways, into retired cells and broken-down hovels, and bring forth names long eminent in heaven, though perhaps unknown to the great world. And even could she find such names, she could not try them as the Church tries them, in a seven-fold heated furnace of inquiry, or weigh them as she weighs them, in the balances of perfection. And how, you will say, can the Catholic Church do this? Simply because the Spirit of God is to guide her into 'all truth.' His is the unerring hand that has raised each saint to the altars of the Church, in the same way that His has been the Voice that had called each to a sanctity as much surpassing natural virtue, as the New Jerusalem, that shall have its foundation in the everlasting hills, shall surpass the cities that are founded on the ephemeral rock of this world.

"It would be an insult to your historical and geograpical know-ledge to talk to you of the universality of the Church. Truly, most truly is she Catholic, and that in the widest acceptation of the term, for she covers the earth as the waters cover the sea ! She enters with her sweet intrusiveness whenever men will let her, teaching ever that one same doctrine which without intermission she has taught throughout all the ages of the Christian era. The world has sent its votaries abroad—so has she. Ambition has conquered kingdoms—she has subdued hearts. Self-interest has conciliated savage tribes—her priests have lived among them, or died beneath their weapons ; and when enterprise and science have gone forth, ploughing the oceans, visiting unknown lands, wandering in arid deserts, and penetrating pathless forests, meekly the Church has followed in their wake, gleaning what they despised for the garner of God. Nor do we find her in these distant lands only in the persons of venturing missionaries, these, and the bones of these, are to be found in every quarter of the globe ; but we find also churches firmly established, congregations ever increasing, complete hierarchies dependent on the See of Rome. Yes, truly Catholic, for as the morning sun passes on its way, lighting up a dawn in every land on which it sheds its beams ; in all the twenty-four hours there is not a sun-rise that is not welcomed at some point of its meridian, by the 'Sanctus, sanctus, sanctus,' of the Mass.

"We reserved the claim set forth by the Protestant establish-ment to be the Church founded by Jesus Christ, and built up by the apostles, that we might consider it with those of the Catholic Church. It would be a protracted though easy task to dispose of the conflicting definitions of the apostolic succession, given by the high, low, moderate, and broad-church party, but as you are only interested in those with whose sentiments you have all your life sympathised, I need say very little on the subject. We will not therefore suffer the breath of inquiry to approach that

fine point, so carefully polished and jealously guarded by the
Tractarians, namely, the valid ordination of two of Queen
Elizabeth's bishops—well may they guard it, seeing it is the one
foundation upon which they build the whole of their arguments.
But this question is only important to that section of Protestantism that looks upon ordination, if not as a sacrament, as at least
the cause of effects that would certainly be sacramental, and such
a belief is confined to Tractarianism and its variations. An
ordinary, or rather a commonplace Anglican, looks upon ordination, simply as a certain serious ceremony, that sets apart certain
serious men, to perform certain serious functions. His ordination
service certainly contains the apostolic charge of binding and
loosing, remitting and retaining, but he betakes himself to the
swallowing system, and says, that it means virtually nothing
more than—'go and be a respectable parson.'

"Still, however, though low-church Anglicans thus get rid of
these words as a *charge*, they still stand as a *text*, and must be
explained, wrested, or distorted somehow. They generally give
us one of two solutions; that is to say, some deny the words
addressed to St. Peter ever to have passed beyond himself, while
others assert that he never received anything more from his
Divine Master, than a charge of elder brotherhood. Now what
could be more inconsistent than the first answer? Would our
Lord have conferred a supernatural power on St. Peter, by
which he might direct souls, forgive sins, provide for the
spiritual sustenance of the faithful, in short, govern the Church
infallibly, if He had intended to take this power away again
upon the death of St. Peter? Did all sin, sorrow, and perplexity pass away with his generation, so that spiritual
guidance should never be wanted more? If those who believe that the great apostle received a supernatural power,
but that it ceased with him, could only see how inconsistent
they make our Lord, they would be positively abashed at their
own irreverence. For they acknowledge with us, that when
Christ ascended into heaven His human ministry was ended, and
yet they cannot see that before He left the world He must have
arranged His Church until the end of time. What would have
been the use of an authority, an infallibility, a miraculous power,
a pardoning power, in short, such a God-like power, as they must
see was conferred on this great apostle and his brethren, if they
read their Bibles, if it were destined to pass away in the course
of a few years, to leave the Church still in possession of such a
gift as the atonement, and yet wandering unguided in the darkness
of such a world as this? More consistent certainly are the second
class of whom I spoke, who deny that anything like a supernatural
authority was ever given to St. Peter at all, though, at the same
time, how they fancy they reconcile such an opinion with the
Scriptures, I cannot understand.

"I remember once, when a very young man, attending a
Wesleyan tea-meeting. After the tea and plum cake had been

discussed, the speeches (perhaps I ought to say the addresses)
began. What the generality of these addresses were, whether
good, bad, or indifferent, I certainly do not now remember, but
there was one I have never forgotten. It was on 'isms,' and
having inveighed against Atheism, Deism, Socinianism, Mesmerism,
and Mormonism, the speaker concluded with two, which as a
telling peroration he had reserved to the last, namely, Rheumatism
and Romanism. Why the latter should have been classed with
wrung sinews and aching bones, I have never yet discovered, it
was certainly an original conceit of the speaker! But the
anecdote with which he wound up his discourse was the cream of
the affair. I will give it to you in his own words: 'Once upon a
time,' said he, 'I took my Bible in my hand and went to visit an
old Romanist. Well, dear brethren, I talked to him a long
time about the sinfulness of his heart, and tried to teach him
how faith in Christ could alone save him, and of how little
use prayers to the Virgin Mary and the saints would be to
save his soul from hell. The poor old man, my friends, only
shook his grey head, and began to talk to me of the Church that
could not err, and which he said would carry him to heaven, if he
only believed and obeyed it. "Look here," says he, catching hold
of my Bible, and fumbling over the leaves till he found the
sixteenth chapter of St. Matthew, "read that." I looked, and
there were these words: 'Thou art Peter, and on this rock I will
build My Church, and the gates of hell shall not prevail against
it.' Just didn't the old fellow look triumphant at me through his
spectacles. Wait a bit, my man, thought I, we'll have you yet.
'Well,' says I to him, 'so you think that warrant enough for
putting your trust in Peter, do you?' "Bless the man," cried the
old Romanist, "isn't it as plain as a pike-staff, that St. Peter, bless
him, was made the head of the Church? and sure he couldn't
deceive us, nor be deceived himself!" 'Stop,' says I, 'let's look a
bit further down in the very same chapter, and what do we see?
why, these words spoken to the very same Peter, 'Get thee behind
Me, Satan, for thou art an offence unto Me.' Upon this, the old
fellow, having nothing to say, could only revenge himself by
giving me a good crack on the head with my own Bible.' Such,'
continued Father Stirling, "was the story I heard at the
Methodist tea-party, though I must say the dénouement seemed
so extraordinary, that even then, though prepared for any
enormity on the part of Romanism, I hardly believed it. A crack
on the head would be a most unconvincing argument in favour of
a religion, and would certainly have given me, had I been the
Methodist, an increased distaste for Romanism! For my own
part, however, were I in the place of his antagonist now, I should
be only too glad to have the opportunity of drawing my opponent's
attention to the beautiful consistency of the teaching of the
Church, as exemplified by this very chapter. Peter the Pope—he
who is to be guided by the Spirit of God, to be led into all truth,
to be preserved from all error—the rock upon which the Church

is to be founded, is one thing. Peter the Man, impetuous, erring, fallible, blindly striving to stay his Master from the salvation of the world, another. An infallible church of fallible men ! No wonder such a prodigy as this sounds strange to unbelieving ears.

"I have already shown you, though feebly, very feebly, that the Church is One, Holy and Catholic. What are her claims as Apostolic? Glance at her as she stands, 'exalted above the hills that all nations may flow unto her.' Look at her machinery with its one universal language (unalterable because no longer spoken), its sacraments unchanged and unchangeable, its ceremonies, its priests, its bishops, its cardinals, its pope, successor of St. Peter, upon whom the keys of heaven itself, in the power of binding and loosing, remitting and retaining, were bestowed, and to whom was given that parting injunction of our Lord, 'Feed My sheep, feed My lambs.' Read the story of the Church, it is very simple. Eighteen hundred years ago, as the iron of the soldier's spear entered the side of Jesus, hanging upon the cross, drops of blood, the last drops of the blood shed for the redemption of the world, trickled from the wound. In those ruddy drops the Church took its source. It was a tiny spring, but grew wider and wider, as age after age it rolled, now through the dark shadows of Paganism, now through the very heart of heresy and of anarchy in the empires of the world, struggling in its course with many a rock, but ever flowing onward, ever widening. Do men ask what is the ocular demonstration of the authenticity of the Church? Its very existence—Behold, I am with you. Who but the great 'I am' could have brought His Spouse, bright and undefiled, as in the first morning of her birth, through the fires of martyrdom, and the blackness and corruption of such a world as this?

"Yet Protestants tell us, that even had such a sacrament existed, the chain of the apostolic succession must have been broken amid the frequent confusion of the hierarchy, and assert that two Popes have ruled Christendom at the same time more than once. But had there been half-a-dozen at the same time instead of one, there would only have been five more schismatics for the true Pontiff to anathematise. The existence of counterfeit money does not make the golden coin more or less valuable. More than this, supposing that the archives of the Church were so confused and conglomerated (which certainly they never were), that looking back through the past ages, from the present day, we could not distinctly trace the apostolic succession from Peter to Pius the Ninth (supposing all this, which is perfectly untrue), would it signify? Should we doubt the existence of a river, with the source and mouth of which we were perfectly acquainted, because part of its course lay through an unexplored territory, through which we could not follow it in all its windings? Impossible! while we had ocular demonstration of its existence in its waters.

"It is getting too late this evening for us to treat this great subject at any length, and the books you are reading enter so fully into it, that I do not feel at all uneasy at leaving you with them. Remember this, however, as a parting word. If there be a Church on earth to whom Christ, who cannot lie, spoke the truth, when He promised to guide her into all truth, it is the Catholic Church, and the Catholic Church alone. It is impossible for a Church to be infallible, and yet to deny its own infallibility, since that very denial is an error in itself, and what Church but the Roman Catholic Church dares, or ever has dared, to lay claim to such a mighty prerogative? No wonder that her enemies gaze in astonishment at her mighty pretensions, so different to the tiny voices of the puny sects that have dissented from the dissenting Church! No wonder that men stare in amazement at this religion that has kept its ground, in spite of persecution, misrepresentation, envy, hatred, malice, and all uncharitableness! Catholicity is indeed an enigma to those without. Despising ostentation, she yet heaps together all that is rich, and grand, and sumptuous. Inculcating Christian charity, she cuts off, root and branch, every soul that differs from one iota of her creed. Preaching humility from every one of her pulpits, she yet cries to every sect beyond her pale, 'I am right and you are wrong.' Yet there is nothing paradoxical in this, though there is one answer only to it all. It is the one given by God Himself through the prophet Habacuc, 'the Lord is in His Holy Temple, let all the earth keep silence before Him.'"

CHAPTER XVI.

THREE more weeks of winter snow and frost passed by, of festivity for the rich, and hard living for the poor. Three more weeks of silent reading, long, deep prayers, and earnest conversations in the presbytery parlour, and again it was Sunday morning. Mass was just over, and the greater part of the congregation had dispersed; only a few pious souls lingered, communing still with Him, from whose bright presence they seemed loath to part. But at last even the most fervent had departed, and our little party alone remained in the church; and then the altar tapers were once more lighted, and Father Stirling, wearing his stole and surplice, appeared at the sacristy door. Marion was led to the altar steps by Mrs. Darrell, while the rest of the family, and the Seymours, knelt round. A recantation was read, the waters of conditional baptism flowed, the words of absolution were spoken, and Mrs. Darrell clasped the Catholic Golden-hair to her heart.

Who can describe the rapture of that moment, when the dreary doubts and misgivings of the past, and the dread foreshadowing of coming anger, and perhaps persecution, are lost in the deep, unutterable joy of the present: "I am a Catholic!" And who can describe the feeling of gratitude that swells, at such a season, the hearts that have fostered the bud, and watched in hourly prayer the expanding of the blossom? Our little heroine's friends felt too much to speak, and they had half reached home before even Emily found words in which to congratulate her; but, the ice once broken, a tide of loving welcome flowed around her, and it was a large and joyful party that that morning breakfasted at The Cedars.

About a week afterwards, Marion was sitting very thoughtfully in her room, with an open letter from her mother before her, announcing her intention of returning to Ennington in the course of a few days. It expressed a wish that she should, at the same time, bring her visit at The Cedars to a close, to assist in entertaining her aunt, who, Mrs. Howard said, purposed returning with her from London.

"What shall I do?" cried Marion to herself; "shall I write and tell her all at once, or wait till we meet? I really do not know which would be best, but I will see what Father Stirling advises."

At this moment there was a tap at the door, and, a servant entering, placed a card in her hand. Marion glanced at it, and read, while the letters danced before her—

"Rev. H. Lisle."

"I will be down directly," she said, with a wonderful effort to be calm, and the girl retired. When she had left the room, instinctively our little heroine sank upon her knees, and remained so motionless for full five minutes, that one might have said a soul had fled in the act of prayer; when she rose, an extreme pallor was the only visible sign of the inward conflict. Marion descended the stairs without encountering any of the family, and placed her hand on the handle of the library door. Twice she withdrew it, but, making the sign of the cross, and, shaking back her curls, she grasped it a third time, with a strong hand, and entered with a firm foot.

Mr. Lisle rose to meet her as she advanced; an unwonted agitation, on his own part, prevented him from observing hers.

"You are surprised to see me," he remarked, after a short and rather awkward pause, which had followed the first greetings.

"Rather, but I am very pleased."

Golden-hair, was that true?

"When are you going back to Ennington?" he asked.

"Mamma has written for me to go next week."

"So I understand, from a note I received, in answer to a letter I wrote, asking her permission to come and see you here. The Ennington people will be very glad to have you back, the old women are calling out sadly for flannels this cold weather, and poor Mrs. Dobson is overwhelmed with needlework and teaching. In the latter department I have helped to set things to rights, but the former was rather out of my province. The school-treat, too, has been waiting for your presence; the children would not think half so much of their buns, if Miss Howard were not there · to distribute them."

Marion tried to smile, but the attempt was a sickly one.

"You do not look well," said the curate. "I am afraid you have been keeping late hours."

"Yes, I have," answered Marion.

"You must get home as soon as you can, we can ill spare your roses in these winter days. How have you enjoyed yourself?"

"Very much. Every one has been very kind."

"Is Mr. Stirling living here still?" asked the clergyman, after a short pause.

"Yes. I do not suppose he will ever leave."

"Poor fellow," cried Mr. Lisle, in a tone of deep commiseration, "do you often see him?"

"Yes, very often."

"Has he ever mentioned me to you?"

"Not once," said Marion.

"I have been entrusted with heaps of messages, from all sorts of people," said Mr. Lisle, and he commenced a long description of the events that had taken place in Ennington during her absence, for which Marion felt profoundly thankful, so difficult she found anything like conversation.

"Shall I go and fetch Mrs. Darrell?" she asked, growing more confident, as she found that the visit she had taken at first for one of espionage, was beginning to wear simply the aspect of a friendly call.

"Not yet," said the curate, hurriedly, "I have several things to say to you first."

Marion's heart sank within her.

"I have not told you, yet, the object of my visit."

"No," said Marion, turning very sick.

"I have come," replied he, "because, unless I had run over to visit you to-day, I should not have seen you for a very long time. I start the day after to-morrow for Sandiham, in the south of England. Marion, my ministry at Ennington is ended!"

Had those words been uttered in Marion's ears a month before, life itself would have seemed a blank; as it was, she did not appear to understand him, but looked at him strangely, almost vacantly. Hope rose within his heart, for he misunderstood her.

"Yes, I am going away," he continued; "it seems a strange thought to me, though, that I shall never minister in Ennington church again. I preached a little farewell sermon last night to my dear old friends: I think there are many who will be rather sorry."

Marion remained silent.

"Dr. Stebbing will have to get another curate, directly; I hope you will like him."

"Why are you going so soon?" she asked at length, abruptly.

"Because I must take possession of my new living at once, the one that you know has been promised me for nearly two years. It is in a lovely part of Devonshire; the gentleman in whose gift it is, is one of my oldest and dearest friends, and the parish being largely populated, there is, he assures me, a large sphere of usefulness open to a Christian minister. If it had not been so, sincerely

I may say, I would not have accepted it, much as I require an advancement on my present very limited income. The living is worth about £500 a year, a wonderful increase, is it not," he added, smiling, "for one who has been 'passing rich' upon £120? Sir William Temple tells me that the parsonage house is beautifully situated in its own grounds, and the society round is all that the most difficult to satisfy could desire. Am I not fortunate?"

"Very," said Marion, whose poor little head was whirling.

"Suppose I tell you I am not satisfied."

"Then you are very hard to please," replied Marion, with a touch of her natural manner. "But they say people never are contented here below," and rising as she spoke, she walked to the window and stood looking out into the foggy twilight.

Her companion rose and placed himself beside her; Marion trembled as his hand was laid softly on her shoulder.

"It is in your power, Marion, to make me quite contented."

The hour had come at last.

"It was to speak to you of this," he continued, "that I came here to-day. Marion, dearest, there has been one bright thought that, ever since you were a child, has made the very sunlight of my heart. It is for this that I have been so anxious to get the living—this that has induced me to quit my labour of love at Ennington, for, looking back on many little incidents in our intercourse, I cannot bring my heart to think that I am altogether indifferent to you. May I come and fetch you, Golden-hair, in a little while, to be the mistress of my new parsonage,—my own little wife?"

A sudden shake of the golden ringlets made him fall back. Had he miscalculated his power? Did she not love him after all? The face she turned on him was so white, so death-like in its agony, that the curate fairly quivered with perplexed emotion. In an instant the golden dream of each life lay shattered, as, with every muscle rigid with determination, she exclaimed,

"Mr. Lisle, it is impossible."

"Impossible!" he repeated, "do you not love me, Marion?"

"It is not that," she replied, shaking her head slowly, "it is not that, but the will of God has separated us,—I am a Catholic."

"A Catholic!" he exclaimed, recoiling in horror; "what do you! what can you mean!"

"That, being convinced it is the one true Church of God, I have embraced the Catholic religion."

He could not answer—he did not attempt it, but seating himself upon the sofa and pressing his hands to his throbbing temples, he gazed at the wreck of his happiness, as once when a boy he had gazed at the fragments of a beautiful vase he had just shivered.

Marion continued. "Had it not been for this, I would have lived and died for you, and my only aim in life should have been to have made you happy. What you have been to me, what you are still, God only knows—He, too, only knows what I feel in speaking as I am speaking now. 'But whoso loveth father or

mother more than Me, is not worthy of Me ; ' if even they are to
be given up for God, what must be said of any other earthly tie or
affection ? Do not, pray do not look like that, any burst of anger
would be better than that strange stony look."

A groan was the only reply.

"Could I have borne anything myself, to have saved you this,
I would have done so ; I would have died a thousand deaths rather
than have caused you and mamma this suffering, but it was not to
be ! Poor, dear mamma ! You will go to your new home, and
soon forget me ; but she—it is too dreadful to think of—should
she feel it as much as you do ! Perhaps, however, she will
remember that this is the first time I have ever acted in opposition
to her, and will let me follow the dictates of my own conscience
undisturbed. I have dreaded meeting you more than I can possibly say, though I never thought that it would be like this. But
I am very glad that the first shock is over ; when mamma and
Edward know it, I shall be comparatively happy."

"In their misery !" broke in Mr. Lisle. "O Marion, what are
you made of ? "

"Of something very weak, I fear," she returned, "or human
sorrow at the pain I am causing you would not triumph as it does
just now, over the happiness of having found God in His own
bright and beautiful Church. But, dark as my future prospect is
at this moment, I would not change it for any lot on earth, had I
to be a Protestant again. The happiness of being a Catholic com-
pensates perfectly, I am convinced, for any misfortune that can
befall us here below."

"Oh, why is it," cried Mr. Lisle, almost wildly, "that this awful
delusion, this mockery of a religion, should thus be destined to
cross my path ? What have I done, that those I love should be
swept from me by a doom far worse than death ? Marion ! I
could have knelt by your grave and said, ' Thy will be done !' but
now years will not bring me resignation. The thought of what
you were, compared with what you soon will be, will haunt me
like a spectre, for, depend upon it, all that is most beautiful in
woman, tarnishes beneath the influence of such a creed as Romanism. Yet even now it is not too late, I am sure it is not ; come
home with me, Marion, come back to Ennington, and let me show
you all the fallacy of these arguments that have blinded you, bright
but cold as winter sunshine. Such a mind as yours may be bowed,
but it cannot yet be utterly broken down to the depths of their
superstition ! Do not let this fearful blow fall on your mother, no
longer young ; do not let that brother, who is looking forward to
the moment when he shall clasp his little Golden-hair to his heart,
find her separated from him by a deeper gulf than the ocean waves
that now divide them ; and if anything I can say from the depths
of my own poor heart can move you, do not let the one dear hope
of my life be blighted, for, O Marion, my darling, I love you next
to God !"

It was a moment of temptation ; and perhaps the black angels smiled in triumph at the white-robed guardian that hovered around his charge. Queen of the angels, protect thy child !

"Do not ask me," she replied, at length, in a voice of such determination that he knew his last hope had fled. "God will be with you all, in His strength you will carry your cross."

"Then I will waste no more time in words. All that remains for me now," he added, after a pause, "is to return to Ennington and write to your mother. Thank God, you are not yet one-and-twenty."

"That makes no difference," replied Marion ; "were I only five years of age, my thoughts, my mind, my prayers, would be beyond control. Even if mamma were to force me to attend her church, and kneel with her at prayers, what would be the value of such a foolish victory ? If argument and persuasion cannot show me the truth of your religion, coercion never will !" And the spirit of her mother shot from her father's eyes.

"At any rate, we will see !"

She held out her hand, but, without appearing to notice it, he turned away and walked quickly from the room.

As he crossed the vestibule, Mrs. Darrell met him.

"Mr. Lisle, I believe," she exclaimed ; "I thought Marion would have brought you in to join us in the drawing-room. We dine at six, and I hope you will favour us with your company to dinner, even if the long ride compels you to leave us directly afterwards."

"I thank you," said the curate, with constrained politeness, "but I have already dined."

"So we shall have to lose our little friend next week, I hear ?" observed Mrs. Darrell.

Mr. Lisle made no reply, except to reach his hat from the stand.

"Are you sure you cannot stay ? At least let me offer you a glass of wine, it is such a cold evening."

"Nothing in this house," was the rejoinder ; "I wish you good evening," and, without another word, he opened the door himself and passed out into the gloom.

Mrs. Darrell remained on the spot where he had left her. "Now, poor child," she whispered to herself, "her troubles have begun. God help her ! At any rate, come what will, she shall have a home and a mother here."

Her ruminations were cut short by the sudden calling of her name, and the pealing of the library bell. Running to the room, she found Marion extended senseless on the sofa, and Joe calling for assistance, and pealing the bell with all his might.

It was some time before she was restored to consciousness, and longer still before she could tell them that Mr. Lisle knew all, and had departed to do his worst.

"I thought he was very ungracious when I asked him to stop to dinner," said Mrs. Darrell ; "but no wonder he looked black."

"If he was black, Marion was white !" exclaimed Joe. "I had been hunting on the shelves for a book I left here, for at least two minutes, before I saw her, and, in the half light, I thought she was dying, if not dead."

"I almost wish I was," said Marion, who overheard him.

"Hush, my child," said Father Stirling, who had just entered the room, "or I shall have to scold you for trailing your cross instead of carrying it. That would be a great pity, for you would have all the weariness of its weight, without the merit of the sacrifice. Cheer up, and remember that the troubles of this world are small in comparison to the great joys our good God will give us in heaven if we are only faithful. No, my dear child, you must love to live till God shall call you. And you will do so, I am sure, for your bravery in this first conflict gives me every hope that you will be worthy of the 'valiant woman' who will stand beside you in every struggle."

Two days later, a letter was placed in Marion's hand, bearing the London post-mark. It was from her mother, and enclosed a note from Mr. Lisle to herself, which ran as follows :

"DEAR MRS. HOWARD—You have no longer a daughter. Marion has given you up to follow an idol of her own imagination. She has become a Romanist, and (backed, I suppose, by her priests) defies us both, that is, she refuses to listen to anything I can say, and declares that no power on earth can coerce her soul.

"Dearest mother, for come what will, such is the tie between us, much as I love her, I do not counsel gentleness, for I think a little salutary severity may bring her back again. Let her see what she has given up in your love ; refuse to meet her except as a Protestant, and, believe me, natural affection, with such a heart as hers, must triumph in the end. My head is throbbing so fast that I cannot see to write, I feel as if I were on the eve of some fearful illness. Come home as soon as you can, for I cannot leave till I have seen you. Your affectionate son,   HENRY LISLE."

The letter from her mother to Marion, ran thus :

"The enclosed, received this morning, from Mr. Lisle, has told me of my misery. Yesterday I rejoiced over a letter that gave me, as I thought, a son, to-day I stand transfixed over another, that informs me I have 'no longer a daughter.' Be it so; if you can live without me, it is enough. Go ! Those who have so kindly provided you with a new religion, must furnish you also with another mother, and a fresh home. What Henry Lisle advises, I adopt. When you can say, 'thy God shall be my God,' you shall once more be my child, but not till then. In this I am even more inexorable than himself, for he would make this a kind of essay to drive you back to me again, a decision to be replaced by something more lenient, should harsher measures fail. But I do not mean it so. It is my ultimatum. O Marion, what have I done that you should treat me thus? You knew me well in not apprizing me of your intention; had I had a thought of such a thing as this, I would have put a stop to it, whatever had been the result. I hate the Catholic religion; I hate Catholic priests; but, more than either, I hate the presumption of my own child, who thus sets at nought my parental authority! Mind, however, I only write to you thus on the representation of Mr. Lisle; he may be wrong, for you may be only waiting to ask my pardon, and do my bidding. If so, welcome; if not, farewell.

"M. Howard."

"What am I to do?" asked Marion, almost wildly, as she placed the letters in Father Stirling's hand.

"Wait and see," said the priest, quietly, after he had perused them. "He whom you have obeyed, will not forsake you. Dominus providebit. Mrs. Darrell will take care of you for the present, and, after a little time, perhaps mamma will relent."

"Never, I am afraid," said Marion, "she has never written nor spoken to my father's mother for twelve years, because she once offended her. She prides herself upon her pride; and, to tell you the truth, I have often felt proud of it, too. There is something so majestic in her unbending character. Out of her own family, Mr. Lisle is the only person with whom she is really familiar; for although she has made acquaintances of a chosen few, she always makes them keep a certain distance. Then, again, she is so determined; you see what she says (and I know it is true), that if she had known my intentions beforehand, she would have prevented it, whatever had been the result. She would have come and fetched me away, I know; and if I had been snatched, in that unsettled state of mind, from every person and everything Catholic, firm as I thought myself, I might have wandered, especially with Mr. Lisle straining every nerve to win me back again; for, O Father, though those letters say a great deal, you do not yet know all," and Marion related the scene in the library.

"Poor child! Poor child!" said the sympathising priest. "Does Mrs. Darrell know this?"

"No; I do not wish any one but you to know it, for it would do no good. But if you did not understand all my troubles, you would not be able to manage so well for me."

"Certainly not, it is no use showing a physician half a wound. Poor Lisle! I feel very sorry for him, too. Well, you will stay here for the present?"

"Not for long," replied Marion, firmly; "no, Father, I must be a governess."

Father Stirling looked rather surprised, but for some few minutes made no reply. "A governess!" he repeated, at length, musingly; "what do you think you could teach?"

"I hardly know, I have never thought about it," replied Marion.

"Well, do so, and let me know for what, on consideration, you consider yourself qualified, and I will write to a priest that I know in London, and see if he can do anything for us."

" What shall I do with regard to mamma ? "

" Write her just the affectionate letter your own heart will dic-
tate, telling her how, if she will only alter her resolutions, you will
devote yourself, heart and soul, to her, as you have always done.
Tell her what it has cost you to give up Henry Lisle, and ask her
not to increase the severity of this trial, by spurning you from her.
Tell her, however, that you must remain a Catholic, but that, if she
will only see you, you will give her such good reasons for the
change you have made, that you are sure she will admit your sin-
cerity, even though she herself may remain unconvinced.   Tell
her that her God *is* your God, and that for Him only would you
cause her the sorrow now wringing her heart.   Say this, or something like this, and surely she will relent ; at any rate, you will
have done your part."

Marion shook her head.   "She will never relent.   O mamma !"

"Come, come ! this will never do !" said Father Stirling, blowing his nose, "I must let you make your first communion, and
then you will be stronger."

Marion smiled through her tears.

"Next Sunday week, I think, and meantime we must make a
novena for you."

"What is that ?"

" A nine days' prayer to obtain an intention."

"And will you make one for me ?"

"We will, that Almighty God may give you strength to bear
your trials as a Catholic ought.   Good-bye, my child.   Poor little
thing," he murmured to himself, as he watched her down the
garden path ; "an angry mother, and a broken love-dream, are
heavy trials for eighteen !   But, no cross no crown.   Mater dolorosa, ora pro eâ."

CHAPTER XVII.

MARION was right ; the sweet letter that reached her mother, in
reply to her own, was unheeded, save by a brief note which accompanied a packet from Mr. Lisle, and informed her that she
had already had her decision.

As for the clergyman's budget, it was something tremendous ;
a long tirade of abuse against everything Catholic, and of flimsy
arguments against every doctrine of the Church.   One after the
other these melted away into thin air, or thinner imagination,
beneath a few telling words from Father Stirling, as he and Marion
conned them over on the afternoon of the Sunday of her first
communion.

"So much for Protestantism, if they have nothing better to
say than that," said Mr. Darrell, who had been listening atten-
tively to the conversation.

"I suppose I shall have to answer these objections," observed Marion.

"I do not see any occasion for your doing so," replied Father Stirling, "though, perhaps, if you do not, Lisle will say that you have not looked into both sides of the question. But I should imagine the very fact of a person living till the age of eighteen in communion with a Church, ought to be a guarantee that she knows what its doctrines are, and what the grounds of its belief."

"She would be clever if she could determine what are the doctrines of the Church of England," observed Mr. Darrell, "among such a mass of contradiction. I was reading an article yesterday on the 'Broad Church,' which has lately sprung up into notoriety, heralded by its 'Essays and Reviews.'" *

"The 'Broad Church,' what is that?" asked Mrs. Darrell.

"Something quite new, 'just out,' in fact, but already growing fashionable, and patronised, they tell me, by those who sit in high places. We shall have the narrow one next, I suppose."

"But who are they, what do they teach?"

"Why, nothing; that is, they seem to be doing all they can to pull Christianity to pieces altogether. Among other things, some of them take away the inspiration of Scripture, and others deny the eternity of hell, so I should think a good many sinners will become broad-churchmen. It will be rather amusing, if not edifying, to watch the rival operations of the Broad-Church and High-Church. Where one party seems intent on pulling off every doctrine it can lay hold of, the other is equally busy in putting as much on as the institution will carry without growing restive; while the Low-Churchman, in his turn, can do nothing but denounce each party alternately, at Exeter Hall and tea-meetings, in common with Romanists and Mormons. Poor Church of England, what will it come to in the end? The poor fellow, of whom Æsop writes, whose old wife pulled out the brown hairs, while his young one worked away at the white, was nothing to it, nor the unfortunate caterpillar, in whose body the ichneumon fly has deposited her larvæ. I always felt a great deal of commiseration for these two victims of misfortune; but the Church of England will soon be more pitiable still. What can one do whose foes are those of his own household? Dissent! Disunion! Infidelity! Could we have a sadder picture of a house divided against itself?"

"Hear, hear!" cried Joe, from the other end of the room. "Who says my father ought not to be in parliament. Wouldn't he 'confound their politics, and frustrate their knavish tricks,' with a vengeance!"

"Why, Joe, you have been so quiet," said Edith, "that I really did not know you were there."

"Rather impertinent, sister mine, any one would think I was habitually noisy, to hear you talk."

* Written in 1864.

"Or to hear you shut a door, open a window, come downstairs or "——

"Come, come, Edie, that will do, I plead guilty; I was born to make a noise in the world, and Father Stirling says we must fulfil our vocation."

"Remarkably cool," exclaimed Father Stirling, "to make me the apology for his love of racket."

"Joe can be quiet sometimes, though," said Emily, looking proudly at him.

"Yes, when he is either hungry or sleepy," said his father.

"Or thoughtful," added Emily.

A smile passed over Joe's handsome face.

"Which have you been all the afternoon, Joe?" asked his father.

"I know," said Emily, "he has been thinking, poor boy, that this is his last Sunday but one with us."

"Nonsense!" cried Mr. Darrell, sitting upright in his chair. But Emily was right; in a fortnight more, Joe must be once again upon the sea.

A very deep silence fell upon the little party, for all felt that much of the home sunshine would pass away, too.

"But this will never do," cried Mr. Darrell, at length; "suppose somebody sings us a song. Look at Marion, she is getting quite mopy."

"No no!" exclaimed Marion, trying to withdraw from the tell-tale blaze that sprung up, as Mr. Darrell stirred the fire. More than one saw a very big tear in the blue eye. Joe saw it, and a flash of pleasure shot through his heart. And yet, poor boy, what had it to do with him?

A few nights after this, there was a little family party at the Seymours, and the young people from The Cedars walked home through the frosty air. They had spent a cheerful evening, but they did not feel quite as bright as usual, for Joe had but a few days longer to be with them, and Marion was becoming daily sadder and sadder beneath her heavy load. "She must have something to distract her, or she will sink," Father Stirling had that morning said to Mrs. Darrell.

The twins walked on in front, talking of Marion and Joe alternately, while the subjects of their thoughts lingered behind in deep and earnest conversation. Joe felt that to-night or never he must speak and learn his fate. He fenced about for a long time, he talked of the sea, of the people in the neighbourhood, of the weather, of his sisters, of his dog, but from each and every topic the subject seemed equally unapproachable, and all the while they were nearing The Cedars, and his golden opportunity was gliding away.

"I shall hear of you sometimes through my sisters, Marion," he observed, at last.

"Of course you will."

"I wish you would write me just a little letter sometimes your-self?"

"There will be no need for me to do that. I can send you any message I wish through them."

"I do not like things second-hand," said Joe, half crossly.

"Well, we shall see."

"If it were not that it makes you unhappy," continued Joe, "I should be half glad that your mother is angry with you, it will be so nice to have you always with us."

"You are mistaken, Joe," replied Marion, "I shall not stay much longer at Harleyford."

"Why? Where are you going?"

"To be a governess."

"Marion! what do you mean?"

"Only what I say, Joe, Father Stirling and your mother both know my intention, and approve of it."

"The Mater does! It was only a day or two ago, Marion, that she said our house should be your home until you returned to your own."

"You need not tell me of your mother's kindness," replied Marion; "but she agrees now with Father Stirling, that I must have some active employment to keep me from brooding over my troubles, which really sometimes seem more than I can bear."

"Poor dear girl," said Joe, affectionately, and pressing the hand that lay upon his arm. "Marion, I shall often think of you when I am many miles from here."

"But you must not do so in sorrow, Joe," she replied; "Father Stirling says that mine is a very mild case of persecution; where one suffers less than I do, twenty suffer more."

"I wish you would make up your mind to stay with my mother and the girls. Father Stirling would soon find active work for you in the parish; if not, there are plenty of little things to distract you. You should see how much they find to do at home, with the house and garden, and with their needlework for the church and for the poor. No one ever spends an idle minute at The Cedars, I can tell you, except, of course, at holiday times like these. I can promise you, you should have plenty to do. Ah! Marion, you are not straightforward with me, this is not your only reason for leaving us."

"Perhaps not, Joe; I think there is another, stronger still."

"Tell me what it is, remember what an old friend I am."

"It is, then," said Marion, "that over and above what I have just said, nothing could induce me to remain a burden on your family, as long as I have the means, by either my head or my hands, of gaining my own livelihood."

"Marion, this is pride, one of the deadly sins."

"Then it is proper pride."

"You had better not talk of such an article as that; Father Stirling would tell you there was no such thing in existence."

"Then, self-respect."

"Equally wrong. 'Now you are in Rome, Marion, you must

do as Romans do.' The Church makes humility the very watch-word of perfection, and you must practise it by consenting to remain at The Cedars."

"I know very well, if it wanted nothing but loving hearts to detain me here, I should never leave the dear old house ; but we need not talk of this now ; you, at least, will not be pained at seeing me go forth to seek my fortune. I shall probably remain your mother's guest for some little time to come yet."

"And do you think my feeling about you is such a selfish one, that I only care not to witness your discomfort? How little you know me, Marion !"

There was a short pause, as both walked on in silence, broken only by the subdued voices of the girls in front.

"Do you mean to say," cried Joe, at length, "that you actually mean me to go back to sea, leaving you in this determination ? "

"What else can I do ? "

"Promise to remain with my mother."

"That I never will. O Joe," she continued, "do not, I beg of you, make my weary path more difficult."

"More difficult, Marion ! there is nothing I would not do to render it smooth. It is you who persist in walking over the stones, when the green sward lies ready for your feet."

"Simply because I know that duty leads me across those stones. Have you forgotten the story Father Stirling told us the other day of St. Jeanne de Chantal, who took her first step upon her path of duty across the body of her son ? "

"She was a saint, Marion, one of those set up to be admired, but far beyond our imitation."

Marion smiled. "A convenient doctrine that, Joe, but I am afraid the line of demarcation must be sometimes rather hard to be determined between what we are to admire, and what to imitate."

"Marion," cried Joe, stopping short in his energy, "I have made one resolution ; unless you promise this, I will not stir to join my ship."

"Joe, are you mad ? "

"I think I am," replied her companion, excitedly. "Listen, Marion, if you had a claim upon our family, a real claim of rela-tionship, would you scruple to form one of its circle ? "

"Candidly, Joe, I do not think I should. It would then be only a question of pride, now it is one of principle."

"Then let it be so no longer, but take your place amongst us as a sister and daughter."

"But I cannot, Joe ; why go over the same ground again ; how can I do this ? "

"By promising to be my wife ; " and poor Joe poured forth the whole secret of his love, with all the enthusiastic ardour of twenty-two.

Marion was perfectly overwhelmed with astonishment and regret. The passing thought that had stolen over her the night of the party, had been so completely lost amid graver scenes and subjects, that this declaration came upon her like a thunder-clap.

"Joe," said Marion, as he paused for her reply, "you must believe me when I say, that of all the troubles I have had to bear, this is not the lightest. Had I liked you less, it would have been easier to grieve you, easier to inflict a blow, that I fear will be a severe one to you, for dear, dear Joe, I can never love you with more than a sister's love."

"Marion !" he exclaimed, in a voice so strange, she could hardly recognise it ; "Marion !"

Neither spoke for some seconds, and now, having entered the gates, they began to ascend the drive.

"Could nothing, Marion," said Joe, at length, " could nothing, do you think, change your feeling for me ? I will give up the sea and accept the appointment offered me the other day, if you shrink from the harassment always experienced by a sailor's wife. I will be what you like, and do what you like, if you will only try to love me."

"Do not talk so, Joe, I beg and pray of you," cried the poor girl, bursting into tears, "or you will break my heart. If you only knew all, you would see how impossible it is."

"You are already engaged," cried Joe, with a start.

"No, I am not, but mamma was not the only one I gave up to become a Catholic."

"I never thought of this, Marion," he said, very gently, after a long pause : "tell me one thing, is it Henry Lisle ?"

Marion bowed her head.

"You are right," he whispered, as they reached the hall door, which his sisters had already entered, "inactivity would be too much for you ; as for me, a month more on shore would kill me. Go wherever you can be happiest, and may God Almighty bless you." Stooping down, he kissed her forehead, and before she could recover from her surprise, hurried upstairs to his own room, and the silent sorrow of his own heart.

Before many days the "old house at home" was very quiet, almost dull, for Joe Darrell had gone to sea again.

"He has felt the parting dreadfully this time, I never saw him so downcast in my life as he has been the greater part of the week," said Mrs. Darrell.

"Poor dear boy !" said Emily, to whose sympathies all had been confided by the young sailor.

More than a month rolled on after his departure, yet nothing was heard of suitable to Marion Howard. More than once Mrs. Darrell tried to dissuade her from an idea so fraught with difficulty, but Mr. Seymour, whom she called in to attend her, for Marion's health was beginning to suffer, also counselled change of scene. Still Mrs. Darrell felt loath to part with her, and once again sought Father Stirling and his advice.

"Endeavour to place her in a good Catholic family, where she may find occupation for talents never yet called into play, but which I feel sure she possesses, and, believe me, my dear friend, you will have done a greater kindness for Marion Howard, than in leaving her in a position where her high spirit would be constantly chafing under a sense of her dependence."

At length Marion thought of writing to her grandmother in London, intimating a desire of spending a short time with her, but leaving it to an interview to tell her of her determination to seek an engagement, and of the events that had rendered such a course of action necessary. Nor did the remembrance of the unfriendly feeling entertained by Mrs. Howard for her aged relative deter her from the idea, for she felt justly that she had no cause to shrink from her father's parent, whom in her early years she had so deeply loved. There was another reason that made Marion turn to old Mrs. Howard. She knew that her mother's family would entirely coincide in her decision with regard to her refractory child, and consider the line of conduct she had adopted as only wholesome severity, and she therefore felt that in her present circumstances this grandmother was the only relation to whom she could look for assistance. Nor was she mistaken, return of post brought so warm a welcome from the old lady, that Marion grew almost buoyant again under its influence. Bitterly both had felt the estrangement, for old Mrs. Howard had never seen her grandchild since the moment she had left Ennington in anger with the mother, and though little periodical birthday messengers, and new year's gifts, had invariably reached the grandmother, they must have been but a sorry substitute for the privilege of clasping her little Marion to her heart.

It was on a cold foggy morning that Marion left the roof that had so hospitably sheltered her during her days of trial, and the party who assembled to bid her goodbye, was at best a melancholy one. Edith, silent in her sorrow, Emily, the impulsive, sobbing, as though her heart would break, while from Mrs. Darrell's soft eyes the tears fell thick and fast.

"Good-bye, darling," she exclaimed, "God bless you. You promise me one thing, remember. If you find anything hard to you, you will come back. Here is your home."

"I will, indeed," cried Marion, smiling through her tears. "This is only half going out to seek my fortune, while I have so many kind friends. Heroines, to be romantic, ought to be quite forsaken and alone."

"Ah, but you see, my dear, heroines went out of fashion with knight-errants and dragons. Good-bye."

Marion took her seat by Robert, for Mr. Darrell was not well enough to drive her, as he had intended, to the station, which lay at some little distance from Harleyfold. As the dog-cart wheeled off, the tears flowed fast behind her gauze veil, and the slow walk down the steep path, brought back so many happy rides and drives, that little Golden-hair felt desolate indeed. At the lodge, Turner and Eliza, animated by different feelings, were standing to bid her good-bye. The former saw only the child she had nursed and fondled as her own, turned into a world of strangers by a mother, whom Turner had never learned to love; while Eliza, with all the ardour of a new convert, saw only suffering for the cause of Christ. But though proud of the martyrdom, her woman's heart mourned over the martyr, and more than one tear fell on the left hand Marion extended to her, as with her right she grasped that of her old nurse.

"Good-bye, nursey," she exclaimed, kissing her, and bending so low that Robert trembled for her equilibrium. "Good-bye. There, don't cry, all will be well. I am coming back to see you all at mid-summer. You must pray for me, Eliza, for I shall indeed need prayers."

"That I will, indeed I will," cried Eliza ; "but, O Miss Marion, things must come right at last."

"Will you not bid me good-bye, nursey?" asked Marion.

"I can't, I can't, deary ; why did I live to see you go away like this, my own sweet, precious child, you who never did anything to anger her? Ah, deary, but the missis has a hard cold heart."

"Turner!" cried Marion, withdrawing her hand, "how can you, how dare you speak like that!"

"Well, this is the first time I ever said a word agen her, but surely, Miss Marion, it is enough to make one forget one's duty to one's betters, to see such a thing as this."

"But not to one's mother, Turner!"

"God bless you, child, you are right," sobbed the old woman, "and I will never vex you with my foolish old tongue again. Oh, deary, deary me!" and she thought of the Christmas eve when she had watched Joe drive her up to the house, so full of life and spirits.

"Good-bye," said Marion, once again, and the carriage rolled off amid an hysterical sob from the old woman, that rang in Marion's ears for hours.

But a farewell visit had yet to be paid to Father Stirling, whose mass was just ended. Marion sprang from the vehicle and entered the church, where, after a little prayer before the Blessed Sacrament, in which it seemed as though the very earnestness of a lifetime was concentred, she sought the priest in the sacristy. Father Stirling, who had heard the carriage stop, and seen her pass the window, was expecting her. He stepped forward to meet her, and held out his hand. "Going?" he asked.

Marion bowed her head, for she could not trust herself to speak.

"Going," he repeated, gently, "away into the world of which as yet you have only heard and read. But keep up a brave heart, you have kind friends in the background."

"I am not afraid," answered Marion, "but everything seems so dull, even the weather, and I have never travelled alone before."

"Nor will you now, my child, you will have two Companions, two who have travelled before."

Marion looked up inquiringly.

"Yes, and a darker, drearier road, for, let the fog be ever so cheerless, it will never equal the gloom of the Via Dolorosa, along which a Son and His Mother travelled eighteen hundred years ago. They will be with you to-day, will not their company suffice you?"

"Yes," said Marion.

"I have offered my mass for you this morning."

She thanked him with her eyes.

"Will you pray for me?"

A sob was the only answer.

"God give you His grace, my poor child, to bear up bravely. Are you afraid your grandmother will refuse to receive you when you tell her all?"

"No, it is not that," said Marion, striving to recover her firmness, "but everything seems so uncertain. I feel as if I was stepping off firm land into a little boat."

"So you are, but you have a good Helmsman. You must write and tell me all your troubles. I have been thinking that you had better not write just yet to your brother, though, I suppose, if you do not, Mrs. Howard will. You must be guided by circumstances. Here is a little book to make you remember Father Stirling in your prayers," and he placed a beautiful Missal in her hand.

She tried to thank him, but the effort was too great, and subsided into another sob.

"Hush, hush," said the priest; "if everything I do to make you happy, makes you cry, I must begin to scold."

Marion smiled.

"Now, really, you are a woman, every inch of you," exclaimed Father Stirling; "crying when I pet you, and laughing when I am angry. I will have no more to do with you, so run away. You will be late for the train," he added, "if you stop another minute."

"Give me your blessing first," said Golden-hair, sinking on her knees.

He gave it, and in two minutes more she and Robert were whirling on behind Black Prince, who trotted as fast as his four legs could carry him.

The country through which the panting engine bore Marion and her fortunes, was not more varied than her thoughts. There was the past, with Emnington and its associations, with her mother and their last railway journey together, and with Henry Lisle and those thousand thoughts of him, half memories, half dreams. Then came the present with its heavy sorrows, yet grand religious influence brooding over all, as the shadow of the crimson glass falls on the cathedral aisle, flecking alike the living and the dead. But, oh, the future! How she strove in imagination to raise the jealous veil that shrouded it from her sight! Refractory children, naughty mothers, the dreaded, because untried, monotony of teaching. Like many other young persons, Marion had a horror of the discipline of the schoolroom, of the hard and inky forms, the torn books, dirty maps, and all those thousand uncomfortablenesses that seemed to make the sum and substance of school life, as she remembered it. Then this brought her back to those very early days at Ennington, to the pretty breakfast-room, the old piano, crayon-heads, the mother-governess, and the lesson interrupted by the knock that made her heart beat quicker even as a child. Golden-hair looked at the vision till it became a living scene, and, "mistaking memory for hope," it seemed as though it could not all be passed. All was so vivid, the house, the garden, Turner—even Tyrza brought memories and tears. Roused from her reverie, she looked through the carriage window. "How like the future is a foggy day," she thought. "Objects in the immediate vicinity are tolerably distinct, but a little further off a dense curtain veils everything from our eyes. Nor does the metaphor end even here, for in the recesses of the mist I could fancy spectres and dreadful forms, which, as we approach them, are only trees and houses. And what will these things be, that now stand out in the future, so black and mysterious, but commonplaces? For what is a life-time, after all, but a simple chain of events, a succession of days and nights!"

At last the fields, and trees, and cows, began to disappear, the fog grew thicker, and the houses more numerous. Uncomfortable-looking places were passed by, the back windows of low tenements, tall, gaunt warehouses, and dingy people. Dull-looking thoroughfares were crossed on high railway bridges, to be succeeded by a cutting with a wall on either side, above the top of which rose houses again, while boys' heads, peeping over the parapet, cried "hurrah!" to the passing locomotive. Then came large desolate expanses, dotted with empty trucks, rusty iron, navvies, and snorting engines, that, like busy-bodies, seemed wondrously intent on doing nothing, unless it were making "day hideous" with their yells. And then came London, busy, bustling, never-quiet London, with its rolling wheels, its ceaseless footfalls, its Babel of shouts, and calls, and cries. Its rows of shops, and streets, and terraces, its thoughtful men and earnest women, its crimes and virtues, its palaces and alleys, its fearful poverty and its wondrous wealth. The winter afternoon was falling, and lights gleamed redly through the fog, and Marion grew tranquil as she felt herself one of the living moving mass. In a world where all have aims, should she have to live without one? No, she took the resolution, that come what might, she would be happy, even though she built the foundation of that happiness on the wreck of the loved and lost. The train neared the terminus, in the midst of that long, strange, weird-like whistle, that, varying with a kind of quivering wail, always brings with it either the joyful feeling of a journey ended, very comforting to one's bones, or the supposition of a collision, very discomforting to the same. Its mournful cadence died away in the fog, the train stopped, and two minutes later, Golden-hair was clasped in her grandmother's arms.

CHAPTER XVIII

MRS. HOWARD, senior, was not rich ; the greater part of her income had passed away with her only son, and a moderate annuity
was the old lady's sole resource.   But it was amply sufficient for
her every want, and many a silent deed of charity besides, and
in her quiet old-fashioned home at Islington she lived alone, a
little quizzed, much loved, and very much respected.

Marion was soon installed in the little parlour, where her grandmother at last succeeded in placing her full length upon the sofa,
beside a very cosy fire, while she bustled off to hurry in the tea.
Very characteristic was the dear old lady's parlour.   The maho-
gany chairs, covered in horsehair and inlaid with brass, the piano
to match, towering up to the ceiling, whose antiquity it set one's
very teeth on edge to compute, the round table in the middle,
and square one under the window, the crimson curtains bordered
with black velvet—all were redolent of lang syne.   A closer
scrutiny revealed cases of stuffed birds, rare and oriental shells,
fans, heathen gods, carved ivory, feather flowers, and various
curiosities, all of which, gifts many years ago from her son, embellished the apartment, with the old lady's work-box and tea-
caddy, and an endless variety of paper roses.

But the family portraits were the glory of Mrs. Howard's heart.
There was her husband, with very black hair, a coat collar rising
majestically above his ears, and a most elaborate shirt frill, that
must have cost the artist a world of trouble and white paint, not
to speak of his eyes, which were so natural that they followed
you into every hole and corner of the room ; and there was herself, looking most benignly at a pink rose, glorious in a satin
dress, lace cap, and a most wonderful array of jewellery.   And
there was Captain Howard on one side of the piano as a baby,
very fat and sulky, and on the other as a boy, not much improved
by years, and over the mantelpiece as a young man in full regi-
mentals.   As, however, in this case only one side of his face was
visible, and that rather dark in complexion, it was difficult to say
how he did look, or whether, in fact, he looked at all, his eyes
being left completely out of the question.   Then came portraits
more antiquated still, portraits of a generation farther off, of
uncles, aunts, and bosom friends.   Marion could not help wishing
that the gentlemen would have combed up their hair before
honouring the artist with a sitting, and came to the conclusion
that it would have been an infinite improvement if the ladies'
bodices had aspired higher, or condescended lower.   But they all
looked very solemn, all seemed intent on impressing the beholder
with the fact that he was in the midst of very respectable people.

It was not until Marion had eaten as much as she possibly
could, to be grumbled at affectionately for not eating twice as
much, that the old lady allowed her to begin upon the subject of
her visit to London.   Not that she was an unworthy daughter of

her great progenitress, for she felt wonderfully curious to learn
what could have induced Mrs. Howard, junior, to send her
daughter to visit her uninvited. Marion told her story plainly and
quietly. She spoke of the Darrells warmly; of her religion
firmly; of Mr. Lisle she said little, but Mrs. Howard understood
her with the intuition of parental love. With regard to her
mother, she simply stated the fact that she would not see her,
but there was that in Marion's manner when she spoke of her,
such a perfect sympathy with her feelings, although grief at her
decision, that the old lady dared not blame her to her child,
although she was secretly boiling over.

"And you mean to say your mother has disowned you,
child?"

"She will not let me go home to her, grandmamma. Is it not
a dreadful thing for me?"

Mrs. Howard dared not trust herself to reply. Both sat in
silence, during which the little copper kettle on the hob sang
merrily, as though he did his best to raise their spirits, while
Marion said many a Hail Mary to his music.

"Thank God, I am living still!" said the old lady, at length.

Marion slipped from her chair, and taking a little stool, placed
herself at her feet.

"And so you are a Catholic, Marion?" said her grandmother,
reproachfully, but stroking her hair at the same time.

"Yes, grandma. Are you very sorry?"

"Yes, dear, I am very sorry," she replied, "because there are
many things in that religion opposed to the word of God. I
think Catholics may be very sincere in their love of God and
Christ crucified, but they mix up a great deal of nonsense with
it, which I feel very sorry you should have learned to believe.
But I think I shall be able to show you all this. At any rate,"
she added, "let you believe what you may, you are still my own
dear child, my poor dear Edward's little one. I have so longed
to see you; indeed, I had just made up my mind that now you
were a woman, and could act for yourself, and travel alone. I
would invite you to come and visit me this very summer, and
see, here you are quite unexpected, but welcome as a swallow in
spring."

Marion smiled, and the old lady continued.

"You look pale and thin; you have suffered a great deal, I
can tell."

"Yes, I have, grandma; but things will be brighter now."

"But I am afraid, dear, you will be very dull here alone with
me. I know no young ladies but Miss Tompkins and her
sister, and they are quite different girls to you; besides, they must
be a good deal older."

Miss Tompkins and her sister Miss Jemima were two highly
respectable young ladies, very neat, very genteel, and very proper,
but they *were* rather older than Marion.

"Grandmamma," said Marion, looking suddenly up, "I have

M

only come to visit you for a little time. I mean to look out for a
situation as governess," and Marion told her what Mr. Seymour
had said. But it was a long time before the old lady, in whom
dwelt all the pride of the Howards (as she phrased it), could be
brought to listen to such a course.

"Well, never mind to-night," she said at length, after vainly
striving to persuade Marion to give up her intention, "there is
ten o'clock striking, and if you will not have any supper I must
put you to bed."

And, having lighted her to her room, the old lady stayed with
her, fondled her, folded up all her things, kissed her fifty times,
cried over her, and never left till she had tucked her up with her
own hands, bidding her say her prayers in bed, for that was not
wrong at all when anybody was so tired. The instant, however,
that grandmamma's last footfall had died away downstairs, Marion sprang out of bed, said her night prayers, then laid herself
down on the couch that had once been her father's and slept
soundly till the morning woke her with its carts and cries.

Marion lay and watched the winter morning struggle in, and
light up her quaint little room, with its old-fashioned chintz and
dingy looking furniture. Weary at last, however, of shaping the
roses and tulips that adorned her curtains into all kinds of eccen-
tricities, she arose and dressed herself. She had just finished her
toilette and ended her prayers, when her grandmother slipped
gently in to see whether her little visitor was awake. And now
that Marion was arrayed in her natty morning dress, with the soft
shining ringlets arranged on each side of the bright speaking face,
old Mrs. Howard must be pardoned if a momentary glow of parental pride passed through her heart, to be replaced by even a
stronger feeling of indignation against the mother who could cast
away so sweet a little flower. But, restraining herself to silence
when comment must be reprobation, and reprobation wrong, she
contented herself with kissing her fondly, and leading her
down to breakfast, where, seated on either side, with the little
copper kettle singing forth his very heart, they discussed their
eggs and coffee, and many a past event and future plan besides.
Before the meal was concluded, won over by Marion's reasoning,
Mrs. Howard had consented to her seeking an engagement, provided she spent a week or two with her first, during which time
anxiety of every kind was to be banished, for, added she, "I must
see a little colour in those cheeks, before I let you go away from
me again."

And so Golden-hair tried to banish intruding cares, and passed
even three weeks with her grandmother in what the old lady considered very gay doings. For what with morning walks and calls
in all imaginable parts of Islington, and evening tea-drinkings at
home and abroad, it seemed to her a perfect whirl of dissipation.
But she for whom all this gaiety was planned and indulged, grew
thinner and paler still, in spite of all, and notwithstanding her
love for her kind relation, pined for the liveliness of The Cedars,

and still more for the dear home life at Ennington, with its thousand interests. Who can say how the gossip of those monotonous tea-parties wearied her young spirit, or how sick at heart she grew of the listlessness that could find no relief except in a little embroidery? Sometimes she had to play, but what piece or song in her little repertoire was not mingled, as music only is, with almost an agony of associations?

Old Mrs. Howard was all that could be desired in aged womanhood—but her friends! On more than one state occasion, when the best china and the silver teapot figured upon the table, and Anne, in "best bib and tucker," handed round the fragrant hyson, and almost imaginary bread-and-butter, "Surely," thought Marion, "grandmamma must have a fancy for disagreeable-looking people." And they were an unpromising selection, from the two old ladies in the corner, who were discussing church and parish matters like veteran vestry-men, down to Miss Jemima in the white muslin. It was only when they were gone, and they generally went early (there being only one of Mrs. Howard's coterie who had masculine protection at command), that Marion found her tongue. Then she laughed and made her grandmother laugh, till one would have wondered how two people could find so much merriment, where, half-an-hour before, there had been nothing but state. So it never once struck Mrs. Howard that Marion was dull, that the daily walk in Highbury had something of sameness in it, or that the conversation of her friends to-day was the same as yesterday and the day before, and would be, in all probability, the same to-morrow and the day after.

But this same conversation of Mrs. Howard's friends was destined to find fresh fuel. On the Monday morning after Marion's third Sunday in Islington, a certain Miss Snagg called on the Misses Tompkins, and after a few minutes' chat, during which time it remained poised on her tongue, like the tit-bit on an epicure's fork, out came a most tremendous secret. No sooner had she departed than on went their bonnets, and down went the secret to Mrs. Smith, and up to Miss Brown, then to the little woman at the Post Office, to the lending library and wool-shop at the corner of the street, crossing and recrossing the circle of Mrs. Howard's friends in Islington, like the flux and reflux of the sea. Then the storm burst. The Rev. Mr. Glumley called from Mrs. Smith, and the Rev. Mr. Singles from Miss Brown; the former groaning in spirit over the defection of the age, the latter simpering and sighing in the deepest sympathy. Both were entertained by grandmamma, both drank two or three glasses of port in consoling her, and both departed without seeing the object of their call and curiosity, who sat in her own room reading Thomas à Kempis. Then tracts enough to have lighted the fires at The Cedars for a week poured in from "sincere well-wishers," while such a "No Popery" cry was raised through Barnsbury, that one would have said the Pope was going to send over another cardinal, or found a second hierarchy in Great Britain.

At first grandmamma was amused, then vexed, then evidently
tired of the question, which was fast making herself and her little
home the butt of the slanderer. She loved Marion dearly, the
child had tightly twined herself round her old heart ; but she did
not want to lose her friends, or still less her high prerogatives as
general umpire and universal favourite. Marion soon saw that
there was but one way to restore affairs to their pristine calmness,
and commenced in earnestness her proposed plan. She inserted
advertisements, and answered them, "personally and by letter,"
rode miles crushed and stifled in omnibuses, and trudged many
weary ones on foot. But to what purpose? To be told, after
crossing London, that the "lady was suited," to be questioned like
a housemaid, and then dismissed to hear no more, to be buoyed
up by a sweet lady face one day, who thought she might suit, and
then receive the gentle note next morning, regretting "that she
was too young." Then she applied to men agents, who shrugged
their shoulders at the word Catholic ; to women agents, who
talked loudly, and told her that, as her qualifications were so few,
she must be contented with a salary from which she knew Mrs.
Darrell's cook would have turned away. Then she called on
priests, who promised to do what they could, but who smiled
sadly, and talked of twenty or thirty converts already on their
lists, and who sent her to convents, where the nuns congratulated
her, shook her two hands, kissed her two cheeks, longed to help
her, but, except with their prayers, could do no more.
At last a daily governess was advertised for in Islington itself,
salary liberal, exactly Marion's qualifications required. The poor
child put on her bonnet. Perhaps she might get this, which
would at least prevent her being a burden on her grandmother, if
it did nothing else.
The lady was a widow, rather stiff and business-like, but kind
in her manner, and was evidently struck by our little heroine's
tout ensemble. She asked for references. Marion wrote Mrs.
Darrell's address upon her card, saying, however, that except with
regard to her position, it was, of course, valueless, as she had
never taught in her life.
"I understand that," replied the lady, "but my children are
young, and if you are naturally systematic, we shall manage very
well. If the reference be satisfactory, as I feel sure it will, you
shall hear from me deciding the day on which we shall commence."
Marion replied by one of her own bright smiles, and rose to
take her leave.
"Pardon me," said the lady, "there is one thing I have forgotten
to ask : I presume you are a member of the Church of England?"
"No, I am a Catholic," said Marion, firmly.
"A Catholic!" repeated the lady, "then excuse me, but I will
return your reference. A Catholic! That would not do at all.
And you would have allowed me to engage you without mentioning
this?"

"I did not think it would signify in daily tuition," replied Marion.

"But it does signify very much," returned the other, angrily. "How fortunate I should have asked you! I would not subject my little ones to Catholic influence for all I could see on earth. Of course I cannot expect you to see this; it is difficult to open the eyes of one born blind."

"Difficult, but no more impossible now with God than in days gone by," returned Marion, "for I myself was a Protestant once."

"Then take my advice, young lady, go home and study your Bible, which will soon bring you back again. This you have not done much as yet, I am certain, for no girl who read her Bible ever became a Romanist."

Thoroughly Catholic as Marion Howard was, she had yet to learn detachment. The gift of Henry Lisle had been too dear to relinquish, and the little black book still lingered in her pocket, though, looking on it as a spurious version of the Word of God, its religious value had departed.

"There is something I should like to show you, if you will look at it," said Marion, quietly.

"What is it?" asked Mrs. Gordon, recoiling, for what small specimen of Romish superstition might be coming, she did not know. "What is it?"

"Only a Protestant Bible."

"A Protestant Bible! You surely do not mean to say your priests let you carry that about with you?"

"I keep it for the sake of an old friend," replied Marion; "but what I want to show you is this. Take it in your hand, and tell me if it has been unread. Every mark is mine, made in my Protestant days, under texts that I loved best. Believe me, when I tell you, that that Bible has been deeply, earnestly, prayfully read, and yet, I am a Catholic!"

"Strange!" said the lady, as she turned over page after page, black with pencil marks, "but so much the worse. I consider you a real loss, the more so that I think you are intelligent."

"I wish I was," said Marion, "I should make all the better Catholic."

"Catholic!" repeated Mrs. Gordon; "Roman Catholic, you mean! We are Catholics!"

"And yet," said Marion, smiling, "if a man asked you the way to the Catholic church, you would not direct him to your own."

"Perhaps not, because even Protestants get into the silly habit of misapplying the term. But it is not the less a misapplication for all that."

"I shall not convince her if I contradict her," thought Marion, so she held her peace.

"You think I am very hard upon you, do you not?" asked Mrs. Gordon, gradually unbending.

"Rather," said Marion.

"I have so much reason to be so," replied the lady; "I once

lost an old and valued friend by such a step as you have taken,
for we have been strangers since."

"Was that her fault?" asked Marion, with rather a piercing
look.

"No," said the lady, hesitating, "it was neither my friend's
fault nor mine, exactly. My family feared this influence for me
in the same way that I fear it now for my own children," she
continued, listlessly turning over the leaves of the book. "This
very morning I have received a letter in which this Catholic
religion figures very painfully. It is dreadful to see the havoc
this evil is making in the bosom of families. One hears of it,
really, on every side now."

"Because the Catholic religion is spreading," replied Marion.

"But its day is over, nevertheless," rejoined the lady; "you
know, the expiring lamp always gives a bright gleam before it
dies."

"It flickers," returned Marion, "but does not grow silently and
surely brighter every moment. For my own part, I believe the
trial of the Church, inflicted for the sins and irregularities of her
children, is passing away, and my own deep conviction is, that
England will be Catholic again. Not by any sudden convulsion, but
that she will glide back into the bosom of the old faith, man by man
renouncing error, till the truth shall gleam like one of our own
altars, that has been silently lighted, taper by taper, till the whole
shines forth in a flood of mingled light." The last sentence was
lost in an exclamation from Mrs. Gordon.

All the time that Marion had been speaking, she had been
turning over the leaves of the book, and now sat looking at the
title-page, transfixed with astonishment.

"My child, how came you by this book?"

Marion was too much surprised by the suddenness of the
question, to attempt a reply.

"I ask you," continued Mrs. Gordon, in an agitated voice,
pointing to the initials already mentioned, "because, oh because,
that is my handwriting! How, in the name of heaven, came it
yours?"

Marion trembled like an aspen. In whose presence was she
then? Mrs. Gordon! The truth flashed upon her in an instant,
but she made a tremendous effort, and was calm.

"You wrote those initials?"

"I did, many years ago. Who gave the book to you?"

"Your brother, for I know now that I speak to the sister of
Henry Lisle."

"And you!" asked Mrs. Gordon, grasping her arm.

"I am Marion Howard; have you heard of me?"

"You shall see," said Mrs. Gordon, rising as she spoke, and
opening an escritoir. "Read that," she continued, putting a letter
into Marion's hand. She did read it, read it to the very end, though
her heart was wrung as she read it. It was a long and bitter
letter, written by Henry Lisle, in the extremity of his grief, and

ended with these words: "Perhaps of all living beings, you,
Agnes, can best sympathise with me in my trouble, since the
dark waters now surrounding me, once flowed so deeply over your
own soul. I know that he is with you, now, only a memory of the
past, and therefore I may tell you of one drop of bitterness in
my cup, not the least bitter, perhaps, of all. It is, that the author
of this poor child's perversion is George Stirling! It is said,
that the sweetest wine makes the sharpest vinegar; and it is true,
for it is hard to look from the dear friend of the past, to the plot-
ting priest of the present, and not to detest him. O Agnes! if I
dared, how I should hate him! I can only seek from Him who
prayed for His murderers upon His cross, strength to conquer
this feeling. Strength to look still with brotherly love on the
murderer of my life's happiness—if not of Marion Howard's soul,
for the darkest shadow of all is, that we are perhaps separated for
both time and eternity! I leave Ennington for my new parish
to-morrow. 'Man proposes; God disposes.' What is it now to
me, that the Rectory is all that I could desire? They wanted me
to hasten down, that I might be consulted in the papering and
painting of my new home, but I wrote and told them to do what
they liked, for that I was easy to please. I am so very wretched!
You will tell me to pray for resignation; so I do, but I seem hard
and wicked when I pray. Mrs. Howard is unaltered—the same
as ever, but there is a kind of shadow over her, that one feels
rather than sees. She has a proud high spirit, but she is not
warm-hearted, and though I admire her for qualities I know her
to possess, were she not Marion's mother, there would be but
little sympathy between us. Even now I sometimes fear the
ruling feeling with her is offended pride, for she has never once
spoken of this sad affair to me in a spiritual light. But I may
mistake her, she is so thoroughly undemonstrative. I tremble for
Marion; so young a creature, wandering alone through the great
world! But what is to be done? She has cast us off; we have
not rejected her. I will write again from Sandiham. Good-bye."

Marion did not raise her eyes from the letter, even when she
had finished reading it, but sat looking abstractedly at the words,
even while she no longer read them. They had given her both
pain and pleasure. Pleasure that she was still so deeply loved,
pain in the depth of her separation from him; pleasure that her
mother bore up bravely, but pain in the creeping shadow, in
the isolation she so well understood of that cold proud heart.

Mrs. Gordon looked fixedly at her, as though striving to read
her very soul.

"This has been a strange meeting," she remarked at length.

Marion's only reply was a burst of tears.

In an instant, Mrs. Gordon's arms were round her neck.

"Marion! little sister," she exclaimed, "look up! A Catholic
governess for my children was one thing, the object of my
brother's love another. He may spurn you with that same rash
prejudice that once embittered my own life, but Agnes Gordon

never will. I can see as clearly as any one, the errors of the faith
you have embraced, but at the same time I see also the still
deeper one of striving to force you back to truth. If my mother
had been living to have counselled a different treatment with poor
George, things might have been very different. I have no doubt
a little leniency would have led him back to re-examine for
himself the doctrines of our purer faith, and would have saved us
years of sorrow and heart-burning, and him a life-time of error."
   Marion did not answer, but clung to her new friend.
   It was late that evening before she returned to Mrs. Howard's,
and later still before she and the old lady retired to rest. For she
had a strange tale to tell. A tale of how she had found the sister
of Henry Lisle in the pale quiet widow, and how that sister had
received her with open arms, and had sympathised with her in
her deep grief, though she could not enter into her deeper
enthusiasm. And then she spoke of the bright and beautiful
children, and how the spirit of the father still seemed to cling
around the home, so recently bereaved. For though he had not
been her first and girlish dream, Agnes Gordon had loved her
husband with a wife's truest devotion, and mourned for him as
those only mourn, who, were it not for the Father in heaven, and
children on earth, would sink beneath their load. Since her
bereavement, her life had been very lonely ; friends she had few,
for those she loved were far away, and the quiet reserved Scotch-
woman cared not to make acquaintances in her adopted home.
And yet she clung to London, and the old house in Islington,
that had been the scene of her married life, every room of which
was so endeared by the shadows of the past. She loved to sit alone
in the winter evenings, before the lights came in, and imagine
another chair not vacant, and to fancy a voice now hushed in
death, still floating round her. And the narrow garden where he
had loved to work, the room where he had kept his things,
the corner where he had sat, the bed whereon he had died,
and from which the sweet white face looked up so peacefully to
heaven, these were to Agnes Gordon the sunniest spots on earth.
Still, even amid the relics of such a devotion as this, the widow
clung instinctively to Marion, not only for Henry's sake, but
because she suffered now, what she herself had suffered once.
   Old Mrs. Howard opened her eyes at the recital, and might
have failed to realise it, had not Mrs. Gordon made her appearance the next morning to ask her to spare her little visitor, to
spend a few days with her. The old lady consented, sorry to lose
her pet, but not loath to give the chatter of her friends a chance
of subsiding.

   "Mrs. Gordon ! Please do not send that letter," cried Marion,
as she finished reading one, just placed in her hand, "really, really,
it is too severe."
   "Too severe, Marion ! I cannot see it."
   "But it is indeed ; what could a Catholic girl be to him now, a

Protestant clergyman, and what claim have I on his forbearance?"

"The claim of Christian charity, the claim of old friendship, the claim of a girl whose affection he has won. I do not say more, for I know that more is impossible; but what right has he to be so angry with you? And why, worse than all, should he excite your own mother against you, when you have only done what you believe to be your duty? Marion, it was Henry's counsel to my father that helped to blight so many years of my own youth, and that drove a bright and genial spirit into gloom and isolation. For that I have forgiven him, for he was young and impetuous then, but now he is older, and ought to have grown wiser with his years. Yes, let the letter go, I want him to see that though I pity his sorrow, I do not endorse his conduct. I should like to tell him how we met, and that even now a certain little lady sits in my own parlour facing me, but you think it would make your mamma more uneasy if she heard that you had left Mrs. Darrell."

"I am sure it would," replied Marion. "She looks upon me, I know, as comparatively safe at The Cedars. As for the letter, I wish it was a little less severe," continued the little pleader.

"Not a whit, my love! It is not often I get angry, but anything like intolerance rouses me at once. My poor dear husband helped to disperse many of the ideas Henry had instilled into me. But if I am liberal, I am not blind, and if there be one thing for which I have an especial distaste, it is the Catholic religion."

"Perhaps you do not understand it," suggested Marion.

"Yes I do, very well; I have heard the subject so often handled and re-handled."

"By Catholics or Protestants?" asked her visitor.

"By Protestants, for it is a strange thing, perhaps, but I never remember having a Catholic acquaintance in my life."

"Did you ever go to one of our churches?"

"Never."

"Will you come with me some evening?"

"You little Jesuit!" cried Mrs. Gordon, laughing, "what would poor Harry think the world was coming to, if he saw you sitting there, with your wicked blue eyes, making me such a cool request as that? Well, we will see."

Mrs. Gordon did see, and the result was, that she went to Benediction with Marion the next Sunday evening.

"What did you think of the service?" asked Golden-hair of her companion, who had been walking by her side for some time in profound silence.

"This; that unless I wished my children to become Catholics, I would never suffer them to enter a Catholic church. I never saw anything so beautiful!"

You are right, Mrs. Gordon. But it was not this beauty that bowed into obedience the great mind and high spirit of George Stirling, nor that conquered the home-love in Marion Howard's heart! Look again, there is something more than this.

CHAPTER XIX.

It was a boisterous day at sea, and the packet-boat running from Newhaven to Dieppe danced on the waves, till every glass in the steward's cabin jingled. The English shores had not yet faded, but already a most forlorn and miserable party were lying prostrate in the ladies' cabin, and most wretched, when all were miserable, was little Golden-hair. "Even the stewardess is ill," whispered a strong-minded passenger, as she arranged an incapable friend in her berth: "dear me, how ill you look! why I am never sea-sick," and she once more returned to her seat on deck. "Eau sucrée!" cried a French belle, and the poor pale stewardess compounded the abominable beverage; "a little brandy," cried an English one, and once again the unfortunate attendant stumbled about the cabin.

"O dear! O dear! what shall I do?" sobbed a poor little girl. "Mamma, do come to me; I cannot bear it any longer."

"But you must, my dear, and you must not disturb the ladies. You will be better soon," expostulated the stewardess.

Mamma was on deck, and nurse unable to lift her head, so the poor child fell back again on her pillow with a groan of despair. Again there was silence in the cabin, if it could be called such, amid the blustering of the wind, the rattle of the engines, and the clatter of plates and dishes from without. O those people! How could they eat? Yet eat they did, and that with as much nonchalance as though they had been in their dining-rooms at home. And so the hours dragged on, only enlivened by the arrival of some fresh sufferer from above, amongst them the hardy lady, who would have been ashamed of her weakness, had she not been too ill even to blush.

But all things have an end, even sea-sickness; and by the time Marion had dressed herself, and the packet had touched at the landing-place, she almost wondered what had become of the suffering that had bowed her so helplessly during the last few hours. It was not long before she was in the train, whirling through picturesque Normandy, still sad however in its winter bareness, and growing ever moment less and less distinct in the early March twilight. But Marion, as she passed along, saw many a village, dotted among the hardly budding trees, nestling round the patriarchal tower, that rose like the presiding genius of each little hamlet. Uncouth specimens of architecture were they almost all, but Marion knew that beneath each tower and steeple that she passed, the Lord God Omnipotent was reigning in the Sacrament of His Love. She was in a Catholic country! The idea was almost too exquisite to be realised! Every man, woman, and child she saw, thought as she did, prayed as she did, loved as she did!

Then she leaned back in the carriage, and thought and dreamed as she had done from Harleyford to London, but even since then the kaleidoscope of life had shifted for her, and though she had a friend the more, she had many a hope the less. Her London confessor had at last found her an engagement in Paris, and she was now on her road thither to undertake it. Notwithstanding her horror of Catholic governesses, Mrs. Gordon would willingly have kept Marion with her, but she saw plainly that it was the young girl's duty to fit herself for the future. She had, however, insisted on sharing with Mrs. Howard the expenses of the journey and outfit, and it only remained for poor little Golden-hair to pack her new dresses, sob her thanks to each loved donor, and take her departure for her dreaded sojourn in the land of strangers.

It was so late when the train reached the Gare St. Lazare, that Marion determined to stop at an hotel with a lady who had been her fellow-traveller during the journey, and not to proceed to the establishment of Mme. le Brun until the morning. After a tussle with certain men in blue, who insisted on an extra coin, of the value of which Marion was profoundly ignorant, the drive through Paris commenced. Except, however, a constant variation of long streets now bright with gas, now deep in shadow, now loud with the hum of voices, now silent in midnight stillness, Marion could distinguish little.

"The Louvre"—"the Tuileries," said her companion. A vast building surrounded by a gilded rail, was our heroine's impression of the palace of kings, but she thought of Louis the sixteenth and the howling revolutionists, and trembled to find herself in Paris.

"The Seine," said the lady, as they crossed a bridge. Marion looked down at the silent waters in which the lamps and stars were reflected, and wondered how much was true of the story of St. Bartholomew's Day. But they soon stopped at the hotel selected by her companion, and before long, Marion was lying in the neatest of French beds, dreaming of Ennington and The Cedars all in one.

She was only just dressed the following morning, when her companion knocked at her door.

"I have been thinking," said the lady, after the morning's salutation, "that it is time we knew each other's names."

"Certainly," said Marion, presenting her with a card.

"I do not happen to have my card-case with me," returned the other, "but I am Miss Hobart Jones, —— Place, Belgravia." The manner with which the name and address were given was so pompous that Marion was obliged to bow very low to hide the smile, which her sense of the ludicrous brought to her lips. "As I informed you last night," continued Miss Jones, "one of my trunks, which I did not register, is lost, and I must return to the Gare to look for it. If you are not in a hurry to arrive at your destination, perhaps you will accompany me."

"I shall be very happy to do so," said Marion.

"We will breakfast then, first at the table d'hôte ; but I suppose, as it is Sunday, you will want to go to church."

"Indeed I shall," replied Marion, "shall not you?"

"As for that, it will only be a matter of half an hour for me," replied Miss Jones. "We will go to the Place du Havre first, and see about my box, then I will take you to the Protestant church in the Rue d'Aguesseau; I shall just catch the Messe de Midi for myself at the Madeleine, for you must know that I am a Catholic."

"So am I," said Marion.

"Capital!" exclaimed her companion; "then we will get Mass over first, directly after breakfast, and then we shall be free to do as we like."

Get Mass over! One would have imagined she was going to have a tooth drawn. Marion thought of Father Stirling and the little chapel at Harleyford and sighed.

They breakfasted and set off to the Madeleine. Here, however, Marion was disappointed, for hers was a nature that associated pillar and arch, and "dim religious gloom" with church architecture, but following her guide, who stepped on before with the air of one accustomed to the place, she entered a row of seats. But here a difficulty presented itself; for how could she possibly hear Mass seated on her chair, and yet how kneel in the limited space allotted her? She looked at her companion, who, however, solved the problem by tipping up the chair before her, and accommodating herself on the rail. Marion tried to imitate her, but oh, the misery of that first Mass in Paris, as she knelt, trying to steady the chair with one hand and hold her book with the other.

It would be difficult to say through what streets her companion did not drag Marion, or what lions she did not show her. And yet, by the afternoon, except a glimmering idea of streets with many people, but comparatively few vehicles, of open shops that had wrung her heart for Catholic Paris (but into which Miss Jones peeped with the utmost unconcern), of large churches with shifting congregations, of houses bearing unfamiliar sign-boards, of women wearing caps instead of bonnets, and many men in blue, Marion had but a very faint idea of Paris.

"You will like Paris," observed Miss Hobart Jones, as they stood in the Place de la Concorde, looking up the Champs Elysées, at the Arc de Triomphe, "do you not think so?"

"I cannot tell yet," said Marion; "it seems very gay. Is it always like this?"

"Yes, always, only a great deal gayer. Do you not think you will be very happy?"

"Not unless the place I am going to is quieter," said Marion, and she mentioned a quarter at which Miss Jones turned up her nose.

"You never mean to say you are going there? Quelle vie! Why it is the dullest quartier in all Paris. Nothing but schools and convents."

"That is just what I like. I am a country girl, and am accustomed to a quiet life."

"Well, chacun a son gout !" exclaimed her companion, "as for me, I cannot understand such things. I like life, gaiety, bustle ! Quite time enough to sit and mope when you are too old to do anything better. I think while we are young we have a right to think more of pleasure than anything else. I do indeed," she continued energetically, as though somebody were contradicting her. "For one thing," she continued, drawing herself up, "the circle in which I move is very high, my friends in Paris being chiefly among its aristocracy. I am only over here now by the especial invitation of the Comtesse de Pierrepoint. She is a charming creature, an old bosom friend of mine, and has promised to let me do just as I like. I am an invalid just at present, and am to be quiet, therefore she has promised mamma not to take me out to more than two dinner-parties a week."

Marion glanced at Miss Hobart Jones, and thought it was almost time for her to be out of mamma's jurisdiction. She also thought of the steam-rate at which they had been traversing Paris, and wondered how fast Miss Jones walked when she was well. The idea too, struck her rather forcibly, that the bosom friend of the Comtesse de Pierrepoint might have stopped short a few stairs lower the previous evening. It was all very well for Marion Howard, the little governess, to mount to the cinquième, but for Miss Hobart Jones, ——— Place, Belgravia—moving in the most exalted circles in Paris—it was rather too much ! Marion knew very little of the world, but she knew better than this, and was naughty enough to wish that her new acquaintance was anything but a Catholic. Silly little thing ! She had yet to learn that though the sunbeam may thaw the icicle, the icicle, with all its frigidity, has no power to lessen the life-giving warmth of the sun, but it was hard, in the burst of her first fervour, to understand a tepid or indifferent Catholic.

Marion was not sorry to bid Miss Hobart Jones good-bye, and find herself on the road to the establishment of Madame le Brun. The bell rang, the gate opened, the luggage was deposited in the cour. It was not till Marion had paid her coachman, and heard the voiture lumber back over the ill-paved streets, and the great gate close with a bang, that she felt she was really alone in a foreign country, and in a house of strangers.

Never, perhaps, had Marion met a form of more quiet dignity, than that of the mistress of the house, who now advanced to meet her. She was simply but elegantly dressed, in the black so loved by Frenchwomen, and her pretty lace cap, with its delicate ribbons, was arranged over her large curls, with the studied carelessness a Française only understands. But notwithstanding her gentle manner and soft words, the softer, perhaps, that they were spoken in musical broken English, and notwithstanding a smile that shone in every feature, Marion did not like her. There was a hard coldness in the light grey eye, that somehow reminded her of a snowy peak rising amid the sunshine of a tropical land. She received Marion kindly, though certainly a great part of the

warmth of her manner subsided, when she found the newly arrived
was simply la maîtresse Anglaise.

After a few inquiries concerning her. voyage, madame, summoning one of the elder girls, deputed her to lead mademoiselle to
her room. The child complied, and showed her a small chamber,
to which her boxes had been already conveyed, and then, retiring,
left her to herself. Marion looked round. It was a square room,
paved with red tiles, and containing a little bed, three chairs of
different patterns, a chest of drawers, and a washstand. Muslin
blinds shaded the windows in the French fashion, and Marion
saw that her prospect was the single street of ————, not
uninteresting to her, with its inhabitants in Sunday costume,
grouped round its doors and on the narrow pathway. Glancing
again round her little room, she was not altogether displeased
with it, comfortless as it was. She had half dreaded something
worse, and, determining to be brave, she followed her little guide,
who soon reappeared with a light foot. The child chattered as
she went, but though Marion possessed sufficient knowledge of
French to understand, she had not confidence enough to attempt
a reply. But, satisfied with nods and signs in return for her
communications, the little prattler led Marion from dortoir to
lavabo, from the lingerie to the garden, and finally landed her in
the salon, with la petite maman, as madame was styled by her
establishment. The room was thoroughly French, and to Marion,
thoroughly uncomfortable-looking, and as she glanced at the bare
floor and hard chairs, with the little round green mat in front of
each, she felt very strange.

"You will dine with me, as it is the first day," said madame,
condescendingly.

Marion bowed, but never felt so much inclined to go without
her dinner.

Madame talked and tried to make herself agreeable, but as
Marion seemed frightened, dull, and—must we confess it?—
proud, she grew tired of the attempt, and proposed that Eugénie
should conduct mademoiselle to the garden.

Sunday being a jour de réception, many of the children's
parents were walking about the garden, which was large and in
tolerable order, and Eugénie, seeing her companion wish to avoid
them, turned into a thicket of trees.

"La chapelle de la Sainte Vierge," she remarked, as they paused
before a little building. It had once been pretty, but it was very
dirty, and fast falling into decay. Marion thought of the chapel in
the garden at The Cedars, and felt sadder than ever. But she
entered, and, to the surprise of Eugenie, who imagined that every
English girl must be Protestant, knelt down before the altar,
though it must be owned that the broken vases and dingy roses
gave her many distractions.

At this moment the elder girls returned from vespers, and
Eugénie, leading her into the recreation ground, where all were
assembled, introduced the maîtresse Anglaise to both pupils and

teachers. It was a hard task to be looked at and questioned without a word to give in reply ; to be in the position of a teacher, and yet to feel as bashful as a new pupil, amid the ebb and flow of the strange language round. They, however, meant to be kind, and did their best, though it was a real relief to Marion when the summons to dinner arrived. But she soon found that she had only exchanged one discomfort for another, for what with the strange people, strange dishes, and strange tongue, Marion had never felt so weary as during the two hours that Madame le Brun and her friends remained at table. But the dinner came to an end at last, and by nine o'clock Marion had sobbed herself to sleep in her little red-tiled room.

It would be impossible to describe the utter loneliness of Marion's life in the French school. The time occupied in giving her lessons, weary as they were to her from the frivolity of her pupils, hung perhaps the least heavily on her hands. In the evening, her only place of refuge was either her cold, comfortless little room, the dirty noisy classes, reiterating with cries of "taisez-vous donc, bavardes !" and "voulez-vous vous taire, mesde-moiselles ?" or else the even noisier lingerie, with the lingères and sewing women for her companions. Of this miserable selection the latter was generally Marion's choice by day, though all three were tried by turns. And what a choice it was ! Nothing but litter and uproar, with the younger children, to whom it formed a kind of nursery, constantly trotting in and out. But in the evening it was different ; for then it was that a circle was formed round the table near the heated poële, with the shaded lamp in the middle, all busy with their needlework. Why, then, did Marion, just coming up from that cold salle-de-piano, where she passed the earlier part of her evening practising, why did she turn away from the merry party, and run upstairs to her room, where, wrapped in her winter mantle, she sat sobbing, in spite of the morning resolution to be brave ? Marion Howard could bear the noisy children, she had learned, after a struggle never known on earth, to take her meals in a refectory, the description of which would not be believed by unsophisticated ears, she could tolerate the hundred other inconveniences of a second-rate or third-rate French pensionnat, but she could not bear the conversation of this hour of license, although the party only consisted of the disengaged sous-maîtresses, and the prim-looking little lingères.

"Qu' est-ce qu'il-y-a de mal ?" asked the mistress of the second class. Poor little soul ! she cannot see that the conversation is wanting in womanly reticence ; and so, while Marion sits upstairs, preferring the cold bedroom and the loneliness of her own pure little heart to the warm lingerie, with its busy tongues, made-moiselle continues her tale, amid such peals of laughter, that even la petite maman herself is at length aroused by the noise. Poor sous-maîtresses ! Surely, when God shall make up His jewels, they who in this life of slavery, shall have kept their faith, their hope, their charity intact, and their hearts unspotted from the world, shall shine lustrously indeed.

CHAPTER XX.

It was a dreary afternoon in the beginning of October. The leaves were fluttering down fast from the trees, and the chrysan-themums fell heavily and untidily across the paths, beaten down by the autumn rains. It was the last week of the long holidays, which had seemed doubly long to Marion, passed, as they had been, in the dingy classes. Had she been alone, she would have felt her solitude less, but about a dozen of the most unruly children had been left behind, under the melancholy guard of the sous-maîtresses, who were expected to return to what was truly for them a house of bondage, for alternate fortnights, during their holidays. Miserable companions were they, each and all, as, groaning for the hour of their emancipation, they occupied them-selves meanwhile in reading romances and scolding their awkward squad.

Hardly a glimpse of the great city had Marion had, beyond the race over it with Miss Hobart Jones; for though she had been unoccupied during the whole two months of her holidays, she had not dared to venture forth alone. Utterly weary, therefore, of doing nothing, there being nothing to be done, the poor girl looked forward with positive pleasure to the recommencement of her humdrum occupation. Anything would be better than idleness, and she quite longed for the moment when the classes should be again echoing with their usual hum. Already la petite maman, all the fresher for her sea-side trip, was looking into everything and everywhere, while the lingères, in renovated dresses, were working faster than ever, as they told stories of their holidays by the dozen. Marion had grown so tired of the uproar in the class, that she had stolen away to the music-room, and seated herself at the piano, but she could not play. Every chord she struck seemed mournfully akin to the dreariness of the dirty room, with its three shabby pianos, and the faint smell of dead leaves, creeping up through the open window. She rose, and descending to the garden, strolled along the wet paths towards the little chapel, that looked more dingy and neglected than ever, with its muddy footprints and rain-splashed windows. But Marion knelt and took out her rosary. Dust and dirt had lost their disturbing influence since her residence in the Pensionnat of Madame le Brun.

"Ma'amselle," said a voice behind her, and a letter was placed in her hand.

It was well she received it as she knelt, well that she read it there, well that the servant walked away without observing the sudden paleness of her cheek, as her eyes caught the black border of the envelope. Marion opened it; old Mrs. Howard was no more.

The letter fell from the young girl's hand, but for many minutes she neither moved her position, nor uttered a word in her sudden sorrow, almost too sudden and too great to be realised. Tears came at length to her relief.

"Grandmamma! grandmamma!" she exclaimed passionately; "my only friend! I have nobody left me now!" but, as she spoke, her eyes fell on the meek white face above the altar, and the hand presenting the little Child to the sorrowing world, and she felt that the words uttered in her first great grief were false.

The intelligence contained in Mrs. Gordon's letter to her young friend, was only too true. Old Mrs. Howard had passed suddenly away, the previous Sunday, on returning from church, so suddenly that she could not even leave one parting word for the child she loved so well. Nor was this trouble, heavy as it was, the only one our little heroine now found herself called upon to endure. For a long time Mrs. Gordon's letters had spoken of her declining health, and Mrs. Howard's death had occurred just as she was on the point of sailing with her family for the Bermudas. It was a hard trial for the widow to leave the home of her married life, but her physicians told her that it was her only chance of saving a life so precious to her little ones, and she left without a murmur.

"Would that I could stay to comfort you, my darling," she wrote to Marion; "but the London fog, rising as I write, warns me that I have already lingered too long. I have every hope that the gentle climate, to which I am hastening, will renovate my health, and that in a year or two we may meet again. Meanwhile, with many prayers, I can only commend you to God, and your kind friends at Harleyford. Over and above the business of our removal, a most important subject has been occupying my attention for some time past; in my next letter I hope to be able to tell you more of this, but at present I must say farewell."

Marion walked to her little room, where she remained all the evening, the laughter from the lingerie below jarring painfully upon her overwrought nerves. She wrote to Father Stirling, telling him of her bereavement, wrote to him in that strain of wavering hope, that the Catholic must employ, who sees beloved ones pass away in error but good faith. So engrossed was Marion in the one idea of her grandmother's sudden death, that it was not till she lay sleeplessly tossing on her little bed, that the concluding paragraph of Mrs. Gordon's letter stole into her mind, and she began to wonder what her subject of consideration could be. "I wonder if she is contemplating a second marriage," thought Marion; "I hope not, but I do not see anything else that she would not have spoken of outright."

Hardly a week after the receipt of Mrs. Gordon's letter, Madame le Brun summoned Marion to her private room, and informed her that having lost several pupils unexpectedly, she desired that the next month should bring their engagement to a close. Marion bowed and walked calmly from the majestic.

N

presence, but in her own little room the brave heart at last gave
way. All that she had borne there availed nothing, for she was
even now but an indifferent French scholar. How could she
return to England with her limited purse ; and even if she
returned, what could she do, still so unqualified as a governess ?
Looking steadily forward to this end, she had worked incessantly
at her French, and had associated with those from whose society
she shrunk, and now, must the work remain unfinished ?

Suddenly Marion remembered an Englishwoman who had
called on Madame le Brun, and to whom that lady had introduced
her as a compatriot. Miss Tubbler had informed her that she
contemplated resigning her lessons in the autumn, and should be
glad to dispose of her pupils. To her, therefore, our little heroine
now applied, though with sundry misgivings, for Miss Tubbler's
appearance was by no means prepossessing.

It would be a long dry story to tell of Miss Tubbler's promises
and their shortcomings ; of the handsome salary in perspective,
which degenerated into little more than the quarter of the sum,
out of which Marion had to pay Madame le Brun good terms for
remaining "pensionnaire libre." Nor will we tell of the lessons
in miserable pensionnats, nor of children from whom Golden-hair
fairly shrunk, all used as she was to the pupils of Madame le
Brun. Nor was this all we leave undescribed, for we could also
tell of harassing journeys to give these lessons, which were
scattered over the length and breadth of Paris, from Belleville to
Mont-rouge, from Vincennes to Vaugirard. Of the bitter morn-
ings when the snow lay thick, and Marion had to rise and trim
her lamp in the still heavy darkness, and then, half-breakfasting,
to find her way through fog or frost to the first omnibus, and its
crowded freight. Of the teaching all day after her flimsy morning
meal, and the return in the evening, often wet, faint, and sick at
heart, to the half-cold dinner in the school refectory, amongst the
uncleared plates and dishes of eighty pupils. And for this Miss
Tubbler asked the fourth part of the first year's earnings, and so
Marion plodded on by day, and lay awake at night, wondering
whether, with all her slavery, she was making enough to pay both
Miss Tubbler and Madame le Brun. The lessons dropped away
by degrees, and the items fell below the mark. What should
she do? The thought of debt, with Madame le Brun's frigid
politeness before her, and Miss Tubbler's dragon eyes, was something fearful. Summoning courage, she wrote to Miss Tubbler,
telling her how the lessons had fallen off from their original value,
and begging a little grace. "Pay me what thou owest," was the
reply, mingled with reflections so impertinent, that Golden-hair's
spirit was roused, and she sent her the hard-earned francs, with a
letter worthy of a Caractacus.

Should she now speak to Madame le Brun, asking her in her
turn to wait, or write to her mother? She resolved to try the
latter, and commenced, but her courage failed her, and she laid
the attempt in her desk, with an hysteric sob.

"What will be the end of it ?" cried the poor child. "Shall I write to Mrs. Darrell ? "

"No," said pride, and Marion thought no more of that.

"To Father Stirling?"

"His spare money must be for charity," said principle, and she shook her head.

"Lie down and die !" said passion, and, in a paroxysm, Marion tore Miss Tubbler's last letter to pieces.

Again it was the day before Christmas Eve, and Marion was looking out into the dirty street from the window of her bed-room. She had just come in from a long wet journey across the rough pavements of Paris, and her wet boots and mud-stained dress were lying beside her. She had not yet spoken to Madame le Brun, or written to England, but her lessons were even fewer, and her employers more exacting than ever. Instead of going down to her dinner, she stood still in the half-dark room, thinking of Ennington and Harleyford, and of that very day twelve months ago, when she received her mother's last kiss, before that happy drive with Joe to The Cedars. All were remembered, and Marion leaned her head against the window-frame and wondered what she would not give, except her religion, to be folded in that mother's arms again. And then she looked so sadly forward to the Christmas Day amongst the unruly few who were to be left behind, and thought of dear old England with its John Bull Christmas, its holly and mistletoe, roast beef and plum-pudding. Of the joyous gathering of friends, the songs, the dances, and romp of little children, for, child-like in her simplicity, Golden-hair clung to these simple pleasures still. She loved Christmas—loved it for God's sake, for home's sake, for England's sake. And as the glowing fire and beaming taper only make the winter night more dreary to the traveller without, so those memories of the past made the present more desolate still, and little Marion thought of England till her life seemed too hard to be endured.

"On vous demande, Ma'amselle," said a voice at the door.

"Who ? I ?" cried Marion, starting ; "a visitor for me ? Im-possible ! There must be some mistake." But she was very quick, nevertheless, in arranging her dress, and having washed her face to hide the traces of her tears, she descended to the reception parlour.

A small flickering lamp was burning on the centre table, but it yielded sufficient light to enable Marion to see that her visitor was a gentleman, and a stranger. He was apparently a military man, about thirty years of age, intelligent and thoughtful looking, though, perhaps, hardly to be called handsome. He advanced to meet her as she entered, but still more assured than ever that there was a mistake, Marion drew back.

"Miss Howard ?" asked the stranger, inquiringly, and she felt that he was scrutinising her in the uncertain light.

Marion bowed in great astonishment. Who could he be, what could he want with her ?

The stranger advanced and took her hand, looking very strangely
into her eyes. Marion tried to withdraw herself, but in vain, for
an arm was already round her waist.

"Golden-hair," said the stranger, softly, "are you afraid of
Edward?"

In another moment she had fainted at his feet.

"Water! water!" he cried, opening the door.

Several of the scholars, with Madame le Brun, ran quickly at
the unexpected summons. The latter looked very blank at finding
her petite Anglaise in the arms of the imposing-looking stranger,
for he had raised her from the floor, and, unconscious of spec-
tators, was kissing her forehead as he endeavoured to restore
her.

"Comment, Monsieur!" began Madame.

Alarmed, as he was, by Marion's fainting-fit, Edward awoke to
the necessity of an explanation. "I am her brother," he said, in
cool, calm English, "and have come to fetch her home."

"Son frère!" said Madame, much surprised, for she had no idea
that Marion had so near a relation. Madame le Brun took
another glance at the gentleman, read that in his eye that she did
not care to question, and bowed very graciously. Before many
minutes, Marion was once more conscious, and Madame le Brun
having departed with her pupils, she found herself in a large arm-
chair, and Edward, real, genuine brother Edward, face to face.
She looked at his dark piercing eye, his complexion olive from
exposure to Indian suns, his strong frame that had never suc-
cumbed even to that dreadful climate, and read in the frank look
and honest glance the pure soul that had expanded uncontamin-
ated, even in that land of luxury and ease. Edward Howard was
a grand realisation of Golden-hair's fairest dreams. As he called
her "little sister," and told her he had come to fetch her back to
England, to be with him always if she liked, for an instant the
pain of the last few weary months seemed already only an ugly
dream. But then came the thought of the disclosure that must be
made, and Marion thought of her mother and Henry Lisle, and
shook like an aspen.

"In ten minutes he too perhaps will have left me! Can I bear
this?"

Edward was talking very fast of the difficulty he had had to find
the school, but Marion heard very little of what he said, she was
thinking of the sweet cup about to be dashed from her lips, almost
untasted. Should she tell him now? Yes; it would be easier,
while they were comparatively strange.

She felt faint again with the first effort to speak, but placing her
hand upon her heart to still its beating, she rose from her chair.

"Edward," she said, "you have found Golden-hair, but you do
not know her yet. Listen, I have done that that has made mamma
and almost every one give me up; and when I tell you what it is,
you will perhaps leave me too."

To her surprise, he remained perfectly calm and silent.

"I would have written and told you, but my life has been so very sad lately, that a letter would have been nothing but grief; so I waited. Edward, I am a Catholic!"

"And I am a Christian," cried her brother, almost fiercely folding her in his arms. "Golden-hair, you tell me nothing new, so run and pack up your things, for I shall bring a carriage round for you in half an hour. We shall stop in Paris till after the jour de l'an with some friends of mine from Calcutta, who are living in the Rue de Grenelle. After that, we shall start for London, where we will set up house-keeping together. Poor dear grandmother! I just arrived in London in time to save the few little things she had left us; for you and I, Golden-hair, are her only heirs. What a sweet, pretty, little sister you are!"

CHAPTER XXI.

EDWARD Howard had been born in England, but from infancy India had been his home. His earliest associations were connected with the luxuriant vegetation of its tropical climate, and his first remembrance was his ayah. His mother and an unmarried sister had accompanied her husband to India, the former only to die there, but the latter married soon after her arrival, and having no children, adopted her nephew as her own. Under her fostering care, the little Edward grew to man's estate, and when the news of the fatal calamity that had befallen Captain Howard, was brought to her, it seemed that he was more solemnly than ever entrusted to her protection. When old enough to decide on a profession, he selected that of arms, and joined the regiment in which his father had held the rank of captain. Here he soon won the esteem of all, and few officers were more noted for true chivalrous spirit than Edward Howard. "Whatever I may be, I owe it all to you," he would exclaim, embracing his aunt: "what would the orphan boy have been, with his stubborn spirit and fierce passions, if you had not tamed him?" And he spoke truly, for it was her teaching only, that had changed his stubbornness into firmness and determination, and converted the impetuosity of youth into earnestness and zeal in the cause of truth and honour. Many times had the young man been tried in the furnace of temptation, but he had passed through his ordeal, and had come forth unscathed. And yet he had had his tribulations; one heavier than the rest, in the death of his mother-aunt, and soon after in that of her husband also. All they had, was left to the child of their adoption, who now that he had no longer any ties to bind him to India, began to glance towards the land of his birth. Having, therefore, "sold out," with a moderate fortune, Edward started for England, to seek the little bright-haired sister, whose letters had always won his heart.

It was towards the end of October, that Edward landed in England. Late one drizzling afternoon, just as the street lamps were beginning to glimmer through the mist, he arrived at the door of Mrs. Howard's house in Islington, with two cabs crammed inside, and piled high on the roof, with all kinds of heterogeneous luggage. A bill in the window, "To be let," startled him at first, but finding it still inhabited, he drew breath more freely, and leaping from the vehicle, the instant it stopped, rapped smartly at the door. After the summons had been repeated twice, a woman's head appeared in the area, and then as rapidly vanished from his sight. In a few minutes a youngster, bearing evident marks of "dirt pies" and bread-and-treacle, opened the door.

"Does Mrs. Howard live here?" asked Edward, who began to think he must have mistaken the address.

A finger thrust in the mouth, was the only response.

Edward repeated the question, but the finger remained unmovable. Out of all patience, he rapped angrily with his stick, and the result was the appearance of the dirty woman, whose head he had already seen, and who now came from the regions below, wiping the soapsuds from her arms with her wet check apron.

"Go to the baby, Johnny, you young worrit! one 'ud think you hadn't got a tongue in your head," and bestowing a hearty box on his ears, that young gentleman disappeared in his turn, scrubbing his eyes with his coat-sleeve.

"Does Mrs. Howard live here?" once more asked Edward.

"She did live here, sir, but she's dead and buried this month."

"Dead and buried!" repeated Edward, in a half-stupefied voice.

"Yes, sir, I'm in keeping the house. There's going to be a sale, I think, though I don't know. It was Mr. Twidgett, the lawyer, as put me in. Would you like to see the house, sir?"

"No, thank you," replied Edward; "can you give me this gentleman's address?"

"Yes, sir, there's an old henvelope in the parlour: if you'll be so good as to wait a bit, I'll get a candle and get it."

"Camberwell," said Edward, reading it, "is that far from here?"

"Indeed it is, sir, just the other hend o' London."

Thanking her for her information, Edward returned to his cab, and ordered the man to drive to the nearest hotel; when his baggage was stowed away for the night, and he found himself seated to a solitary meal, he gave way to his disappointment.

And was this his welcome to England?—death and desolation? The dinner went away almost untasted, and an hour later, Edward was on his road to Camberwell.

It was late when he returned, a heavy gloom was on his countenance. He looked gravely displeased, but he rang the bell and ordered tea.

"The rascal!" he exclaimed, as he stirred his tea, "a day or two more, and I should have been too late! Poor old soul, her little things would have gone to feather his nest!" He sat in deep thought for nearly an hour, but his brow grew more placid as he grew warmer, for the London fog had chilled him through and through, in spite of his wrappers. "Perhaps he has a large family," ruminated Edward, as the waiter having cleared away the tea-things, he prepared his cigar ; "poor fellow, he did not seem overburdened with this world's gear. But 'honesty is the best policy' after all, my friend."

"Forgive us our trespasses, as we"—the soldier paused that night in his evening prayer. But not for long, the victory was soon won, and Mr. Twidgett forgiven. "I must see about Marion to-morrow," was his last thought as he fell asleep, "my little Golden-hair!"

It was again a damp autumnal evening, as Edward and his portmanteau were landed by the stage-coach at Ennington ; but this time the fog rose clear and white from meadow and mill-stream, undimmed by the smoke of half a million fires. He walked briskly down the little street, "observed of all observers," for a stranger in Ennington was too rare an occurrence to be suffered to pass unheeded. But had a very legion turned out to scrutinise him, they would have stared unnoticed by the object of their curiosity, so thoroughly was he absorbed in the thought of the anticipated meeting.

"Which is Mrs. Howard's house?" he asked of a little girl he met, who was hugging a loaf almost as big as herself. The child, whose mouth was full of hot bread, nodded to the white house.

Edward walked up the little garden, usually so neat, but now half buried in dead leaves, while china-asters, Michaelmas-daisies, and chrysanthemums straggled over the wet paths, beaten down by the rain. The house, too, looked cheerless and uncomfortable, with its soiled blinds and ill-arranged window curtains. He could not have said why, but half the pleasure of his excitement had vanished by the time he reached the door. A grey cat sprang away through the bushes as he knocked, and glared at him angrily ; one could hardly have recognised in it the sleek-looking Tyrza of other days.

"Is Mrs. Howard at home?" he asked of an awkward-looking girl, who opened the door.

"Mrs. who?" asked the girl, roughly.

"Mrs. Howard."

"Never heerd on her, so I dunnow. I only came from t'other side of the country last week."

"Who is that, Lydia?" screamed a shrill voice over the balusters.

"Dunnow, miss. He says he wants a Mrs. Somebody."

The speaker descended ; a venerable spinster, to judge by her appearance, which was more ill-tempered even than her voice.

"I fear there is some mistake," said Edward, saluting her politely, "but I was informed that Mrs. Howard lived here."

"So she did," replied the lady, shortly, "but she has gone to live somewhere else, and I have taken the house furnished for twelve months."

"Excuse me," said Edward, whose countenance was below zero,
"but could you not give me her address?"

"No. I have lost it, and forget what it was—somewhere in
Clifton, I think. But she has behaved so unhandsomely to me,
that the less I hear about her the better, till I am obliged, so I
don't much care! Good evening to you," and the door closed
heavily.

This time, there was not even the London hotel to turn to, and
poor Edward stood at the little green gate, speculating as to his
next course of action. At this moment, our old friend, Dr. Stebbing, appeared in view, and Edward immediately crossed the
road.

"Excuse me, sir, but do I speak to the clergyman of the
parish?"

"You do, sir," replied the rector, taking off his hat, with old-
fashioned politeness.

"Then I hope you will be able to assist me in my unfortunate
position," replied Edward. "My name is Howard; I have just
arrived from Calcutta, and my welcome is a very sad one. Of my
three only relatives, one is dead, and my mother and sister, whom
I expected to find in that very house, are gone, I know not
whither."

"For the first trouble, I can, of course, only offer you my sympathy, Major Howard," replied the rector, extending his hand;
"with regard to Mrs. and Miss Howard, I can, I am happy to say,
assist you. But first, let me in their name bid you welcome to
England, for they are old friends of mine; I am too old-fashioned
to stand upon ceremony, but I shall be glad to see you home to
dinner with me. It is just about ready, and though you must
take us as we are, I think you will perhaps stand a better chance
in risking your bill of fare with me, than with mine host at the
inn. I will tell you the whole story. It is a fortunate thing that
you chanced to light upon me, as I dare say I know more about
Mrs. Howard's movements, just now, than any one."

Edward needed no second invitation, but accepted the first as
heartily as it had been given, and they were soon on their road to
the parsonage. It was a short walk, but it was the commencement of a long friendship.

"We will not enter into the subject, I think, till after dinner,"
observed the Rector, as he led the way into his sanctum, a very
learned-looking apartment.

"Certainly not," said Edward; "you have a splendid library."

The old gentleman looked much gratified, and finding his visitor
a kindred spirit in his bookworm propensities, it was not long
before a dozen curiosities of literature strewed the table.

"See, here comes my wife," exclaimed the doctor, breaking off
in the middle of a dissertation upon a new edition of certain
Greek tragedies, "I must introduce you." He did so, describing
how he had met his new friend alone and disconsolate before his
mother's door.

"You did not get much of a reception there, I will warrant," said the doctor, laughing. "Miss Smith and her mother, are, to say the least, very peculiar. They live like recluses, and generally contrive to get a maid as formidable as themselves. Unhandsome indeed ! I happen to know all about that piece of business, and were it not that Mrs. Howard is too high to enter the lists, I would soon force them to their first agreement. They are paying her about two-thirds of the terms arranged."

"And everything is getting ruined for want of cleaning," said Mrs. Stebbing.

"Oh, a little soap-and-water will soon set all that to rights, my dear ; and now perhaps that Major Howard has come, the other affairs may be set straight also."

"That is not the only family business that required righting," observed Edward, and he described the manner in which his grandmother's property had been left in the hands of her attorney. "She left few things of value," he continued, " but a great deal too much to throw away. The whole affair is a mystery to me, from beginning to end."

"When you have had your dinner, I shall be able, I have no doubt, to help to clear it ; so come, for I hear it is ready. You are naturally curious, but Harpocrates himself was not more discreet than I shall be, till you have well dined, and fortified yourself with a glass or two of my old port. I do not know how our edibles stand to-day, especially for one accustomed to Indian luxuries, but be they as they may, you have a hearty welcome, and as we used to say at school, *fames optimus coquus est.*"

According, however, to the doctor's idea of a good dinner, Edward did but little honour to the meal ; his single glass of wine especially outraged his worthy host, but he pressed him to another in vain.

"It is a custom I acquired in India," said Edward, "where a man, to be anything, must be very temperate."

"To be sure, my dear sir," returned the doctor, "there is nothing like moderation, but there is such a thing as the opposite extreme. A man with such a frame as yours, requires more than one glass of wine to keep up his stamina."

"It has been kept up on less than that in India," replied Edward, smiling, "for I drank very little besides water there."

As soon as Mrs. Stebbing had left them, the doctor began. "You have been looking so anxious, my dear young friend, for the last half-hour, that I can see the sooner I commence my tale the better. Really, however, I hardly know where to begin, for it is a long story, and in some things a sad one."

Edward started, and the dark complexion grew so pale, that the doctor wasted no more words, before satisfying his anxiety. He told him all. Of Marion's visit to The Cedars, of her conversion, and of her mother's stern determination, on hearing of the step her child had taken. He told him also, partly from surmise, and partly from words dropped by Mrs. Howard, of the unfortunate

termination of Mr. Lisle's wooing. He told him all he either knew
or guessed, and this was more than sufficient to prove to Edward
the lonely situation of his only sister. "I have often tried to
reason with Mrs. Howard," said the doctor, in conclusion, whose
honest eyes bore testimony to his sympathy, "but she is inexorable. To me, there is something fearful in casting off a young
girl into such a world as this, simply because she has embraced
an error. This is surely no way to dispel the infatuation!"

"Cruel! Abominable! Most unnatural!" broke in Edward,
with an energy that startled his host. "Can you tell me where
she is now?" he asked.

"I do not know, but I can give you Mrs. Howard's address, and
you can write to her."

"I would rather do anything else—poor dear child, I will try
and find her without a word from her mother if I can. What a
fortunate thing she has left this village, for how I could have met
her face to face, I cannot imagine; I know my fiery temper well,
and should, I am certain, have said to her what I might have
repented afterwards, for let her behave as she may, we must
remember she is Marion's mother, and was my father's wife."

There was silence for a few moments, broken at last by the
doctor.

"The last time I heard of Miss Howard, she was staying with
her grandmother in Islington. She wrote to me herself from there."

"And may be with that grandmother in her grave, for aught
we know," cried Edward passionately. "Forgive me," he added,
"but sorry as you are for me, you cannot tell what I feel. The
months that I have been upon the sea, for I came by the Cape,
have seemed short, in the one bright thought of seeing and knowing Marion. The idea of a simple-hearted English sister, to one
whose only experience of women has been the sickly enervated
girls of India, has been something more than a bright dream. But
now—it is dreadful!"

"Nonsense, my dear boy! Cheer up, you have only to look for
her; let us hope she is all right somewhere, though it will be, of
course, a grief to you to have her a Catholic."

"Oh, let her be whatever she likes! I shall not complain if I
ever find her."

"There is one thing I can do," said the doctor, brightening up,
"I can get you the address of her Catholic friends, who undoubtedly know where she is."

"If you only could, my dear sir," cried Edward, warmly, "what
thanks should I not owe you!"

"I will go this moment," said the rector, jumping up from his
chair, "there is an old cobbler here who goes over to Harleyford to
church every week, he will be sure to know it. I shall be back in
no time. Keep up your spirits, and go to Mrs. Stebbing in the
drawing-room. She was a great friend of your little sister, and
will tell you many things about her."

The doctor went, got the address, and, as good as his word, was back in no time. Despite his agitation, Edward passed a very pleasant evening with his kind entertainers, who insisted on his staying all night, but notwithstanding the softness of Mrs. Stebbing's spare bed, and the soporific influence of the "nightcap" that the doctor forced upon him, not for an instant did their visitor close his eyes, or lose the consciousness of his trouble. It was not that he did not hope eventually to find Marion, but the thought of what she had suffered, and must be suffering still, was most painful. Then there was his bitter disappointment, in finding everything so different to what he had anticipated, and—let him say what he would—if there was one thing on earth he hated more than another, it was the Catholic religion. "But I will win her back by kindness," said Edward, turning over to the other side, under the delusion that he might go to sleep.

He rose the next morning so haggard and feverish, that the doctor begged him to postpone his visit to The Cedars, till the following day. Edward was, however, fixed in his determination to lose no time in gleaning tidings of his sister.

"But I feel ill, nevertheless," he added, "I have caught a severe cold, and fatigue, excitement, and change of climate are doing their work. I shall perhaps be worse to-morrow, therefore I must work while I can." So saying, he took an almost affectionate leave of the doctor and his little wife, and walked towards the inn, at which he had already engaged a post-chaise to take him to Harleyford.

It was the first bright day that Edward Howard had seen since his arrival in England. Though very few leaves lingered on the trees, and those were brown and withered, and although the scene altogether, notwithstanding the yellow sunshine, looked damp and autumnal, there was still sufficient beauty lurking in the country through which he drove, to raise his drooping spirits. Still, as he remembered all he had anticipated in his little sister, and the pretty home she had so often described, that he had learned it almost by heart, and contrasted these pictures with the sad reality of the death of his grandmother, the tyrannical parent, the forsaken home and wandering Golden-hair, he felt that though his sadness might pass away a little, it would take something more than a gleam of sunshine to bring anything like a real joy into his heart. As the wheels crushed the dead leaves, thickly strewn in the narrow lanes, he could not help comparing them with his own bright anticipations. "I am glad it is October," he exclaimed ; "I could not have endured flowers and waving trees, they would have seemed to mock me."

After a drive of two hours the post-boy stopped at the lodge gates, and in answer to his summons Turner quickly appeared, smoothing her apron, and shading her eyes from the sun. There was something so picturesque in the unstudied attitude of the old woman, that Edward could not but look at her with interest, agitated and excited though he was.

"Does Mr. Darrell live here ?"

"He do, sir; but he and missus, and the young ladies are all away from home."

"Good heavens !" cried poor Edward, "what shall I do ?"

Turner shifted her position to get the sun out of her eyes, and looked at him, but Edward did not notice the scrutiny, as he leaned forward in the chaise, pondering within himself what he should do next. A sudden prance of the horses, followed by a sturdy "Wo ! will ye ?" recalled him to himself.

"When do you expect them home ?" he asked.

"Every day, sir; for they have been gone near upon a month, but they may stay a good bit longer for all that I know yet. It all depends on Miss Edith, sir; for it's only for her health that they are gone at all. She's weakly, rather, poor dear, that she be. Will you leave a message for them, sir ? I'll be sure to remember to give it them when they come back."

"Why, no," said Edward, "that would be of no use ; it is the address of a friend of theirs that I want."

"I see," said Turner ; "well now, sir, I'm a thinking that p'raps they know it up at the house. If you'll give yourself the trouble to write it down on a bit of paper, I'll step up in a minute and ask Betsy, for she have lived so long in the family, that I believe she knows all about their friends every bit as well as they do theirselves."

"Do you think so ?" said Edward, taking out his pocket-book with great alacrity. "Well, it is a Miss Howard, who was staying here some time ago, that I want to find out."

"Miss Howard !" cried the old woman, falling back, "what ! Miss Marion, my own darling child ! Is it her as you want ? Oh, deary, deary me, but you'll have to look far enough for her. Lawa, sir ! she be miles and miles away from here, my own precious child !" And old Turner sobbed heavily.

"What ! do you know her then ?" cried Edward, who could have hugged the old woman with all his heart.

"Do I know her !" echoed Turner, half indignant at the question. "Wasn't I the first as ever nursed her in this blessed world ? Wasn't it me as taught her to walk, and say her own mother's name ?"

"Well, I am her brother," said Edward, bluntly.

"Her brother !" exclaimed Turner, "Mr. Edward ! my poor master's son ! To think of that, now ! Oh, deary, deary me, what queer things does come to pass. O Mr. Edward, but it does my old heart good to see you, that it does, for now I look at you I can see my poor old master once again. Ah, sir ! but it was a weary day for many hearts when he got drowned."

"That it was," said Edward, with a sigh.

"And then you see, sir, it was double bad for me, because my poor man was lost at the same time."

"Then you are the widow of that old faithful Turner, that my father used to mention in his letters, and who was coming out with him to fetch me."

" To be sure I am, sir ; after he came to live with the master, I came to be Miss Marion's nurse."

And here followed the history of their life with Captain Howard, and hers with his widow, the whole so interlaced with eulogiums on her pet and nursling, that Edward's heart beat more warmly than ever for his little Golden-hair.

" And a dear faithful old soul you have been, I know," said Edward, holding out his hand, which Turner kissed most devotedly, to the amusement of the post-boy, who walked round the horses' heads to hide a very broad grin.

. " Mr. Edward ! Mr. Edward ! only to think of you're being here ! " she cried, again and again.

" Well now," said Edward, " can you get me the address ? But perhaps you know it."

" No, I don't, sir," replied the old woman, shaking her head slowly, " them gimcrack foreign names never would stick in my head, and if they did, it wouldn't be of no use, for I couldn't get them out."

" Foreign names," cried Edward ; " you do not mean to say she is abroad ? "

" That she is," answered Turner, sorrowfully, " all across the sea, where they speaks no English, and is all black, I believe, and pagans too, I dare say."

" Black and pagans ! Why, that misguided child can never have gone to Africa ! "

" No, sir, that's not the name ; it's in Paris, I'm thinking."

" But they are not black there," cried Edward ; " though I am not so sure about the paganism," he added bitterly.

" Ar'n't they, sir ? Well, I didn't know. But, Mr. Edward, it seems all one and the same thing to me, whether they are black or white, so long as she's in a forrin country. I only know I couldn't walk to her now, nor get a lift in a cart, even if she was dying, and the thought of her breaks my heart. O Mr. Edward, sir, but it do seem to me real cruel, that her mother should cast her off like an old shoe."

" I think you and I had better say nothing about her, Mrs. Turner."

" So we had, sir, much better ; besides, I promised Miss Marion I wouldn't ; but for all that my blood boils above a bit, when I hear the wind at night, and think of her all snug and comfortable-like in her bed, not knowing where her own flesh and blood is."

" Come, come," said Edward, smiling, " you are breaking your promise, even now."

" Am I ? then the Lord forgive me, and her too."

" Now," said Edward, " will you get me the address ? "

This time Turner fairly started, and in the interim Edward, alighting from the chaise, paced backwards and forwards before the gate.

. " Have you been able to get it ? " he asked, as Turner re-appeared.

"No, sir, that I haven't; nobody here knows it at all, but Betsy says she has no doubt Father Stirling could give it to you."

"Father Stirling! Who on earth is he?" asked Edward, knitting his brow.

Turner hesitated. "He is the priest, sir, and has had a great deal to do with Miss Marion," replied Turner, "for it was him as baptized her, as they call it."

"Was it?" said Edward, stamping his foot; "then if I cannot get the address except from him, I will do without it. Sneaking villain!"

"O Mr. Edward, sir, but, indeed, he is a real gentleman. Now, please don't take on so, because you see it can't do no good. I tell you what," added the old woman, soothingly, "go up and wait at the house, and I will run down to the Father myself, and ask him. I'll be bound he knows."

"The Father!" cried Edward, sneeringly, "one would think you were a papist too, old woman!"

"No, no, Mr. Edward, I'm not a papisher, really!" exclaimed Turner, alarmed for her orthodoxy; "but my Liza is, and that's how I come to know him; and somehow, one gets into the way of speaking like other folks does. Besides, he has been real kind to my Liza and the dear boys. Now, go up to the house, there's a dear good young gentleman, and just wait in the drawing-room, and I'll run up to him and be back in no time; Bennie there will mind the gate. He don't live far off, and you'll see how quick I'll be."

"No," said Edward, after a pause, "I will not trouble you, I have altered my mind. I will go myself, and just tell him what I think of him and his rascally proceedings. A girl of eighteen to be duped into separation from her own mother! That mother may have been harsh in her judgment, I know," he added, half speaking to himself, "but that makes no difference in his crime. 'Leading captive silly women.' Ah, St. Paul, how truly spoke the words of inspiration there! But, we shall see; I shall be much astonished, sir priest, if I do not surprise you a little before I have done with you! Well, good-bye, old woman," he exclaimed, turning suddenly to Turner, who stood by looking anxiously at him. "I am very glad to have found you, for you have been a very ray of brightness to me in my trouble. I shall run in and see you again, if I can, though as yet I hardly know what my plans may be. If my sister is in France, as you seem to think, I may go over there at once, and never visit this part of the country again. But Edward Howard will never forget Marion's old nurse, come what may." He held out his hand as he spoke, and, after a warm, affectionate grasp, two shining sovereigns glittered on the old woman's palm.

"Mr. Edward, sir, Mr. Edward, please don't!" cried Turner, holding out her hand.

"Hush, just for a remembrance, you know," cried Edward; "perhaps I shall never see you again."

"Yes, but you will though, I know you will. I shall live to have you come to see me yet, with my own sweet darling hanging on your arm. The Lord Almighty bless you, and may you see her very, very soon."

Without waiting to see the carriage move off, Turner rushed into the house, and, seizing up Bennie, began crying over him as if her old heart would break.

",What's the matter, grannie?' asked that young gentleman, rather surprised at this sudden burst of affection.

"Oh, but he's the image of his father, that he be!" cried Turner, kissing the sovereigns, while Bennie looked as if he did not quite understand this answer to his question.

When Eliza came home that night, and the boys were in bed, she heard a story that made her open her eyes.

"But even now, mother," said Eliza, at the end of the recital, " I can't tell whether he is angry with Miss Marion or not."

"Well," said the old woman, "the fact is, child, I don't think he knows hisself. He's angry with her mother above a bit, I can see, although he is too gentleman-like to say so to the likes of me. He's furious agen the Father, but he has got the poor, dear old captain's own heart, bless him, that he has ; and he loves his sister so well, that he's ready to forgive her anything. Why, bless you ! he's talking already of going off to France after her, and it ain't likely he'd go all that way to tell her he'd have nothing to do with her ! No, he's sorry she's a papisher, but he don't forget she's his sister, for all that. And very nat'ral, too, I say, for that's just how I feel about you, Liza, my girl."

CHAPTER XXII.

FATHER STIRLING was seated in his study, so deeply engrossed in the perusal of a certain heavy folio, that he did not remark the unusual apparition of a post-chaise standing at his gate. It was not until his housekeeper had placed a card bearing the name of Major Howard, under his very nose, that he raised his head, and, to his no small surprise perceived the phenomenon.

"The gentleman is waiting in the parlour, Father."

"Major Howard ! Who can he be ?"

"Don't know, sir, I never saw him before," answered Martha, whose breath had nearly been taken away with astonishment. "I wonder who he is ?" she continued, after her master had left the room, and she turned the card over about half-a dozen times, as if she expected it to solve the enigma.

Edward was standing when the priest entered the apartment, and, as he refused the chair offered him by the latter, there was, of course, no alternative left for Father Stirling but to stand also.

"Mr. Stirling, I believe ?" said Edward, haughtily, and drawing himself up to his full proportions.

Father Stirling bowed gravely, and waited for whatever was to follow so formal an announcement.

"You know my sister, I believe," continued Edward, finding that the other still remained silent.

"I have the honour of knowing a Miss Howard, a Miss Marion Howard, if you allude to her ?"

"I do," replied Edward. "Well, sir, I want to know where she is."

"In Paris, I believe," said Father Stirling; "at least she was there when last I heard of her."

"Well, sir, and how came she there?" asked Edward, in an overbearing tone.

"Really, Major Howard, I should have enough to do, were I to attempt to fathom all the motives by which my friends are actuated in their proceedings. But I do not suppose I should be very far wrong, if I were to say I suppose she went to learn French."

"An evasion, sir," cried Edward, in a loud voice, "and you know it."

For an instant the hot, proud blood rushed through the veins of George Stirling, but he controlled himself by a great effort, and only looked very much surprised.

"Are you aware, sir, you are giving me the lie ?"

"I nevertheless repeat it !" cried Edward, in the same tone. "It is an evasion, for you know it was not to learn French that my sister went to Paris."

"Then, sir, I can only say, since you understand her motives so much better than I do, it is a great pity you should waste your time in asking me about them. I have given you my own impression of her reason for going, but, as it seems I am mistaken, perhaps you will not think it too much trouble to enlighten me ?"

"Well, then," returned the other, "my sister went to France because she had no longer a home in England."

"Indeed," replied Father Stirling, "I am sorry to hear it, though how this could be the case, I can hardly understand. The door of her mother's house was, I know, closed against her, but there were three homes, to my knowledge, open to receive her. Two permanently, and the third certainly till she could provide herself with a suitable engagement as governess."

"Engagement as governess !" replied Edward; "and what should make the daughter of Captain Howard require a situation as governess, I should like to know ?"

"That which reduces the daughters of many captains to a like exigency—the force of circumstances. Notwithstanding the kind entreaties of her friends, she steadily refused their invitations, and went to Paris to fit herself for a profession that would render her independent of their assistance ; I must say, sorely against their desire."

"Acting for once by her own free will," said Edward, sarcastically. "There was no advantage to be gained from coercing her in this instance, I suppose?"

"Nor in any other," replied Father Stirling. "Miss Howard possesses one of the firmest minds I ever met with in a young person, it would be difficult to coerce her."

"I am sure, sir," said Edward, curling his lip, "your opinion of my sister's strength of mind is very flattering to her, and ought to be very gratifying to me. What indomitable will and courage in so young a girl! To seek a new religion, embrace it, defy her mother, become an exile in a foreign country, and all this, with no other aid than her own firm mind and will! Why, Mr. Stirling, my sister must be an eighth wonder!"

"She would be, Major Howard, were this all true, but you have mistaken me. Your sister found a new religion, and she embraced it in this very chapel. She bowed to her mother's decision, though she did not defy it, for she loved her too well for that. She lives even now an exile from England, but she has not done all this by her own mind and will."

"By whose then? Yours?"

"Mine! That had been as weak, even weaker perhaps than hers. No, all that she has done, and is doing, was and is in the strength of Almighty God."

"And you dare stand in the face of daylight, in the presence of God Himself, and utter such words as those? Speak of Him, 'too pure to behold iniquity,' as counselling and encouraging disobedience, and the want of all natural affection! O Popery!" he continued, clasping his hands, "can we be surprised at its fruits, when such are its ministers!"

Father Stirling's lip was almost bitten through with determination. "Whoso loveth father and mother more than Me, is not worthy of Me."

"Even Satan," replied his visitor, "can wrest the Scriptures to serve his ends."

"I cannot see what I have wrested in that quotation," observed Father Stirling.

Edward laughed scornfully. "Not in the letter, perhaps, and thus it is that Romanism wins over silly girls. But I should be sorry to insult your common sense by thinking, for one moment, that you yourself believe half the nonsense you profess and teach."

"And yet I would a thousand times rather that you did insult my common sense, than insult God in my sacred calling, as you have done, ever since you entered my house, Major Howard."

"When a man acts as you have done, with regard to my sister, he cannot expect to be treated with anything but contempt."

"You are begging the question, sir, but as I am willing to believe you are misled, partly, perhaps, from prejudice, I will tell you what I really have had to do with Miss Howard. Some few years ago, when quite a child, your sister came here to visit Mrs.

O

Darrell, and was, I believe, even then rather struck with the ceremonies of our worship. I myself, upon one occasion, had a little
conversation with her, about the Catholic Sunday, I remember,
but that was all. A few days after, she and I were severely
injured by the upsetting of a gig, and I did not see her again for
five years. At the end of that time, she again visited Mrs. Darrell,
and one morning, while that lady and her daughter went on a little
errand of charity, Miss Howard remained with me in this very
room. Our conversation was upon religion, but the subject was
commenced by herself. She asked me many questions, which I
answered to the best of my ability, meanwhile praying earnestly
that God might enlighten her. Not another word was said by
either of us on the subject, though we frequently met, until she
called upon me one Sunday afternoon, and told me, that being
thoroughly convinced that the religion of the Catholics was true,
she had resolved to become one. Then three weeks later, having
instructed her, I received her into the Church. You know, it
seems, as well as I, the persecution that followed ; I trust some
day you may hear her trials from her own lips. This is all I have
had to do with her conversion, but I candidly tell you, that could
I think my poor prayers, or imperfect explanations, had been
instrumental in it, I would thank God on my bended knees, for
having condescended to use so poor an instrument in so great a
work. But I cannot felicitate myself on this, for my share in the
work was very small. And yet, Major Howard, you come to my
house, and as though by some unlawful act I had led away your
sister into a course of crime, you insult me, nay, almost brand me
as a liar. Nevertheless, I can willingly believe that you are a
gentleman. I can well imagine that your ordinary accents are
those of courtesy and politeness, but many a man fails to see that
it derogates from his position as a gentleman, to treat a priest
with opprobrium and insult. You say, I do not believe half the
doctrines I profess. Why then do I profess them ? Is this lowly
roof and quiet life, think you, a great reward, for the pain and
trouble of such a life-long deception as mine must be ? If I do
not believe this religion, why did I, like your own sister, give up
everything the world holds dearest, to embrace it ? Perhaps you
think that I am only holding fast the error in which I was reared.
You are mistaken. I too am a convert. You have charged me
with falsehood, would you like me to accuse you of cowardice ?
My father was a soldier ; supposing, like him, I had taken up the
arms of this world, I believe I do not err in saying, that you would
not have dared to cast an innuendo on the officer, where you have
so strangely insulted the priest. But while the soldier of this
world resents his injuries, the soldier of Christ must bear them
patiently. When the general of an army lies on the bare earth,
his followers must not murmur for a softer couch ; and the disciples of Him who was 'spit upon, and reviled,' must look for
persecution, and complain not when it arrives. I place my cause
in the hands of Him, who is even now judging between us."

There was a long pause. " Mr. Stirling," said his visitor, walking up to him and offering him his hand, " you are right ; I have grievously wronged and insulted you. Believe me, though, nothing but the blow I have received in finding my sister so alienated from her family could have made me forget myself as I have done. But I am truly sorry."

Father Stirling smiled one of his own peculiar heart-smiles, as he warmly grasped the proffered hand. " I can well understand, my dear sir, what you feel, aware as I am, of the horror with which our religion is regarded by the generality of Protestants. Let me say, however, that it is for want of knowing it better. Protestants see a genuflection, and they cry 'Idolatry !' they hear that we worship the Virgin Mary, and they cry 'superstition ;' while confession and absolution are defined by no loftier epithet than 'tom-foolery.' Is not this true ? "

" It is not far wrong," replied the other, smiling.

" And yet see what men give up for this 'idolatry, superstition, and tom-foolery,'" returned the priest, " and this, not only the ignorant and weak, but men of high mental power and education. Perhaps, Major Howard, in India, the following fact may not have come under your notice, but during your sojourn in England, just remark this. A change from the Protestant to the Catholic religion, is rarely, if ever, attended with any worldly advantage to the convert. It frequently entails upon him the loss of home, friends, position, and property, sometimes, indeed I may say often, of the whole four combined. When, on the other hand, do we hear of a person giving up the Catholic religion, who does not with the change, gain some worldly advantage ? It may be the wife to please the husband, and ensure the harmony of the domestic circle, or *vice versâ*, or else the starving Irishman who gives up, or *pretends to give up* his faith, for bread to feed his little ones. It may be temporal interest that is the bait, such as that gained by the apostate prelates and courtiers, who, under Henry the Eighth, fattened on the sequestrated revenues of the Church. Should a priest of our own day fall from his high estate, it is, I might say without exception, because he has grown weary of his vows, and can find no respectable way of breaking them, but by apostasy. Do we ever see a man suffering for Protestantism ? I do not say there is not such a man, but I do say, that with all my experience of the world, I have never met with one. I have seen the apostate priest the hero of the platform, hugged, courted, caressed, by the credulous public, but never have I seen a man leave the high places of our Church, just as all lay fair before him, to creep into an obscure Protestant curacy for his conscience' sake. But I have seen, and do see every day, Protestant clergymen give up good benefices to become obscure priests, or, if married, even to glide silently into the secular life, into some employment perhaps most contrary to their tastes, and only sufficient for their daily bread. And why ? Because when God says 'come !' they dare not tarry. And in this, my dear sir, I am not speaking from what I think or

opine, but from what I *know ;* and if you will look into the subject
for yourself, you will see that I have spoken truly. But come,"
he added, changing his tone, " I do not see why we should still
stand facing each other in this antagonistic fashion, sit down and
tell me all you wish to know about your sister. Nothing could
give me greater pleasure than to render you any assistance in my
power in finding her, for I know no one in whom I am more
interested. I may truly say, her troubles have been mine, poor
child."

Edward took a chair. " It is her address in Paris I want, for I
must go and see her at once, though my plans are as yet so uncertain that I hardly know what my course concerning her will
eventually be."

" You have not seen her for some years, I believe ? "

" I have never seen her," replied Edward.

" Never seen your own sister ! How very extraordinary ! Then
let me tell you, you will find a little body as good as she is clever,
and as pretty as she is good ! She is a universal favourite here."

Edward's eyes sparkled. Impulsive fellow ! He was beginning to like Father Stirling wonderfully. " Do you think she is
happy in France ? " he asked.

Father Stirling hesitated. " Well no," he said at length, " I do
not think she is. Mrs. Darrell showed me a letter from her the
other day, throughout which, though it was cheerful, we could
both see the tone of cheerfulness was assumed. I know what
French schools are, and I cannot see how a girl tenderly nurtured,
as she has been, can possibly be comfortable there. I know she
must fret after home."

" And she shall have one ! " cried Edward, impetuously ; " I will
stay in England as I at first intended, and she shall be my little
housekeeper. But I tell you candidly, I shall leave no stone
unturned to root out her new ideas. Before six months are over,
you will find her as good a Protestant as ever."

" I can trust her," said Father Stirling, laughing, " she is too
humble in her own strength to fall, you too strong in your fraternal
love to tyrannise. There was a tremendous bow-wow when you
first came in, but you are too much like Marion for it to last long."

Edward laughed. " Well, I was thoroughly savage with you, I
know. Everything I had set my heart on, seemed to have
vanished like the ' baseless fabric of a vision,' and I certainly
traced all my troubles to you. But things seem much clearer
now. I cannot tell you what a relief it is to me to find it was not
necessity that drove her abroad. It is also a comfort to know
that one of my poor grandmother's last acts was to befriend her."

" Which she did most tenderly, I can assure you," replied the
priest. " Although herself not oppressed with this world's goods,
Miss Howard's determination to become a governess was highly
distasteful to her grandmother. She was ready, she said, to
retrench in any way for the pleasure of having her with her. But
though she was liberal-minded, her friends were not, and your

sister soon perceived that her religion was the cause of no little discomfort to her kind relation. This decided her course at once, and she went to France."

"Do you think Mrs Howard knows of her mother-in-law's death?"

"I cannot say. Old Mrs. Howard has been dead a month, has she not?"

"Yes; so at least Mr. Twidgett, her lawyer, informed me, who is the only person from whom I have received any intelligence concerning this sad event. He says that he wrote to Mrs. Howard informing her of it, but that he did not receive any answer from her. At first I attributed this, rather harshly perhaps, to indifference, but I now think it probable that the people who have taken her house at Ennington, and who have a very unfriendly feeling towards her, may have neglected to forward the letter. I shall be glad if it be so, as it will remove one great cause of displeasure I have entertained against my step-mother."

"Yes; it does not do to judge harshly," observed Father Stirling, "it is always safer to hear both sides of the question before giving the verdict."

Edward smiled. "The cap fits," he remarked.

"So does mine," returned the priest, "for within the last half-hour, I prejudged somebody very severely."

"And with good reason," replied the other.

"I did not know that Mrs. Howard had left Ennington," observed Father Stirling, "nor do I think your sister is aware of it, for she did not mention the circumstance in her last letter."

"Probably not," said Edward, "seeing that there has been no communication between the mother and her child. I have no doubt myself, that Mrs. Howard left Ennington because the place and its associations were too much."

"Do you purpose finding her out also?"

"Certainly not. I shall leave her to herself. She has no claim upon me, and as she is amply provided for, I need not trouble myself about her. I could not be decently civil to her if we met, and, therefore, for her sake, Marion's, and mine, I had better keep out of the way. No, I shall see my affairs a little straight, and then start for Paris. Will you give me the address?"

"I will go and look for it," said the priest, rising, "it is in my study." He left the room as he spoke, but in a few minutes returned empty-handed.

"I am sorry to say I have put it away with some letters, but I will make a search and send it down to you in the course of the evening, that is, if you purpose passing the night in Harleyford."

"Such is my intention; perhaps, as I am a stranger, you will recommend me a hotel."

"The Green Dragon is generally considered the best, I believe," said Father Stirling.

"Then the Green Dragon let it be; may I have the pleasure of your company to dinner with me at six?"

"With the greatest pleasure. I trust by then, I shall have found your sister's letter. Au revoir!"

Father Stirling watched the chaise drive off from the little green gate, a smile on his lip, and a strange earnest light in his calm grey eyes.

"What will be the end of it? Will there not be danger in her constant contact with such a spirit as that? No, Marion Howard, I do not fear for you! Truth shall triumph! God only knows; perhaps he too will become a Catholic!"

He walked back into the house, and taking up his breviary, turned over the pages abstractedly. At length, laying the book upon the table, he passed into the chapel, and walking slowly up to the rails, knelt before the altar.

What was his prayer? Something so earnest, that the time passed unheeded, and the October sun was casting a slanting shadow on the image of Mary, investing it with a ruddy life-like glow, before he rose from his knees. "This one, even this one," were his last whispered words, as, rising to his full height, he once more bowed his knee as though loath to quit that Presence, the Faith, and Hope, and Love of his lonely life.

CHAPTER XXIII.

"An ostler from the Green Dragon wants to see you directly, Father," said the housekeeper, opening the parlour door, the afternoon after Edward Howard's visit to the priest.

"The Green Dragon!" cried Father Stirling, opening his eyes, "the Green Dragon—to be sure, but whatever can be the matter? Major Howard has left me a message, I suppose. Show him in."

"Please, sir," said the man, entering, and pulling a piece of hair that seemed to grow on purpose for salutations, "please, sir, warn't it you as dined with a Muster 'Oward at our place last night?"

"To be sure I did."

"Then, sir, the Missus sent me to tell you, as how the gem'men is uncommon bad. He's took off his 'ed altogether, sir, he be."

"When was he taken ill? He complained last night, but I did not for an instant apprehend anything serious; I thought he would have left this morning, or I would have gone to see him the first thing. Have you a doctor for him?"

"No, sir. I went for two on'em as I comed here, but they was both out. He was feverish when our Polly, the chambermaid, went to call him, though he didn't get real, to say bad, till about an hour or so ago."

"Tell your mistress I will be down directly, and will bring Mr. Seymour with me. Poor fellow, what a dreadful thing! Stay, here's something for your trouble."

"Thankee, sir," said John, pulling his lock and vanishing.

Edward Howard's illness was no slight attack, and within a few days from the time of his arrival at Harleyford, life and death seemed poised upon an equal balance, and battled stoutly for the victory. As he himself had said, fatigue, excitement, and change of climate, had worked their will on a constitution not too strong, and two sad faces bent over the young soldier's bed.

"It is certainly the crisis," observed Mr. Seymour, taking out his watch and lifting the burning hand.

Father Stirling sighed.

"This is too much for you," said the doctor, "we shall have you knocked up next."

Except to say Mass, Father Stirling had hardly quitted the sufferer's bed.

"I wish now I had written to his sister, but I was afraid of alarming her needlessly, poor child."

"You acted for the best in not doing so, but no one can tell how these things terminate. I apprehended no danger yesterday, now I must say I feel very uneasy. You see the lucid intervals become rarer and rarer. He is a fine young fellow, it would be a great pity."

"Sua voluntas fiat," said Father Stirling, "but the idea of his passing away in his Protestantism, is a very sad one."

"And yet I fear it must be so," replied the doctor, "for even were his mind to become clear, as is sometimes the case at the last, it would not be the moment to attempt his conversion."

"God's ways are not man's ways," replied Father Stirling, almost sternly, "nor are our seasons His. We never know; I have seen stranger things than even this would be. But I hope he will recover."

"I shall be glad when Jarvis comes, for I begin to feel very anxious," said Mr. Seymour.

At that moment Dr. Jarvis and another medical man entered the room, and Father Stirling walked down stairs to leave them to their consultation. At the foot of the stair-case he was met by the landlady, who told him that Mr. and Mrs. Darrell had just come, and were waiting for him in the parlour.

It would be impossible to describe the real pleasure with which Father Stirling welcomed his friends.

"We have only just arrived," said Mr. Darrell, "but as soon as we reached the gates, Turner gave us your message, asking me to come to you here. It seems the man told her that Major Howard was ill, and the old woman has been in a dreadful state ever since, especially as the answers to Eliza's inquiries have grown more and more unfavourable. So I sent the girls in, and Mary and I drove down at once. Now tell us about him. Is he in any danger?"

"Very great danger; Seymour says, humanly speaking, the chances are equal."

"Poor fellow."

"Have you a good nurse?" asked Mrs. Darrell.

"That we have not : if I could have left him, I would have gone to look for another. She is a dirty, deaf, snuffy old woman, about as useless and uncomfortable in a sick chamber as you can well imagine."

"You shall have Turner."

"Now that is an act of real charity," said Father Stirling. "I was wondering how we should manage to-morrow, for I must be away all the morning, and I could never have found it in my heart to leave him with Mrs. Brown."

"But you have not yet told us anything about him," said Mr. Darrell ; "what sort of a man is he ?"

"Thoroughly good," and here followed the story of Edward's visit to him, with its stormy beginning, and tranquil termination. "I dined with him afterwards, in this very room," continued Father Stirling, "and I must say, I never passed a more pleasant evening. He is a man of first-rate education, good sense, and universal intelligence, while his ordinary manners are those of a well-bred gentleman. I can understand his illness very well, for I am sure his excitement must have been something very tremendous, to induce him to transgress the rules of social politeness, as he did at first with me. Will you go up and see him as soon as these gentlemen come down ?"

The creaking of boots on the stairs announced that the consultation was ended, and our little party mounted to the sufferer's room. When Mr. Seymour joined them a few minutes later, they saw plainly that his hopes were vanishing fast.

"One of the most acute cases of brain fever I have ever known," he remarked to Mrs. Darrell, "but we must hope for the best."

"I think I had better stay with you," replied that lady, who had already seated herself in the nurse's chair, and was arranging a pillow as only a woman can. "I can do so very well," she added, placing her cool, soft hand on the young man's throbbing brow.

"Indeed, you must do no such thing," replied Father Stirling, "it would be a great deal too much for you after your journey. Mr. Seymour will, I know, agree with me."

"I am sure it would," replied the doctor, "only let us have Mrs. Turner, and we shall manage very well." And so having straightened the bed, and dismissed the obnoxious nurse, Mrs. Darrell departed with her husband, and about an hour afterwards old Turner set out, on what was truly to her an errand of love.

Father Stirling and his new assistant passed a dreadful night, as side by side they watched their patient, now raving in delirium, now prostrate from utter exhaustion. Mr. Seymour came and went the whole night through, snatching from time to time an uneasy sleep in an adjoining room. The hours rolled on, and as the danger became more imminent, the doctor's face grew more anxious still ; Turner wept bitterly, and Father Stirling prayed long and earnestly. Another hour of watching, at the end of which the sufferer fell into a doze ; not a breath was heard from the watchers, and gradually the slumber grew deeper and more peaceful. When the morning broke, Edward was sleeping like an infant, and the three faces, lately so sorrowful, were radiant with delight. The crisis was over, and the patient saved.

It is not our intention to pass with poor Turner through all the dull monotony of the sick chamber, as her charge slowly recovered. He did recover, and before the end of three weeks was sitting in a large chair before his bedroom fire, pale, it is true, and still very weak, but looking very bright indeed for an invalid. Old Turner, at the further end of the room, sat knitting, looking up occasionally from her work, comparing her patient with the dear old master, and rejoicing in the happy chance that had made her his nurse during his sickness. In the front of the fire, mulling some claret, stood Mrs. Darrell, while Emily was just unpacking a perfect harvest of grapes and nectarines on the little table.

"You are too good!" exclaimed Edward, turning to the latter; "you do not know what I have been thinking of all the morning."

"No. Something very deep, I suppose."

"Deep and simple too. I have been thinking of the story of the good Samaritan. I need not tell you what brought it into my head."

"The sight of some good old man on a donkey in the street, I daresay," replied Emily.

Edward smiled. "It was not a sight at all that suggested it, but rather a thought. The thoughts of the kind hearts among whom a certain wayfaring stranger had fallen. But the stranger I was thinking of, was even better off than the traveller of the parable, for where he found one good Samaritan, I have found many."

"You! I see then, Mr. Egoist, you have been thinking about yourself. If you were a Catholic, you would not be allowed to do that."

"Indeed, what then do Catholics think about?"

"Other people."

"Ecce signum!" said Edward, pointing to the fruit, "well, then, I must be half a Catholic, for I know I think very often of all of you. If Marion be only half as good, I shall be satisfied."

"Marion! She is a little angel, Major Howard, you will be delighted with her."

"When I see her, perhaps I may," said Edward, moving restlessly in his chair, "but I wonder when that will be, I gain strength so slowly. I can hardly cross the room yet."

"Nevertheless you are strong enough to bear the journey to The Cedars, I am sure," said Mrs. Darrell, turning round from her claret, "and I shall call and speak to Mr. Seymour about it this very afternoon."

"What! hamper yourself with a sick man, my dear Mrs. Darrell!" expostulated Edward, "indeed, this must not be."

"But indeed it must," said Mrs. Darrell. "Come now," she added, merrily, "you have borne such a good character for

patience during your illness, you must not grow refractory now.
You are very dull here, and want fresh air and society, and you
must have them.   Three weeks in one room is enough for
anybody."

"Have I been ill only three weeks?" asked Edward. "It
seems an age. I wonder what poor Marion is suffering all this
time. I am afraid she is very unhappy in France."

"I hope not, otherwise I should be anxious for her to come to
us at once. As it is, I think it would be better that she should
remain, until you are well enough to fetch her. The journey
from Paris is long and dreary for a young girl alone. It seems
strange not to let her know any of these late events, but to tell
her you were here and ill, would make her very uneasy; and of
course, if she knew you were in England, we could not account
for your not going to see her in any other way."

"Besides," rejoined Edward, "I know it is a silly idea, but I
have set my heart on surprising her."

There was another thing too, on which he had set his heart,
and that was on making her a Protestant, before he again
subjected her to the influence of the Darrells. Grateful as he
was to them, he still shrank from their religion.

The very next evening saw Edward on the drawing-room couch
at The Cedars, where a cheerful party were gathered round the first
fire of the season. What is there, gentle reader, in a first fire?
Nothing more than usual, surely. And yet you and I both know
well, how brightly it burns and dances up the chimney, and how
it laughs among the cups and saucers, putting the very lamps and
tapers themselves to shame. Another will be lighted to-morrow,
and it will be a cheerful, bright, and homely fire, but it will not
be as redolent of comfort, as ecstatic in its sparkles, as last night's
blaze. Is it the first gushing melody of the home spirit, the first
kiss of his lip, as he nestles afresh upon the hearth? Perhaps; I
know not, but I do know, that one has brighter thoughts and
dreams beside the first autumn fire, than perhaps anywhere else
on earth.

Happy as they were, our little party were very quiet, the three
ladies busy with their needle-work, and Mr. Darrell and Father
Stirling with their chess. Edward looked from one to the other;
poor fellow, it was the first English fireside he had ever seen, and
he thought of Marion, and formed a bright vision of many
evenings such as this. Was he not satisfied, when in all human
certainty he might soon expect the vision to be realised? Men are
strange beings! riddles in their longings, riddles in their dis-
content—not quite. He could not have said why. Perhaps, dearly
as he loved his little sister, another idea, indefinable even to
himself, had entered the soldier's heart. For Marion he had sold
his commission, and crossed the ocean, and left the friends of his
childhood, and yet, at this moment, perhaps for the first in his
life, he felt as though her affection would not content him. He
glanced round the room again, and covered his face with his

hand, and thinking that he slept, the voices grew more hushed. But he was awake, keenly awake to every sound and word, especially to the music of two girlish voices, though he could not tell which was the sweeter of the two.

"You must take your medicine, for you know Mr. Seymour has made me head nurse," said Emily, handing him the glass. "Stop, let me shake up the pillow."

It was soon done, and Edward sank back again, thanking her with his eyes; had it been a block of stone placed to receive him, the touch of those light fingers would, he believed, have made it a bed of roses. As it was, he nestled in the down, and, for the first time in his life, wove a romantic story.

The days flew by, till the couch was exchanged for a chair, and that again for the carriage. Then came walks, and even rides on horseback, until the full tide of life and strength returned, and Edward was himself again. Yet not himself, for though the red blood mantled in his cheek, and the light shone in his eye, he was an altered man. The soldier who had been impregnable to the battery of so many Calcutta seasons, had yielded without a struggle to the first English glances, though strange to say he could not tell which of the two sisters had conquered him. "Who could choose between them?" he asked himself, as a morning or two before his intended departure, they tripped into the room, radiant in their new winter bonnets, to take him to see a water-fall a mile or two from the house. "One might as well try to decide between the red and white rose, or the morning sunshine and evening moonlight!"

The walk to the waterfall was a merry one, for the girls laughed and chatted all the way, and Edward was exuberant in the joyousness of recovered health, and the happiness of the present moment.

"If it could be always like this," he whispered; but when he thought of Marion, a pang of reproach shot through his heart. "My darling Golden-hair!" and the truant sped back to his allegiance.

"Papa and mamma talked of coming to meet us," observed Emily, as they were returning, "if they do so, I suppose we shall see them very soon. What a delicious heap of leaves to walk in!" she exclaimed, suddenly bounding like a kitten, to the other side of the road, and rustling them with her feet. "I do so love this. Come, Edie."

"No, thank you, I do not like to trouble the dead. 'Requiescant in pace.'"

Emily laughed, and continued her walk. "I wish all sacrileges were as harmless as this."

"'Requiescant in pace,'" repeated Edward, "it is sweet to repeat those words over forgiven injuries, old sorrows, and dead friends. It is a good wish uttered in pretty words."

"Very," replied Edith, "especially in our religion, where the words are a prayer as well as a wish."

This was almost the first time religion had been mentioned to him by any of the family, and, coming as they did, from Edith, the words made him look up in surprise.

"I mean what I say," she added, smiling. "It seems to me, Mr. Howard, that a religion that does not pray for its dead, must be very cold and comfortless. If those I loved were to pass away, my only consolation would be to pray for them."

"Am I simply to bow, or am I to answer what I think?"

"The latter, certainly."

"Then forgive me, if I say, that the beauty of the idea is no excuse for the falsity of doctrine. We do not pray for the dead, because we do not believe in the efficacy of such prayers. As the tree falls, so it must lie."

"Most assuredly, for there is no repentance beyond the grave. A man dies only once, and then he dies for either heaven or hell."

"So we say, but you go further, and imagine a third place," rejoined Edward.

"Indeed! Where is it?"

"I do not know; it would be rather difficult to decide, but I mean purgatory. You believe in that, do you not?"

"I should hope I do," replied his companion, smiling, "but I look on purgatory as heaven."

"What can you mean, my dear Miss Darrell? If your idea of purgatory be what I have been told it is, it must be a peculiar kind of paradise!"

"Perhaps so," replied Edith, "but it is part of paradise, nevertheless. Is not the certainty of heaven, think you, paradise in itself? Suppose, Major Howard, you built one mansion with a porch and another one without, how many houses would you possess?"

"Two, of course."

"Then call one of these houses hell, and the other heaven, with its porch purgatory; and you will understand what I mean. For what would centuries of suffering be, compared to an eternity of joy, but a little, little porch? It has always amused me, from a child, to hear people outside the Church talk as though three distinct hereafters lay before a Catholic. What can there be for a saint but heaven, and for a sinner but hell?"

"But if heaven be limited to saints, it will be but scantily peopled," observed Edward.

"And yet it certainly is limited to them," replied Edith, "for we know that nothing defiled can enter the kingdom of heaven; and what is the world at large, but fearfully, dreadfully defiled?"

"The Blood of Christ cleanseth from all sin," exclaimed Edward.

"Yes, I know that, for the Catholic looks to Christ and to Christ alone, for the remission of his sins through the merits of His Blood shed for the whole world on Calvary. Without this, there would be no treasure in the Church, no grace in any

Sacrament, no efficacy in any contrition, no salvation, no heaven for any of us. Nothing but hell, black, and yawning for all."

She paused but her companion made no reply.

"You did not think our Christianity was so simple, perhaps," remarked Edith.

"Candidly I acknowledge, I did not. I did not expect half such a clear bright confession of the great Gospel Truth. But you are an exception, Miss Darrell. Upon what do the generality of Catholics build their faith?"

"Upon 'Jesus Christ and Him Crucified.' Do you think, Major Howard," she suddenly asked, turning upon him the full light of her dark earnest eyes, "that I would tell you an untruth?"

"I am certain you would not," was the reply.

"Then believe me when I tell you, that in that name the faith, the hope, the heart-love of every Catholice centres. The sunless world, the soulless body, the sightless eye, would be but faint types of a Christless Catholicism. You might as well talk of heaven without God."

"But if then your faith in the merits of your Redeemer be so strong, where is the need of purgatory?"

"I can simply repeat what I said before, that nothing defiled can enter heaven."

"But can anything be defiled, that has been washed in the Blood of the Lamb."

"Certainly not," replied the young girl, "hence it is, that there are souls that pass at once to the presence of God. Souls that have lived in such union with Him, have toiled so incessantly at the work of their salvation, and sought so constantly the cleansing stream to wash away each speck and spot of contamination, that by the grace of God, who gave them this disposition, they have passed straight and undefiled into the Beatific Vision. Clean in heart, they see God. But what shall we say of the tepid, the negligent, the slothful, the timid believer? Shall such a one be wafted straight to that heaven, for which, perhaps, he has hardly ever sighed? And yet that man was a believer. There have been moments in which he would have died for his religion, others when he has even wept over his sins, because they had offended a Father, whom with all his carelessness, he really loved, and dying, he has called on Him for pardon, and on Christ for help and grace. Shall that loving soul, although so feebly loving, be cast into hell, to become the prey of the devil and his angels? Who could love our dear Lord and believe in His love for us, and imagine such a thing as this? But when he shall have expiated his sins, shall have been tried in the furnace seven times heated, and when he shall have been purified like fine gold, then we believe he shall be hailed in the mansions of eternal rest, and find a home among the 'Everlasting Hills.'"

At this instant they were joined by Emily, who seemed rather surprised at the turn the conversation had taken.

"I am glad you have come," said Edward ; "Miss Edith is trying to convert me."

"I wish she could," replied Emily, "though I am afraid that is more than she will manage in one morning's work."

"Well, certainly, purgatory is not a very inviting doctrine to begin with," answered Edward, "I must say I infinitely prefer the Protestant idea of stepping quietly and comfortably into heaven at once."

"There now," exclaimed Emily laughing, "you yourself have exactly given the difference. What we believe is a *doctrine*, what you believe an *idea*. You could not possibly have given a better definition."

"I did not intend it as such, I can assure you," returned the gentleman ; "my definition would be just the reverse, of course."

"You do not make any distinction between mortal and venial sins ?" observed Edith.

"Decidedly not. 'Sin is the transgression of the law ;' so says the Bible, nor does it say more. I find nothing of the words mortal and venial."

"Do you believe, then, that when you have an uncharitable thought, or practise a little act of selfishness, you are on a par with Nero or Caligula ?"

"No ; I have too good an opinion of myself for that."

"And yet rash judgment and selfishness are sins, are they not ?"

"To a certain extent they are, and consequently displeasing to God, for which reason I should do my best to avoid them."

"But suppose you do not avoid them, for human nature, remember, is very frail ; what then ?"

"I must repent."

"But suppose you do not even do this, for human nature is also very blind, and little sins glide through our consciences, very much as the metal held in solution passes with the water through the sieve. What then, do you expect to go to heaven in spite of the 'transgression of the law,' or is your portion to be with Nero and Caligula ? You see you must make a distinction in the gravity of sins. Shall I tell you our doctrine on the subject ?"

"Yes, do. I like to hear you talk about your religion, you look so earnest. I am not surprised at Marion changing hers, with you for her pioneers."

"Major Howard," said Edith, pausing in her walk, and looking at him stedfastly, " you must not give either Emily or myself the credit of Marion's conversion, for she never spoke to either of us on the subject until she had quite made up her mind. We prayed for her very hard, just as we are doing now for you, but we never said a word to her."

"You do not mean to say you pray for me to become a Roman Catholic !" said Edward, laughing.

"To be sure we do," replied Emily.

"Then heartily, most heartily do I thank you ; but, believe me, that prayer, sweet as are the lips that breathe it, has never yet pierced the 'golden pavement,' though may God grant, that as it sinks back to earth, it may fall in blessings on the heads of the two fair supplicants."

"Shall I tell you, Major Howard, what a little angel whispered to me last night?" asked Emily, "just a little secret."

"Do; angels' whispers and ladies' secret are worth hearing."

"Well then, he told me you would one day be a Catholic."

"Did you believe him?"

"I did; and mark my words, if ever you are a Catholic, you will be a priest. Mind, you are to say your first Mass for Edith, and your second for me."

"Agreed," cried Edward, laughing, while Emily joined him with all her heart.

Why did another little figure bow her head, and rustle the dead leaves in her turn?

"And so you wish me to be a Catholic?" continued Edward, musingly. "Well, I can thoroughly appreciate the kindness of the hearts that breathe the wish, believing as those hearts do, that in the word Catholic is concentred all that is most glorious in God and goodness, but it will never be. Catholics cling too much to the merits of their own good works for me, seeing, as I do, in the word of God, that 'salvation is by faith alone.'"

"I cannot understand that," replied Emily, "for the 'devils believe and tremble.' For myself, I cannot imagine how the two can be separated, for 'faith without works is dead,' and works without faith would be only heathen virtue. People blame us a great deal for our reliance on our good works, but after all we must all be saved by them; we cannot be saved without. It is not only the atonement that is necessary, but the application of that atonement to our souls; for though Christ has died for the whole world, many thousands fall into hell every day in spite of Him. And why is this, but simply because they hate God and love sin. Now, it is a bad action to do either the one or the other, and they are lost. Every day, let us hope, many souls are welcomed in heaven. Why is this? Because they loved God and hated sin. Here are two good actions, and they are saved. I can only tell you what I think in very simple words, for I am not so used to talking about religion as Edith is, and cannot express myself so well, but do you see what I mean?"

"Perfectly."

"Then, when the great good work is performed, and the sinner is in a state of grace, we believe that any other good work he may perform expiates the temporal punishment due to him, and merits for him a greater increase of glory in that heaven that Christ has opened for him. But if Edie explained our doctrine of mortal and venial sin to you, you would understand this better. I do not pretend to be a controversialist, and it was she who entered the lists with you. I am only the 'squire, to carry the shield and hand the weapons."

"I am sure I know very little of controversy," replied Edith, smiling, "but I know what I believe as a Catholic, and why I believe it. Voilà tout. A mortal sin is a grievous offence against God, which deprives the offender of the friendship of God and sanctifying grace, and renders him deserving of eternal punishment in hell. Venial sin is a smaller offence against God, which does not deserve hell, but which must nevertheless be expiated before entering heaven. This may be by repentance and suffering here, or by purgatory hereafter."

"I see. Then purgatory has nothing to do with mortal sin."

"Yes it has, in this way. The temporal punishment due to every grievous sin will be inflicted there, if not expiated before in this world. I see you do not understand this. The Catholic Faith teaches that, besides the eternal punishment due to sin which, as all believe, was turned from us only by the death of Christ, there yet remains another, over and above, and this is what is called the 'temporal punishment.' I can show you what this is, by an example from the Old Testament. David committed a sin, and Nathan the prophet, sent by God, visited him. The king repented : 'I have sinned,' said he, 'against the Lord.' And Nathan replied, 'The Lord hath taken away thy sin ; thou shalt not die.' Thus was the eternal punishment remitted, but see what followed after. 'The child that is born to thee shall surely die.' Here was a temporal punishment inflicted to satisfy the offended majesty of God, though the sin had been forgiven. Again, do you remember how in his pride David once numbered the people ? Once more he repented, once more he was forgiven, but once more was the temporal punishment inflicted. Seven years of famine, three months' flight before his enemies, or three days' pestilence. He chose the last, but imagine what an alternative ! Is it not enough to make one tremble, for how shall we stand if a penance such as this was inflicted for a sin comparatively slight, and that after it was forgiven ?"

"But this was not purgatory."

"It was not inflicted in the place, or rather state, that we call purgatory, but it was a purgatorial or cleansing punishment, inflicted to render David once more pure in the sight of God. Temporal punishment is not by any means invariably inflicted after death. God frequently sends it here in the form of some heavy cross. More than this, we may even anticipate it in this life by some penance, voluntarily borne, to disarm the vengeance of God. It may also be forestalled by good works, as when our Lord says, 'He that converteth a sinner from the error of his ways, shall save a soul from death, and cover a multitude of sins ;' and again, 'give alms, and all things are clean unto you ;' and when St. Paul says, 'charity covers a multitude of sins.' We may anticipate it by prayer, as we have once more an example in King David, for part of the penance inflicted on him in the three days' pestilence was remitted upon his prayer at the threshing-floor of Araunah the Jebusite."

"There is one thing I should like to know," said Edward, after a pause of some minutes' duration ; " do you believe God forgives a sin, however great, upon the repentance of the sinner ? "

" Certainly ; provided it is a true repentance, not only a horror of hell, or a remorse caused by human considerations, or a regret springing from personal suffering, caused by one's own sins, though these are all well and right in their place. It must be a true, deep, earnest compunction for having offended so great a God, and so good a Father."

" And this you believe is enough to save the soul ? "

" Undoubtedly it is."

" Then why confess your sins to a priest ? "

" Because the sacrament of penance is the medium God has Himself chosen for the confessing of the sin, and the according of the pardon."

" I do not see this," replied Edward.

" ' Whose sins ye shall forgive, they are forgiven ; and whose sins ye shall retain, they are retained ;' and again, ' Whatsoever ye shall bind on earth, shall be bound in heaven ; and whatsoever ye shall loose on earth, shall be loosed in heaven.' "

" Of course I knew, my dear Miss Darrell, that these two texts were coming ; if it were not for these, your doctrine would indeed be unsupported. But, just look here. Can you imagine anything more likely to have a demoralising effect upon the mass of the people, than the idea, that let a man's sins be what they may, he has only to go and whisper them to a priest, and then, these forgiven, commence afresh his course of crime and iniquity ? "

" Not more than your own doctrine of faith and repentance is demoralising," replied Edith. " There is only this difference between you and ourselves. The Protestant who repents, kneels down in his own chamber and confesses his sins, to go forth and sin afresh, while the Catholic has the additional trouble of going to the priest. Rather, therefore, than an easier process, the Catholic's confession is the more difficult one of the two. But if you imagine that a few words whispered, for form's sake, in a confessional, will ensure forgiveness of the sins confessed, you are grievously mistaken. A humble gesture, a bowed head, a sad voice, may deceive a priest, and the absolution may be pronounced, but God looks at the heart, and if sorrow for sin be wanting, that absolution will not be ratified in heaven. 'To err, is human ; to forgive, divine.' Man, weak, erring man, may rise from his knees, and quit the confessional, only to sin again. But if while he spoke those words, 'I confess to Almighty God,' he did confess his sins, resolving, with all the steadfastness of his heart, to keep from evil, as from his Father's most bitter enemy, both you and I, Major Howard, know that that repentance was genuine, however signally he may fall afterwards. If, however, that man should content himself with a cold, callous confession, unaccompanied by sorrow, or if he should wilfully conceal one grave sin, that man would leave the church, even deeper dyed in iniquity, for he would have added sacrilege to his former guilt. What the pen is to the writer, such is the priest to the hand of God. A weak, frail instrument, it is true, but the medium of great and glorious things. Of all the seven pillars of the Church, there is not, after the Holy Eucharist and Baptism, such a sacrament as this. You are, I believe, Major Howard, a Christian ; you have led, I do not doubt, a consistent, conscientious life, but there must be shadows on your conscience you do not like to look at. Could you once hear those words, ' go in peace,' as the door is closed, you would understand why I feel so deeply as I speak to you of this. Could you but glance into our religion for one moment with the eye of faith, you would see what great and beautiful things there are in it. They lie like pearls and precious stones at the bottom of a river, but the water is transparent, and he who looks may see them shining through, while he who dives for them, may draw forth a shining store ! "

"Sweet enthusiast !" thought Edward, as he glanced at the beaming eye and flushed cheek of the young speaker. But he said nothing, and our little party moved on in deep silence, broken only by the wind as it creaked the leafless branches, and by the discontented twitters of the sparrows overhead. But a fervent prayer was rising from one heart, long since detached from earth, and a strange new day-dream was flitting round another, while Edward, as he strode on between them, found that the walk to the waterfall had decided a wavering balance.

Soon after Mr. and Mrs. Darrell appeared in sight, and the girls and their escort hurried forward to meet them.

"Have you enjoyed your walk ? "

"Immensely," replied Edward, and he spoke the truth.

CHAPTER XXIV.

HARDLY an hour had elapsed from the moment of Edward's arrival at the school, before Marion found herself packing her trunks in the little room at Madame le Brun's. Even now she was obliged to pause occasionally in her task, to reassure herself that she was in reality up and awake. "Supppose it should be a dream, after all, and brother Edward only a phantom of the imagination !" But the garments strewed around were sufficient to prove that it was a veritable packing-up, and her boxes were just deposited downstairs, when she heard that Edward had returned, and was waiting for her.

It was difficult for the brother and sister to imagine that they had only just met, and had never met before. Having left the luggage at his friend's house, Edward drove back to a grand restaurant on the Boulevard, all light and glitter, that they might have the few first hours of their meeting all to themselves. They had a great deal to say, and before they left the table, Edward had sighed over her conversion, stormed, in spite of his good resolutions, over her banishment from home, and had nearly laughed himself into a fit over Miss Tubbler and her exactions. But Marion could not imagine that he saw the gravity of the case.

"Listen, Edward," she expostulated, as they walked home along the brilliant boulevard; "if I do not stop and go on with the lessons, Miss Tubbler will expect me to pay her, I do not know how much money."

"She is quite welcome to do that," rejoined her brother; "now, just explain the whole affair to me, for it seems a most complicated piece of business."

Marion did so.

"And how much have you already paid her?" asked Edward, in conclusion.

Marion named the amount.

"Then she may return you a few pounds, if she likes, for conscience' sake, or retain them in remembrance of a silly little girl. Oh, deliver me from Miss Tubbler; what is she like?"

"A woman, I suppose," answered Marion, laughing.

"I question it," replied her brother.

At this moment Edward hailed a voiture, and they were soon driving towards the Champs Elysées.

"Golden-hair," asked Edward, in a low voice, "what is this story I hear of a certain curate?"

Marion's face, which had been raised to hear the question, was suddenly turned away.

"What is it?" he asked again.

"Only that he has given me up, too."

"Were you engaged to him?"

"No."

"Then how could he give you up?"

"He came to Harleyford to ask me to be his wife, and I told him I was a Catholic," said Marion firmly.

"And what then?"

"He went away, and I have never seen him since."

"And do you care for him?"

Silence gave consent.

"Well, cheer up, darling," cried Edward, "it will be all right yet. I do not at all despair of seeing you a Protestant again. When we are settled, I will get you some thoroughly good books on the subject, and take you to hear some of the very best preachers, and we shall see if they do not convert you back again."

Marion started up with such energy, that she fairly startled him. "Do you suppose," she exclaimed, "that I would read a Protestant book, or enter a Protestant church? Do you think I want to be converted back again? I would rather ten thousand times stop here and work at Miss Tubbler's lessons all my life. Edward, my brother, let us understand each other at once! I have longed for you, looked for you, prayed for you, as earnestly as I should think a poor shipwrecked sailor looks for land, but, unless you promise to leave me free, quite free in my religion, I dare not go back with you. Even if it killed me to see you go without me, I would welcome death before apostasy ! "

"Golden-hair," said her brother, "you misunderstand me. I promise, before God, to leave you free to serve Him, as you will, when you will, where you will. Is that enough ? "

Her head drooped upon his shoulder. "I will try to be all you can wish in everything else."

"That promise is more than enough," said Edward ; "for I only want a sister's love."

The time in Paris passed quickly by. The sea was soon crossed again, some of the furniture removed from the little house in Islington, more bought, and, before many weeks, our little heroine found herself the installed mistress of a very pretty villa, in one of the sunniest suburbs of London. Edward's vision was realised, and he thought so, as one windy evening in February he and Marion sat in the neatest of little parlours, learned-looking with his books, home-looking with her nicknacks, and bright with their grandmother's Indian curiosities. The little copper kettle sang merrily between them, just as he had done a year ago, when Marion and the dear old lady, now so silent in death, had discussed her conversion and future plans. His song was a merry one too, although he had commenced at first with rather a melancholy whirr, as though in heart he still lingered among the shadows of the past, with the little coterie at Islington, and was not yet accustomed to his villa home. But soon he bubbled gaily, and Marion, who had been for some time watching his red nose very earnestly, rose to make the tea.

"I shall be getting jealous of that book soon, Edward," she exclaimed, as he sat, after the fashion of all bookworms, hastily conning the last few words of the chapter, before laying it by.

"Buckland" closed with a bang, and in two minutes they were as merry as the cricket, whose song reached them even there, from his home under the kitchen hearth.

"I had a letter from The Cedars to-day," observed Marion, as she handed him his tea.

"How are they all ? "

"Very well. It was from Mrs. Darrell, and she tells me two pieces of news."

"What are they ? "

"One is that Joe is coming home next month. It appears he has been ill, and has been recommended to return to England ; but Mrs. Darrell seems to think that he is, in reality, tired of the sea, and wishes to settle down at home."

"And what is the other piece of intelligence, if I may ask ? " inquired her brother.

"Something that ought to make me very glad, but it seems so strange, that I cannot realise it at all."

Edward began to feel strangely nervous, and wished she would come to the point at once.

"I suppose I may tell you," she continued, "though as yet it is, to a certain degree, a secret. One of the girls is going into a convent. Guess which."

"Good heavens!" cried Edward, as though a fearful catastrophe had been related to him.

"Well, which is it?" asked Marion.

"Edith, of course," said Edward, crossly, beginning to weigh his tea-spoon on the edge of his cup.

"Then you are wrong."

The teaspoon was just balanced, but it lost its equilibrium in an instant.

"What, Emily!" cried Edward; "well, you do astonish me! I never could have thought it. I am no judge, of course, in such matters, but I should have imagined Edith the very girl likely to be taken by the fancied charms of conventual life; while, as for that laughing, chattering, beautiful Emily, she seems the very antipodes of a nun."

"This is because you do not know them yet: those who know Emily best, say she lives constantly in the presence of God. With all her light-heartedness, I am certain you never heard her say a giddy word, nor do a giddy thing."

"Never; on the contrary, the real earnestness of her character often shines through those very words and actions, but, for all that, Edith is much more sedate."

"Not in reality, but she is very much quieter. But she is a more general favourite than her sister, demure as she is, especially with gentlemen."

"Is she?" ejaculated Edward, rather drily.

"Which do you like best?" asked his sister.

"Emily is decidedly the nicer-looking; indeed, I do not think I ever saw a prettier girl in my life; and her manners are very winning."

"Am I to infer from that, that she is the favourite?" asked Marion, laughing.

"No, not at all; mind has always a great charm for me, and I consider Edith highly intelligent. It is a pity she is so quiet, for when she comes out, she shines."

"I know that," replied Marion.

"I have heard of light being hidden under a bushel," said Edward, after a long pause, "but I never heard of a greater sacrifice than for that beautiful girl to shut herself up in a nunnery. If she were a fright, it would be a different thing."

"Edward, Protestant though you are, you would not surely offer only ugly, worthless things to God."

"Certainly not: in anything I thought He really cared to accept I should, of course, consider nothing too good to offer Him. But He has never asked people to become monks and nuns, and never will. It is a useless, unnatural life."

" How so ? "

" In the stupid vows they make, to be sure."

" And yet, dear Edward, of these three vows, the first, on a certain occasion, was a command of Christ Himself, the second was enjoined by an apostle, while the third is added to enable frail humanity to carry out the other two."

" How do you mean ? "

"Simply this. A young man once came to our Blessed Lord, to ask what he must do to be perfect. Not merely to lead a good consistent life mind, for that an easier answer might have been returned, but to be *perfect.* The answer was, to sell all he had and give it to the poor, and follow Jesus. Here, then, is the nun's first vow of voluntary poverty. With regard to the next, of celibacy, St. Paul speaks of those who marry as doing well (as of course they must, for matrimony is a sacrament), but he speaks of those who marry not, as doing better. And who was it, who, with His own lips, said the better part should not be taken from her, who, giving up even the lawful cares of this life, sat at His feet instead ? Surely, what Christ has approved, and St. Paul enjoined, must be right ; and hence, as I said just now, the second vow of the recluse. But this was not following to the letter that divine command, ' let him deny himself, and take up his cross, and follow Me.' True self-denial is difficult to practise, for naturally a man is tender to his own flesh. The horse without a bridle often runs to its own destruction, and where could such a bridle be found for man as obedience ? Another man sees our faults, and is a beacon to us ; he sees our virtues, and can encourage us on our way; he sees our dangers, and can warn us. Moreover, if we would learn to practise self-denial in its intensest form, we must give up our will. Heart, liberty, life itself, is nothing to this ; for until a man knows what it is to do everything at the bidding of another, he can never realise the full sternness of the command ' leave all and follow Me.' Thus the religious makes the greatest of sacrifices, gives up all, and makes the third vow of obedience."

There was another long pause, filled up by the little copper kettle, who sang as vigorously as a choir of nuns.

" I wish you would look a little, just a very little, into our religion," remarked Marion.

" Now, Golden-hair, I declare that is too bad. Just think how sharply you were down upon me, when I asked you to examine mine."

" Because you asked me to *re-examine* a religion in which I have lived nearly all my life, and doctrines which, having thoroughly understood, I saw good reason to disbelieve, or I never should have disbelieved them. I, on the contrary, ask you to look into a subject on which you have never perhaps thought seriously for ten minutes together."

" How do you know that ? "

" Of course, I do not know it, it is only a surmise. Tell me, however, that you have seriously considered it, and I shall be satisfied."

"Candidly then, I never have, and equally candidly it has been, because I have never thought the subject worth the trouble."

"Are you afraid to read one of my books?"

"Not at all. Indeed, I should rather like to do so, that I might understand your arguments better."

"Then I will bring one to your room this evening."

That night the well-worn, shabby "Keenan" lay on Edward's toilette.

It was about a month after this, that Marion, who was writing a letter, heard her brother's step in the passage much earlier than he usually returned from the British Museum, where he spent the hours that would otherwise have hung heavily upon his hands.

"Edward," she exclaimed, springing from her chair, "how early you are! Is anything the matter?"

"Nothing, you little nervous thing!" was the reply, as he pulled her back in her chair to the no small disarrangement of her curls. "There, just order tea an hour earlier, and go on with your letter. The fact is, I want to catch the train, for I am going away for a few days. Shall you be very dull without me?"

"I shall miss you, of course, but I daresay I shall find plenty to do. I might have the garden altered while you are away : shall I?"

"Do, it will give you occupation;" and here followed a long list of instructions, very precise in detail, but nothing to do with either you or me, dear reader.

"I am glad you are going," said Marion, when he had concluded, "for I think you require a change of some kind. You have been looking pale, almost ill, for the last few days."

"I know that, but the change I most want is something to do. Where do you think I am going?"

"I have not the slightest idea."

"To Harleyford."

"To Harleyford! What! to The Cedars?"

"Yes; I am going to be introduced to Joe, and if I like him, I shall make a proposal to Mr. Darrell."

"I am sure you will like him; everybody does; but what are you going to propose?"

"Well, to tell you the truth, I have been cogitating very much over a letter his father wrote me yesterday concerning him. I have been thinking that, as he has energy, I a little experience of the world, and both of us a moderate capital, we might enter into a partnership in which these three qualifications might be very useful."

"Edward, I should like it so much," cried Marion: "what a first-rate idea!"

"At first I thought we would go together; but as the weather is still cold and cheerless, I decided that we would ask the girls here first, and that you should go back with them to Harleyford, when you would have brighter days for a country visit."

"I should like that much better; you always guess my wishes exactly."

"It would be hard if I did not study my 'lone and only bird' a little, I think."

" I do not know when Emily goes into the convent," said Marion, "but ask her to come and spend a little time with me first."

"I will. And now come and help me to pack up my portmanteau, for I must be off in half an hour."

Marion did miss her brother very much, notwithstanding her horticultural labours, for she had more time than usual to think, and she thought incessantly of her mother. Although, as a rule, she said but little to Edward on a subject in which she felt he could not naturally sympathise, the sad thought of their estrangement cost her many a sleepless night and bitter tear, though gratitude to him kept her always cheerful in his presence. Now, however, that she was alone, she gave way to her sorrow, much to the contempt of her maid, who informed the servant next door that her mistress "couldn't take on more if her young man had gone to sea, and all because her brother had gone away for a week." Ah, Golden-hair, you are not the first person whom the world has misjudged, or whose affairs have been canvassed over the garden wall.

The week had lengthened into a fortnight before a cab one evening drew up before the gate, and Marion, radiant with delight, once more welcomed Edward home. Again the little kettle sang, it seemed to Marion, a dreamy song of expectation, as she watched her brother, who was making the viands disappear with wonderful celerity.

"And now I suppose I may begin to talk to you," she exclaimed, as he laid down his knife and fork. "What do you think of Joe?"

"He is a capital fellow : I have no doubt that we shall eventually enter into an arrangement, perhaps after Christmas, but his father wishes him to travel a little on the Continent first. Emily, I find, enters the convent in May. I suppose you know she is to be in London."

"No, I did not."

"Mrs. Darrell will bring her up, and they will stay with us for a week. It is expected she will take the veil about July, when the whole family will come to town. After the ceremony Joe and Edith will spend some little time with us, and when he starts on his tour we shall go back with Edith to The Cedars."

"A very nice arrangement," said Marion; "I am so delighted that Emily is to come here."

"And now, Golden-hair," said her brother, "I have a strange piece of news for you."

"About whom?" she asked, with a faltering voice, for his manner half alarmed her."

"You must guess ; but do not be afraid, it is nothing in any way tragical."

Marion did her best, and there was not an event, likely or un-likely to transpire at The Cedars, that she did not imagine.

"You are not near it," said her brother; "I will tell you this much, it has something to do with Father Stirling."

"He is going to leave Harleyford."

"Not that I know of."

"Some one has left him a legacy."

"No such luck."

"Edward!" cried Marion, suddenly, the blood rushing through her heart like a wave, "he is reconciled with Henry Lisle."

"No, dear, he is not. What a wild idea!"

Marion could not attempt another guess after that.

"He received somebody you know into the Church last night, somebody you know and love."

"My dear old Turner."

"No," said her brother, looking strangely at her, "somebody dearer still."

"Edward, my own darling brother!" she exclaimed, springing towards him with a low hysterical cry.

A deep and solemn silence reigned in the room, as she knelt before him, with her head upon his knee, while more than one tear fell down upon the golden ringlets—a silence broken only by the song of the little kettle, who sang in Marion's ears a "Gloria in excelsis."

"This has been 'Keenan's' work," said Edward, when Marion was once more seated soberly vis-a-vis; "at least it was your little book that first put the thought of going to Harleyford into my mind. Though I wanted to see Joe, my real intention was to see Father Stirling; but I would not say a word about it, for I was not at all sure, till yesterday morning, that I was convinced."

"And so Father Stirling received you. Is he not very much pleased?"

"I never saw any one look happier than he did when he bade me good-bye at the coach this morning. Marion, of all the men I ever met, I never loved and admired one as I love and admire him. And to think that it is not yet six months ago since I abused him in his own house! But it was his gentleness and forbearance on that occasion that first drew me to him. One seldom meets with a more beautiful character than his."

"And it seems to me that the greatest charm in that character is the way in which he adapts himself to the various spirits around him" remarked Marion. "A scientific man could not find a more genial companion than Father Stirling, and yet a child is at home with him in two minutes. He is truly 'all things to all men.'"

"He has been everything to me," said her brother.

Bright indeed were the blue eyes that evening, and long and earnest was the conversation that followed; he, in the flush of his first enthusiasm; she, no longer isolated in her faith and love. In spite of the shadow that her mother's alienation cast upon her life, the path of the future was not so dark, even amid that shadow. No more lonely walks to church, no more silence when the heart, full of some thought of beauty, longs to speak; but union in thought, and word, and deed, in all things.

"I shall go to Mass with you to-morrow morning," said Edward as he bade her good-night at her chamber door; "take care you do not forget to call me."

She did not forget, and as, side by side, they knelt at the Elevation, Golden-hair felt that truly this was the happiest moment of her life.

CHAPTER XXV.

"AND so you saw them off by the train, and left your mother brave to the last?"

"Brave to the last!" repeated Joe Darrell, throwing himself into a chair by the open window of the little parlour at Streatham, "but I consider that we have all been cowards, except her."

"I do not see that," replied Edward; "it is no play work to part with one of two sisters for life."

"It is not so much that, for of course I know that her choice is a right one, and I feel sure she will be happy; but I cannot help thinking how she would have shone in the world. I could have given her willingly to a husband."

"But not to God."

"How sharp you are upon a fellow. Remember, Ned, she was my favourite sister, my little confidante, and I cannot think what I shall do without her. Just suppose it were Marion, how would you feel?"

"Will you believe me if I say, that of all things I should most like to see her in a convent?"

"Now that is just because you are a red-hot convert, and nothing else. Tell the truth, would you not rather see her married?"

"No, indeed I would not, and that for many reasons. First, nuns are almost always happy, which cannot be said of wives; secondly, the Spouse of the nun never changes, which earthly husbands do. Thirdly, the nun is provided for for life, which is not always the lot of the wife and mother in this world of change. Then the nun can never be widowed, never be led into extravagance; in short, the convent is safe, which married life is not. So you see, my dear Joe, leaving the high vocation out of the question, even my worldly prudence would rejoice if my sister entered a convent."

"Which I think she is very likely to do," said Joe, half savagely, "do not you?"

"About the most unlikely person I know. Marion likes the world too well to fly from it, and yet with too reasonable a love to fear it. So that in all probability she will remain in it, though I trust not of it, all her life."

"I wish Edith would get married," said Joe; "I do not want to have two of them nuns, I can tell you, however good it may be, as that reverend mother said, to have one's sisters always praying for one. I would much rather have them to talk to, if it's all the same to her. God bless my poor little Em, what shall I do without her!"

"Come, Joe," said his friend, "you are tired and that makes you cross. Lie down on the sofa."

"Well, so I will till supper-time," replied Joe, suiting the action to the word. "Where are the girls?"

"Gone out for a stroll. The fact is, they are in rather an April mood; we had two showers over tea. But they are not such heathens as you; their uppermost feeling is one of true happiness when they think of Emily. It is strange though, that while they can talk calmly enough of her future, even should she be sent abroad, the very mention of this morning's ceremony melts them at once."

"And no wonder," cried Joe. "What on earth do they want to tantalise her friends for, by dressing a girl up like a bride, and making her look like an angel, before cutting off her hair, and making her a fright for life? I call it a refinement of cruelty."

"And I call you a heretic."

"Bother it, but I am not, though," cried Joe; "I'll answer for it there never was a more out-and-out Papist."

"And you cannot see the reason of the ceremonies observed in a clothing?"

"Not a bit of it," replied his friend.

"Well, I have only my own ideas to guide me, but it seems to me that as of course it is a sacrifice, it ought to be made in a solemn manner."

"Ah, as solemn as you like," cried Joe: "if they dressed her in deep black I could understand it."

"And where would then be the type of the spontaneous offering of her young life to God, or of the purity of the virgin heart about to unite itself to Him for ever? Why, Joe, your argument might be used to every ornament employed in religious worship, until, having taken away all things beautiful, you brought us down to the four walls of the conventicle, and Brother Brown in the simple glories of his go-to-meeting superfine. Would that suit you?"

"I don't know," said Joe, "I'm asleep."

"The best thing for you," replied Edward, "so I will not try to convert you any longer."

He was soon once more deep in the book he had laid aside at his friend's entrance. After a time, however, the falling evening brought his reading to a close, and rising from his chair, he walked to the window. The movement aroused Joe to something between a groan and a yawn.

"Are you awake, Joe?" asked Edward, looking round.

"Humph," said Joe.

"Do you not think the girls ought to be in?"

"Humph," said Joe again, with a plunge that sent Marion's work basket over upon the ground, where it lay, a heap of melancholy confusion.

For another ten minutes there was silence, during which Edward looked out very pensively at the moon, just rising above the houses.

"How long have I been asleep ? " asked Joe suddenly.

"About an hour."

Joe again relapsed into silence, but not into sleep, for with his hands joined above his head, he lay and watched his friend, who was standing with his back to him.

"You have a nice little box here, Ned," he observed at length.

"Yes, it always looks bright and cheerful, thanks to my home-fairy. Nearly everything in the room is her work."

"She is indeed a home fairy," cried Joe, kissing the edge of the anti-macassar.

"Joe !"

"Proceed."

"Did you mean what you said just now ?"

"Don't know," returned Joe. "I say a good many things, but I seldom mean half. Do you mean what I said about poor Em ?"

"No, about Edith."

"What did I say about her ? I forget."

"That you would like to see her married."

"No, I don't want her to be married particularly, except to keep her out of a convent."

"Joe," said Edward again, after another pause.

"All right," replied his friend, "what's the matter ?"

"I want to say something to you."

"Go ahead, old boy."

"I think you had better give her to me."

"What ! " cried Joe, springing off the sofa ; "you don't mean to say you "——

"Have been overturning my work-basket," exclaimed Marion, opening the door. "Only look, Edie, at the litter these two boys have made ! What have you been doing ?"

"I don't know exactly," said Joe, who looked as if he spoke the truth, while Edward began gathering up tapes and cottons to hide his confusion.

"Ned, you clumsy fellow," cried Joe, who was shaking with laughter, "you are only making things worse. Shall I do it, Marion ?"

"By way of improvement ?" cried Edith. "If Marion has any respect for her treasures she will not let either of you touch them."

"Yes, they may, because, if they prick their fingers with the pins, it will be a very just penance for upsetting it."·

"Joe did it ! " cried Edward ; "he went to sleep, and kicked it over in the fervour of his dreams."

"What did you dream about, Joe ?" asked his sister.

"That a horrible old nun was going to cut my hair off, which I was determined to resist."

"Now, Joe, is that the truth?"

"Truth; of course it is, and what is more, I don't expect to dream anything else for a month to come."

"And what has Edward been doing?" asked Marion, laying her hand upon his arm,—"dreaming too?"

"I am afraid so, Golden-hair."

"A waking dream, I suppose," returned Marion,

"Not half so grand an institution as a sleeping one, I should think," said Joe, "but I suppose they are considered more romantic."

"Romantic!" cried Edith; "I question whether you know what the word means, Joe, you are so thoroughly matter-of-fact."

"Give me your definition of the word first, sister mine."

Edith hesitated. "The spirit of the beautiful," she answered, shyly.

"Now, Ned, what say you?"

"The innate poetry of a prosy world."

"Marion."

"I do not know."

"Nonsense; a young lady without a definition of the word romantic! Impossible!"

"It is true, Joe; though when I was younger I was very fond of thinking and talking about it."

"Give us the result of those juvenile cogitations, then."

"Well, it used to seem to me that romance was the blossom, and reality the actual fruit of life."

"Not a bad one, for the blossom fades to make way for the fruit, and I am sure romance gives place to reality as we grow old."

"Now, Joe, give us your idea on the subject," cried Edward.

"A slice of cold mutton and a glass of ale for reality, the romance you shall have after supper, for the fact is, I am waxing hungry."

"Poor fellow," exclaimed Edward, ringing the bell.

Marion hurried out to give certain little private directions, and Edith, who was wonderfully interested in her companion's ménage, followed her.

"What say you to a turn for five minutes?" asked Edward, "while they lay the supper cloth."

"Capital!" exclaimed Joe, "just what I was going to propose."

It was a calm quiet evening, such a one as often closes in a sultry August day; a freshening breeze rustled the leaves in the pretty gardens as they passed along, and the last rays of the setting sun poured a refulgent stream of gold and crimson across the horizon. Both gentlemen walked on for some time in silence, for the theme of their interrupted conversation was still uppermost in their thoughts.

"Ned," exclaimed his companion at length, "do you really mean to say you like Edith?"

"I do, and have done so from the first moment I saw her."

"Shall I tell you a secret?"

"She is already engaged!" cried Edward, catching his breath convulsively.

"No; something far brighter for you than that. Ned, my dear old fellow, Edie likes you."

"How do you know?" asked Edward, stopping short in his energy.

"By a thousand little things I myself should never have discovered, but which poor Em noticed, and told me of, as one of her greatest troubles, for she thought you far too clever to bestow a thought on our quiet little Edie. She, of course, poor child, has never suspected that her secret has been read."

"But your father, Joe, what would he say, for she might, I have no doubt, make a much better match?"

"About a month ago he told me that, could he fashion a husband after his own heart for either of his girls, he should choose no higher standard than Edward Howard. So it seems that in this case, in spite of the old adage, the course of true love does run smooth. Well, Ned, I must say the idea of a brother-in-law has sometimes rather bothered me, but now the case is altogether different. This is a kind of set-off against this morning's business. Poor Em! I would put up with something uncommonly stiff in a brother-in-law though, to get her out in the world again."

"Now, Joe," cried his friend, "don't get cross about that again. Very little reflection will soon put that straight for you. Of course it seems hard at first, but you will cease to regret it, the very first time you see her bright face in the convent parlour."

"Through a grating!" cried Joe.

"Through a grating, and why not? Is that much to put up with for the love of God?"

"Not for a saint like you, perhaps, but very much for an ordinary every-day sort of fellow like me."

"Nonsense, Joe. You are fifty times better than I am. You have little idea what a convert is, with his miserable doubts and fears. You have always been my beau-ideal of a young Catholic Englishman; so don't be scandalising me now."

"Ah, Ned, you do not know all I have to bear. You have told me something about my sister, now I will tell you an owre true tale about yours." In a few words Joe told him of Marion's rejection of his suit. "And this," said he, "is a trouble that has not passed away; my heart is as true to her as ever, and mine to-day is a strangely mingled sorrow, for I have met my sweet little sister again, to part with her for life, and I can see in Marion's eye, after an absence of two years, the same fatal glance of sisterly affection. Ned, my dear boy, there is no chance for me, is there?"

"None, I fear," said Edward, in a voice husky with emotion.

"I thought not; indeed, I may say I knew there was not. And

yet, Edward, night and day I never forget her, and I think I could die just to see one little flush on her cheek when I meet her. And that wretched Lisle can give her up with his bigoted stupidity. I don't believe he really cares for her."

"Yes he does, for I saw a letter the other day that he wrote to his sister, when Marion first became a Catholic. He has been intolerant, very, but at the same time there has been something very noble in the way in which he has sacrificed affection to principle."

"I cannot say I see it," replied Joe; "but don't you think she will outgrow her fancy for him?"

"Never. Joe, I would give you hope if I could, but it would be cruel to deceive you. Marion's is a true woman's heart, and her love for Henry Lisle will only cease with death."

Once more they relapsed into a silence which was not broken till they stood before the garden gate.

"Ours has been but a poor exchange, Joe," said Edward, pausing, with his hand on the handle, and looking sympathetically at his friend. "You have made me the happiest of men, while I have only deepened a wound for you."

"Can't be helped, old fellow. Besides, it's only what I knew before. I cannot imagine how I can be such a fool as to stand crying over spilled milk. I know she will never like me, and I can't think what I have come here for, except to make myself miserable by looking at her, like an old cat at a bird in a cage. But, somehow, I couldn't help it, though I made a dozen resolutions to go straight back to Harleyford after the clothing, instead of coming to see you. Do you know, Ned, I sometimes wish she was married, for while there's life there's hope; and, while there's a gleam of hope, I shall never be fit for anything. Will you answer me one question candidly?"

"If I can."

"Do you think, if Marion had never known that parson, she would have liked me?"

"That is a difficult question, Joe; what can I say?"

"The truth, to be sure."

"And make you more miserable?"

"Then you think she never could, in any case, have fancied me?"

"On the contrary, were her affections free, you are, I believe, just the wild, dashing spirit that would have captivated her. But is this idea a consolation to you? It would be just the reverse to me."

"Yes, it is. It is a consolation to me to flatter myself that there is anything in me that under other circumstances might have won her. Perhaps, of all men a sailor, who, by his very profession, is left to brood and dream, who is led across the wild waters by the pole star, and directed by the fragile finger of a compass on his course; he, perhaps, of all men, knows most truly what is the value of a woman's heart. But, Ned, it is better as it is, for I sometimes think if Marion had loved me, I should have ceased to look for heaven."

"My poor, dear fellow, no, that you never would," cried Edward, in whose eyes heavy tears were standing. "But cheer up, you will find some one much prettier and more clever than my little sister. I shall live to see you with a sweet little wife even yet."

"No, that I swear you never shall. By George! Prettier and more clever than his sister! I wonder the words didn't choke him. You ought to have said better while you were about it."

"Well, come in now, and let us have some supper; I am afraid you forget you are hungry."

"It is not the first supper the thought of her has spoiled, nor will it be the last. I sometimes think, Ned, I shall have to give up the idea of the partnership business, it would bring me too much into contact with her."

"We shall see; you will be stronger both in mind and body after your tour. Have you quite made up your mind to start to-morrow?"

"Quite," said Joe as they passed into the house.

Not one member of the little party was in good spirits. The exciting scene of the morning had rather unstrung them all, and the conversation of the two young men had not passed over without a saddening effect on both. They, however, did their best to be gay, and before the conclusion of the meal, all had in some measure recovered their usual cheerfulness.

"Play us something," said Edward, and the girls sang the familiar duets and the same sweet ballads that had so often echoed through the old house at The Cedars. One or two were laid by, almost reverently. They could not even open them, for the voice that had borne its part in them could not be replaced by another. Yet could they, with the moon, have penetrated the chapel in the Enclosure at that very instant, so bright a face was smiling beneath the novice's veil, that they would have sung her old songs in very joy at her happiness, while she sung the matins and lauds to the glory of her God.

"Joe, will you come and sing 'All's Well' with Marion?"

Poor boy! It was hard to sing such a lay as that, with his heavy heart. But Joe Darrell seldom thought of himself, and he moved directly to the piano, and took Edith's place.

"I hope we shall not make such a blunder as we did that evening at Mr. Seymour's; do you remember it?" asked Marion, laughing.

Did he remember it! Was not each event of that night burned into his brain?

They sang it very nicely; old as was the song, and simple as was Marion's untrained voice, there was yet a charm in the duet that would have pleased many a lover of better music, but Edward and Edith must have been more than stoical, for the conclusion of the song actually found them talking. It was some little time before they seemed even to be aware that the music had ceased.

"It would not be polite, I suppose," exclaimed Joe, "to talk of pearls before"——

A laugh from Marion aroused them to a sense of their short-coming.

"Thank you," said Edward, starting, and pulling a leaf, not half withered, off his favourite geranium, "very well sung indeed."

"Beautiful," added Edith.

"It is a lovely night," observed Edward, opening the French window; "would you girls be afraid of a walk round the garden?"

"There is nothing I should like better," said Edith, "it is just what Joe and I do every evening at home. Will you come, Marion?"

"Of course she will," replied Edward, offering Edith his arm: "come, let us set them the example."

Joe rose, but he did not follow them, he only took up one of the duets that had been laid aside, and read it until the notes and words danced before his eyes.

"Poor Em!" he ejaculated, laying it down, with a very heavy sigh.

The words awoke a slumbering thought in Marion's heart, and they talked of the little nun for half an hour. He, seated with his hands resting on the piano, looking at her profile, she dreamily playing strange wild running chords. But the words that fell among the notes were sweet and soothing, and while Edward and his companion walked round and round the grass-plot till they ought to have been giddy, Marion talked to Joe of his sister, and tried to show him how weak it was to murmur at the will of God.

"But I cannot help it, Marion."

"Yes, you can. When I was a little child, studying with mamma, there sometimes came a lesson that I declared I could not learn. As she never excused it, I sat down with a full deter-mination of conquering the difficulty, and I always did so, for there are some of those lessons I could repeat even now. So it is with resignation; it is, indeed, a lesson hard to learn, but say once, with a mighty effort, 'Thy will be done," and, believe me, you will never retract the words."

"Do you speak from experience?"

"I do, from bitter experience. I have had hard and heavy trials, Joe."

"I know it, Marion, and pity you from my very heart. Over and above this morning's business, I have had one that has nearly crushed me. I never have been, never shall be, resigned to that."

"Yes you will; whatever that trial may be, you will bear it patiently, if you only try."

"Impossible, Marion; I have tried, but it is of no use."

"You have tried in your own strength and failed."

"That is true. My own strength is all that I have had to trust to, for my trouble, from its very nature, must be borne alone."

"Do not say so, Joe; if it is really a trouble, it has been already

Q

carried up Calvary.   Like the Cyrenian, you have only helped to
carry the cross."

"It is of no use talking to me like that, Marion," cried Joe,
almost pettishly, " when its weary weight is on me day and night.
And it will never be lighter till you speak one word."

She turned and looked at him with an eye so full of sympathy
and sorrow, that for an instant he was mistaken.

"Is it possible, Marion," he exclaimed, leaning forward and
snatching her hand from the keys, "is there a hope for me?"

"Joe, dear Joe!" she cried, gently extricating her hand from his
grasp, "why will you not let me look upon you, think of you, love
you, as I do Edward?   Believe me, this I do ; more is not mine to
give.   I am unchanged, and unchangeable."

She rose as she spoke, at the same instant Edward and Edith
entered from the garden, and five minutes later the two girls
were upstairs in Marion's room.

Neither spoke for full ten minutes after the door had been locked,
but each seemed busy with her own thoughts, Edith, radiant with
smiles, combing out her long black hair, and Marion arranging a
drawer of house linen.   At length, however, the latter turned from
her task, and the looking-glass revealed the smiling face, with its
wonderful expression.

"Edie, darling, what is it?" asked Golden-hair, laying a hand
on each shoulder.   In an instant Edith had turned, and was
sobbing in her arms.

"Why, what a funny child you are!   What an April day!   You
were laughing just this minute.   Are you thinking of Emily?   I
am your little sister now, remember!"

"So he says," whispered Edith.

"Who?"

Another sob was the answer, and then the truth flashed on Marion.

"Edie!   My darling!   What, has Edward"——

"Hush!   Marion, do hush!"

But she saw how it was, and, with a long fond kiss, welcomed
her new sister to her heart of hearts.

"Joe," said his companion, some few minutes after the girls had
retired, turning to that young gentleman, who, extended upon the
sofa, was fast becoming misty in the smoke of his own cigar, "had
I not better write to your father?"

"Yes, but to make things quite sure, you had better speak to
Edie first, I think."

"Bless the fellow!   Why, Joe, I should have thought you
might have guessed that that piece of business had been managed
already!"

"What a blockhead I am, to be sure ; I recollect now how you
came in from the garden, she like a wet pink rose, and you, for
all the world, like a peony that couldn't hold its head up.   If I
had not been thinking of something else, I should have wondered
what was the matter with you."

"I have been thinking, Joe," continued his friend, "that I will go back with the girls to Harleyford next week, and speak to your father."

"Capital! Be sure to write and tell me what the governor says on the occasion."

"I will. How long do you think you will stay abroad, Joe?"

"Till I recover my senses. Don't laugh, I really mean what I say. I am going in downright earnest to study resignation."

"God bless you, my poor dear fellow, and make the hard lesson easy."

"Amen," said Joe, "now shall we go to bed?"

CHAPTER XXVI.

"THERE! didn't I say so, Mr. Edward? Didn't I say so, deary? Didn't I say I should live to see my own child hanging on her brother's arm?" And old Turner's dim grey eyes almost sparkled again in their glee.

"Ah, yes, you were a truer prophetess then, than I gave you credit for, old lady; but, look, you ought to have foretold the two while you were about it, for, you see, I have a pair of arms and a lady to each."

"To be sure you have. Two good, strong, stout arms, like your father's. God bless the poor gentleman. And now, tell me, Mr. Edward, what do you think yourself? Could they be better filled?"

"No, that they could not," said Edward, glancing alternately at his white and red rose.

"That they could not," repeated the old woman, slowly; "but there's one sweet face I miss to-night, and shall have to miss, I'm afeard, for many a long day, for I suppose we're never like to hear Miss Emily's sweet voice, nor see her heartsome smile again. Poor dear! Poor dear! Well, they may say what they like, but I don't understand them there sort o' things at all."

"She is very happy, nursey," said Marion, "we all three went to see her last night, and she looked as bright as a queen."

Turner shook her head.

"Oh, but she did, though, really," continued Marion, "and sent her love to you, and said I was to ask you to take care of her geraniums next winter."

"Did she, now?" cried Turner; "to be sure I will take care of them. She's not obliged to stop, is she, Miss Marion?"

"Not at all, she can come out any moment she likes for the next twelvemonth."

"Then we shall have her with us again, even yet, for all as is come and gone."

"Is that a prophecy, Turner?" asked Edith.

" No, no, Miss Edie, because, as I said just now, I don't know nothing about these sort o' things. I only mean, I hope as how she won't stop. I beg your pardon, Miss Edith, but when is Mr. Joe coming back ? "

" I do not know, Turner—why ? "

" Because I miss his merry, bright face about here, and because I think, too, that Mr. Edward would be better if he had one arm to himself, like. Two's company, you know, Miss Marion, and three is none."

" Quite true, nursey," replied Marion, laughing, " so suppose I stop here with you ? "

"Indeed, you will do no such thing," cried Edward, magnanimously detaining her, while a little flush ran over Edith's happy face. " What a mischievous little mortal you are ! "

" Mischievous ! Just because I want to do what you and Edie would like better than anything in the world, if you dared say so. Look how nursey is laughing ! she is mischievous, if you like. We shall have another prophecy directly, will you stop and hear it ? What are you thinking about, Turner ? "

" Something that makes my old heart very happy, deary ; and if you will stop a bit with me, and let Mr. Edward and Miss Edith go on, I will tell you all about it."

" Now, I am jealous," cried Edward, looking, however, anything but displeased, as his sister bounded from his arm into the little cottage. "Well, if she will go, we cannot help it," he added, pressing his companion's arm ; " I dare say we shall be able to amuse ourselves," so saying, he closed the gate, and five minutes later they were rambling through the prettiest lane in Harleyford.

" And so my own pet has come back to the old woman, fresh and blooming as a rosebud," cried Turner, flinging her arms round her baby of other days. " I did sometimes fear when I thought of you all across the seas, that I should never live to see this blessed day. But here you are, safe and sound, thanks be to God, and just the same as ever."

Marion only replied by a French kiss, again and again repeated. Then a chair was pulled out and dusted, though Marion refused even to look at it till the old woman was in her usual corner. But when both were fairly seated, there followed such a tale on the one side of France, the French school, Miss Tubbler, and last, not least, of the pretty little home at Streatham, and, on the other, of Edward's arrival and illness, Emily's departure, and all the events, past and present, at The Cedars, that the twilight was deepening fast before Marion thought of moving.

"Must you go yet, deary ; won't you wait for Miss Edie and your brother ? "

" Well, yes, I suppose I had better do so, nursey. They will not be long now, I should think."

" I shouldn't think so," said the old woman, " but I don't know, young people holds time with butter-fingers, you know, deary, specially sometimes," she added, smiling.

"What are you looking so pleased about, nursey?" asked Marion.

"Just my own thoughts, Miss Marion : I was thinking how very happy Mr. Edward seemed, as he turned to shut the gate. Ah, deary, we shall be having the church bells ringing before long, I'm thinking. Well, they be made for one another, that they be."

"What has put such a funny idea as that into your head, grannie?"

"Just my own two eyes, child, that saw this same thing afore ever Mr. Edward went over to fetch you. There is only one thing, deary, that makes me quake like, when I see them so happy together."

"What is that?" asked Marion nervously.

"Miss Edith's cough, dear. Oh, but it goes right through me, that it does."

"But only when she has a cold."

"Well, it may be so, and I do hope I shall live to see her Mr. Edward's wife, but I feel afeard when I hear it. Poor Miss Emily used to worrit herself very much about it, because, you know, Miss Marion, there is consumption in the family, Betsy tells me."

"Well, Turner, we are all in the hands of God."

"So we be, deary," returned the old woman.

"Besides, it seems hard," continued Marion, "to think of this to-day. I know I may tell you, nursey, because I always look upon you as my second mother. It was only this morning that Edward asked Mr. Darrell's consent, and this is the first day of their engagement."

"Is it, though?" exclaimed the old woman, with a glistening eye; "may God bless them, then, and spare them to one another for many, many years. Aye, deary, but everything looks bright to young folks when they're keeping company; it's a time they look back upon with light hearts, even when they're old and grey. Them two will never forget this evening in all their lives, Miss Marion, that they won't. God bless them for ever, I say."

"Amen," arose from the heart of her little visitor, who had risen and was standing in the porch amongst the pink roses, "for ever and ever."

The old woman also stepped out to water her flower-beds, too intent upon her task to speak for a few minutes, and Golden-hair looked at the setting sun, and dreamed. Of what? The sunset was bright, but the reverie was very shadowy. It was a mingled dream, of a mother's kiss long unknown, of a few words once spoken in the library at The Cedars, of her grandmother, and the dreary French school. Was that all? Was there not also one little thought that the "home fairy" might not perhaps be what she had been, that the married Edward might not be brother Edward still? Sweet little Golden-hair. After all, the smile that welcomed the truants was not a very jealous one.

"A goodly parcel of letters!" exclaimed Mr. Darrell, as he emptied the post-bag at the breakfast table one morning. "Behold," and he held up a budget of all shapes and sizes. "One from Joe to me, and one from Joe to you," tossing the letter in question to Edward. "One from little Em," he added, laying it almost reverently beside the mother; "another for Marion, forwarded from London; the rest, I can see, a parcel of rubbish about farming and farm matters, to be opened as time and convenience shall suit."

"Emily writes on behalf of Mother-Abbess," said Mrs. Darrell; "she says she is happy as the day is long. I should like a Protestant to read that letter. It is business-like, bright, and yet pious as a sermon, at one and the same time."

"May I read it, mamma?" asked Edith.

"Certainly, dear, and answer it too, if you like. Do you think you will be able to think of any news to tell her?"

The smile that ran round the table, made Edith glad to take refuge in Emily's letter. Edward, too, became very deeply interested in his.

"Joe talks of stopping for some weeks in Paris," said Mr. Darrell; "he seems to like his companions very well on the whole."

"Yes, and of going from thence to Switzerland, and of ascending Mont Blanc," observed Edward.

"Hope he will enjoy it," said Mr. Darrell. "Silly boy, to waste his breath and shoe-leather for the pleasure of getting above the clouds, into a little deep snow. Never could see the fun of that sort of thing myself. What is the matter, Marion?"

He might well ask, she had laid her letter down with such a strange expression on her face.

"Mr. Darrell!"

"Miss Howard!"

"It is from Mrs. Gordon; you remember my writing to you about her, do you not?"

"Perfectly well; you mean the lady who went to the Bermudas."

"Yes. Well, I will read you her letter."

"'What have you thought, dearest child, of the letters I have lately written you, congratulating you on your brother's arrival and affection, yet so studiously silent about myself, in spite of your many questions? Marion, I would not tell you anything, when I could not tell you all. I would not weary you with my doubts and fears, and I had nothing else, peculiar to myself, to speak of. But the case is altered now, the blindness of Saul has passed away. I believe. Marion, my sweet little sister in sorrow and heart, we are sisters now in faith. I will tell you no more, for I am about to return to London, my health being nearly re-established; and then, face to face, you shall hear all. All the strange by-paths and tortuous ways through which the truth has followed my flying steps, until, like the jailer of Philippi, I have cried,

amid the flashing of God's own light, and the rending of prison
bars, what must I do to be saved? What will my brother say?
I must not,—will not, care. In a letter I received from him a few
days since, he said he thought of spending a few weeks on the
continent to recruit his health and spirits, which are, I fear, poor
fellow, at a very low ebb.'"

The voice of the little reader began to fail, and she passed the
letter to Mrs. Darrell.

"There is nothing more of any consequence," she observed;
"but has it not been a wonderful conversion, she was so very
determined?"

"Gloria in excelsis Deo!" cried Mr. Darrell. "Marion, you
must show that letter to Father Stirling. What a good thing he
has returned."

"He will, indeed, be pleased," said Mrs. Darrell, "she is a very
old friend of his."

"Yes, I will take him the letter after we have seen Edward off
this morning," said Marion.

"Can you not stop a day or two longer with us, Ned?"
inquired Mr. Darrell, while from Edie's eyes also there stole a
very pleading little glance.

"Indeed, I fear I must not do so, there are one or two gentlemen
I have promised to see this very afternoon, and business must be
attended to, you know. More than ever now," he added, with a
proud, bright smile; "I have a double reason for trying to make
my fortune as soon as possible."

Edith and Marion smiled, and, breakfast being over, passed
with Mrs. Darrell through the window upon the lawn.

"And you will succeed, Edward," said Mr. Darrell, as soon as
they were alone, "you will succeed. The man who could give up
inclination for business, never went to the wall yet. Mark my
words, Ned, my boy, you will get on bravely in the world."

"I have such a bright guiding star," replied Edward, "I can
well understand Jacob's fourteen years of servitude, if Rachel was
only half what Edie is. What do you think of the partnership,
now?"

"We must see how Joe comes back. There seems to be, I am
happy to say, a more settled tone in this last letter. He talks in
it of the future, something like a man of business."

"He will do well enough in a little time, you will see,"
remarked Edward, soothingly.

"I wish he were more like you," replied the father.

"You forget he is some years younger. Joe will come out yet
quite to your satisfaction, I know."

"Then it will have to be in the firm of Howard and Darrell."

"We shall have even that, if we have patience, and God thus
wills it."

"I trust so, most sincerely, my dear boy," cried Mr. Darrell,
warmly shaking his friend's hand. "I should be very happy in
the idea that both my children's lives were linked with yours.

But, allons," he added, rising, "do you think you have time to come and look at the thrashing machine that was set up yesterday in the lower barn? it is on quite a new principle, and I should like to hear what you think of it."

"Plenty of time, though, with regard to my opinion; machinery is a subject in which I am more interested than wise. But I should very much like to see it."

After half an hour's very learned conversation on flails, fly-wheels, cylinders, and horse-power, and another of very sad and somewhat sentimental adieux, Edward was on his road back to London. Shortly after his departure, Marion was standing with a letter in her hand, waiting for the presbytery door to be opened.

"I am very sorry, miss, but the Father is out; he went away on horseback directly after breakfast, and told me he could not say whether he should be back to dinner or not. He said, if you called, I was to tell you he would try to get up to The Cedars this evening to see you."

"Thank you, Martha, how is your rheumatism?"

"Much about the same, thank you. Do you know, Miss Howard, but I am very glad to see you in these parts again. It seems a very long time since you were here."

"More than a year and a half, and everything seems to have been standing still during my absence, for I see no alteration in anything, except in Eliza's boys at the lodge, and that old Turner seems a little infirm."

"We must expect that, miss, at her age, but she's a good old creature. It's a pity but what she was a Catholic."

"She is very happy as she is, and loves God so truly, that I do not fear for her. It seems a strange thing, perhaps, but, much as I love her, I care less for her conversion than that of any one else that I know. I look upon her as God's own ignorant, happy child, to whom, for reasons of His own, He has never yet shown the full light of His truth. But He may speak to her even at the eleventh hour; should He do so, I always feel sure that Turner will do His bidding. I am very sorry that Father Stirling is out to-day. It seems such a long time since I saw him."

"Yes, miss, it does. He was so pleased to see Major Howard last evening. It does seem a pity going away as seldom as he does, that he should have been away just during the few days of the Major's visit to Harleyford. He so seldom takes a holiday."

"Yes, my brother was very much disappointed too. Well, Martha, if you will give me a sheet of paper I will write a note to Father Stirling with this letter, and I shall be glad if you will give them to him as soon as he comes in."

"Certainly," replied Martha, leading the way into the familiar little parlour, where it was some few minutes before Marion could collect her thoughts to write, every object round her was so fraught with old associations.

"May I go through to the church?" asked Marion, as she gave her letter into Martha's charge.

"To be sure, miss," and Marion passed through the little arched door, and knelt before the altar. She had been distracted over her letter, but she was not so now, for the thoughts that crowded round her were woven into her prayer. The past, with her mother and Henry Lisle; the present bright with Edward's happiness and Mrs. Gordon's conversion, the future veiled and mysterious. Nor was poor Joe forgotten in his deep, unrequited love, nor the little nun in her solemn, difficult life of inward joy. All were remembered in a long, deep prayer, but the first and last words of that prayer were "my mother." Shall the prayer be heard? Shall the bright curls nestle once again against the mother's cheek? Patience, Golden-hair, be it so or not, remember, "God does all things well." She did remember it, and passed out of the chapel with a strong heart and firm foot.

"It will seem very strange when Edward is married," ran her soliloquy, as she walked home. "I am afraid I shall sometimes feel rather in the way, as I did last night, and then I shall not always have nursey to talk to. Of course, too, I shall not keep his house, nor make his tea, nor do anything else that I do now. Well, I shall soon get used to it, I suppose. At any rate, I must make Edie think that I like having nothing of the kind to do, or she will feel herself a supplanter, and that would make me very unhappy. How fond Edward is of her, and well he may be; yet somehow, though I love her so much myself, I cannot bear the idea of any one being dearer to him than I am." At this point in her soliloquy, Marion was walking down a very narrow lane, and, in spite of herself, a salt tear trickled down.

"What am I doing?" she exclaimed, stopping suddenly short in her walk; "crying because Edward is so happy! Why, I do believe I am jealous—jealous of dear Edie." And ashamed of her weakness, Marion turned precipitately to other thoughts, and had half arranged the wedding by the time she arrived at The Cedars.

Father Stirling was late home that evening—so late that Martha walked more than once to the little green gate, with an uncomfortable recollection uppermost in her mind, of a certain picnic and a disastrous termination. Bright as usual, however, he came at last, though evidently very much fatigued.

"I am afraid your dinner is half spoilt, Father, but I don't know, for I have done all I could to keep it nice and hot for you."

"I am sorry you should have taken so much trouble, Martha, for I have dined; but I will tell you what you may do—just run over with it to old Biddy while it is hot. She does not often get a dinner, or supper either, poor creature, I am afraid, for she looked so pale and thin just now, as I passed her sitting at the door."

"Oh, but, Father, what am I to give you for your supper if I send this away," objected the housekeeper, "for I'll be bound, notwithstanding your dinner, you're half famished after your ride?"

"Have you an egg in the house?"

"Yes," said Martha, discontentedly, "but I don't feel any way sure they're fresh, for you sent off all the new-laid ones we had to

William Dobson last night, and I can't keep you waiting till I go up to the farm."

"Never mind, run over to old Biddy at once, there's a good soul, and then come back and get me a cup of tea; and, notwithstanding your suspicions concerning the eggs, I think I will venture on a couple."

"Did ever any one see the likes of him!" exclaimed Martha, as soon as she arrived in her own domain, and had begun arranging the tempting little dinner in a basin for Biddy. "I believe, if he had any one else but me to look after him, he would be starved to skin and bone. But I will go up to the farm though, if I break my neck for it; he shan't eat musty eggs while I'm in the house."

Left to himself, Father Stirling began to think, and, to judge by the smile upon his face, his thoughts were very bright ones, as he leaned back in his arm-chair, playing an imaginary accordion on the tips of his fingers. Presently, Marion's note caught his eye, and, breaking the seal, Mrs. Gordon's letter fluttered to the ground. With a calm eye and unmoved brow, he read the ecstatic effusion of the woman, who had been to him in early days what he alone knew, and a strange glad look passed over his face. But that was all. Quietly refolding the letter, the priest rose from his seat, and walking into the chapel, sought his constant refuge in his joys and sorrows, in his usual place before the altar.

Very calmly and warmly did Father Stirling that night congratulate Marion on the conversion of her friend, when he joined the cheerful party at The Cedars, but not a shadow less simply than he spoke of Edward's reception into the Church.

"Is it wrong to wish it had been her brother Henry instead?" asked Mrs. Darrell, aside, as Marion took her seat by Edith, on the opposite side of the room.

"Of course it is, my dear friend, very wrong. Conversions are not human achievements, and to entertain such a wish, is to say to God, 'what doest Thou?' and that, you know, we must not say."

"But would it not be delightful if he could be brought to see the errors of his ways?"

"To be sure it would, and so perhaps he will, in God's own time. But we must beware how we sit in judgment on the decrees of Providence. Fifteen years ago I prayed very hard for the instant conversion of this very lady, but now I thank God, from the depths of my heart, that He did not then grant my prayer. And yet, apparently, there was every reason to suppose that such an event would be in accordance with the Divine Will. And so even now, Henry Lisle's conversion may be a thing predestined in the infinite wisdom of God, though there are two hearts He may see good to try first in the crucible of affliction. Do you not think so?"

"Yes, I do. Already Marion Howard's troubles have given a tone to her character."

"They have done more; they have shown her the fragility of

earthly happiness, and have taught her to make heaven her treasure-house. They have taught her patience and resignation, and given her a yearning after the path of perfection—a path difficult to distinguish when the blossoms of worldly prosperity grow rank and luxuriant. God grant she may follow it !"

"But, Mr. Lisle, Father—what good has his trouble done him ?"

"Taught him to suffer ! Given him, perhaps, part of a weary purgatory here ! If it had not been good for him to be afflicted, his road would still have wound on amid pleasant places. Stay, Miss Howard is coming to speak to you."

The conversation now became general. As the evening wore on, Father Stirling seemed wonderfully pre-occupied, and fidgeted from one place to another like a spirit of unrest.

"It seems like old times to have Marion here again," exclaimed Edith.

"Yes, and any one can see that she is not sorry to find herself once more amongst you."

"That indeed she is not," replied Marion.

"There have been many changes since her arrival here with Joe, that cold winter's evening," said Mrs. Darrell, musingly.

"There have indeed," replied the priest.

The little party grew silent with their own thoughts, the mother of her children, Edie of Edward, while Marion's ideas were a conglomeration of the reveries of the rest.

"Will you be very jealous if I ask Miss Howard to take a turn or two with me round the garden, before it gets dark ?" asked Father Stirling.

"Well, considering how long it is since you saw her, I do not think we shall, so you may monopolise her for half an hour. Am I not generous ?"

"I never knew Mrs. Darrell anything else," replied the priest, smiling.

"Thank you," exclaimed the lady, "but I am afraid even Father Stirling was polite then at the expense of truth !"

It was not until they found themselves in the very green alley that had been the scene of Marion's childish conversation with him about the Catholic Sunday, that Father Stirling broke silence.

"Do you not wonder, my child, what I want you for ?"

"Rather," replied Marion.

"Do you remember our last drive together ?"

"Of course I do ; neither of us could easily forget it, I should imagine."

"Would you be afraid to trust yourself to my charioteer-ship again ?"

"Not at all."

"Well. I think the journey I wish to take you to-morrow would be worth even a broken head or arm."

"A journey ! Where ?" asked Marion, opening her eyes very wide.

"Not far. To a little village a few miles off; one that you have not seen for some time. Will you go?"

Marion looked at him without speaking.

"As you do not answer, I shall conclude that silence gives consent."

"Father Stirling, what do you mean?"

"What do I mean? Why, my dear child, that to-morrow morning I shall call round for you, in old Jackon's gig, to drive with me to Ennington."

CHAPTER XXVII

FATHER STIRLING's surmise had been a true one. Mrs. Howard had left Ennington because its associations had been too much for her. She had loved her child more deeply than she imagined, and the loneliness of her little home had been more than she could bear. She had therefore resolved to try change of scene, and having, as we have already seen, let her house furnished, had passed a year at Clifton.

Irrespectively, however, of the annoyance she received from her unprincipled tenants, Mrs. Howard found her new mode of life anything but a pleasant one. Too reserved to seek new friends, too indifferent to wish to please those with whom chance associated her, too cold to excite interest in strangers, hers was a lonely life. Even her pride, for which she had sacrificed the very sunshine of existence, she found but a poor substitute for happiness. Nevertheless, she hugged it to her heart, each day intrenching herself more strongly in her determination never to see her daughter until she should yield to her will.

Her year of exile having terminated, she returned to her own house in the early spring. The renovation was hard work, but Dr. Stebbing's recipe of soap-and-water, applied by Sally's strong arms, soon made all bright again. Before long, clean white curtains once again shaded the windows, the garden was restored, and even Tyrza became re-civilised.

Still it was in vain that Mrs. Howard tried to banish, amid old pursuits and old familiar faces, the dreary thoughts that fresh scenes had failed to dispel. Perseveringly she arranged and re-arranged the rooms, sat down to her books or needlework, walked in the garden among the spring flowers, yet only to miss the sunny face and busy fingers almost more than ever.

"And yet, I know that I am acting rightly," thus ran her frequent reverie; "my relations say so, and surely, of all living people, my sister Isabel is good. I make no profession, but she, at least, is a religious woman; at least one hardly ever hears her talk of anything but church matters, and she says I have only acted as she would have done in my place. I wonder where Marion is. Somehow I feel easy about her, for I know, even if she has left

The Cedars, Mrs. Darrell will keep her eye upon her. Perhaps she has gone to her grandmother ; if so, the old lady will be only too glad of an opportunity of poisoning her mind against me, I know ; but I must make up my mind to every kind of misrepresentation now, and rest content with the assurance of having done my duty."

At this moment a sudden gust of wind fluttered her cap ribbons far behind her.

"I shall catch cold if I stay here any longer," she exclaimed, shivering, and so she passed into the house, and wandered slowly from room to room, unconsciously seeking some distraction for her thoughts. Presently a letter-rack, Marion's handywork as a child, caught her eye.

She unlooped it from the wall, and a rare store of bills and papers she turned out, deposited by her late tenants, and, to her surprise, at the bottom of all, a letter addressed to herself, and bearing the date of the previous October. It fell from her hand before she had fully perused it, for it was Mr. Twidgett's letter, announcing, in lawyer-like style, the death of her mother-in-law.

"Dead ! Mrs. Howard dead ! Impossible !"

A pang of remorse shot through her heart. She began to wish that she too was dead, and buried in that quiet corner of Ennington churchyard, which her husband had chosen for the grave he was destined never to rest in. With this thought, too, there came another, what would that husband say, from his place of unquiet sepulchre beneath the deep waters, could he see how his aged mother had been neglected by her, whose slightest wish had been his law ? Mrs. Howard burst into the first flood of tears she had shed in all her troubles. Pride, as usual, tried to whisper consolation, but in vain, and the haughty spirit sobbed on, unchecked in its agony.

She was only beginning to grow calm, when a sharp rap at the door announced a visitor. It was answered before she could interfere.

"Is Mrs. Howard in ?"

"Yes, sir," and Dr. Stebbing was ushered into the drawing-room.

"What a nuisance !" exclaimed the lady, looking at her reflection in the mirror, with great dissatisfaction ; "how can I go to speak to him such a fright as this ? I must bathe my eyes and see what that will do."

Notwithstanding her ablutions, however, her face bore evident marks of her late emotion, when she entered the drawing-room, and had she only known it, somewhat raised her in the estimation of her visitor. He began to think there was even yet a healthy spot in the warped and contracted heart, and his greeting was consequently a shade or two warmer than it would otherwise have been.

"I should have called on you before," he remarked, after the usual salutations, "but both Mrs. Stebbing and myself concluded that you would not care to receive visitors during the first week or two of your return."

"Well, I really have been very busy," she replied, "for the house was in a dreadful condition."

"So we could see from the outside."

"Nothing would induce me to try the experiment of letting it in a similar way again, although I might be more fortunate another time, for I appear to have come in contact with unusually disagreeable people. I have just discovered that they did not even trouble themselves to forward me a letter that arrived last autumn, for I have this afternoon found it at the bottom of an old card-rack. Unfortunately, too, the letter was both important and pain-ful, for it was one announcing the death of my mother-in-law from her lawyer in London. It has given me a severe shock."

"You did not know it, then, until to-day?"

"Of course not, there was no chance of my doing so. This lawyer was the only one connected with Mrs. Howard, who knew my address, perhaps, even of my very existence; for, with the exception of Marion and her half-brother in India, the poor old lady was the last of her family. I wonder what has become of her little property. Her annuity, of course, ceased with her, but she had many valuable family heirlooms, and, wrong as Marion has been, I should like her to have what has been left to her in the will, if only for the sake of keeping them in my poor husband's family. Edward, too, ought to have been written to, though," she added, striving to appear indifferent; "I do not see why I should trouble my head about it."

"Especially as everything was arranged long ago by Major Howard himself," replied the doctor.

"What do you mean?" she asked, looking at him in blank astonishment.

"Simply this, my dear madam, that the property of the deceased lady is already in possession of the rightful heirs, who have not long since transferred it from Islington to Streatham, where they are now residing."

"The rightful heirs! I do not understand you; there are, I know, no nearer claimants to Mrs. Howard's property than Marion and her brother."

"Who are the persons named in that lady's will, and who are precisely the people in possession of her effects at Streatham."

Mrs. Howard began to think of cases when hereditary madness had broken out suddenly, but the doctor had never looked more sane in his life.

"In plain words, my dear madam," he exclaimed, "do you know where your daughter is?"

"No, Dr. Stebbing, I do not, though I should think, most pro-bably, with her friends at Harleyford, if one can apply the term to those who have so wretchedly misguided her."

'You are mistaken," replied the doctor; "she is not there. After having gone through many troubles, she has found a haven of refuge in this very brother Edward. He has taken a house in Streatham, and she is with him. And now, I suppose, you are

wondering where I have gleaned all my information, and so I must
tell you what happened in this quiet little village of Ennington
about the end of last October. I was one afternoon walking
slowly home from the schools to dinner, when I saw this very
house door closed most unceremoniously upon a gentleman, who
had evidently been making some inquiries. You are perhaps
aware, Mrs. Howard, that though curiosity certainly had its birth
in Mother Eve, it has not by any means been thenceforth confined
to her sex. As I had seen this gentleman alight from the coach a
few minutes before, and had been somewhat struck by his appearance, I was, I must say, a little curious about him. I certainly did
not feel less so, when I saw him stand melancholy and perplexed,
looking up and down the street, with the evening fast closing in.
I was quite gratified when I saw that he had made up his mind to
speak to me, and you may imagine my surprise, when, after very
few preliminaries, he told me that he was Edward Howard. He
said he had only just arrived from India, to find his grandmother
dead, and you and his sister gone he knew not whither; for Miss
Smith informed him that she had burned your address, and did
not remember it. Poor fellow, I never saw such a picture of despair, till I invited him home with me to dinner, and promised to
tell him all I knew of his sweet little sister."

Mrs. Howard frowned.

"Oh, I can tell you, I did not spare you," continued the old
gentleman, smiling, and polishing his bald forehead. "Whatever
my friend Lisle may have said to the matter, my opinion has been
unchanged throughout the whole affair. You have done wrong,
and acted very harshly. Marion has been misled, but I cannot
see that she has committed a fault, for she has only exercised the
proudest boast of our Church, that is to say, the right of private
judgment. Having been biassed by stronger minds than her own,
she may have erred in this judgment, but I have not a single
doubt that a little judicious management would have eradicated
the error in a very short time. Why, even upon Lisle's own ad-
mission, she was slightly touched some five or six years ago, and
you saw how she came round then. But you have defeated your
own end, for I sadly fear Marion Howard will never return to us
now, and I do not speak without a foundation for my words. I
suppose, however, you are thinking that all this is very impertinent,
and has nothing to do with my story."

Mrs. Howard smiled in spite of herself.

"The major stayed all night with us," continued the doctor,
"and I procured Mrs. Darrell's address for him from the old
Catholic cobbler here, for he refused to write to you, or hold any
communication with you, on the subject of his sister."

"So much the better," interrupted his auditor.

"Well, whether for better or worse, so it was. The next morning he took a post-chaise to Harleyford, and I never saw nor heard
anything more of him until about a week before Christmas, when he
suddenly made his appearance. He then told me that he had been

taken seriously ill at Harleyford, that he had been, in fact, almost
at death's door, that he owed his recovery in a great measure to
the kindness of Mr. Darrell's family, and to the Catholic priest of
the place, and that he was then on the point of starting for Paris,
to fetch his sister."

" To Paris ! You do not mean to say that Marion has been
living in Paris ? "

" That she most certainly has," replied the Rector, " for her
brother says, she could not be induced to remain either at The
Cedars, or with her grandmother, and so she took a situation in a
French school as English teacher, where she remained until last
Christmas. But I wonder Mr. Lisle has not told you this, for the
last time I saw your step-son, he told me that while in London,
Marion had become acquainted with his sister, Mrs. Gordon,
who is now, however, in the Bermudas for her health."

" How strange that Mrs. Gordon should never have mentioned
this to her brother ; though now, I remember, she wrote rather
decidedly to him about his angry feeling with regard to Marion,
remarkably so, I thought, for one who had not seen her brother
for years, and who was, as I supposed, a total stranger to the young
lady in question. May I ask when you last saw Edward ? "

" The very day you did."

" I do not understand you," replied Mrs. Howard.

" You remember the flying visit you paid to Ennington, about a
month since, when your friends did not even know you had been,
till you had again taken wing."

" Yes ; I only remained two hours here, and that was spent in
talking to my tenants to no purpose, and then I returned by the
evening coach to London."

" Do you remember who were your companions, coming up ? "

" Let me see. Old Grimble, and Mrs. Greaves, the butcher's
wife. I do not remember any one else : stay—yes, there was a
gentleman also, quite a stranger to me."

" Who was no other than Edward Howard ; he stayed all night
with me before going on to Harleyford, whither he was bound. I
never knew that you had been travelling companions, until I heard
quite by chance of your angel visit to Ennington, when I remembered Major Howard speaking of a lady, who had alighted
in our village, 'one of the most elegant women he had ever met.'
I only wish I had known it was you, I would soon have enlightened him."

Mrs. Howard remained silent with astonishment. She now
remembered perfectly well, the dark-eyed gentlemanly stranger,
whose manners and appearance had greatly prepossessed her, and
the little piece of admiration so naturally expressed by Edward,
and so neatly thrown in by the rector, was not without its effect.
She began to think her step-son might turn out a much more
agreeable person, than she had ever imagined such an appendage
could possibly be.

" He told me of a strange piece of business, in a note I had from him a few days after his return to London, after that very visit here."

"Indeed !"

"Yes, it seems that during his week's stay at Harleyford, he was received into the Catholic Church. I have written him a long letter on the subject, though with a very vain hope of influencing him, for he seems very earnest in the step he has taken. This is why I said just now, I fear Miss Howard will never change again ; this conversion will, of course, help to intrench her in her new opinions."

Mrs. Howard made no reply, and the kind-hearted rector seized the opportunity of her silence, and tried once again his powers of eloquence, to induce her to relent in favour of her child. Finding, however, that his arguments produced no effect, although Mrs. Howard seemed too much stunned to attempt to combat them, he arose to take his leave.

"One thing I have to ask of you," said the lady, as she wished him good-bye, "and that is, that you will not mention to Edward Howard, that he and I have already met."

"Certainly not, if you do not wish me to do so," replied the clergyman, "but I am quite disappointed. I should have liked to enlighten him on the subject of his fellow-traveller."

"But you must not do so, if you please, for I do not wish to be brought before him and Marion in any way. She wishes to forget me—let her do so ! "

"My dear madam," cried Doctor Stebbing, "how mistaken you are ! her brother tells me that she pines for you day and night !"

"Let her come back to me then," replied the mother, "the conditions are not hard ! "

No, Mrs. Howard, not hard, but simply impossible ! Doctor Stebbing did not say this, though, dear reader, for he did not think so. He only took up his hat and Malacca cane, and, with a courteous adieu, walked briskly home to his wife, who was waiting dinner.

CHAPTER XXVIII.

THE snowdrops and crocuses had faded away in the cottage garden in Ennington, and again the summer roses were blooming red and bright in their stead. Once more the new-mown hay perfumed the meadow-lands, once more the hay-maker's song mingled with the murmur of the mill-stream and the droning of the mill, and once again the bees, birds, and butterflies were winging their way through the golden sunshine.

Bright, however, as were the summer days, they were little heeded by Mrs. Howard. Like Ezechias, she had "turned her face to the wall," as the shadow of death fell on her soul, and in untold bitterness of heart, she gazed into his face and trembled.

R

She was very ill, very lonely, very desolate, for Dr. Stebbing and his little wife, who would have tended her so kindly, were away on their summer trip. Even little Miss Leicester would have been useful now, but she was in Bath, dancing attendance on an aged aunt, who ought to have died for the benefit of her nephews and neices at least ten years before. There was no one left in Ennington but the new curate, and he was so awkward and boyish, that the very thought of him fretted the invalid. And so the days dragged on; old Mr. Bernard her only visitor, and Sally nurse and sole companion.

For a long time she had been lying very still, planning ways in which the pattern of her curtains might have been better joined, and Sally, who had mistaken her silence for sleep, was rather startled when her mistress exclaimed abruptly, "I wish you could write, Sally."

"Laws, ma'am, so do I."

"Just give me my desk and I will try and write a few words to Mrs. Dampier myself, I cannot bear this isolation any longer. It is killing me."

The desk was brought, but the pen was hardly between her fingers, before the invalid sank back exhausted.

"There! take it away," she said faintly, "I must get Mr. Bernard to write for me."

And yet before that gentleman arrived, the plan had been discarded, as the vision of her prim serious sister floated before her mind. "She would only worry me, and make me more melancholy still," was her conclusion, "and I should shock her if I did not let Mr. Mason visit me every day. Though I really think I will send for him to-morrow, if Dr. Bernard says I am no better; but I I know I shall not like him," she added, petulantly, shedding tears in her weakness.

The next day found her even worse, and Sally was despatched for Mr. Mason, for though Mrs. Howard did not exactly imagine herself in danger, a strange unwonted gloominess made her long for spiritual consolation, and brought the thought of Henry Lisle many times before her.

Mr. Mason was a quiet, gentle, meek young man, whose want of firmness and energy was fast letting everything in the parish, that was under his immediate care, go wrong. He walked into the invalid's room, looking very warm, and feeling very uncomfortable, for this was his first curacy. His ministrations were precisely such as might have been expected. Weakly and timidly he talked of resignation, and stammered out something about repentance, heaven, and the judgment to come. But though she listened like Felix, like him Mrs. Howard did not tremble, but in her untamed pride only blushed to think that such a spirit as hers should have sought consolation from such a mind as Mr. Mason's. In about ten minutes he left the house, not to return, and Mrs. Howard, closing her eyes, lay still, and brooded once more over the dull mental pain that his visit had by no means helped to allay.

When Mr. Bernard made his call the following day, he shook his head. No wonder. Was his patient likely to improve, while the very thoughts that had laid her low, still hovered round her like spectres? She was very much worse, and poor Sally, her patient nurse, looked white and wearied with watching.

"Go to bed just to-night, Sally," said Mrs. Howard, in a tone she had never from her childhood used before to a servant. "Go to bed, and let little Polly come and stay with me."

"No, thank you, ma'am, I would rather be here," and in two minutes the country girl was stretched on her mattress by her mistress's bed. And now as through the silent watches of the night she lay restlessly awake, listening to the breathing of her weary nurse, Mrs. Howard thought, as she had never done before —thought of her life as it was lying that night, written word after word in the solemn Book of God—not a syllable blotted out of the handwriting against her. For although in the village church she had bowed her head with others at the general confession— where had been her repentance? Although she had said with the congregation, "I believe in God"—where had been her faith? As though a veil had been withdrawn, the utter weakness of her cause in the sight of God lay plainly before her now, and she shuddered as she thought of death.

"Not yet! not yet!" she cried. "O my God! give me time for repentance—time to live to know Thee—time to learn to welcome death, as they tell me Christians welcome it for Thy sake."

Sally was fairly puzzled when she arranged her mistress early in the morning, for she could not determine whether she was better or worse. The old doctor himself looked almost equally nonplussed, and shook his head more vigorously than ever, all the way home.

"Sally," said Mrs. Howard, after his departure, "I should very much like to have some one in to help you."

"There is no need," said Sally, half hurt.

"Yes, but indeed there is. You will be getting ill too, and I do not know how Polly would manage with both of us on her hands at once."

"I feel all right as yet," said Sally, "and I'm sure there's no one about here, as you'd like to have with you."

"No, therefore I shall have to send to London for a nurse."

"Just as you like, of course, ma'am," replied Sally, crossly, "I only know I am very well as we are."

"I want somebody to go to Harleyford for me to-day, how could it be managed?"

"Very well, if Polly could mind you; because I could go myself."

"You! Why how would you get there?"

"Walk."

"What! all the way?"

"To be sure. Unless somebody passed in a shay, and would give me a lift."

"I could not think of such a thing !"

"Do you think you could manage for a few hours with Polly, ma'am ? that's the question."

"Yes, very well indeed ; but you must not go, you are not strong enough to walk to Harleyford, in such warm weather as this, to say nothing of getting back again."

"I shall try," said Sally, grinning, and marching out of the room.

It is very pleasant to drive or ride through country lanes on a warm summer day, but vastly different to toil through them on foot for nine long, weary, dusty miles. By the time poor Sally, with aching feet and glowing face, had arrived within a mile of Harleyford, she felt very much exhausted, and her stout heart began to consider in some dismay, how the journey back again was to be accomplished. She, however, plodded resolutely on, and at length, by dint of much inquiry, found herself before the presbytery door, and a few minutes later, for the first time in her life, actually in the presence of a real, live Roman Catholic priest.

"Well, and what can I do for you, my child ?" asked Father Stirling kindly, as Martha ushered her into the study. "You are a stranger, I see. Sit down—not in that draught though," he added, rising, and placing a chair on the other side of the window.

"There, that will do. Are you a Catholic ?" he asked as he resumed his seat.

"Laws, no, sir !" cried Sally, startled altogether out of her propriety. "I never even heard of such a thing till lately."

Father Stirling laughed. "I see, I beg your pardon. Go on."

"My mistress told me to tell you," answered Sally, who felt rather confounded, "that she would have written if she thought I could not make you understand, sir. She would like to see you —that is if it's convenient."

Father Stirling looked somewhat surprised. "Stop a minute, my child, and take your time. Where do you come from ?"

"From Ennington, sir."

"From Ennington ! How did you get here ?"

"I walked, sir."

"Why, you must be half dead. Who is your mistress ?"

"Mrs. Howard."

"Who ?" exclaimed the priest, who began to think he had fallen asleep over his office, and was still dreaming.

Sally repeated the name.

"Tell me again what she has sent you for."

"To ask you to go and see her, if you possibly can. She is very ill indeed, sir. Mr. Mason, the minister, had to be fetched yesterday, so you may think she's pretty bad. She tried very hard to write, but she almost fainted over the note, so she said you must excuse a message instead."

"To be sure, to be sure. Yes, I will come directly. What is her illness, do you know ?"

"She caught cold, sir, and wouldn't nurse herself, all as ever I

could do. But I think it's more because she worrits herself so.
She has never been the same since "——

"Since when?"

"Well, I don't know that it's manners to say anything about it
to you, sir, but she's never been the same since Miss Marion went
and turned."

"I suppose not," said the priest, half to himself.

"No, indeed, she has not, and no wonder. I'm a quietish sort
of girl, and I say very little to anybody, but I have my feelings,
sir, and I find the house awful dull without her."

"Have you lived long with Mrs. Howard?"

"Ten years, sir; Miss Marion was a little girl when I first come
to Ennington, and seeing her grow up, as one may say, before
my very eyes, it was no wonder as I missed her when she didn't
come back. But it wasn't any business of mine, and this is the
first word I have ever said about it, and I shouldn't now, only
I want you to do good to my poor missus. But please, sir,
don't "——

"Don't what?"

"Why, sir, don't make her a Papisher too!"

"Why not?"

"Because—because it seems so dreadful to do the things they
do!"

"Does it?" asked Father Stirling, looking very much amused,
and rising to ring the bell. "Now, my child, I will tell you how
we will manage. You shall go with Martha into the kitchen and
get some dinner, and then I will drive you back. Just send me
in a crust of bread and cheese," he added, turning to the housekeeper, "let some one run over to Mr. Jackson, and ask him to
let me have the gig; and be as quick as you can in everything,
for this is a sick call, and I am in a hurry."

Sally felt very thankful as she sped over the miles between
Harleyford and Ennington in the old-fashioned gig, even though
her companion was a priest, and the end of her mission to fetch
him to the bedside of her sick mistress. Now that she had a
little leisure to think, she was on the point of commencing a few
speculations on the curious turn events seemed to be taking,
when her cogitations were cut short by Father Stirling himself.

"And so," he exclaimed, suddenly, "Catholics do such dreadful
things, do they?"

Sally hung down her head, but at the same time smiled an
affirmative.

"And what do you think is the worst thing they do?"

"I don't know, sir," she replied hesitating; "worship idols, I
should think."

"You don't mean to say you believe Catholics do that, my good
girl!" cried the priest.

"Yes, sir, I thought they did! Of course there was a bit of a
stir in the place when it got out that Miss Marion had gone and
turned, and I asked Farmer Grimble what Catholics did that was

so dreadful. He told me that they worshipped idols, confessed all the sins they had ever committed, or ever were going to commit, to a priest, and that they starved themselves sometimes almost to death, because then they thought they were sure to get to heaven."

"And you thought this rather a peculiar creed, I suppose! No wonder."

"What, sir?"

"You thought these were curious things to believe?"

"To be sure I did," replied Sally, smiling.

"Well, child, very little of all that Farmer Grimble told you is true; he is quite mistaken, poor man. We neither worship idols, starve ourselves, nor confess the sins we are going to commit; all this is sheer nonsense! But we certainly confess the sins we have committed, and feel very happy afterwards. You would not like to have to do that, I suppose?"

"Laws, no, sir! I shouldn't know which end to begin at."

The priest smiled kindly, and whistled on his horse.

"Why," continued his little companion, "the Bible says, 'our sins are more in number than the hairs of our head,' and how could I ever recollect them?"

Father Stirling replied by explaining in a few simple words, the true doctrine of the Church, and though very far from convincing her of the authenticity of his religion, her last remark, as she sprung from the gig at her mistress's door, was to the effect, that, the very next time she saw Farmer Grimble, she would tell him not to talk of things he didn't understand. "And yet I always thought, somehow, Miss Marion couldn't have come to worship idols, that I did!"

It was with mingled emotions that the priest entered the chamber of the invalid, and certainly, among them all, surprise was not the least prominent. Had the Reverend Adolphus Gardiner offered him the hand of fellowship, he could not have been more astounded than at Mrs. Howard's message. He found her propped up with pillows, very weak and careworn, though lighted up as her face now was by a flush of expectation, and by the strange bright look it had worn all day, there was that in her appearance that wonderfully interested him.

Sally having placed a chair for the priest, and withdrawn, a few moments' silence ensued. It was broken at length by the lady.

"I hardly know how to apologise, Mr. Stirling, for bringing you all these miles, but I have a very particular question to ask you. I could not write it, for I am so very weak, and somehow"— here her voice failed—"I could not bring my mind to let my servant ask it."

"And there was no occasion for her to do so! Rest assured, my dear madam, that the drive of to-day has been only a pleasant excursion. Priests, like doctors, are accustomed to sick calls. I have walked miles in the dead of night, before this, to attend to one."

"But this can hardly be considered a sick call," replied Mrs. Howard, "for I will be candid, and tell you at once that I am as firm a Protestant as ever. I do not want to see you professionally."

He rather winced at the term, but only bowed in reply.

"You will be astonished at my question, I know," continued the lady, "but I lay awake all last night, and determined to ask it, for I do not think I shall ever get well again."

"We must hope for the best," replied the priest, soothingly. "I see no reason why you should not. This very warm weather is against you now, when it passes you will have a better chance of recovering your strength. You seem to me very low; does your medical man permit you to receive visitors?"

"I have never asked him," replied the invalid, smiling, "for the simple reason that I have no one to visit me. I have only three or four friends residing here, and during the whole of my illness they have been from home. I have seen no one all the time but my doctor, and Mr. Mason, the curate, once."

"Only once!"

"Yes, and that was yesterday; I found him so thoroughly uninteresting, that I could do nothing with him. I did not ask him to call again. An overgrown school-boy and nothing else!"

Father Stirling looked very grave. "And have you no one else to offer you spiritual consolation in this weary illness?"

"No one; I must wait until Dr. Stebbing comes back."

"Suppose you die meanwhile," was on the tip of Father Stirling's tongue, but he only shook his head. "And what is the question?" he asked after a long pause.

Mrs. Howard shaded her face with her thin white hand, and remained silent. It was pride's last struggle, and Father Stirling watched her with rather an anxious expression of countenance. But the hand was at last withdrawn—"Will you tell me where to find my child?"

"Will I give you Miss Howard's address?" he replied slowly, striving to seem unmoved; "well, I really cannot remember it at this moment, but I can get it for you very easily. I expect, however, that she will be at The Cedars before long. All Mr. Darrell's family are in London just at present, for one of their two daughters is to take the veil very shortly, and I understand that Miss Howard is to return with Edith Darrell, a few days after the ceremony. I suppose, therefore, she will be in Harleyford in about a fortnight's time."

"Is she much attached to Emily Darrell, do you think?"

"Very much so, they are like own sisters."

"And I suppose she will be present at the ceremony."

"Undoubtedly, seeing that the sister of the nun-elect is at this moment visiting her."

"What a dreadful thing for a young girl to shut herself up in that way, just like a bird in a cage. What will she have to do? Visit poor people?"

"No, the order Miss Darrell is entering, is what we call an enclosed one; they never go out at all, but lead lives of prayer and meditation. It is a very strict, but at the same time a most beautiful order."

Mrs. Howard looked uneasily at him.

"Will you answer me one question candidly?" she asked.

"If I can."

"Do you think my Marion is likely to follow her example?"

"Not in the least likely, I should say," replied the priest, laughing, "so make your mind quite easy on that score. I have never seen the smallest shadow of a vocation in her."

"I am so relieved," cried Mrs. Howard, bursting into tears; "my poor, dear child!"

Was ever woman so altered? As Father Stirling compared her with all the descriptions he had heard, and all the mental pictures he had formed of her, he made quite a meditation on the grace of God.

"There is one thing I cannot help wishing very much," observed the invalid, after a long silence.

"What is that?"

"That you were a Protestant clergyman."

"I am afraid I can hardly say amen to that," replied Father Stirling, smiling, "but may I ask why?"

"Because I should like to talk to you."

"Cannot you do so now?"

"What use would there be in doing so, when we believe such different things?"

"No, no," replied the priest, "you are mistaken, we have many points of belief in common; for although you stop short of my creed, I believe all that you do."

"Hardly, I think," replied the lady, "for I believe the Catholic religion is contrary to common sense."

"And yet you say every Sunday, 'I believe in the Holy Catholic Church.' Come, my dear madam, is there not some little discrepancy here?"

Mrs. Howard smiled. "I know very little of controversy, but I presume what I mean by the Catholic Church is one thing, what you mean, another. To have spoken as an orthodox Protestant, I suppose I ought to have said, that the Roman Catholic Church is opposed to common sense."

"The two titles have precisely the same meaning, my dear Mrs. Howard; but may I ask what particular doctrine, or doctrines, of our Church, you find so faulty?"

"I was afraid you were going to ask me that question, and I do not very well know how to answer it. I have my own ideas, generally, both on your religion and ours, but I will be candid with you, and tell you at once, that though, as one of its members, I prefer the latter, I have thought very little indeed about either one or the other."

Father Stirling looked at her compassionately and a prayer rose from the very bottom of his heart. He thought of Elias and the Shunamite's son in the days of old, and prayed, like him, that the dead might be brought to life.

"I wish it had not been so," she continued, "for those who live as I have never lived, would be happier here than I am now. It would be strange for you to hear a Protestant confession, and yet I feel as if I could almost make you one this afternoon."

"I shall be very happy to hear anything you like to tell me," replied the priest, "and to offer you any advice or consolation in my power."

"I do not know the reason why," returned the invalid, in the same tone, "but all last night I lay awake thinking and thinking, and it almost seemed as if God held the past up before me, and asked me what I thought of it. It was not a bright picture, yet I looked at it very steadily. Mr. Stirling, I have been very wicked, very harsh, and you, as well as I, know in what I have sinned."

"You mean in the matter of poor Marion?"

"Yes, I do, and it is a sin too, that, let me do what I will, I can never atone for; I only wish I could—I only wish I could."

"But you acted upon principle in your severity, did you not?" asked the priest. "You believed her to be in error, and tried to drive her back to what you thought, and still think, to be the truth."

"No, I did not. If I had had any thought of this kind with regard to her, I should not feel as I do now. It was very different. I was angry with Marion for three reasons, first, because she dared to act independently of me; secondly, because of the ridicule and contempt with which I thought so strange a step would be visited; and thirdly, because a certain bright future I had pictured for her, was dispelled by her own perversity. I had had a vision of her, as the mistress of a home all I could desire, moving in a circle I knew she was fitted to adorn, and I almost felt to hate her in my disappointment. But, as to whether the change she had made was pleasing or displeasing to God, on this view of the subject I never bestowed one single thought. But this is not surprising, for, during a life of nearly fifty years, I have never thought of Him at all till now."

"And now?" asked the priest, bending on her the full force of his calm grey eyes.

"I will try. If ever I arise from this bed, it shall be to exclaim, like the prodigal, 'I have sinned against Heaven and before Thee.'"

"You have said it already, for you see the errors of your past life, and are prepared, by the grace of God, to do your best to amend them."

There was long silence, broken at length by the sick woman.

"I do so wish still that you were a Protestant!"

"And again I ask why? Do you think that Catholics cannot sympathise with the sorrows of those who are not Catholics? Believe me, I feel deeply for you in this first moment of your awakening to the thought of God. Your trials have been great, but should they even be greater, you have only to place them in His hands ' who carried our griefs, and bore our infirmities.' "

"You speak of Christ," replied the invalid. "Mr. Stirling, my confession is only half complete, though at what I am about to say, you will, I know, be deeply shocked. Christian, as all have thought me, I am not one in heart. For years I have secretly doubted Christianity. I am not a sceptic, I am not a deist, still less am I an atheist. I should wish to be a Christian, but, in the depths of my heart, I do not believe. Revelation seems to demand an amount of credulity that I cannot bring myself to believe God would ever require from us."

"And yet, unless you believe that the truths of Christianity have been revealed to the world by God, you must, of necessity, attribute to man doctrines that are entirely above his understanding. You even do more, for you make him the author of a religious system which, in spite of the bitter and active hostility of all that is most powerful in the world, and notwithstanding the restraint which it places on natural inclinations, has been embraced in every age and in every region. Thus you see, by refusing to believe in the Divine inspiration of the Scriptures, you are in fact far more credulous than one who admits it."

He paused, but receiving no reply presently continued : "I could show you this in many ways, if I were not afraid of tiring you. As it is, I will only touch upon one point—the one that seems to me the very acmé of the non-believer's credulity, namely, its prophecies and their fulfilment. You know that a very large proportion of the historical events recorded in one part of the sacred Scriptures may be found distinctly prophesied in another. The birth of Christ in Bethlehem, the leading circumstances of His life, Passion, death, and burial ; the destruction of Jerusalem ; the scattering of the Jews, were all foretold long before they happened. If we leave Divine inspiration out of the question, there are only three natural ways in which the exact accordance of scriptural prophecy with historical fact can be accounted for, and the first of these is by chance. Now, I am sure you will agree with me, that a person who can believe in such a chance, or rather such a chain of chances as this, evinces more credulity than one who looks on the prophecies and their fulfilment as the direct work of God ?"

" Yes ; besides, one who believes in God as the Beneficent Father of the universe cannot, at the same time, believe in chance. It seems to me only a disrespectful term for God's Providence."

"Exactly so. Let us suppose, then, that the non-believer gives the second answer, and tells us that ' these historical events were planned to suit the prophecies, and fulfil them.' Why, this would evince a credulity of mind even more astonishing. Just imagine. The whole life of a Man would have to be planned from His cradle to His grave ; a city would have to be encompassed, taken, and annihilated ; a powerful people would have to be scattered over the whole earth, and yet kept distinct from every other nation on its surface till the end of the world! And all this for no earthly purpose, but to fulfil a few texts. What would you think of this answer?"

"That a man who could think it any solution of the question must be mad."

"Well, I do not think you will find the remaining answer more sensible. Our non-believing friend, 'then, might inform you in the third place, that the prophecies—which he would triumphantly show, are seldom consecutive, but are found scattered here and there throughout the Sacred Writings—have evidently been dropped in after the events, to give authority to a newly fledged Christianity. This at first sight, my dear Mrs. Howard, might seem, perhaps, a more sensible answer; and yet, if we examine it, we shall find that the man who could give it, would be quite as credulous as the one who should take shelter in either of the other replies. For can we suppose that the Jews, with their malicious hatred of Christianity, would have silently permitted additions to the sacred books, and especially the interpolation of passages which should support the abolition of the Mosaic dispensation? And even supposing the alterations to have been affected, would they have tamely suffered the destruction of every copy of the original version?"

"One would hardly think so."

Again there was silence, broken at length by the invalid. "I am very glad I spoke to you of this," she observed, in a low voice; "I shall think over what you said very deeply, and God will help me to believe, for I do not want to doubt any longer. But will you do one thing more? Will you teach me something about this Christianity of which I have hitherto been so strangely ignorant? You will do so as a Catholic, I know, of course, but, be that as it may, it makes no difference; I must and will know who and what Christ is."

He commenced to speak to her when the sun was shining brightly—he did not cease until that sun was sinking in the western sky. He did as she asked him—he spoke to her of Christ. He began at the beginning of the story of Redemption, when the first man and woman were rejoicing amid the glories of the new creation, while the echoes of the "fiat lux" were still rolling around the eternal throne. He spoke of their great sin, and how its heavy shadow was to fall on their children through all generations—of the great promise, and how its light was to gladden the hearts of those children till the end of time. He spoke of the old covenant, with its statutes of terror, and rites of blood, leading ever upward to its consummation on the Hill of Calvary; he spoke of the new covenant, streaming downward from that Hill, in those ruddy streamlets that were to fructify the whole earth. And then in simple words he told of the birth, the infancy, and childhood of the Messiah. Of the exile in Egypt, the home life in Nazareth, and the wandering life round Galilee, seeking for souls. And then, as the evening sunset streamed around them, rich and red, he spoke of Gethsemane, of the scattered disciples, of the streets of Jerusalem and their shrieking rabble, of Calvary and the cross. He said no more, but silently sat and watched the shadow on the wall, so silently, that those who saw not the burning and throbbing of the heart within, vibrating still with the echo of the words he had spoken, might have said he was a statue.

But his listener. Strange, he had hardly uttered a word with which she had not been familiar from her babyhood, and yet, when at length he turned to her, she was weeping like a child.

"I am afraid," he exclaimed, in his usual brisk but soothing tone, "that this conversation has been too much for you."

"No, no," she returned, drying her tears, "it was not too much, indeed it was not. I cannot tell you how I like to hear you talk. You have made me feel like a new creature."

Father Stirling smiled. "Will you let me ring the bell for my little friend, Sally? for I fear you will be getting exhausted for want of refreshment. I was very thoughtless not to think of it before. I shall have the doctor forbidding me the house, and I should not like that," he added, giving a vigorous pull at the bell.

"What! do you mean to say that you will come to see me again?" asked the invalid, with a sparkling eye.

"To be sure I will, if you let me come."

"Indeed, indeed, I will! You may believe, Mr. Stirling, that I do not speak to you in the language of compliment, when I assure you this is the first happy hour I have known, since Mr. Lisle wrote and told me that Marion was a Catholic."

At this moment Sally entered.

"It was I who rang for you," said Father Stirling. "If you had seen how pale and tired your mistress looked just now, you would have said I should never come again."

Sally smiled and ran down for the tea-things.

"And now," said the priest, once more approaching his Protestant penitent, "I must bid you good-bye. Shall I write for Miss Howard's address?"

"Not yet, I should like to see you again first, if I can."

"Very well, I will come again the day after to-morrow."

"Thank you very much. But you will stay, now, and let Sally get you a cup of tea?"

"Nothing, thank you; I expect my old Rufus is getting desperate outside. Good-bye."

Rufus was decidedly put out of the way. Never had his master taken such a liberty with him before, as to leave him standing in the sun for three whole hours, and he shook his ears back in a very ill-tempered fashion, half the way home. But never in his life before, had his master heard a "Protestant confession."

"I should think you must be half dead, ma'am," said Sally, as she handed her mistress the tea, "I wish you would just try and eat this piece of toast with it." Much to Sally's astonishment, not only that, but two more pieces disappeared, while Mrs. Howard looked so bright, that her little maid was even more puzzled than she had been in the morning.

"Father Stirling is a good doctor, is he not, Sally?" asked her mistress, with a smile.

"I should rather think he is. Why he has done more for you in one afternoon, than Dr. Bernard has done in a month. I hope he will come again."

"The day after to-morrow, he says. Will you pull the blind quite up?"

The girl obeyed, and the room was flooded with a sea of gold and crimson, from the midst of which the invalid glanced upward, with the radiance of a new hope shining in her eye.

"This is a bright and beautiful world, after all, Sally."

"So it is, ma'am, very beautiful. If the people who live in it was only made to match, we should be very happy, very happy indeed."

"Why, silly child," exclaimed her mistress, "earth would be heaven then!"

CHAPTER XXIX.

ONCE more old Rufus is standing before the green gate, prancing with impatience till the stirrups dance again, wondering what can keep his master so long. Shall we step into the little house and look for him, dear reader? Let us go into Mrs. Howard's room, where Father Stirling sat so long the day Sally first fetched him, talking to the "dreamer awakened." No one is there, nor does it any longer wear the air of a sick chamber, with its even high-piled bed, snowy drapery, and country perfume of marjoram-scented linen. As we seek him down stairs, glancing into each pretty room we pass, all is so bright and gay with flowers, that it seems like a preparation for some grand gala-day. Even Sally's and Polly's whispers, as they bustle about in their own domain, seem to be of something very bright to-morrow. There are voices in the little breakfast-room, and we may enter if you will, for story-tellers and story-readers are privileged persons. They listen to private conversations and confidential communications by the dozen, peep into love-letters, and even dive, with a sort of magical passe-tout, into the very bottom of the speakers' hearts. Yet nobody ever gives them the ugly name of eavesdroppers after all.

And is that Mrs. Howard, she who so lately trembled in the shadow of death? To be sure it is, though, to see her now, sitting erect at the open window, with her workbox and writing materials lying around her, one could hardly imagine her to be the same woman, who only a fortnight ago had almost fainted in trying to write a letter. It is a wonderful change truly, and, under God, Father Stirling has been a wonderful physician.

Mrs. Howard has been talking long and earnestly, and as he listens, Father Stirling rests his arm upon the window-sill, and looks out across the bright country landscape, where the spire in the distance rises from among its ivy and its graves, and the ripening corn is waving like a yellow sea all round it.

"And so our conversation of last Sunday evening was our first Catholic one, you consider?" he remarked, as the lady concluded her observations, and waited for his reply.

"I think so; all you have said at other times is exactly, I know, what Henry Lisle would have uttered. Until last Sunday, I could not have told that yours was a different faith to his."

"And what impression did that conversation leave on you, may I ask? Did the first glance of my cloven foot give you a better or worse impression of us?"

"I cannot say. Once I knew too little to be able to criticise your religion, now I know too much to dare to judge it. Much as I wish to become a real Christian, I tremble still at the word Catholic. If what you told me the other day was all I had to learn, I might, perhaps, some day believe it true; but I have been thinking since of many things I have heard about the Catholic religion, and some of them seem very strange indeed."

"Tell me one of these things."

"Well, the worship of the Virgin Mary, for one instance. It seems—if I may so phrase it—a robbery of God, to worship any other than Him. Indeed, I cannot see how one can do so, and at the same time steer clear of idolatry."

"It would, certainly, be impossible, if our Blessed Lady were worshipped in the sense in which you understand the word. But you are mistaken, my dear Mrs. Howard. We worship God as the source of Light, of Life, and of Truth, as the Almighty Creator, Redeemer, and Sanctifier; we honour Mary as the first created intelligence, but only as a creature after all. To compare ourselves with Mary, would be presumption, to compare Mary with God, would be blasphemy. There is a distance unimaginable between the highest archangel and the Virgin Mother; but there is a distance infinite as the breadth of heaven itself, between that Mother and her Son. Yet we worship her with a fond, devoted, childlike love; if we cease to do so, we lose half our peace and light. But this is not strange. The diamond in the monarch's crown does not sparkle less brilliantly in the sunshine, because the windows of his palace glitter in the beam as well. There is room in the human heart for many kinds of love, for friend, child, sister, parent, wife, and country, and yet, amid all, God still holds His sway in the Christian's heart. Shall we not, then, find a way to love His Mother, without trespassing on His high vantage-ground?"

He paused, but Mrs. Howard remaining silent, he continued.

"I cannot imagine how any one, who contemplates Mary in the immensity of her dignity, can think of her as an ordinary woman. Mother of God! There is that in the very name, that seems to cast us prostrate at her feet. Only show a woman to the world, who should be daughter of one mighty monarch, wife to another, and mother of a child, one day destined to hold the reins of a great empire. Show her, at the same time, matchless in human virtue, skilled in human arts and science, profound in human learning, protectress, moreover, of the oppressed, and common pleader of the cause of all men. How would men regard her, what national homage would be too great, what love could her people testify, that would be too deep for such a queen as this? Yet, let this woman be what she might, Mary is more, for what she would be on earth, Mary is in heaven. Daughter of God the Father, Mother of God the Son, Spouse of God the Holy Ghost, she shines upon us with a threefold radiance, and binds us to her with a triple cord of love. Could we look on her in heaven, we should see her as she is; looking up to her from earth, she is simply a mystery. Threefold in her glory, she is threefold in her power; and prays, as she alone can pray, for her children here below, the younger brethren of her Son."

"But, Mr. Stirling, how can she do this? You say she is only a creature, and yet you seem to endue her with the God-like attribute of Omniscience, else how could she read the thoughts and hear the prayers of people in every part of the world at once?"

"Is the devil a creature?"

"Yes, of course he is."

"Is he omniscient?"

"No; what a strange question!"

"How does he tempt the whole world at once, then?"

"I am sure I don't know, I never thought of this!" exclaimed the lady, opening her eyes.

"Most likely not," cried Father Stirling, much amused at her astonishment; "'we discover things that our philosophy never dreamt of,' every day. You must not imagine, however, that I draw any parallel between the power of Satan and that of our Blessed Mother, for her sympathies are one thing, his temptations another. The prince of the power of the air is, next to Mary, the highest created intelligence, and with that intelligence he directs his myrmidons, those myriads of spirits that fell from heaven with him. But no more. He is a spirit, and as such, being endowed with the attributes of agility, he can pass more swiftly than light, but he can only be in one place at a time. Now, with Mary, it is very different. Her home is heaven, and there as she gazes on God in the Beatific Vision, she sees the reflection of the universe in Him, perhaps in that sea of crystal that stretches far and wide before the Eternal Throne. There lie our troubles, there our joys, and Mary, as she gazes on them in God, prays, for every throb of that Immaculate Heart is prayer."

"Why call her immaculate; did she never sin?"

"Never; could God, think you, He who is of 'eyes too pure to behold iniquity,' could He have been the child of a sin-stained mother ? Impossible. He 'who loves to repose among the lilies,' would not have the lily that He chose, flecked with a single spot of the earth from whence it grew. Mary was that lily. Immaculate from the first moment of her existence, immaculate in her life and death, immaculate she was assumed to heaven."

"But, really, Mr. Stirling, how do you know all this : the Bible says nothing concerning it ?"

"There are many things on which the Bible is silent. Do you think the few pages of the Gospels contain all the words and actions of our Lord ? Certainly not, for St. John expressly says, 'that could all these be collected, the world itself should not contain the books that should be written.' Yet why should one thing that He said, or one action that He performed, be recorded more than another ? Simply because God so willed it. Some things not explicitly recorded in the Bible, we know, by inference; some not recorded at all, by tradition. Nor is it the Catholic Church alone that recognises tradition. Why do Protestants baptize their infants, when not a word is said concerning it in the Bible ; and why do they sanctify the first day of the week, and do their hardest work upon the seventh, when the Bible says, 'remember the Sabbath Day to keep it holy, for the seventh day is the Sabbath of the Lord thy God ?' They do both upon tradition. The Bible is undoubtedly the Word of God, and to act contrary to its commands and precepts, would be to act contrary to Him who gave it ; but it was never given as the common text-book for the mass of mankind. 'They 'who are unstable, wrest over the Holy Scriptures to their own destruction.' These words that the great apostle spoke by inspiration, might be the natural language of us all, even in the present generation, I often think, from the depths of our experience."

"And yet there is enough in the Bible to carry us to heaven."

"If we knew how to use it, undoubtedly ; but where would be the cure, think you, if, instead of consulting a physician, the sick man sent for a pharmacopœia, and studied it himself ? There is, certainly, a probability that he might do himself neither good nor harm, though the chances are, I think, that he would get poisoned. Yet, place that little book in the hands of a mediciner, and strength grows in his patients as he consults it. 'Understandest thou what thou readest ?' asked St. Philip of the officer of Queen Candace, who sat in his chariot, with the Scriptures open before him. 'How can I, was the reply, 'unless some man should guide me ?' Was St. Philip surprised at the answer ? In no way ; we simply hear that he took his place beside him in the chariot, and 'preached unto him Jesus ;' and where the written word had been incomprehensible, the preaching of the Church, represented by the apostle, prevailed, and the 'man of great authority was baptized, and went on his way rejoicing.' The Bible, I repeat, cannot be too much respected, but even as the child must beware how he plays with fire, and tampers with sharp-edged tools, so must the man beware how he plays with the fire of the Spirit, and tampers with the Word of God, 'sharper than a two-edged sword.' And is respect for the Bible, do you think, compatible with using it as a common school-book? Shall the decrees and revelations of the Most High God be read in turn with the history of a few ephemeral nations, and the sayings and discoveries of a few poor worms? While the traveller stands entranced, as he gazes for the first time on Loch Lomond, the shepherd boy, born upon its margin, walks whistling by. What is there for him, but rocks trees, sky, and water! 'Familiarity breeds contempt;' and he who has spelt wearily through the abstruse epistles in his childhood, will find it hard in later years to see their beauty. But we are wandering from the subject we commenced; do you think you see any better yet, in what light we regard the Blessed Virgin Mary?"

"Yes; but still I do not see, notwithstanding all you have said, that there is any necessity to pray to her, or to any other saint at all. You believe that God hears prayers that are addressed directly to Him, do you not?"

"Certainly."

"And answers them?"

"If He sees good to do so."

"Then what need is there of any medium in addressing Him?"

"Mrs. Howard, do you think St. Paul ever prayed?"

"Of course he did."

"Were his prayers ever answered?"

"Yes, sometimes miraculously."

"Then why did he ask his brethren to pray for him?"

She was silent.

"What do you mean when you say on Sunday, 'I believe in the communion of saints'? Do not even Protestants say, that it means a communion of love, and sympathy, and prayers?"

"I really do not know what they think it means," replied his companion, with a slight flush.

"Then take my word for it, such is their version of its meaning. Like us, too, though not so often as we, they pray for their friends, and ask them in their turn to remember them at the throne of grace. They could not well scruple to do so, when they read in their own Bibles, that 'the fervent prayer of a righteous man availeth much.' Therefore, my dear friend, you see plainly that those of your own faith frequently use mediums between themselves and God."

"But these mediums are living people. If I ask you to pray for me to-night, as I shall do before you leave me, that is very different to kneeling down, and saying to one long since dead, Pray for me."

"Very different, because, in speaking to me, you address a fellow-sinner, one who, for aught you know, may be out of a state of grace, and whose prayers, in that case, would be valueless for others, until he himself repented; whereas, in the saint, you invoke one standing in the immediate presence of God Himself. So the

s

question simply resolves itself into this ; can the blessed in heaven hear, see, and sympathise with those on earth ? and the Church says they can.   How else can angels rejoice over a repentant sinner ? and does not the inspired Word itself tell us, that the saints are as the angels of God in heaven, and that they are equal to the angels ?

"There is also a great instance of the intercession of an angel being heard and answered, in the book of Zacharias. I will try and give it you in the sacred words themselves. 'The angel of the Lord answered, and said, O Lord of Hosts ! how long wilt Thou not have mercy on Jerusalem, and on the cities of Judah, with which Thou hast been angry these three score and ten years ? And the Lord answered the angel that talked with Him, with good words, and comfortable words.' Again, in the Apocalypse, we hear that 'the four and twenty elders fell down before the Lamb, having vials full of odours, which are the prayers of the saints ; ' and further on, in the same book of mysterious revelation, we read : 'And another angel came and stood before the altar, having a golden censer, and there was given to him much incense, that he should offer the prayers of all saints upon the golden altar, which is before the throne of God.   And the smoke of the incense of the prayers of the saints ascended before God from the hand of the angel.'   What then must have been the prayers that the angel presented before God ?   Were the saints praying for themselves ? Certainly not ; since they have light, and peace, and joy, and love, in fullest, broadest perfection.   What can the blessed in Heaven pray for, except for their brethren still fighting and struggling on earth ? "

"But you pray more often to the Virgin Mary than you do to God, at least so Protestants say."

"I am not prepared to admit this, but, even if it were so, remember, that in praying to her we pray to Him.   Mary, of herself, has no power to grant us anything, either spiritual or temporal, but God has made her the dispenser of His graces, and in Him, and through Him, she obtains us all things.   Our prayers are cold, faint, doubting—hers, who shall describe them !   If, at the moment of the annunciation, she was 'full of grace, and blessed amongst women,' what is she, after all the graces and glories that have fallen upon her since ?   And if she is too compassionate not to pray, too dearly cherished by the ever Blessed Trinity to pray unheard, shall we make light of such an advocate, and prefer our own cold prayers to hers ?   Like the sun, God shines forth upon His creation, the Source of light and heat, but we cannot gaze on Him with mortal eyes, cannot endure the rays of His glory.   With light reflected from the unapproachable brightness of God, moon-like, Mary shines from heaven, and we gaze without difficulty on her tempered radiance, and pass on our way, amid the calm white rays of her love.   Truly, truly, when the reformers tore away everything bright and beautiful from the ancient Church, and, like foxes and night-birds, made for themselves a home amid the dismantled ruins, fairest of all the sweet things they ravished were the altars of Mary. From the moment that her images were broken, her pictures defaced, her rosaries scattered bead by bead, and that the Angelus ceased to float upon the breeze, from that moment the poetry of religion faded from English hearts and homes."

"And yet," objected his listener, "England is prosperous, and even religious."

"Yes, prosperous with a human prosperity; religious, with a cold, calculating religion, that spends hundreds on its churches, and hundreds of thousands on its homes. That gives its dole of worship once a week to God, as though calculating to a nicety what it must do to be saved. That finds good works supereroga-tory, the pain of fasting contrary to the liberty of the Gospel, and penance food for laughter. That never takes one generous view of religion, nor offers one mortification on its altar. It is an easy thing to kneel in a softly-cushioned pew, and call oneself 'a miser-able sinner,' but it is not so easy to feel the hard wood of the cross pressing into the weary shoulder, and yet take it, as the just reward of those miserable sins."

"You are very bitter against Protestants."

"God forbid. Indeed, my dear friend, you are quite mistaken; I know too well the heaviness of the cloud that obscures their path, to blame them when they fail to pierce it. Some people tell us that the age of miracles is past, but I look on every conversion as a special miracle of God."

"Do you think I shall ever be a Catholic?"

He was silent.

"Do tell me."

"What do you think yourself?"

"I cannot say; your religion is very beautiful, and"——she paused.

"Let me finish the sentence," said the priest—"I will pray to be directed."

Mrs. Howard smiled, and Father Stirling rose to take his leave.

"Goodbye; you will try and keep calm for to-morrow."

"I will; but, Mr. Stirling"——

He bent forward to catch the low tones of her voice.

"Will you pray for me? I should like to be a Catholic, if I could."

"I will, on one condition."

She glanced up, inquiringly.

"That you do not call me Mr. Stirling any more."

"Father, will you pray for me?"

"I will, my child; indeed I will."

"Poor thing," he muttered, as two minutes later he was riding down the street; "poor thing, there is no crucible like the crucible of affliction, after all."

The red sky had not been a false prophet at either Ennington or Harleyford, for when the morrow came, the August sun shone

forth in his most ardent splendour from the bright blue sky above.
Sally had been up and busy from a very early hour, and she and
Polly, fresh and smart as two country posies, were on the tip-toe
of expectation.   Mrs. Howard, with a smile on her trembling lip,
sat before her toilette glass, that reflected a countenance strangely
different to the Mrs. Howard of other days.

The night had been once more a sleepless one, but it had not
been weary, for every hour that chimed had been another nearer
to her child, and the mother, in sweet anticipation, had watched
for the morning light.   As it broke upon the bed, she reached a
book from her pillow, and began to read.   But it was not for long,
for the words that met her eyes, seemed so much like an echo from
her own night thoughts, that she could go no further.   "What is
truth?"   Momentous question, asked by Pilate, who yet tarried
not for his answer.   Should she be like him?   Forbid it, Heaven!
It seemed as though the form of the ancient Roman started from
the shadows of the past, to warn by his unanswered question, those
who, after glancing at the light, pass on into yet deeper darkness.
All she had read and heard, during the last few weeks of her sickness, came back into her mind—strange thoughts and feelings,
growing like the morning light around her, stronger and intenser
every moment.   "What is truth?" she whispered, as she replaced
her book.   "I am the Way, the Truth, and the Life," came the
answer, and with it a new-born faith, a fitful hope, a trembling
gleam of love.   Mrs. Howard rose and prepared to meet her child,
but over and above her calm expectation, there hovered the same
look that had puzzled Mr. Bernard a fortnight before, and had
sent Sally on her mission of love to Harleyford.

"The missis is altered as I never see," said Polly, as she returned
to the kitchen from carrying up Mrs. Howard's breakfast.

"You'd be altered, child, if you had borne all she has, and that
ever since the spring."

"But I don't mean in her face, I mean in her ways."

"What have her ways got to do with you, I should like to
know?   Just you sit down and eat your breakfast, and mind your
own business," cried Sally, in a tone of ineffable contempt.

Polly laughed.   "You haven't altered yourn, any way about.   I
don't believe the missis would have spoken to me as sharp as
that, if I had done ever such a thing to vex her."

"I'd advise you not to try."

"I don't mean to, for I like her now; I used to hate her once,
though."

"More shame for you.   And you call yourself a Christian, I
suppose!"

"Well, I suppose I am.   I ain't a hanimal, am I?"

Sally only poured her tea into her saucer in indignant silence.
"I tell you what it is," she exclaimed, at length, "I shan't be
sorry when you're off.   I'd rather by half do all the work myself,
than be pestered with you; you young girls are so awful aggravating."

Polly, who infinitely preferred her berth at Mrs. Howard's to her father's cottage, with its pinching and penury, began to whimper.

Sally gradually softened. "Come, leave off that noise, and we'll see. I like you well enough about me, when you behave yourself."

The tears ceased, and Polly commenced a vigorous attack on the bread-and-butter.

"What did Mrs. Howard say to you," inquired Sally, "that made you think of her being altered ?"

"She told me I looked very neat and tidy, and asked me how I got on with you."

"What did you say ?"

"I said very well, for of course I did't know you was going to snap one up so, when I come back."

Sally smiled. "I always get cross when I hear a word said against her."

"Why ?"

"Why ! What a child you are, to be sure, for knowing the whys and wherefores of everything ! Well, if you must know, it's just this. For many years after I first came here, I saw very little of Mrs. Howard, and thought about her still less. It was Miss Marion as I had to do with. As you and all the rest of the village know, Miss Marion went away, and you know too, how her mother said that until she was a Protestant again, she should never come back. Now a great many people in the place think that this was all the missis's doings, but I've my eyes about me, Polly, and I know better. There were many days when, proud as she was, the missis would have given way, if Miss Marion had only had some one to speak for her. But she hadn't, poor dear young lady : for as for me, I was, of course, as good as nothing ; I should only have lost my place, and my nose with it, if I had said a word. No, as I said just now, it wasn't Mrs. Howard's doing, but all that Mr. Lisle—you remember him, the parson as used to be here before Mr. Mason. I think, and so does a good many people, that he had somehow been keeping company with Miss Marion, but anyways, he turned against her as bitter as gall. Now, if you like, I do hate him above a bit ! One day I recollect fetching him in a glass of ale : of course they both kept quiet while I was in the room, but as I shut the door, I heard him say, quite plain, 'don't give way ! don't give way !' She had been crying all the morning, I could see by her eyes, but, of course, she said nothing to me, for it wasn't in her nature."

"I know that," interrupted her auditor.

"After Mr. Lisle went that day, she seemed more unhappy than ever, and soon afterwards we left Ennington, she and me, and went to live a lonely life in Clifton. Laws, Polly ! I never was so dull in my life ! Down a strange kind of crooked way they call the Zigzags one day, across the Downs another, or else a little shopping in Clifton, or in large streets in Bristol, which we never seemed to see twice, that was all we ever did, and then we used

to come back to the lodgings for the rest of the day, each to keep
our own company. And amongst it all, the worst was, that I
could see her heart was breaking. If she would only have spoken
to me, I used sometimes to feel that I could have helped her to
bear her great sorrow. But she never said a word to me about
anything but my business, for while we were there, I used to make
her dresses, and do all sorts of things to take up my time. She
wouldn't have had me with her, only she didn't like the looks of
being alone. Well, would you believe, Polly? I grew quite fond of
her, although she never seemed to notice me any more than the
first day I had come. But I determined to make her like me, and
at last the day came. One morning she got a letter from Miss
Smith, the person that took the house while we were in Clifton,
and something in it vexed her so, that she burst out crying right
before me. I only went up to her, as I felt it right to do at the
moment, seeing her so lonely and unprotected, but I felt as if I
could throw my arms round her neck. I don't know what I said,
but I never saw anything so angry as she was for a minute. She
seemed half as tall again, and looked just as I could fancy a great
queen. I tried to beg her pardon, but I broke out into such a
great sob instead, that I always feel quite ashamed when I think of
it. And what do you think she did? Why, she came straight up
to me, and put her two hands upon my shoulders with such an
altered face, that I thought it couldn't possibly be her. But it
was her, and from that moment she grew quite changed to me.
She keeps her place, and I keep mine, and so we always shall, but
in heart we are friends. She is a widow, and I am an orphan, and
there seems to be something more than common that binds us
together. Since her illness she has altered still more, and if she
goes on much longer like this, we shall have her an angel. But
somehow, I don't want that, for then she would perhaps take to
her wings and fly away for ever. Now, Polly, you know I haven't
told you this, to go and tell everybody, but just to let you see how
much there was good in her all the time that she seemed so proud
and cold, for you see it was only seeming."

Polly shook her head. "I like her very much now, and I only
hope she will keep like she is. But people changes sometimes
after they get well, don't they?" ruminated Polly.

"Not such as her," replied Sally: "no, child, it's all the Lord's
doing, this is. Do you know, Polly, what she puts me in mind of,
when I see her so good and so loving?"

"No. What?"

"Of the bright fresh stream that gushed out of the hard rock
when Moses struck it. If it hadn't been for that rod, the water
would have been in it, I suppose, to this day; and if it hadn't
pleased the Lord to smite poor missis with a heavy trouble, the
love that we see now, might have been shut up in her heart till
her dying day. Don't you think so?"

"Yes," said Polly, trying to look as if she understood. "Who's
the gentleman as comes here so often?"

"A minister," replied Sally.

"A minister is he? What a queer cut of a coat he do wear, to be sure!"

"Never mind his coat; it's the cut of his face as I like."

"Does he live far off?"

"Not very," replied Sally, who had been enjoined by her mistress, to say as little as possible concerning their visitor.

"It's him as is coming with miss to-day, ain't it?".

"Yes, he is a friend of hers."

"Is he married?"

"No."

"Perhaps he's after Miss Marion too," said Polly thoughtfully.

"No, he isn't, so you'd better not be making any more guesses. He's a reg'lar right-down bachelor, and no mistake."

"O goodness!" cried Polly; "but, however do you know? he ain't so old."

A ring from the bed-room bell silenced the speaker, and left her to finish her bread-and-butter unassisted.

. . . .

A repentant mother! Reader, the veil must fall! Such was a spectacle for angels, not for men. Even Father Stirling lingered in the porch for full ten minutes, before he ventured in, stroking Tyrza, and humming the "four-leaved shamrock."

That afternoon Sally and Polly kept house alone, and in a lumbering old carriage Rufus bore three happy hearts behind him to Harleyford. A grateful tear twinkled in her eye, as the mistress of The Cedars embraced the friend of her youth, and with no slight emotion bade her welcome to her home and heart.

"How things does change about in this world, 'Liza, my girl!" said Turner, as she that night settled herself to sleep.

"Didn't I say she would come round after a bit, mother?"

"So you did, so you did; the Lord forgive me for all the things as I've ever said agen her. How she do be changed to be sure! Oh, deary, deary me! Miss Marion's as happy as a queen, that she be, the Lord love her!"

And the Lord does love her; fragile instrument in the working of great and glorious things! The bright curls nestle to-night against her mother's cheek, and Golden-hair dreams of heaven.

CHAPTER XXX.

IT was a scene of life and gaiety, brightness and bustle, with the autumn sun shining redly on the red leaves, and the water sparkling and flashing in his beams. Oh, the Bois de Boulogne! Who, who knows Paris does not know it, with its broad roads and gilded gates, its clear lakes and verdant lawns, its waving woods and tortuous bye-paths, its art and nature so magically blended, that one cannot say which is the true charm of the scene? And who, who loves Paris, does not love it, with its flowers and swans, its picturesque islands and falling cascades, its morning chats and rambles, its mid-day drives and state, its evening fêtes and merriment? How often has the Englishman, fairly wearied with lion-hunting, sunk with a sigh of relief into one of its cane-worked chairs, glad for a while to rest on his oars, as he cons his guide-book, or thinks over his day's wanderings in peace!

This was exactly what two Englishmen were doing on a certain September afternoon—two genuine sons of Britain, "doing Paris" desperately. No one would have certainly set them down as Frenchmen, even had "Murray" been out of sight. There was, indeed, no desire on their part to disclaim their nationality, for they were talking animated English, much to the amusement of an honest old lady, en bonnet, seated on the next chair.

"And so you are beginning to get tired of Paris?" remarked the younger of the two, a fine handsome young fellow, with merry black eyes and dark complexion, rendered still darker by exposure to the sun; "I cannot understand that at all; I call it no end of a place!"

The other smiled. He had seen more summers than his companion, and it seemed as though much of his interest in life had passed with its earlier years. His manners were grave and quiet, and his clerical garb made the gravity not unsuitable. The smile excited by the remark of the other soon faded, and a rather melancholy shadow took its usual place upon his brow.

"I am not surprised at your idea of it," he remarked after a pause: "I can fancy that those who can appreciate its gaieties, find Paris a perfect Elysium. As for me, although I can understand its charms, they do not suit me."

"Do you not like this?" asked the other, pointing to the animated scene around them.

"Of course I do, and many things besides, but, usually speaking, Paris grieves and shocks me."

"May I ask if you have been here long?"

"About a week, and as I am making a tour for my health, I do not suppose I shall stay much longer. I have not yet decided whether to go on from here to Switzerland, or up the Rhine."

"I am going to Switzerland," replied the other; "the idea of its mountains is to me a most bewitching one, for though I have traversed many thousands of miles in voyages from London to Sydney, and from Sydney to London, I seem to have seen but little of the really grand scenery of the world. But your temperament is, I should imagine, very different to mine; I can well fancy that Germany would suit you better than glaciers and mountain passes. Yours is, I am sure, just the nature to appreciate the sweet-storied Rhine, with its ruined castles and luxuriant vine-yards—you like dreamland, I know, and one must keep one's eyes uncomfortably wide open in walking along the precipices of the great St. Bernard. But that is just the sort of thing I like. Come, tell me; am I not right in my estimate of you?"

"Yes—no. Mine is a dreamy nature, but I never dream, for it is a waste of time, and dangerous. I am thoroughly matter-of-fact."

"Not as much as you think. Perhaps you would be surprised if I told you, that it was the enthusiastic look of admiration you bestowed upon that beautiful glimpse of scenery at St. Cloud, that first made me wish to speak to you."

"I am very glad you did speak to me," replied the other, "for I had been wishing for a companion all day. I have been in a great measure alone during my stay here, for although I have letters of introduction, I have not felt exactly in spirits to make use of them," and the speaker sighed heavily. "With the exception of an old college friend of mine, a clergyman residing here, I have hardly spoken to any one."

"And how do you get on with this most barbarous lingo?"

"As to that, I can manage pretty well; I was at school for some time in the provinces."

"More than I can : I nearly send the old garçon into a fit, half-a-dozen times a day, though he is polite enough to get black in the face rather than grin. I am afraid I shall be the death of him from apoplexy some day." And the young fellow laughed till the tears came, at the recollection of his various blunders.

It was some time before they left their seats, and the longer they chatted, the more animated they grew. The naïveté with which his young companion descanted upon everything that had fallen under his notice during his sojourn in France, considerably amused the clergyman. Still there was a tone of thought and deeper feeling, wonderfully perceptible in the young man's observations, when the under current of his nature was stirred, that gave his graver companion a great desire to know more of him whom chance had made the companion of the passing hour. The young man, on his side, was quite as favourably impressed with his new friend. Weary of the companions of his tour, youths whom love of adventure had led into the wild revelry of the Quartier Latin, among the students of the Ecole de Medicine, he had gradually weaned himself from their party, and promising to overtake them on their road, had suffered them to depart without him. All this in the natural frankness of his disposition he told his new companion.

"You have quite made up your mind, then, to go on to Switzerland, I presume?" remarked the clergyman.

"Not altogether, though those fellows are expecting me, even now, I know."

"If you take my advice, you will not go. You do not care much for them, I can see."

"Candidly, I do not; the fact is, they are too fast for me. Even those of the party that seemed very rational at first, are as bad now, if not worse, than the rest."

"So much for bad example; you had better not go after them."

"I have more than half a mind not to do so. I was rather upset about one or two little matters before leaving England, and I long to be quiet. Otherwise, I confess, I should have got on with my friends much better; but, somehow, I cannot exactly enter into all that sort of thing just now. I should thoroughly enjoy a quiet party of two or three; or even one friend to travel with would suit me very well."

"You would not care for the company of a dull old fellow like me, or we might go up the Rhine together."

"Yes, I should," cried the other; "I believe we should get on bravely together."

"Then be it so," said the clergyman, rising. "It is getting chilly now, and I think we had better move on. This is truly a pretty scene," he continued, turning to take a last look at the gay groups. "I have been very pleased, too, by my visit of this morning to St. Cloud. There is something to my taste very beautiful in that heavy palace, sleeping, as it were, among its stately trees and verdant alleys. That and the grand old Versailles are among the few things I care for here."

"Do you not like the Tuileries?"

"Yes I do. But it is the air of deep repose that especially charms me at Versailles and St. Cloud. I suppose you will smile if I say I like the dreaminess of the alleys and silent waterworks."

"Have you not seen the waters play?"

"No, and am not likely to see them, since they tell me it will have to be by the desecration of the Sabbath. Abominable!" he exclaimed, striking his foot vehemently, as though denouncing Paris and Parisian impieties for ever.

"The country round Paris is very pretty," observed his companion, as they continued their walk.

"To a certain degree, but to my mind it in no way equals the scenery surrounding London. You will search vainly here for the beauties of our Richmond. The woods of Meudon are well enough, but along what a flat expanse of fields and vineyards, you must pass, to reach it from Paris. How different from the pretty villa-dotted roads that lead out in all directions from our metropolis. A man, to my thinking, must be Paris-mad who would compare it with our grand old London.

"Take her altogether," he continued, "England is a beautiful little country. The castles of the Rhine, and the glaciers of Switzerland, may be all very well, but the charm of English scenery lies in something deeper and dearer still. Although she is now so populous that her large towns intersect her like a mighty network, there is yet room for isolated villages and broad estates; and though she stands highest on the pinnacle of science and discovery, the charms of her little villages are still intact. Railways intersect her like a web, factories pour forth their marvellous floods of wealth, mines probe deep into her bosom, but the country lanes of dear old England wind on just as peacefully beneath their arching boughs, in these days of steam, telegraphs, and bustle, as they did in the times of stage-coaches, highwaymen,

and silence. There is a little village where I once lived, that cannot boast a single charm of scenery; its river is a simple mill-
stream, its hills and valleys are the gentle undulations of the chalk,
and yet I know no sweeter spot on earth than that, with its peaceful cottages, its old grey church, and thick luxuriant trees. I do
not suppose you ever heard of Ennington."

"Ennington !" replied the other with a sudden glow of pleasure,
"yes, I know it very well."

"Indeed. I was curate there till within the last two years."

Had a thunderbolt fallen at his feet, Joe Darrell could not have
looked more utterly confounded.

"Is it long since you were there ?" asked the other, not remark-
ing his companion's emotion.

"No ; — yes ;—some time since," replied Joe, absently. He
was thinking of the Christmas Eve when he had fetched Marion
to The Cedars.

"Do you know any one living there ?"

"No," replied Joe, who did not feel inclined to reckon Mrs.
Howard among his acquaintances.

"Only a passing visit, I see," replied the other.

"Do you ?" thought Joe. "Yes," he added aloud, and with
some bitterness in his voice, "I went there on a commission for
my sister. It was winter time, but I remember I thought it a
very pretty little place."

He remembered, too, that he had thought very little about it,
but very much of a flood of golden ringlets, swaying in the wind
beside him ; and falling every minute more deeply into his remini-
scences, he walked on in silence. Perhaps his companion was
thinking of golden ringlets too, for he also became silent, and full
a quarter of a mile was traversed before they again exchanged a
syllable.

As the slanting sunbeam cast the shadow of his rival across
his very path, Joe Darrell might well be silent, for he felt that
rival's power ; and if a single hope, in spite of all that had come
and gone, still lingered in his heart, it melted at this moment like
frostwork before the sun. One glance at the calm majestic brow
beside him, and he read the iron destiny that had separated him
for ever from the woman of his choice. He was vanquished ; he
knew it, felt it, but half the pain subsided as he gazed upon his
rival. If he had become so strangely interested in him by one
hour's conversation on indifferent subjects, what must be the devotion of the child's heart that had ripened into womanhood under
his influence ! For the first time he realised what Marion's sacrifice had been, and the halo with which his affection had encircled
her, grew brighter as he gazed. It was a farewell glance, and the
last gleam of the sunshine of his youth faded that evening as
the sunbeams set on Paris. But a strange determination rose in
his breast, springing phœnix-like from the embers of his boyish
love, and as his companion walked on still silently beside him, laying his hand upon the crucifix that rested on his heart, Joe Darrell

made a vow. Not a vow of vengeance, gentle reader. Amid the mixed feelings with which he stepped on beside his rival, admiration perhaps was paramount. Not of misanthropy—Joe Darrell loved all men with a deep large love. Not of celibacy for Marion's sake—the possibility of loving another never crossed his mind. What then was his vow? An echo from the days of chivalry, a faint whisper from the desert, and its silent self-devotion.

"A thousand barriers divide her from me; one only separates her from him, and I will strain every nerve to tear it down. For God's sake, for Marion's sake, I will labour for his conversion."

Like oil upon the troubled waters of the sea, the waves of passion gradually subsided, and while his new resolution quivered at his heart, Joe Darrell walked on his way, with a kindling eye and smiling lip, in perfect peace.

As they passed the barrier with its gilded rails, the sun was just sinking below the horizon.

"I feel loath to see him go," said the clergyman, "for on what will he rise to-morrow?"

Joe looked up inquiringly.

"What do you think of Parisian Sundays?" asked the other.

"Many things," replied Joe; "I both like and dislike them."

"More than I can say," answered his companion, "for to me they are positively awful. Were it not that I could not conscientiously waste the day God has given us for Himself, I would willingly sleep it over, and spare myself the grief of witnessing such wholesale desecration as Paris will to-morrow present. What do you think of the open shops, and various occupations going on on all sides?"

"I think it very wrong."

"And what do you think of the theatres and public gardens, sending forth their strains of music on this sacred day, syren-like, decoying men to their destruction?"

"I think them worse still."

"And what do you think of the gadding about in every direction, of the open Louvre, and other places of a similar nature? Of a party of young people positively playing at ball and other games, as I saw them last Sunday in the Tuileries garden, as I passed through, on my road home from the church, in the Rue d'Aguesseau?"

"I think it very right."

"You think it very right!"

"Yes, indeed I do. I think that minds bent for six days over mental or manual labour, require a little unbending on the seventh. I know that 'the Sabbath was made for man,' and I am an advocate for rational amusements upon it. Shut up the shops—stop the work—take away everything that bears with it a trace of sin—and I love what remains of the sprightliness and gaiety of a Sunday in Paris, more than I can say. I am quite in my element amongst it all."

"You are! Then I must say I am greatly disappointed in you.

To me, the universal profanation is sickening. One might say, that the great heart of Paris never beats to one thought of God."

"Many unjust things not only might be said, but are said," replied Joe.

"Pardon me, my dear young friend, but this would not be unjust. Last Sunday I attended the morning service in the Oratoire; there were a few worshippers, certainly, but what are they amongst such a population as this?"

"Not much," replied Joe, smiling, in spite of himself.

"No," continued the other, "not much, indeed, merely a handful of wheat among a weary waste of tares; and the other Protestant churches, they tell me, are no better attended. One Sunday afternoon I went to the one at Grenelle, and found a room that would be discreditable as a school in England, and such a miserable congregation! I came away truly sick at heart. And yet, except for these little bands of faithful ones, scattered here and there through the length and breadth of Paris, the whole mass of this great city is steeped in utter supineness."

"About what?" asked Joe, opening his eyes.

"About their immortal souls. Why, where is their religion?" he asked, seeing Joe looked perfectly aghast.

"Where is their religion?" he repeated; "where all religion ought to be, before their minds, on their lips, in their hearts. You have seen much in Paris, but you seem to have overlooked one item, and that is her Catholic churches. All day long on Sunday, these are more or less crowded, and even during the week the Masses are well attended. For the Catholic religion is no Sunday garment, but is worn all days alike, suits all hearts alike, saves all souls alike. The work done in Paris on the Sunday is without an excuse, a remnant of Voltaire's handywork, a relic of the Revolution; but, believe me, there are those who do not sanctify the Sunday less with prayer, and praise, and good works, because they have brethren who openly profane it. Really, you do not understand what their religion is!"

"Yes, I do," replied the other, bitterly; "understand it to my cost; understand it in all the foulness, blackness, dreadfulness of its deceptions and iniquity! Of all men living, few know Popery better than I do, few men have suffered more from her machinations. I am truly sorry to find a bright, intelligent young Englishman like you, vindicate her. Keep away from her enticements, my dear young friend, for, believe me, she is enticing! Do not, I charge you, by the living God, let the glitter of a few candles lead you astray from Him, into the shadow of error, where He is not, never has been, and never can come!" He paused, and looked at his young companion.

Joe smiled. "I can well understand that, thinking as you do, you are surprised at my vindication of Catholicism, but, before we go a step farther on our road or in our friendship, let me tell you one thing. Do not be startled, but, by the grace of God, I am what I am, and that is a Catholic."

They walked on in silence, broken at length by the clergyman.

"I am, of course, sorry to hear this, indeed, I am deeply disappointed. One thing, however ; as we journey on together, will you promise me not to shrink from religious conversation?"

"I will, but on one condition."

"What is that ? "

"That you, on your part, do not inveigh against my religion as you did just now, but that you let me explain it thoroughly to you, instead."

The other hesitated.

"Are you afraid ? " asked Joe, rather mischievously.

"No, I promise to hear all you have to say, with as much patience as I can muster. I certainly give you full and free permission to make a convert of me if you can."

"That I could never do," replied Joe ; "for conversions, like rain, fall down from heaven. But I shall pray very hard for you."

The other looked strangely at him. So practical a religion in a young man of the world was rather new to him.

"You are a strange mixture," he observed, looking up quietly, after a short pause.

"How so ? " asked Joe.

"In every way. You have the heart of a boy with the head of a man, for you convulse me one moment with an account of your mad-cap escapades, and talk the next of giving up the company of your fellow-tourists, because they are too fast for you. Then after revelling in the idea of Sabbath desecration, you speak, not ten minutes after, with a solemnity I have rarely seen, even in the most serious young persons of your age."

Joe laughed, and, pointing out the figures on the Pont d'Iéna, changed the conversation.

"To-morrow I shall shift my quarters, and come over to you," said Joe, as he shook hands with his new friend at the door of his hotel.

"Will you not come in now and rest ? "

"No, thank you, I am expecting some letters of importance, that I shall have to answer to-night."

"Do you know that we have not yet exchanged cards ? " asked the other.

Joe wrote his two first names, Joseph Fortescue, on a leaf torn from his pocket-book, and received in exchange the card of the "Rev. Henry Lisle."

He knew very well what name the little card would bear, and yet he almost started as it lay in black and white before him. But stifling the rising feeling, and laying his hand once more upon his crucifix, he pronounced his vow again, and walked briskly to his hotel.

CHAPTER XXXI.

Mrs. Howard became a Catholic. A month afterwards the cottage at Eunington was to let, and Tyrza purred contentedly before the kitchen fire of his new dwelling at Harleyford. Naturally enough, Mrs. Howard regretted the sweet little home that had welcomed her as a bride, and sheltered her as a widow, but this regret was but a small item to be weighed against the enjoyment of Catholic privileges, and, like Tyrza, she soon grew accustomed to the change, and very happy. Happy in the society of her old friends, happy in her child, happy in her glorious and new-found faith.

Yet the past was not forgotten. Her new religion taught her too well the value of tribulation, for her to wish to forget its lessons; and often, very often, even when her hope and love were brightest, she looked back. Looked back at the gentle husband to whom she had been a wayward and exacting wife, at the child wandering from her mother's arms, at the outraged relation dying unreconciled, until, fairly wearied with the dreariness of the prospect, she turned to the future for relief, and gazed upon it silently and thoughtfully. "Rejoice with fear," says the apostle, and she trembled as she read and meditated on final perseverance. "Eye hath not seen, nor ear heard, nor hath it entered into the heart of man to conceive, what God hath prepared for those who love Him," and with restored confidence, she walked on her way with a firm foot, while the music of heaven seemed already ringing round her path.

And what did Marion all this time? Was not her cup of joy running over? She too was very happy, and whenever she compared, as she did twenty times a day, the joy of her present life with troubles not long passed by, she smiled very brightly. Nor was even the thought of Edward, left alone in his little home, a serious drawback to this happiness, since she knew that he kept up his heart by promising it a mistress at no very distant day.

And so in the freshly-painted house, half-way between The Cedars and the church, Golden-hair and her mother lived together. There was something even more than filial in Marion's affection, for mingled with her love was a solicitude almost maternal, and truly, most truly, was it appreciated. Perpetual sunshine, Mrs. Darrell called her, and told her one morning as she kissed her, that theirs was now a life without a shadow. Was she right?

"I wonder, my dear," said Mrs. Howard, that very evening, after a long talk about the old days at Ennington,—"I wonder how our old friend Henry Lisle gets on in his new living."

There was no answer.

"Poor fellow," continued the mother musingly, "I should like to see him, but I suppose that will never be."

In an instant the curls were drooping over the table amid such a heart-rending sob, that the name was neutral ground hereafter.

It was a dreary day ; a dull morning had subsided into a still duller afternoon, and the shadows were deepening fast. Mrs. Howard was sitting before the fire, and Marion, no longer able to work, was standing by the window, lost in a reverie.

"He is at home by this time," said Mrs. Howard, suddenly looking up.

"Who?" asked Marion, starting.

"Joe, of course ; what a strange child you are ! were we not just now talking of him?"

"Yes, I remember now, but I did not think of him for the minute."

"You thought I meant Edward, I suppose. I wonder we have not heard from him. Perhaps we shall have a letter in the morning, saying at what time we may expect him. He must come to-morrow, to sign the deeds of partnership. Well, his bed is quite ready, even if he were to come to-night, for Sally has been airing it, and arranging his room all the morning. Dear boy ! I do so long to see him ! I am sure, Marion, I shall grow to love him quite as much for his own sake as for yours, or even your poor dear father's, for his letters could not be more affectionate to me, if I were his very own mother. Just hand me his portrait ; I must have another look at him, though I think I know his face pretty well already."

Marion gave her the morocco case, and a conversation ensued that effectually roused the little dreamer from her reverie. To have talked to her of Edward would have awakened her, had she been one of the seven sleepers. A double knock, however, brought the chat to a sudden conclusion. The door opened, and Mrs. Howard's hand was grasped in Joe Darrell's.

"Dear Mrs. Howard," he exclaimed, "I am so truly pleased to meet you. As you may imagine, your name has been a conspicuous item in every letter I have received from home for the last two months. And how is Marion?" he asked, turning to her, and pressing her hand with the quiet frankness of an elder brother ; "my congratulations come late in the day, but they are very sincere ones. You must be very happy now !"

"I am, indeed," she replied, in a voice trembling with emotion.

"And so are we happy," continued Joe, in the same calm clear tone, "very happy in having you so near us. We shall have the old musical evenings over again now. Won't it be jolly ! We will sing our old duets till The Cedars ring again ! You have not forgotten 'All's Well,' I hope?"

"No," said Marion, looking at him in some amazement.

"We must rout up Jessie and Dora too," he continued, "those were nice evenings we used to have at their house ! 'And so we will again,' as the song says, 'and so we will again' ! "

"You seem quite revelling in the anticipation of your musical evenings, Joe," remarked the elder lady. "Well, they say 'music hath charms,' but perhaps something else in Mr. Seymour's house has still greater ones. Jessie is a nice-looking girl, and they tell me that Dora is very clever."

"To be sure, you see I am no bad judge!"

Mrs. Howard smiled, but there was more of perplexity than mirth in Marion's laugh.

"It is not much more than an hour since I arrived," said Joe, "but I was obliged to run over to have just a few minutes' chat with you. My mother wants you to go back with me to spend the evening. It is not foggy, do you think you might venture?"

"I think so," said Mrs. Howard, rising, and walking to the window, "but now tell me, is your health improved?"

"Very much," replied Joe, "indeed I have come back an altered being," and there was a side glance across the room. "I have had exercise of body, I can assure you, and almost more exercise than I could manage for the mind. But I have accomplished my task," and Joe's dark eyes flashed with unwonted energy.

"You have been alone during the latter part of your tour, have you not?" asked Mrs. Howard.

"No," replied Joe, "not alone, but led, helped, guided, assisted, or my task would never have been completed!"

"Why, what was it?" asked the lady, surprised at his earnestness, "and who assisted you in accomplishing it?"

Joe paused and smiled. "My task!" he exclaimed, "such a one, that when I look back upon the last two months I am lost in wonder. I will tell you," he added, suddenly changing his manner: "I have visited France, Italy, Switzerland, and Germany since August. What do you think of that for a task?"

"Pretty well, and your companion?"

"Did I tell you I had had one?"

"To be sure you did, not two minutes since—a Leader Guide, Director; in short, everything one could imagine to be most requisite in an unknown country."

"Ah yes—though you misunderstood me—but never mind, you are right notwithstanding, for I had a companion. A companion too that I will not attempt to describe, for you will meet him to-night, and be able to judge of his merits for yourself."

"You were very fortunate to fall in with him."

"Very," said Joe. "I met him by—well—not by chance—but suddenly in Paris. Such an eye for the beauties of nature, such a mind to penetrate her works, such a will to overcome fatigue and difficulties, I never met before."

"Is he young?"

"Not very, about five-and-thirty."

"I am glad you have brought him home with you," said Mrs. Howard, "for I am quite curious to see him. Why, my dear boy, he must be a perfect phœnix!"

Joe laughed just as he used to do in the hay-fields, when they were all boys and girls together, Marion thought.

"Then, I suppose," observed Mrs. Howard, "that I am to infer that your trip has been a pleasant one."

"Well, yes," replied the young man, rather hesitatingly, "I suppose you may, upon the whole, though even the Drachenfels, Swiss glaciers, and Paris gaieties have their drawbacks. But Rome repaid me for all,—beautiful, classic, Catholic Rome! I felt as if I never could have left her. Yet here I am, you see, fully prepared to forget my enthusiasm, and buckle to business. Ensconced behind the desk and ledger, I shall soon forget even the Eternal City."

"No, you will not," said a low, timid voice.

"Do you not think so?" he asked, turning to the speaker, while a flush of pleasure shot across his dark features. "Well, Marion, perhaps you are right, perhaps I appreciate such things more than I myself imagine."

"One who could not, would have neither a great mind nor a large heart, and Joe Darrell has both."

Mrs. Howard looked up rather surprised.

Joe laughed. "You did not think your quiet little daughter was quite such a flatterer, did you, Mrs. Howard?"

"She is no flatterer, for I know she speaks the truth; but you must be a great favourite, for she does not often speak her sentiments so unreservedly."

"He is everybody's favourite, mamma: you do not know him yet; when you do, you will not be surprised at hearing everybody praise him."

Joe turned over the leaves of a book that lay on the table, to hide his emotion. Fully did he appreciate the words of the speaker, but fully also did he understand that every encomium was another stone raising yet higher the wall of separation between them. But Joe had learned his hard lesson of resignation to good purpose, for in two minutes he was himself again.

"Edward is coming up to-morrow, I believe," said Mrs. Howard.

"So I hear, to sign the deeds of partnership; then hurrah for Howard and Darrell!"

"In more senses than one!" said Mrs. Howard.

"In more senses than one," repeated Joe. "God grant that both partnerships may prove happy ones."

"It will be your turn next, Joe," said Mrs. Howard.

"What to do?"

"To follow Edward's example, to be sure."

"And get spliced! No, I was cut out for a bachelor. Wouldn't be bothered with a wife for all I could see. But you have not told me yet how you like Harleyford," he added, changing the subject rather abruptly.

"I have good reason to like it," answered the lady.

"That's no criterion, Mrs. Howard. When I was a youngster they always told me that I ought to like Latin and Greek, and the master's cane, and the doctor's physic; but I had a wonderful aversion to them all, nevertheless."

"Then I am not so difficult to please, for I love Harleyford dearly, both for its own sake and your mother's. I do not know what I should do without her now."

"There are not many like her, that's my private opinion," said Joe. "Young fellows.talk a great deal about independence nowadays, but those who talk loudest are the very first to run home to their mothers when things are not straight with them. As for mine—I could never say what she has been to me, or what I should do without her."

"May it be very long before you solve the sad problem by experience, my dear boy."

Merry as Joe naturally was, his observations not unfrequently turned even the gayest conversations into a serious channel. Perhaps from the simple fact that they were rarely speculative, but came freely, impulsively from the depths of his own heart, and from their very artlessness and simplicity, found an echo in the experience of those with whom he talked. Had Joe Darrell tried to make a speech on a mother's love, he would signally have failed, but volumes would not have furnished such a testimony to the value of his own, as did the glistening eye and kindling cheek with which he spoke of her.

Many were the questions that Mrs. Howard and Marion asked concerning his travels. He gave them a graphic but thoroughly characteristic account of his wanderings, humorous when told in his own way, strangely evasive when given as an answer. Mrs. Howard was charmed, but Marion thoroughly bewildered. It was not until the clock struck five that they noticed how time was passing.

"By George!" exclaimed Joe, starting to his feet, "I promised my mother only to stop ten minutes, and I have been here an hour."

"Our toilette shall not detain you long," said Marion, as she tripped upstairs with her mother; "make friends with him, Tyrza."

Joe did not care much for cats, and yet in half a minute Tyrza was arching his back upon his new friend's knee, and rubbing his cold nose in his whiskers.

"Cool," exclaimed Joe, stroking him; "do you know you're smothering me with hairs?"

"By the by, Marion," said Joe as they came in sight of the presbytery, "Father Stirling asked me to tell you that he should like to see you for a few minutes, if you could spare the time."

"This evening?"

"So he said."

"Then I had better run in now."

"I think so. No time like the present, you know."

"But, my dear," objected Mrs. Howard, "I cannot possibly let you come to The Cedars afterwards by yourself. It will be quite dark! If Joe will kindly wait for you, I can go on very well alone. Will you, Joe?"

"We must first see whether Marion will consent to such an arrangement."

"Certainly not, mamma. If I am at all timid I am sure Martha will come with me. Besides, very likely I shall only stay a minute, and be at The Cedars as soon as you. Good-bye for the present."

"At least let me open the gate for you, Marion," said Joe, stepping forward, "and shut it after you, too," he added in a low strange whisper. "Good-bye! yes, for ever!"

She did not hear the words, but turned from him with one of her brightest smiles, to hurry up the little path. Neither did Mrs. Howard notice the ashy whiteness of Joe Darrell's face as he offered her his arm, and with a quickened step led her towards The Cedars.

"I wonder what Father Stirling wants that child for this evening?"

"Shall I tell you?" asked Joe.

"Do," said Mrs. Howard, fairly puzzled by her companion's strange earnest manner. "I had no idea that you knew."

The answer was a long one—so long that though both knew they were waiting tea at The Cedars, they walked past the lodge, and back again almost to the church, and even then retraced their steps only to return. When at length they entered the gate Mrs. Howard's brain was whirling.

Father Stirling had himself received Marion at the door, and led her into his little study.

"Are you in a hurry?" he asked.

"Not particularly, but I am going to The Cedars to spend the evening, and should not like to keep them waiting longer than I can help."

"I see. Well, there is a woman in the hall just at this moment, and I must speak to her. Will you come into the next room and stay a few minutes, till I am disengaged?"

"Certainly," said Marion, moving towards the door.

"Stop a minute; there is a gentleman there already, but you need not mind him, it is only a very old friend of mine who has been spending an hour or so with me." He entered the room as he spoke, drew his arm-chair of state, as he called it, to the fire, and bade her make herself at home.

"I shall not be longer than I can help," he said smiling; "I daresay I shall be able to despatch my visitor in ten minutes or a quarter of an hour. Will you do the honours for me?" he added, turning to his friend, "and remind me to introduce you to this lady in due form, when I come back. I will not stay to do so now."

The afternoon had faded into a dull dingy twilight, and the flickering fire cast an uncertain light upon the objects in the room. The stranger, who had risen upon their entrance, resumed his seat by the window, at the further end of the apartment, and sat looking out into the garden, as though quite engrossed in its dimly visible grass-plot and flower-beds. So perfect a silence reigned, that Marion soon forgot her companion's presence, and sat looking very tranquilly into the red coals, trying to read Joe Darrell. For once in her life she found this a difficult task. Accustomed as she was to his frank, careless manner, she had never before seen the vein of strange determination that now seemed to pervade every word and action, and our little heroine was puzzled. Whether or not she would have succeeded in deciphering Joe must remain a secret; certain it is, she had not proceeded far towards doing so, when a low voice from the other end of the room startled her from her thoughts.

"This is a very quiet spot," observed the stranger, who had again risen, and was standing with his back against the shutter, looking out with folded arms into the fast-increasing gloom.

Slight as was the remark, there was a distinctness in the tone, a pathos in the voice, that thrilled Marion through, and she started perceptibly.

"Very quiet," continued the gentleman, as though talking to himself, "and so peaceful, one might almost imagine it exempt from the usual penalties of sin and sorrow."

"But such would be a false imagination," replied Marion, recovering herself; "our people on the whole are very good, but they both sin and suffer."

"So I suppose. If it were not so, many a weary man would seek to pitch his tent in such a valley of repose. I, for one, the weariest of the weary."

At another time it would have struck Marion as peculiar that a stranger should thus allude to the sorrows of his own life. As it was, she was alive to nothing but the tones of his voice, that quivered through her heart like the echo of some old familiar song. She knew that she was in the presbytery parlour, but she knew no more. The past and present surged around her, her heart beat almost audibly, her very identity seemed fast forsaking her. There was again a silence broken once more by the voice.

"Father Stirling has great influence here."

"Very great," she replied, making a mighty effort to answer calmly.

"Is he much beloved?"

"He could not be otherwise, for he loves every one."

"Even his enemies?" asked the stranger.

"He has none, except the world, the flesh, and the devil."

"Three too many for any man. But if Father Stirling has such influence with his children, will he employ it, do you think, for me?"

"Why should he not?"

"Because I deserve nothing at his hands. Over and above his three great enemies, for many years he has had a fourth, and that fourth has been myself. He has forgiven me, and we are friends; but could he, think you, gain me the forgiveness of another, one who has been even more wronged than he?"

There was no answer.

"Listen, you shall hear. One day I came to this very town full of a bright hope, I left it that same evening in bitterness and wrath. I spurned a treasure I had coveted for years, and trampled under the foot of my pride and bigotry the heart the only woman I had ever loved had yielded me."

He paused, but a marble pillar could not have been more motionless than his listener, and he went on.

"She was a fragile creature, but withstood like a rock the storm of persecution I called down upon her. She went on her bleak strange path, and meekly fought her battle with the world. Could Father Stirling's mediation, do you think, gain me the forgiveness of this loving, bright-haired, injured woman?"

He crossed the room as he spoke, and stood beside her.

"No," replied Marion firmly.

He started visibly.

"No," she continued, "for forgiveness must follow the commission of a fault, and he who acts from conscience, however blindly, never does wrong."

"What would she do, then? Golden-hair, God has shown me the truth, and I too am a Catholic now. What would she do?"

"The will of God"! and the dancing firelight shone on a flood of golden ringlets bowing very low over hands that were joined in mute thanksgiving.

"Will you not forgive me, Golden-hair?"

The head was raised, and never did dancing firelight fall on two more radiant faces.

CHAPTER XXXII.

ANOTHER year had passed away, and once again the leaves that had budded bright and green in the spring were blowing hither and thither with a mournful rustle, as the autumn wind swept by the turnpike road, and through narrow lanes, and across the wet dismal fields. How he soughed, and whined, and creaked, and whistled, that same sad spirit of the wind! now roaring with a demon voice across the forest and athwart the ocean, now moaning his low sad story far away among the distant hills. But no where did he howl among the chimneys, rattle the casements, or sough among the branches, as he did at The Cedars, one dreary wet November night.

And yet, except from the echoes of the wind, the old house was very hushed. Soft were the footfalls that trod the stairs and corridors, and low the whispers that fell from time to time from anxious voices. It was evening, just the hour of the usual social tea-party, but no light hearts were gathering to-night. A dark shadow hung over the old house, and the day of music and laughter had gone by, for the sword of the destroyer was already half unsheathed, and the light of the home already quivering in its socket.

Edith was dying. The cloud, large as a man's hand, had waxed larger throughout the year ; the little cough had borne its fruit of death, and old Turner wept over the fulfilment of her dread. Yes, Edie was dying. The truth had dawned at last on all, and the frail hope that had borne them up, in spite of every fatal symptom, had given way in the face of the stern reality.

Ten minutes before all had been around her bed, the grey-haired father, in the bitter agony of grief restrained, and the mother, in the silent stupor of a life-long dread, realised. Joe, too, had been there, changed in a few weary days, as only those can change who die, or watch the dying. But all these had left her now ; one by one they had stepped away from where they dared not linger. Not for worlds would they have called back to one throb of human sympathy the half-emancipated spirit, nor disturbed by human grief the raptures of her superhuman joy. One watcher only was there, Edward Howard, and he so changed and worn and wasted, that when he had arrived that afternoon, they had hardly recognised him.

Edith was asleep, and as he gazed on the face, changed by suffering, but still warm and young, not yet fixed, as every feature soon must be fixed in death, tear after tear rolled down his cheek. Must she go ? Could he live to lose her ? With what a wild yearning wish he longed to clasp her to him, and defying even mortality, to cry, " I will not let thee go ! "

" Is this resignation ? " whispered a still small voice. It was unheard ; what had resignation to do with him ; was not Edith dying ? Was not the day-star gliding from the firmament of his life ? Falling on his knees, he poured forth a wild and passionate, almost complaining prayer, that even at this, the eleventh hour, the one joy of his life might be spared to him.

" Edward," said a voice, almost a whisper, " has Edward come ? "

In an instant he was at her side.

She extended her thin white hand to him, and smiled, as, kneeling beside the couch, he pressed it to his lips.

" Have they told you I am dying ? " she asked.

" Hush, hush, Edie ! do not talk so ; you are very ill just now, but it is only a fresh cold ; you will get better, love. You look better even now than when I first came, indeed you do. Keep up your spirits, and all will be well."

The young girl smiled, not a sickly smile, but a bright rapturous one, like a sudden flash from heaven. " No, Edward, you must look bravely at the truth. I am sinking very fast. But you must not give way to grief, for I look to you and Marion to make all the others bright. Will you try and do this, for my sake ? "

He only bowed his head, but the tear-drops rained fast upon the fingers he held in his.

" Edward," she whispered after a long silence, broken only by

the ticking of the clock and her own short, panting breath, " I
did not expect this from you. You must be stronger."

"I cannot, Edie, I cannot ! Oh, why cannot I die too ? "

"Because it is not the will of God. Listen, Edward : do you
believe I love you ? "

"Is not your love my one sunbeam ? "

"And yet I am glad to leave you, and to leave papa and mamma too, and those I have loved at home, who have been more to me
than I could ever say. But God and heaven are dearer, dearer
far ; and much as you were to me, Edward, in the world, I would
not change my prospect of dying so soon, even to be to you all we
once thought I should have been. Is it not a consolation that we
shall meet again, if both are faithful, in heaven ? Not as we have
been here, in sunshine and shadow, meeting and parting, but as
pure, bright, and yet identified spirits, basking in the perpetual
presence of God ! Edward, mamma is more resigned than you.
She, with her mother's love and weak woman's heart, says bravely,
' Thy will be done ! ' Will you not say so too ? "

A groan was the only reply.

" Papa can say it," she continued, " and yet I was the darling of
his old age. Joe whispers it a hundred times a day, and Emily,
dear Emily, although I cannot see her, I know well she says it
with one of her brightest smiles."

"Edie," he replied, "these are not alone ; linked together, they
bear their griefs in common ; but I, fancy my lonely life without
you ; I, who have worked early and late to make you a home,
shall I live in it alone and desolate ? "

"No, Edward, for I believe God calls you to higher things. Do
you remember Emily's prophecy two years ago ? "

"No, darling."

"Not while she was rustling the dead leaves in the Mill Lane ?
She said, ' You will be a priest, and you must say your first Mass
for Edith, and your next for me.' I do not think I should remember these words, so lightly spoken, just now, if they had
passed with their echo. This, I believe, Edward, is your true
vocation. ' Man proposes, God disposes,' and He never meant
that I should be your wife. As I look forward, I seem to see your
future. You will not forget me, I know you never will ; but my
memory will be a chastened thing with you, and when you shall
be a priest of the Most High God, you will cease to regret one who
would have kept you from Him. I believe that you will live to
see, even on earth, that the stroke that has severed us from each
other, has united us both to Him. Is this thought a bright one ? "

" A little star, Edie, on a very dark sky, that is all, and even this
star only a thing of the imagination."

" It may be so, but the thought makes me very happy. It is
enough to satisfy me that the first glimpse of the idea has been to
you even as a little star. I feel, in my own heart, that the bright
spot will grow larger and larger when I am gone, until the beauty
of one grand thought shall flood your soul ; the one grand thought

of living for God alone. All that is most beautiful on earth hovers
within the vocation of a priest. After the words of ordination, one
who before was only simple natural man, goes forth on his mission,
God-like in his powers and graces. For he speaks, and the Lord
of heaven and earth lies beneath his hand, to be given to hungering
and thirsting multitudes at the altar, or to be borne in his bosom,
as our dear Lord will soon be borne to me, to light up the dark
valley of the shadow of death. Again he speaks, and chains of
sin that have rusted around their victim fall from the sinner at
his word, and he who was bound in iron fetters goes forth free.
To attend the sick and dying, to comfort the weary, to feed the
hungry, to teach the ignorant the one bright truth of God—is not
this a higher, a far higher future than to spend a few short years
with me? O Edward! my first, my last, my only love, the latest
thought of earth that will cling to me here below, will be a thought
of this!"

She sank back exhausted, and closed her eyes.

"This has been too much for you, Edie," cried Edward, starting
to his feet seriously alarmed, "and it was all for me!"

"No," she returned gently; "I am only a little tired; I shall be
better directly. I cannot talk more to you now, much as I have
that I could say; but remember my words, Edward, although for
nothing would I have them bind you. Not one earthly motive
must mingle with such a thought as this. A vocation is the voice
of God, and the power to follow it God's work alone."

"Yes, yes," he whispered hoarsely and absently, as once more
sinking on his knees he buried his face beside her.

"May God bless you for evermore!" said the young girl, and
collecting her remaining strength, she raised his cold hand from
the bed, and pressed it to her lips.

For two more days the lamp of life wavered and flickered. But
as the night of the second day closed in, all plainly saw that
another sun would never rise for Edith Darrell. And yet not a
sob, far less a murmur, broke the sweet silence of that chamber,
when the angel of resignation hovered hand in hand with her
sister death. Calmly, even as in days gone by, she had helped the
twins to arrange their altar; Marion, with noiseless footfall, placed
a table, with a crucifix and four lighted tapers, by the bedside; and
as Father Stirling entered the room with slow and reverent step,
even death was forgotten in the presence of its Victor, Who shall
describe the thrill of rapture that ran through each weary heart,
even in this dark hour of desolation, as the Sun of the Christian
life flooded with His beams the shadows of the sick chamber?

Edith had been administered, and had received her last communion; and now, upon her mother's arm, slept her last earthly
sleep. Father, brother, lover, friends, were grouped around her
bed, and Father Stirling, very white and sad, knelt beside the child
he had moulded with such earnestness for heaven. At length she
stirred.

"Mamma."

" My child ? "

" You will not stop long, not very long, will you ? "

" I hope not, darling."

" Where is papa ? "

A pressure of the hand was the only answer.

" Father Stirling."

Even the mother made way for him, and he bent over her.

" Tell Edward——" the words were lost.

" Tell him what, dear child ? "

" Tell him," she whispered, collecting all her remaining strength, " to do the will of God—only the will of God."

They were her last words. Five minutes later, amid the sobs of breaking hearts, Father Stirling was praying for the dead.

It was in the little chamber where Marion had first seen her, eight years before, that Edie was laid in death, calm and cold, yet even more beautiful than life. Two watchers were there, Marion and her brother, the latter kneeling and gazing on the marble face, striving to realise his loss.

" Will you stay here for a few minutes, if I go downstairs ? " she asked, for she felt that he wished to be alone.

" I will. O Golden-hair, you alone are left me now ! " He rose and sank into a chair, and drawing her to him, rested his head upon her.

What could she say to comfort him, while death lay there beside them in all its iciness ? She stooped and kissed his forehead.

" You have been very brave, dear, and she was so happy to go, that it would be wrong to sorrow much. Edward, my brother, how many times darker your shadow would be, if you were not a Catholic."

" I know it," he replied, " but it is very heavy as it is ; very, very heavy, Golden-hair. But I must not keep you, my child," he added, rising, " for I fancy Lisle has arrived ; if so, I would not detain you from him for a minute. Go and see. God bless you ! "

When she had left him, he once more approached the bed, and removed the veil that Marion had laid over the face of the dead. Again he sank upon his knees and tried to pray, but he felt hard and stony, and far away from God.

" How can I pray for her ? " he whispered at length—" pray for her as one still suffering for sin ? I cannot do it. I cannot fancy her anywhere but in heaven. O Edie, Edie ! pray for me instead ; " and a paroxysm of passionate grief burst from his lips. As he grew more tranquil, shocked at his own vehemence, a hand was laid upon his shoulder.

" Is this as it ought to be, my friend ? "

Edward glanced for an instant at the speaker, then buried his face once more in his hands.

" Is this as it ought to be ? " repeated Father Stirling ; " or, is it as she would have it be ? "

There was no answer, and the priest, walking slowly round the bed, in his turn raised the handkerchief from the face of the dead.

"She looks very happy, very peaceful," he said softly, after a few moments' pause.

The young man rose, and placed himself beside the priest, who still held the handkerchief in his hand. "What else could the sunset be of such a life as hers," he asked, "but a peaceful one ?"

"Will you say the *De Profundis* with me ?" inquired the priest.

"Why should we say it, father ? she does not need it."

"How so ?" asked the priest with a sad smile.

"What sins has she to expiate ?" demanded Edward almost fiercely.

"The heavens are not clean in the sight of God, and His angels He charges with folly. What then is earthly purity ? Do be reasonable, dear Edward. What would she say to this, in her sweet humility, think you ?"

"You are right," replied Edward, " grief has made me mad, I think ; " and he responded as calmly to the prayer as though it had been offered for a stranger.

"Do you remember," asked the priest, when it was concluded, "that I was the last person to whom Edith spoke ?"

"Of course I do."

"Shall I tell you what she said ?"

"Yes, do, pray do."

"These, then, were her last words ; tell Edward "—

"Edward ! Did she speak of me ?"

"Tell Edward to do the will of God ; only the will of God."

"Was that all ?"

"Yes, all, and it was her last request, dear Edward ; but, indeed, indeed you are not fulfilling it."

"You believe her words meant resignation ?"

"Undoubtedly."

"Yes, but they meant more ; sit down, and I will tell you all." And in the chamber of death Edward Howard told the priest the whole of his last conversation with his betrothed. No one disturbed them, all by intuition left them to themselves. The daylight faded quite away, and the waxen tapers cast a sad funereal glow upon them ; still they talked on, in low whispers, as though they feared to wake the sleeper at their side. But not till peace, and hope, and perfect resignation reigned in the bosom of his sorrowing friend, did Father Stirling leave him and the silent chamber, to join the mournful party in the hardly less silent drawing-room below.

"Is he better ?" asked Henry Lisle, grasping the priest's hand, as he entered.

"Much better, almost himself."

"Thank God !" cried Mrs. Darrell, " for I began to fear we were to lose him too."

He was better ; the bitterness that had tortured his soul had melted away before the soft words of charity and gentle reproach

that had been poured into it, and he could even look on the sweet
white face before him with a smile.

"Tell Edward to do the will of God," he repeated softly.
"Amen ! Amen ! Yes, whithersoever it shall lead me, Edie, even
to giving you up willingly ;" he paused ; "yes, willingly, to God.
Father, in this, as in all things, may Thy will be done !"

CHAPTER XXXIII.

"Father Dunstan ?"

"Plait-il, Monsieur ?"

"Le père Anglais."

"Ah, oui, oui, monsieur. Traversez donc la cour, et entrez au
petit parloir là en face, je le ferai appeler." And the Englishman
and his bride crossed the square of the old Dominican convent,
and entered the plain little parlour to await "le père Anglais."

"It is very quiet here," remarked the lady, taking one of the
rush chairs.

"Very ; one would hardly imagine that the life of a great city
whirled past the doors. But it is very dull and gloomy-looking,
even to-day. Indeed I think this June sunshine falling upon the
white unshaded flags, makes it look even more so by the contrast.
Much as I admire the Order of St. Dominic, I cannot imagine a
vocation that would have led me here."

"No one can say what he would or would not do under other
circumstances," replied the lady ; "for myself, I fancy if I were a
religious, this is just the spot I should like to be in. Solitude in
the very midst of a large sphere of action."

"O Marion, if you had only seen the lovely convents I have
sometimes met with, sheltered among hills embowered in trees, or
buried in peaceful valleys bright with flowers, you would not say
so."

"Yes, Harry, I would. In this world I love and admire these
things very much, but were I consecrated to God, I would not
have nature itself divide my love, but would wish to live and
labour for Him, and Him alone."

"Enthusiastic child !" exclaimed the husband, smiling; "but to
come down to commonplace affairs, do you know that I have had
two letters this morning, one from Edward and the other from
Joe? I meant to have brought them with me," he continued,
"but I find I have left them on my dressing-table. It is a pity,
for I could have read them to you, as we are sure to be kept
waiting some time. That is, I believe, 'a rule without an exception,' observed with regard to convent visitors."

"Did either of them say anything particular ?"

"Nothing. Edward's was full of young men's associations,

clothing societies, and poor schools ; Joe's like himself, John Bull to the letter as usual."

"Poor, dear boys ! I am glad they are well. Did you not think they both looked particularly happy the day we were married ?"

"Edward did and was, for I believe he thought Golden-hair's happiness secured, and I trust in God that his confidence may not be misplaced, but Joe was masked to the life."

"Do you think so ?"

"Do I not know it, you little puss ? Ah, Marion, if ever you get half the devotion from your husband that you have had, and still have, from him, you will be one wife in a hundred."

"Harry !"

"You will, for Joe Darrell did that for your sake and your happiness that, dearly as I love you, I never could have done."

"In what way ?"

"He laboured with every energy to remove the obstacle that lay between you and another. Marion, I have known that boy steal into my room after I have been in bed, and stand beside me half the night, trying with all his powers of eloquence to teach me some Catholic truth. At one time, in Germany, he slept in a room next to mine, where he had a little iron bedstead that creaked if he only stirred. Often, for two or three hours after he has left me, I have not heard a sound, and once I grew so fidgetty about him, that in my turn I rose and went quietly to his room, and I found the bed still undisturbed and Joe upon his knees. And his prayers and perseverance did their work, for, stranger as I believed Joseph Fortescue to be to me and mine, I felt there must be something in a religion that could make a young man as earnest as this. Looking at you by my side, Golden-hair, my own little wife, I feel there is nothing I could not have done to gain you: but to labour to lose you ! only an angel, or Joe Darrell, could have done that."

"Poor Joe ! How sad to think that he is not happy."

"I do not say that, for a nature such as his must be happy in the odour of its own good actions. Joe will be a rich man too, and universally loved and respected, but his will be a lonely life."

"I wish he would take a fancy to Jessie Seymour, for I am sure she likes him."

"But is in no way suited to him," replied Mr. Lisle.

And here followed such a long dissertation on the suitability and unsuitability of husbands and wives in general, that though a full half-hour passed by, it was not until a church clock in the neighbourhood struck the hour, that Henry Lisle remembered he was waiting, and had a right to be impatient.

"Really, these holy fathers keep their visitors waiting a most tremendous time," he exclaimed, rising to survey the quadrangle through the open glass door ; "why, this is worse than going to see Emily."

"I wonder whether he is changed."

"Not much, my dear, I should imagine ; he has only left us, remember, twelve months."

At this moment a door opened suddenly, and a friar in the Dominican habit stood before them.

"George !" cried Henry Lisle, grasping his hand.

"Father Stirling," and joy inexpressible beamed from Marion's blue eyes, "I am so glad to see you."

"And so am I glad to see you," returned the friar, "and would not have kept you waiting so long, but we were at Office. When I heard that an English lady and gentleman were waiting for me, I immediately guessed they were Mr. and Mrs. Lisle," and he laughed as in old times as he pronounced the latter name.

"You look very well," observed Mr. Lisle.

"And seem very happy," added Marion.

"So I am, dear child, so I am ; well, you look happy too."

"Ought I not to be so ?" asked Marion, behind her curls.

"Most decidedly ; but you think I have not such good reason to felicitate myself, I can see."

"No, I do not, for I know you will be happy wherever you are ; but I think you might have stayed with us ; you could not be better than you were."

"Does she flatter you like that, Henry ? But now tell me, have you two been so engrossed in each other, that you have forgotten to bring me any news ? You know, I am a regular old gossip. First of all, please to remember I am quite in the dark as to the chain of events that have given me the honour of this visit. Not very long since I had a letter from a certain friend of mine, speaking of himself as neither flesh nor fowl, clerk nor layman, and lamenting his limited resources, which, unless he could find something to augment them, must postpone his marriage *sine die*. Most sincerely he had my sympathy, and I wrote and told him so, although, looking on his lot from a Christian point of view, it was so rich in crosses that I could not help slyly congratulating him in my heart. Not six months afterwards, I get a hurried scrawl, telling me to expect a visit from him on his wedding trip. Now, I certainly have enough of mother Eve in me to want to know how all this has come about."

"It will not be a very long story. Do you remember my father's old uncle, Saunders ?"

"Very well ; and what a comical old soul he was."

"You remember his quarrel with my father upon some point of Sabbath observance ?"

"Of course I do, and that he actually altered his will in consequence."

"Yes, in favour of some very distant relations. Well, then, he died about four months since, and they, in their turn, having offended him, he has left the whole of a very substantial fortune to my sister Agnes and myself. As the disinherited parties are already rich, and there never was a shadow of justice or common sense in the alteration of the original will, most thankfully have I accepted my portion."

"And where do you propose pitching your tent ?"

"Now, you must prepare for a surprise. Ever since Edith's death Mr. and Mrs. Darrell have contemplated a change. They have just bought a house for themselves and Joe in London, and we are to take The Cedars."

"And long may you live to enjoy it, my dear friend. Changes! changes! changes!"

"Changes!" repeated Henry Lisle, "there have been so many lately, that I sometimes begin to question my own identity, and feel ready to declare, like the old woman in the story-book, 'I'm sure it can't be I.' Imagine, George, if on the day of my ordination I"——

"Just hark at him, 'my ordination:' when were you ordained, I should like to know?"

"Well then, on the day I thought I was ordained—will that do? Imagine if I could have looked forward and seen myself a layman, calling on you a monk!"

"The latter would not have surprised you much, would it? for I had shown you my hoofs and horns by then."

"I know you had, but strange as I thought you, I never dreamed of such a step as this."

"Nor I," said the religious gravely. "God unfolds His purposes very slowly. How is Edward?"

"Just as you would have him, heart and soul in his work. He will soon have his tonsure. I called on him the week before last, to tell him which day had been fixed for the wedding, and I saw the superior of the community. He told me that he had rarely met with so earnest a character as Edward Howard's in his life. His one grand thought seems to be the preservation and reclamation of young men. To hear him talk, one would imagine that he had never had another aim in his life."

"He could not have a higher aim, nor a wider field to work in, than he will have in London. I suppose he did not mention Edith."

"Yes, he did, in congratulating me."

"What did he say?" asked the priest, bending his grey eyes anxiously upon him, for he was thinking of a struggle he had once witnessed in a very still room.

"These were his words, 'I could never have imagined that the day could come when I could say truthfully, I do not envy you. But I say so to-day; Edith was right, this is my true vocation. All my life, even her love, has been a preparation for it. The shadows of the past are now quite merged in the glory of the great work that lies before me.'"

"Thank God, thank God," said the priest. "Truly you have a noble-hearted brother, Mrs. Lisle."

Marion started at the name so unfamiliar on his lips.

"Ah, my child," he continued, rubbing his hands, "once upon a time we little thought you would ever bear that name!"

"Or that somebody else would be called Father Dunstan, instead of his good old Scotch name, that had served his family so long," exclaimed Henry Lisle.

"See how he is down upon me," cried Father Dunstan, laughing heartily. "Do you mean to say you are not yet Catholic enough to have a devotion for St. Dunstan? Why, man, he was one of the greatest champions the Church ever had."

"So I suppose, but I have somehow an unpleasant association with him of a hot pair of tongs, that I cannot quite get rid of."

"Ah, little lady, this husband of yours carries a good share of Protestantism about with him even yet, I can see."

"No, really, father, he is getting a very good Catholic, though I think yesterday you would have been rather shocked at us both, if you could have heard the very unorthodox meditation we were making in the train. Shall I say what it was, Harry?"

"If you like; but prepare yourself for a scolding."

Father Dunstan laughed. "What a dragon you make the old father out to be! Come, Mrs. Lisle, I am not going to scold, so give me the result of the meditation."

"It was only this, that what is so often said by people out of the Church about Protestant countries being more civilised than Catholic ones, seems really to be true. How is it?"

"First of all, I am not going to admit the statement, you may rest assured, though, if it were true, and Catholic countries were in the lowest condition of civil, and if you will of literary degradation, and if all Protestants once were models of human advancement and research, I should only reply that it proved that the good things of heaven and the good things of earth are in the inverse ratio of each other. If it were not so, if religious truth and human prosperity always went hand in hand, what a glorious worship that of the sun must have been, if we are to judge of it by its temple at Palmyra. What an amount of holiness too, must have concentrated in the Egyptian's adoration of his cats, dogs, and mummies, if we are to gauge it by the breadth of his cities, the height of his pyramids, and the glory of his sciences. There have been Hindu temples, Carthaginian temples, Mexican temples, whose magnitude and grandeur one must have seen to realise— was the Shadow of God in them, or in the tent of badger skins, over the Mercy-seat in the wilderness?

"Then, again, what may be said of men collectively as nations, may be said of them individually. Was the truth with the rich and prosperous citizens who rambled through Nero's pleasure-grounds to enjoy his feast, or with the miserable Christians who burnt in wax and resin to light up their amusements? Is it Dives who inherits the reward, or the beggar Lazarus who lies at his gate?—the poor man with his woes, his want of civilisation, and his ignorance of this world's lore, who shall find it hard to enter heaven, as 'the camel to go through the needle's eye,' or he who is rich in goods, deep in wisdom, standing in the high places? Human prosperity the touchstone of religious truth? What nonsense! Henry Lisle! Henry Lisle! divine of the English Church! student of the Protestant Bible from your youth, surely,

surely you must have read it bottom upwards, or you could have answered your little wife yourself."

"Perhaps I did," exclaimed that gentleman thus apostrophised, laughing heartily, "the worthy father must have made a mental reservation, though, Marion, when he promised not to scold you, that he would give me a double dose instead."

"Well, it is rather too bad, I must confess," replied the priest, "though, if I am too hard upon you, you must forgive me, just as you used many years ago, when I sometimes gave you an extra dig in an amicable fight. You have not told me yet how you like my successor."

"I have seen very little of him, but Marion says he gets on very well."

"Very well, though he finds it no enviable path to follow you. He is young and inexperienced, and must spend many more years of love and strength before his flock will love him and obey him, as they loved and obeyed Father Stirling."

The priest's eyes glistened, but he only raised his rosary, and pressed a wire.

"God bless them all, my poor dear children," he murmured gently, as he let it fall. "Is Turner a Catholic yet?"

"No, just as far off as ever, but just as firm in her 'creed of faith, hope, and charity' as you once styled it."

"Enough to take her to heaven, simple old soul! How is Mr. Gardiner?"

"The same. He has been lately preaching a set of sermons, to prove every word of the Anglican prayer-book conformable to her creed."

"What a clever man he must be! Of course he commenced by defining that creed. The best way to do that, I should imagine, would be to add High Church, Low Church, Middle Church, and Broad Church up together, and take the average. If I had been in my old post, I think I would have proposed that to him before he began. It might have given him a wrinkle. How is his cara sposa?"

"What Joe says she always was—his master."

"Poor man, he has his good points though, and so has she. When did you last see Emily?" asked the priest, turning to Marion.

"About a month since."

"And how did she look?"

"More beautiful than ever, if possible, and so bright and cheerful. Something brought up poor Edith's name, and she talked of her just as naturally, as I should talk of seeing mamma when we go back. It almost seemed, as she spoke, as though death were a white angel."

"Do you always then fancy him a black one?"

"Yes, always. Does he not seem so to you, father?"

"No, no. Lustrous in his whiteness, bright and flashing as the chariot that bore Elias to his rest. It is a great mistake, my child, to invest this radiant form with aught of gloom or terror, or to look upon our greatest friend as an enemy. It is good for us to be here, but better to be in heaven."

Marion stole a glance at a pair of eyes bent fondly upon her.

"Yes, better to be in heaven," he repeated smiling, "though it is hard, I know, to think so, in the first flush of a great earthly joy. But, as I said just now, it is good for us to be here. Good, whether our path shall lead through the sweet communion of married life, or the silent life of the cloister, provided it be ever onward, upward, heavenward, Godward. You must not forget that this is no abiding city, and you will not forget it, but, side by side, you will pass to that better heaven, helping each other forward. All that I wish for you," he added solemnly, almost reverently, "I cannot speak. For Henry Lisle, son of my benefactor, and friend of my youth, or for his little wife, my own child in Christ. No, no; I cannot tell you all I wish, all I pray for. On earth," he continued with a kindling eye, "the spirit cannot find utterance for its greatest thoughts, its strongest sympathies, its deepest yearnings, but in that Better Land, that shining, lustrous realm of the Hereafter, the spirit's voice shall be loosed, and then, if we be but faithful, you shall read the uttermost depths of what I this day feel."

"Father," whispered Marion, after a short pause, "do you mean to say that you will never come back again to England?"

"In all human probability, never."

"Does not this grieve you?"

"No, my child; if a little feeling of home-sickness ever comes over me, I think of the Land we were just now talking of, the only Fatherland of the Dominican."

"But you have not yet taken the step that binds you irrevocably to this Order," said Mr. Lisle anxiously.

"Not yet, but I trust soon to do so."

"Then let me say just one word, George, my dear old friend. Had your life in England been a useless one, I could have rejoiced in it; had it been an unconsecrated one, I could have understood it; but living as you did, every thought and sympathy given to God, why should you leave us?"

"Because He so willed it."

"I cannot think it; indeed, indeed I cannot, your life at Harleyford was so useful! Who is to convert the Protestants there now?"

"Father Dalton, while I do my best to reclaim infidels."

"But your poor?" pleaded Marion.

"Are round me here," replied the priest.

"But we miss you so much, father, so very much; the whole place seems altered now."

"Poor Father Dalton, I am sure, from what I saw of him, he is a most zealous young man, and yet you quite leave him out in your calculations."

"Yes, he is very good, but he need not leave, even if you came back; he could stay and help you."

"Little temptress!"

"No, indeed—if you had only told us, father, that you were going for good!—but to leave us for a month, and then never to return—it was very cruel!" And Marion burst into tears.

"Come, come. What! crying in the honeymoon! Henry, do you allow this?"

"I cannot blame her for what, if I were a woman, I should probably do myself."

"I must not rely on your assistance, I can see," replied the priest smiling: "the last injunction, then, that the old father lays on Marion Howard of other days, shall be, that if ever she gives him a thought, it shall be with a prayer, not a tear. Will she obey it?"

"She will," said Marion, drying her eyes.

"And now," said the priest, "there is one thing I have just remembered I had to say to you. Notwithstanding the careful inventory I have just made of all my worldly goods, one item, and that rather a bulky one, has been omitted: if you will accept it, Henry, it is yours: it will, I know, bring back many a treasured reminiscence to your wife."

"Of course I will accept it properly, and with thanks."

"Do not be too sure; it is by no means either a treasure or a beauty."

"What is it?"

"Old Rufus."

"O father!" cried Marion, "I would rather have him than anything in the world. I will ride him myself as long as he lives."

"Or as long as you do, which would probably be five minutes after you mounted him. They say you must not 'look a gift horse in the mouth,' but I would advise you to look at him on all sides before you accept him, for he has neither beauty, value, nor temper."

"But he belonged to George Stirling, and while there is corn and grass-land in my possession he shall have his share," replied Henry Lisle.

"You will find him then in the paddock, behind the presbytery, whither he was transferred last week from the stables of the Green Dragon."

"Yes, I saw him in the paddock the day before we left," said Marion, "nor was I the only one who did so. If you could have heard the exclamations of our school children when they recognised him through the hedge, you would never have forgotten it. 'Father Stirling's horse!' Father Stirling's horse!' I am sure they fancied he was only a herald to his rider. Father, father, how deeply you are loved in Harleyford! how can you leave us?"

"No man living, my child," he replied solemnly, "has not his earthly fetters, and mine indeed were wreaths of flowers. How I loved you all, God only knows. 'The lines had fallen to me in pleasant places.' Do not think your pastor has left you without regret; many a tendril was wrenched and broken when he tore his heart from its old resting-place, but it is over now, and truly he is a happy man."

"And so am I happy," said Henry Lisle, laying his hand on the shoulder of his little bride.

"And so are you happy," repeated the Dominican, smiling benevolently on them. "Each of us, I trust, fulfilling his vocation as God would have him."

Half an hour later Father Dunstan stood alone, while the echo of a closing gate still rang upon his ear. It is not often monks indulge in reveries—what could he be thinking of? It would be hard to guess, gentle reader, for athwart his face there ran a varying expression, like the lights and shadows of an April landscape. Did the words of an old friend and the pleading glance of a little fragile figure still hover around him? Perhaps. It may be that the reverie was a thing of human regret and superhuman hopes, of earthly temptations and celestial trust and confidence. But even as he lingered, the sound of the vesper bell stole along the corridors, and home, friends, and kindred were soon forgotten, as the glorious notes floated upward from the white-robed choir :

> "Laudate Dominum omnes gentes,
> Laudate eum omnes populi."

And Golden-hair tripped through the streets of the foreign city by her husband's side, joy in her step, light in her eye, love in her overflowing heart. Sweet little Golden-hair! Twenty times a day Henry Lisle pressed the little hand to be sure of its identity. Was it possible! Could it be true!

Old Rufus has now, for many a day, been trotting round his new master's fields, and has grown so subdued with increase of years, that even a little Marion has been held upon his back. For many a day too, a son of St. Dominic has been passing silently on his humble path, little known in the land of strangers. And yet he is not forgotten. Not forgotten in the little church with the gilded tabernacle, in the cottage homes of Harleyford, or beneath the cedars ; for kindly words, and loving deeds, live long in the hearts of men. Not forgotten in the Fatherland, where the Lord of the harvest with His own hand garners the sheaves that have grown on this poor earth, and where, at the great Harvest-Home, the labourers who shall have borne the heat of the day shall find the fruit of their toil faithfully stored for Eternity.

THE END.

www.ingramcontent.com/pod-product-compliance
Lightning Source LLC
Chambersburg PA
CBHW021219270326
41929CB00010B/1197